C H I N A
N
W
E
S
BHUTAN
I N D I A
BANGLADESH
KACHIN
Myitkyina
C H I N A
SAGAING
Hakha
Mandalay
Sagaing
CHIN
SHAN
VIETNAM
MANDALAY
MAGWAY
Taunggyi
NAYPYITAW
Magway
Sittwe
RAKHINE
NAYPYIDAW
Loikaw
L A O S
KAYAH
BAGO
Bago
KAYIN
AYEYARWADY
Pathein
YANGON
Hpa-An
Bay of Bengal
Yangon
Mawlamyine
MON
T H A I L A N D
Dawei
TANINTHARYI
CAMBODIA
Andaman Sea
Gulf of Thailand

A-MAZE

Myanmar's Struggle for Democracy, 2011-2023

Balestier Press
Centurion House, London TW18 4AX
www.balestier.com

A-Maze: Myanmar's Struggle for Democracy, 2011-2023
Original Title: အံ့စရာ ဝက်ပါ
Copyright © Ma Thida, 2024
English translation © Maung Zaw, 2024

First published by Balestier Press in 2024

A CIP catalogue record for this book is available from the British Library.

ISBN 978 1 913891 48 0

Edited by Brian Haman
Cover design by Maung Medi

All rights reserved. No part of this publication may be reproduced, stored in a retrieval system or transmitted in any form or by any means, electronic, mechanical, without the prior written permission of the publisher of this book.

Cover description: The unwavering stare of Chin revolutionary medics confronting barbaric soldiers vividly highlights the shock experienced by civilians witnessing the cruel and unjust treatment inflicted by the state army on its own people. It also showcases the extraordinary bravery and resolve exhibited by even young civilians in the struggle against military dictatorship, advocating for a future founded on federal democracy. This young woman is one of the nine medics from the People's Defense Force (PDF) in Chin State who were apprehended on November 16th, 2021. Like her, individuals involved in the Spring Revolution in Myanmar (Burma) are tirelessly working to dismantle all barriers imposed by military dictatorship, akin to navigating a maze rather than seeking a way out of it.

A-MAZE

Myanmar's Struggle for Democracy, 2011-2023

Ma Thida

Translated from the Burmese by
Maung Zaw

Balestier Press
London · Singapore

Foreword

Amidst the myriad nerve-racking challenges I faced before embarking on the journey to prepare this book, the most pressing question weighing on my mind was one that incessantly demanded the right decision: Where should I draw the line? The Spring Revolution, the focal point of my literary endeavour, continues to unfold in Burma (Myanmar), with its momentum unabated as forces of the armed revolution persist in their fight against the military junta.

First and foremost, it's crucial to clarify the purpose of this book. It does not aim to serve as a historical record nor as a scholarly research work. So why did I write it? Following the publication of "The Roadmap" in 2011, my politically dormant pen had remained idle in regards to the democratic trends in Burma. However, in February 2021, the attempted military coup occurred, prompting some political analysts to assert that the trajectory of democracy had regressed. Yet, it can only be deemed a "U-turn" or a regression if the country had initially embarked on a linear path, reached a certain point, and then backtracked from its original direction.

This raised two significant questions: firstly, how far have we progressed in Burma's Journey of Democracy from 2011 to 2021? And secondly, in what direction have the tumultuous events post-February 2021 been steering us—further away from the Goal of Democracy or closer towards it? This book endeavours to address these questions in an effort to unearth a deeper understanding. Effectively, I sincerely hope that this book sheds light on the political upheavals that Burmese society has endured for decades. Indeed, delving into the entire story of the ongoing Revolution, which has yet to achieve its ultimate victory, would be a vast and unwieldy undertaking. Therefore, I ultimately decided to focus solely on the two-year period of the Burmese people's struggle against military dictatorship and their unwavering quest for democracy. Specifically, the book will cover political events in Burma up to February 1, 2023.

It's important to note that from February 1, 2023, onwards, the momentum of the Spring Revolution has been remarkably swift. The Revolution will undoubtedly continue its course, but I have chosen not to document its further progression. Instead, I felt compelled to present this book to international readers, who may not yet have a comprehensive understanding of Burma's political landscape. Initially, I considered writing in English, but it took me some time to finalise the format of the content. Ultimately, the decision to write in Burmese, my native language, was the obvious one. However, since it has taken additional time to produce an English translation of the book, the focus has necessarily been limited to the two-year period of the Revolution.

An astonishing array of events involving thousands of real-life characters have unfolded within the span of these two years. Any attempt to detail and allocate a role to each and every individual within the confines of this compact volume of real-life stories would be impracticable. As previously mentioned, this book does not aim to serve as an exhaustive historical record or scholarly research work, and I therefore extend my humble apologies to any scholars who may identify perceived flaws or omissions within its pages. Conversely, this is not a work of fiction, and, as such, I refrained from embellishing it with fictitious characters and events. It is imperative to emphasise that the Spring Revolution itself represents the collective action of the Burmese people, characterised by countless poignant sacrifices made for the betterment of their nation. Admittedly, a significant number of lesser-known individuals, organisations, and events may have gone unnoticed.

Given that the primary aim of this book is not to serve as a historical archive, it is possible that the names of some individuals who made contributions to the cause of the Revolution through their involvement in organisations and events may not be explicitly documented within these pages. To these brave souls, I offer my sincere apologies for any oversight in acknowledging their efforts. I firmly believe that numerous writers will explore this historic phenomenon from diverse perspectives and in various literary forms. It is my earnest hope that this book will make a meaningful contribution to portraying the living essence of the Spring

Revolution, but I still urge you, dear readers, to consult other books by other writers for a deeper understanding of this complex subject. I also cherish the hope that individuals who experienced these tumultuous political upheavals and traumas firsthand will document and share their unique experiences in writing, which will further allow international readers to gain a more nuanced understanding of Burma's recent past and possible future.

The ongoing Spring Revolution, which has surged forth for over two years now, represents a monumental task aimed at addressing the deep-seated issues and challenges that have long plagued the land of Burma. As both a close observer and one viewing from a distance, I see this book as my attempt not only to grasp the complexities of the past and present leading up to this momentous undertaking, but also to shed light on its origins, direction, and the diverse array of allies contributing to its cause. For readers from distant lands who have not directly participated in this Mission, I anticipate that they will become deeply immersed in the unfolding events chronicled within these pages. However, I must concede that in the process of writing this book, certain ideas have developed wings of their own and flown away, disappearing into the ether before I could commit them to paper. It is a common experience for writers to find that real-life events can present themselves as far more intricate than initially anticipated.

Although this book may not offer a comprehensive depiction of the entirety of the recent past and mutable present, I dare say that it can provide, at the very least, a broad overview of the task at hand. If this book succeeds in contributing to the better understanding of those who have been disconnected from the political landscape of Burma, lost amidst the intricacies of the Maze, then I believe my purpose in writing it will have been, to some extent, fulfilled. I have written this book with a heartfelt prayer on my lips, hoping that, through the collective negotiations and collaboration of all participants in this Revolution, the intricate political landscape of Burma will swiftly unravel, paving the way for the nation to navigate out of the Maze and ultimately achieve the aspiration of Federal Democracy. My earnest desire is that such a resolution would render it unnecessary for me to delve into heart-rending subject matter of a similar nature in my future writing and books.

I extend my humble apologies and heartfelt acknowledgments to every news agency, Facebook post, and individual whose data, information, personal stories, and events I have referenced within this book. Regrettably, I had no opportunity to seek formal permissions for their use, but I am deeply grateful for their contributions nonetheless. I am also indebted to Maung Zaw for generously dedicating his time and effort to translate the entirety of my text. My thanks also go to editor Dr Brian Haman, lecturer at the University of Vienna and the editor-in-chief of *The Shanghai Literary Review* for helping me editing this manuscript and reaching out to the publisher the Balestier Press.

I would also like to express my sincere appreciation to Professor James Scott and Professor Erik Harms for giving me the chance to do research in the peaceful environs of the MacMillan Center, Yale University. And my heartfelt thanks also go to the Martin Roth Initiative scholarship (Germany), its team (especially Verena Harpe) and the team of two host organizations — The Association of Friends of Schloss Wiepersdorf (Dr Norbert Bass and Elisabeth von Haebler) and Berlin Literature Action (Martin Jankowski and Lars Jongeblod), for providing me the chance to finish writing this book during exciting days in Berlin.

Ma Thida

O Guardian Spirits of the World,
O Guardian Spirits of Groves with flowers unfurl'd,
I invoke thee all!
O Guardian Spirits of Hills and Mountains,
O Guardian Spirits of Villages and Fountains,
O Yoke-ka-soes, Guardian Spirits of Trees,
I invoke thee, please!
O Guardian Spirits of the Land and the Water,
O Guardian Spirits of the Buddhist Sāsanā,
O Guardian Spirit of the Ocean,
I invoke all thy hoary, surging motion!
O Five Devas of Cloud-dwelling, O Deva of the Heavens,
O Four Guardian Angels of the World with amazing legends,
I do invoke thee, wild with emotions!
O King of Celestials, Brahmas, O King
Of the Asurā deities, O King of hell realm,
I do invoke thee all!

Having the Guardian Spirit of the Earth as the Witness,
I fling a volley of my curses merciless
Onto the devilish soldiers who demolish our religion!
May the despot Min Aung Hlaing, blessed with the heart of a pigeon,
And his rotten-hearted accomplices, good-for-nothing junks,
Who have caused the bloodshed of our people and monks,
May they all fall backwards, and vomit cuds,
And drop dead in the pools of their dark blood!
And their offspring, too! May they meet the bang
Of Fate sans merci, and die in heart-breaking pangs!
Just like the blue flames die, their souls molested,
So, their bodies shall soon turn into a smouldering wreck!

It was a moment when a young lady, aged about fourteen or fifteen, stood before the crowd, reciting these lines with a voice filled with raw emotion, cascading forth like a mountain torrent. The video capturing her impassioned speech went viral on February 1, 2023, marking the second anniversary of the attempted military coup in Burma. Since February 2021, following a brutal crackdown on peaceful strikes, the people of Burma, particularly the country's youth, have continued to mobilise in various forms as part of the ongoing Spring Revolution against the military junta. This unique video, featuring the young lady's fervent curse, reminiscent of Minister Min Nan Thu's, was a poignant expression of defiance aimed at the military dictators and soldiers who callously extinguished thousands of innocent lives.

The last part of the Min Nanda Thu stone inscription reads as follows:

The wanton hand so reckless, so destructive,
that would do damage to my donation of this religious edifice,
May he or she, when travelling by water way,
be attacked by whale sharks and manta rays,
and get killed by ferocious crocodiles
and other underwater predators wild!
May he or she, when travelling by land,
Get devoured by lions, or leopards with sharp fangs,
trampled by elephants, or attacked by wild boars
the body torn apart, in blood and gore!
May he or she suffer the venomous bites
of banded kraits and Indian cobras with fangs gleaming white!
Come, saw-scaled vipers, the Russel's vipers,
bite the destructive hand black and blue, and slip and slither!
Should he or she happen to fly by air,
May the crooked beaks of mythical garudas dare,
May falcons and eagles swoop at lightning speed,
And his or her soul the claws clutch and squeeze!

May whirlwinds and tempests blow him or her mad,
May the Eight Kinds of Dangers fall right on the head,
May Nemesis in ten different forms get the victim swept,
And snap and fling the soul into the Flames of Death!

The young lady continued to recite the lines of curses with fervour, her voice tinged with bitterness. The genesis of this defiant act dates back to March 6, 2021, when the atrocities committed by the military regime continued to escalate on a daily basis. On that day, a group of women from upcountry Burma, spanning generations, gathered amidst the ancient ruins of pagodas. Balancing bowls of bananas and coconuts on their heads, they staged a demonstration, echoing the curses of Minister Min Nanda Thu. This display of curses seemed to provide an outlet for the pent-up frustrations of a populace compelled to suppress their anger, as the policy of peaceful protest was unanimously adhered to at the time. However, as time progressed, it became evident, particularly among the younger generations, that neither the curses nor peaceful demonstrations were effective in the face of the military's threats. It became increasingly clear that armed revolution was the most potent weapon against these armed oppressors. It was on the second anniversary of the attempted military coup that the curses uttered by a young lady, symbolising Generation Z, captured the attention of the media and rapidly spread across various platforms.

O wretched, woebegone military dictator,
May thy life, thy family be no peace, but a disaster!

Double, double, trouble thy heart,
Eleven Fires burn thy physical rampart!
May all thy wealth ebb and flow,
May thy heart be laden with woe!
Thy starving soul shall suffer in Hell,
and be born inside a dumb creature's shell!
Double, double, trouble thy heart!

Rues shall press thy physical rampart!
Like the curses of Min Nan Thu split thy head,
Thou shalt never be bless'd
with an opportunity to pay reverence

to Ariya Metteyya's Noble Presence!
In woes we are now lying prone,
but on thy head these woes shall be thrown
till the end of the world!
We fling curses to thee, Fascist ogres,
Thy life shall be an endless calamity,
thy end up being an unlamented tragedy!

This video was a collaborative effort between the Students' Unions of three universities, serving as a moving reminder of the profound impact of loss and injustice on the Burmese people. When stripped of beloved idols, robbed of land, property, wealth, and power, and deprived of fundamental rights and values such as equality, mutual respect, and justice, the resulting bitterness festers deep within the collective consciousness. Passed down through the generations, these sentiments of bitterness are a testament to the enduring legacy of oppression in Burmese society. Bitterness, a constant companion borne from bitter experiences under military dictatorship, has nurtured a Poison Tree, corroding the very essence of humanity. Are the military dictators powerful enough to ensnare us in a Maze of conflicting emotions, trapped amidst the tumultuous currents of love and hate?"

"Absolutely speechless, mate! Yesterday, it was like a ghost town out there, not a soul in sight on the streets or roads! Just check out Google Maps, mate, it tells the whole story! The day before, the whole city was gridlocked with traffic, but yesterday? Not a peep, just shiny black roads, deserted. Only the 'Dogs' were out and about, you know what I mean."

"And it wasn't just our city, mate! Listen up! Every town, city, and even villages across the entire country! That was the Silent Strike in action! This is the true essence of the Spring Revolution—we're determined not to back down but to keep flying our banner high!"

The informal tea party inside the roadside tea shop buzzed with excitement as they exchanged news of agitation amongst themselves.

"Oh, by the way," chimed in a man sporting a red T-shirt, "have you seen the Min Nan Thu Curses video?"

"I was over the moon, mate," replied another guy, eagerly sharing the latest scoop he'd seen on Facebook, "people actually obeyed and stayed indoors for the Silent Strike, the whole day!"

"Yeah, mate, it's fantastic news! The better-off folks stepped up and supported the hawkers and peddlers, who were barely scraping by, to participate in the Silent Strike. A day beforehand, they chipped in some money to help supplement their meagre incomes. And on the actual day, they did their part to ensure the success of the Silent Strike by purchasing goods from these street vendors, helping them make ends meet."

Seated on rickety wooden stools around a small, cluttered table adorned with empty tea cups, a flask, and plain tea cups before them, these individuals were completely engrossed in discussing and exchanging information about the resounding success of the Silent Strike that had swept across the entire country the other day. For those who had gradually withdrawn from active involvement in the Revolution due to pressures faced over the past two years, the relative success of the Silent Strike served as a significant psychological boost. It revitalised their dormant spirit, reaffirming their belief that if the circumstances demand it, our people, always united, are still prepared to rise and respond. However, witnessing the conflicting narratives of certain politicians and armed revolutionary fighters, there was growing concern among the populace that such lack of unity among leaders could jeopardise the Revolution's progress. The public perception of the Silent Strike deeply resonated with those who had orchestrated the mission, imbuing them with newfound strength. It was a powerful reminder that despite enduring the brutal realities of oppression, the people remained steadfast and unified, ready to join forces in any mission against dictatorship.

"You know the story of the taxi driver, right?" interjected a young man who had been quiet during the tea party. "He jokingly posted a request for pocket money to cover his daily car rental fees since he wouldn't be working on the day of the Silent Strike. But when people offered to help pay his rental fees, he had to decline. And then there's this family I heard about—they were determined not to work that day. They said they'd be happy with just some Nga-pi to go with their rice, you know, that cheap pounded fish paste used in cooking."

"Well, some companies gave their staff the day off yesterday. And those who stayed indoors kept things quiet, avoiding noisy activities to show solidarity with the Strike," added another participant.

These people didn't wait for one speaker to finish before eagerly interjecting their latest information into the ongoing discussion about the riveting topic of the Silent Strike—a subject that would undoubtedly be recorded in the future history of the country. They were deeply moved by the acts of compassion among their fellow citizens and were inspired by the loving kindness displayed by comrades and the unwavering loyalty to stand together until the Strike achieved success. What made this Silent Strike truly remarkable was its complete absence of hate speech, which served to unite the public more strongly than ever before.

"Isn't it ironic?" remarked one of the attendees. "Those who foolishly staged the Counter Strike in support of the military were a complete failure! They looked utterly ridiculous, standing there all alone on the deserted main roads with no audience to applaud them. Even the funeral of a wretched decoy from a village drew a larger crowd than those demonstrators who joined the strike as a paid job! Barely a hundred of them, holding photos and placards! Can you believe it? Police cars and ten military vehicles were deployed to provide security, guarding those party stooges! What a disgrace to those shameless security forces!"

"Absolutely shameful!" echoed another participant. "Imagine going abroad and having your entire clan see you off at the airport, only to realise that there were more people present than those VIPS—Very Idiotic Persons! From what I've heard, those so-called honourable individuals were paid, initially 5,000 kyats, now 10,000 kyats, for their 'honourable' mission! It's laughable, considering they used to organise much larger demonstrations in support of the military in the past. It's absurd, isn't it?"

"It's safe to say that the number of those supporting the military has significantly dwindled on the ground compared to online platforms. Information about this counter strike against the Silent Strike was disseminated online, outlining transportation services and refreshments for the demonstrators. However, to the dismay of the sponsors, the turnout was far fewer than expected."

"As you know, the Silent Strike has been staged four times now. Each mission has been a step up from the last, truly unprecedented on a nationwide scale. No other country has done anything like it!"

"Absolutely, brother. We participated because it was a mission born out of mutual understanding and a shared sense of responsibility among our citizens. We've shown our unity and resilience by staging this strike multiple times. There's a quote from a Danish film director—I can't recall his name—but he said, 'Silence is the loudest sound in the universe.' One thing's for certain, brother, the military can't withstand our united voice."

"Wait a minute! Wait a minute! I'll read out Min Ko Naing's poem to you. May I have your attention?"

When the day like this comes,
They fear the voice of our people,
They fear the silence of our people, too.
When our people are out in the streets and on the roads,
They are seized with nerve-wracking horror;
When our people shut the doors and keep themselves indoors,
They are seized with maddening fright.
Who are they?

My countrymen, my noble countrymen,
Each of you has done your bit,
and carried out your collective duties and responsibilities.
Our Silent Strike, a huge success,
has shaken the whole world in rumbling vibrations!

Clap! Clap! Clap! In the realm of imagination, the applause resounded loudly in the mind's ear. However, in reality, the entire tea party remained silent, expressing their delight by mimicking applause without making a sound, a reflection of the Silent Strike. Even customers at other tables, hearing the recitation of the poem, gestured their applause silently, displaying the three-finger salute in protest of the military coup.

As the Curse against the military dictatorship was chanted, fueled by primal rage and burning worries, and expressions of unity, compassion, and humanity were conveyed through silent gestures, both actions unfolded simultaneously. Thus, Hate and Love were the dual reflections of the Spring Revolution. Once, Burma was known for its "Grace under pressure," but what of its present image? Has it faded from the political landscape? How does the world perceive Burma now, enduring bitter rancour and silent anger under cruel brutalities? Has the world become disconnected, deaf to the cries of our suffering people? Where do we stand on this arduous Journey of Democracy?

On the Road, or Getting Stuck in a Maze?

We've embarked on this journey, and if we aim to reach our destination at the end of the road, we must stay on course and continue our march forward.

The Road to Democracy has been a nearly four-decade-long endeavour for the citizens of Burma, starting from 1988. We made a promising start, but as history often repeats itself, the military coup swiftly quashed the nationwide demonstrations after a mere six weeks. Under the guise of the State Law and Order Restoration Council, the military junta announced plans for a future general election, inviting all political parties to register. Despite scepticism among the people, they participated in the 1990 general election, overwhelmingly supporting the key opposition National League for Democracy party (NLD), led by Aung San Suu Kyi. However, our hopes for progress towards democracy were dashed when the junta, instead of honouring the election results, refused to convene parliament and initiated a national convention to draft a new constitution. Only 14 percent of the convention attendees were elected MPs, with many representatives being arrested or forced into exile. It felt like winning a lottery prize only to have the ticket stolen away. This national convention was clearly a diversion from our path to democracy. I was among those vehemently opposed to this plan and paid the price with a twenty-year prison sentence.

Since the inception of this national convention, our journey towards democracy has hit a dead end. It took a staggering fourteen years to finalise the draft constitution, which was eventually approved by a 2008 referendum. We found ourselves at a roadblock. However, in a bid to alleviate mounting international pressure, particularly following the 2003 Depayin massacre, the military junta released many youth leaders from the 1988 generation in 2005. This gesture reignited hope among the general public, suggesting a potential path back to our democratic aspirations. The '88 generation leaders began mobilising society under the guise of humanitarian activities, creative endeavours, and community development assistance. It was akin to uncovering a tunnel leading back to our road to democracy. However, in 2007, spurred by sympathy for donors facing adversity, a significant number of Buddhist monks spearheaded the Saffron Revolution. They marched in long processions through streets and roads, chanting the Metta Sutta and Pali texts to dispel dangers from all beings. This action caught the attention of the junta, but it also kept the public politically vigilant despite severe oppression and fear gripping their hearts.

Even in the face of adversity, countless locals rallied behind and supported the Saffron Revolution. With the advent of new technology, the world became acutely aware of the dire situation unfolding within our borders. We found ourselves halted at a crossroads on our journey. The brutal crackdown instilled terror and apathy among our people, threatening to derail our progress. Yet, despite these challenges, we stood firm in our resistance. In 2008, just over a week after Cyclone Nargis wreaked havoc on the southern part of the country, causing catastrophic destruction and claiming the lives of at least 150,000 people, the military junta seized the opportunity to hold a referendum on the 2008 constitution. Exploiting the nation's misery and grief, they manipulated the referendum process. Discrepancies emerged between the announced voter turnout by the military junta and the actual population census in 2014. In 2010, a general election was conducted under the 2008 constitution. The National League for Democracy (NLD), led by Aung San Suu Kyi, chose not to participate in what they deemed an unfair election. As a result, the military proxy political party, the Union Solidarity and Development Party (USDP), secured the majority. This left us standing at a critical juncture on our journey.

At this fork in the road to democracy, one path leads to what some call "Stingy Democracy," permitted by the military junta under the guise of "disciplined democracy." The other route, "Make-up Democracy," is governed by a new administration, composed of current civilians dubbed "Baung Bee Chut" (meaning "shedding their military uniforms") and in-service army personnel known as "Baung Bee Wutt." Another challenging path, "Khwa Tee Khwa Kya Democracy," remains unclear—a tumultuous clash within the government itself, pitting civilians advocating for justice and democracy against army personnel with entrenched political ideologies. There's always the looming possibility of a U-turn towards autocracy, given the military junta's potential to reverse gears at any moment. However, recent events have shown that we're no longer at the fork in the road.

On February 1, 2021, the Commander-in-Chief, alleging electoral fraud in the 2020 general election, invoked sections of the 2008 constitution to declare himself Chairman of the State Administrative Council (SAC). This move, widely viewed as a coup aimed at reinstating military rule, led to the overthrow of the elected government. Despite the SAC's claim of "state power control" and promises of a new election, their actions breached the constitution and amounted to an attempted coup, potentially constituting high treason. We're now in a situation where our road to democracy seems lost. It's akin to the aftermath of the 1988 uprising, where we find ourselves trapped in a Maze without an exit. Despite our weariness from this prolonged journey, we still cling to the hope that we're on the path to democracy.

Indeed, the Spring Revolution has been tirelessly engaged in dismantling the walls of the Maze and paving the way for a new highway towards a federal democratic union. This endeavour involves various strategies and actions aimed at achieving comprehensive change in both the political system and the cultural norms of Burma. One significant shift in the revolution's motto from "Down with the military dictatorship!" to "Down with any form of dictatorship!" underscores its broader objectives. Beyond simply overthrowing the existing military regime, the revolution seeks to uproot all forms of undemocratic practices and outdated cultural conventions that no longer align with modern principles.

The people of Burma are resolute in their determination not to remain trapped within the confines of the Maze, whether thick or thin. They are committed to toppling any barriers that obstruct the path to democracy and equilibrium. This determination extends to the collapse of the entire Maze, symbolised by the Burmese term "Wingaba," representing all walls and barriers hindering progress. The people of Burma are in fact forging a new highway towards a federal democratic union. They are taking charge of constructing this road, shaping it according to their aspirations, and steadfastly advancing towards their destination. This collective effort involves persistent activism, grassroots mobilisation, and a steadfast commitment to democratic ideals.

Through such concerted efforts, the Spring Revolution is not only challenging the entrenched power structures but also laying the groundwork for a more inclusive, equitable, and democratic society. It is a journey marked by resilience, unity, and an unwavering belief in the possibility of transformative change.

Wall:

The Climax of the Maze: January 2021

"As many of you are aware, Section 215 of the State Constitution and Section 43 of the Union Government explicitly state that the President is not subject to accountability to either the Hluttaw or any court for the execution of their powers and functions as outlined in the Constitution or any law. Let's reflect on the consistency seen in past elections – the 1990, 2015, and the recent 2020 elections – all resulting in landslide victories. The public support has remained steadfast for decades. Frankly speaking, those who are now raising objections to the election results are simply disgruntled parties unable to accept defeat. I must caution these parties and individuals that their reckless remarks may lead them down a path of political suicide," declared U Zaw Htay, spokesperson for the State Counsellor's Office, during a press conference held on January 8, 2021.

These remarks came in response to legal actions taken by the Union Solidarity and Development Party (USDP) and the Democratic Party of National Politics, a newly formed party led by former military generals. Both parties filed lawsuits against the President and the Union Election Commission, submitting applications to the Union Supreme Court. Htay's tone was confrontational as he questioned these parties' adherence to the 2008 Constitution.

Section 417 of the 2008 State Constitution outlines the conditions under which a state of emergency can be declared, stating that if circumstances arise that threaten the disintegration of the Union or national solidarity, the President, in coordination with the National Defence and Security Council, may declare a state of emergency. Section 418 (a) dictates that in such cases, the President shall transfer legislative, executive, and judicial powers to the Commander-in-Chief of the Defence Services to restore order swiftly. Section 421 (a) further stipulates that the President must submit the transfer of sovereign power to the Commander-in-Chief of the Defence Services to the Pyidaungsu Hluttaw. Section 421 (b) allows for extensions of the prescribed duration of emergency measures.

Observers widely interpreted these constitutional provisions as limiting the military's ability to seize power without presidential consent. Htay's pointed question underscored the gravity of the situation, hinting at the potential consequences for constitutional integrity and democratic stability.

However, the USDP not only protested and lodged complaints about the 2020 election outcomes but also continued to hold press conferences and stage demonstrations in cities. What was striking was that on January 20, the military regime issued a statement annulling the 2020 election results, alleging voter fraud: "If political parties, including the Tatmadaw, can prove that it was a free and fair election, this would reflect the desires of the Burmese people, and the Tatmadaw would accept the election results in line with the desires of the people." The statement emphasised the need for coordination among the Hluttaw, the government, and the UEC for a positive outcome. The phrase "political parties, including the Tatmadaw" instead of "the Tatmadaw, together with some political parties," wrongly implied the military regime's status as a political party that participated in the election and did not accept the results.

One week later, on January 28, the UEC issued a 15-point statement addressing voters regarding the electoral process. It acknowledged some errors and shortcomings but stated that any cases of fraud were being addressed and that the Election Tribunal was resolving disputes over the results. The statement reiterated the UEC's status as the national-level authority responsible for all election matters and emphasised its independence from political parties and the government.

However, the initially small demonstrations against the UEC gradually morphed into support for the Tatmadaw (state army). The following headlines from newspapers and journals published about ten days before the attempted military coup on February 1, 2020, reflect the evolving political situation in Burma:

Michael Kyaw Myint in Exile will Lead Demonstration in Nay Pyi Taw (January 20, *Myanmar Now News*)

Two USDP Members Demonstrating for Tatmadaw Arrested in Myawaddy (January 22, *Myanmar Now News*)

Tatmadaw Denites No Involvement in Michael Kyaw Myint's Activities Tatmadaw Threatens the Military Coup May or May not Happen. It Depends (January 26, *Myanmar Now News*)

Demonstrators for the Military Attack the Police Force in Yangon (January 27, *Myanmar Now News*)

Commander-in-Chief Blurts Out State Constitution, if Not Followed, to be Cancelled (January 27, *BBC News*)

Diplomats Object the Attempts to Alter Election Results (January 29, *DVB News*)

The Tatmadaw will Safeguard State Constitution (January 30, *RFA*) Two Wounded by Demonstrators for the Tatmadaw (January 30, 2021, *Myanmar Now News*)

More Demonstrations for the Tatmadaw in Yangon (January 31, 2021, *BBC News*)

After the military coup, demonstrations supporting the military's role in Burma's political landscape took place, with some groups of mercenary fake nationalists, including chauvinistic monks, supposedly participating for financial gain. These demonstrations occurred from January 21 to February 25, totaling 22 in number, with 11 before the coup and 11 after. It's noteworthy that the orchestrator behind these activities, aimed at agitating peace-loving people, was ironically former Police Major General Khin Yee, who later became Vice-Chairman of the USDP after retiring. He was appointed as Minister of the Ministry of Immigration and Population under the State Administrative Council, as detailed in the book *Democracy-dutiya-Asoeya-thit nint Myanmar-Naing-gan* ("Second

Phase of Democracy under the New Government and Burma") (Vol.2), authored by U Soe Thein, a former member of Peace Centre (Source: December 22, 2022, *The Irrawaddy News Agency*). According to the book, U Khin Yee organised demonstrations supporting the Tamadaw in Lower Burma, while those in Nay Pyi Taw Council Region were organised by Lt. General Wai Lwin, former Minister of Defence during U Thein Sein's Government. U Khin Yee retired from his ministerial post in 2022 and was appointed as Chairman of the USDP on October 5. During his tenure as Police Major General, he supervised the violent suppression of the 2007 Saffron Revolution staged by Buddhist monks, and he later became Minister of the Ministry of Immigration and Population during the Rakhine conflicts in 2012.

The revelations in the book shed light on U Khin Yee's political manipulations, previously unknown to the public, and exposed U Soe Thein, formerly praised as a supporter of political reforms in Burma, as a mask-wearing writer. The military has often emphasised the presence of control freaks manipulating events from behind during critical turning points in Burma's democratic journey. After the attempted coup, it became even clearer that many such control freaks had been leading the country into the Maze since the post-2012 period. People began to realise that they had mistaken the Maze for the path towards their goal.

Passage:

The Rise of the Spring Revolution

"In accordance with Section 417 of the State Constitution, the State is declared to be in a state of emergency."

At 8:00 pm, this breaking news was announced on all government televisions.

At exactly 8:00 pm, the cacophony of banging pots and pans, clanging iron plates, and whatever makeshift instruments could be found, reverberated through the air, breaking the profound silence of the night. These sounds echoed from buildings on every street and road, denouncing the military coup and seemingly driving away the malevolent spirits from human dwellings in the old traditional way (Taw-htoke, in Burmese).

Perhaps it was the frequent aggressive demonstrations by the Tatmadaw's stooges before and after the coup that kept people across the country on the brink of staging anti-military protests or strikes. Some political observers suggested that they were misled by false propaganda spread on Facebook, advising them to wait and observe any changes silently for 72 hours. Another reason for their silence could be their preference for peaceful demonstrations, fearing harassment by the "aggressive mobs" that roamed the main roads daily, coupled with apprehension about COVID-19.

However, *Voice of America News* reported that from the evening of February 2, car horns and the clamour of pots and pans emanated from buildings on certain streets and roads in cities. On February 3, a historic campaign was launched: the Civil Disobedience Movement (CDM) began with participation from medical staff and government employees, quickly spreading across the entire country. The banging of pots and pans in protest also proliferated nationwide. Campaigns against the use of goods produced by the military were initiated. On February 4, around thirty youths, led by Dr. Tayzar San, gathered in front of the University of Medicine, Mandalay, staging a strike. Following the strike, four young men were arrested. The military issued orders to internet service providers to restrict users' access to Facebook pages or accounts.

"Respect Our Votes!"
"Give Us Our Power Back!"
"Who is our President?" "It's U Win Myint! U Win Myint!"
"We are Youths. Youths have a Future!"

There arose thunderous chants of protest slogans in rhythmic beats, resonating not only from the main tar roads but also from every corner—streets, pavements, lawns, and narrow lanes alike. The sun shone radiantly, illuminating the spirited masses, young and old, their hearts pulsating with newfound hope for monumental change. Protest signs and banners of various hues and designs, representing diverse professions, departments, schools, universities, and regions, adorned with messages not only in Burmese and English but also in foreign languages like Chinese and Korean, filled the air.

Marching in throngs stretching for miles, protesters fervently chanted slogans, eliciting collaborative responses from the cheering public lining the pavement, their applause resonating loudly. One group of protesters would pass by, chanting, "Mother Suu!" to which the people would respond, "Release her now! Release her now!" Another group would stride by, chanting, "What do we have on our side?" met with the resounding reply, "We have Truth on our side!" Motor vehicles driving along other roads joined in by honking in solidarity, drowning out some of the slogans. As the buses and cars receded into the distance, the throng of protesters sang in unison the famous protest song "Thway Thissa" ("We Make a Vow as Blood Brotherhoods"), its lyrics resounding: "The time has come, Bro! Blood brotherhood! Get united! It's time we stood together!"

Cheering onlookers seized every opportunity to read the messages on the placards, conveying sentiments like "Defy Any Unfair Order," "Wish Mother Suu Happy and Healthy," "We Want Justice," "We Want Democracy," and "Free Our Leaders." They enthusiastically supported the activists with slogans like "No Office-going! Get Yourself Free!" and

"Down with the Military Dictatorship!" There, on the pavement, a young mother and her preschool daughter sat, snacking beside their homemade protest signs—hers reading, "No More Junta!" and her daughter's proclaiming, "No More Bad Guys!" Nearby, a young woman held a sign with graceful handwriting, declaring, "Spring Flowers may get plucked, but Spring can't be stopped!" Her friends sported similar attire.

In front of an embassy, about twenty protesters engaged in a sit-down strike. A sign hung from a nearby tree, mocking the Commander-in-Chief Min Aung Hlaing with the words, "Nann and boiled peas, eat it! Hey, Shortie, beat it!" A young lady lay on the road, her placard reading, "I don't wanna go back to 1988, so keep it up guys." Beside her, a resolute girl held a sign stating, "F...* the military coup! I am still single!" A young man, resembling a film star, lay on a grass mat, his sign appealing to the UN for support. Joining them, a foreigner held a sign around his neck, expressing solidarity: "This is not my home, but this is already my home. So I have a problem like yours!"

> "Our bones and flesh
> must be the cause of the Dictator's death!
> Fear can no more silence the call
> For our people, ready to wage war!
> Those guys so power crazy
> Set Justice and Truth a-blazin'!
> We all must keep ourselves alert,
> Dictatorship must be totally crush'd!"

The spirited song filled the air, accompanied by a symphony of protest signs bearing similar messages yet occasionally revealing individual reactions, like one reading, "My hands play DJ, but I never thought these hands that play DJ would have to strike the pans and drive out the evil spirits!" The Spring Revolution had taken shape without pressure, urgings, or instigations from any external sources. It was fueled by individual decisions, unshakeable convictions, and surging feelings, epitomised by the slogan, "Every carriage is the locomotive," reminiscent of Karl Marx's

The Rise of the Spring Revolution 29

quote, "Revolutions are the locomotives of world history."

Amidst the bustling crowds, light trucks brimmed with an assortment of food—fried vermicelli, rice, Indian platters, bread, desserts, coffee, tea, fruits, and snacks—distributed by middle-aged men and young women. Meanwhile, diligent volunteers collected used containers and garbage, maintaining cleanliness amidst the chaos. Two shirtless, tattooed men stood by a three-wheeler, already filled with bulging garbage bags, their sign proudly proclaiming, "We are not municipal workers. We are volunteers."

Nearby, a luxury car opened its boot, offering water and refreshments for free, with a plea to dispose of cans responsibly. The car's owners, what looked like a brother and sister duo, held placards urging action against the military coup and questioning consciences: "Knock out the Military with CDM!" (Civil Disobedience Movement) and "Are you sure you have a clear conscience?" An ambulance labelled "Emergency Clinic" stood by, manned by young men and women in duty coats and nurse uniforms, ready to assist. Street children joyfully partook in the free snacks, even helping with garbage disposal—a heartwarming display of civic duty.

It was also heartwarming to witness a young hawker, despite her modest appearance, offering slices of watermelon to the sit-down strikers out of her own generosity. But a young man, looking like a teen, suggested buying half of her watermelon slices and sharing her donation, saying, "Little Sis, I'm proud of you, but don't give away everything for free! You'd be busted, with no dosh to restart your business. This is my offer. I'll buy some from you, and we can make the donation together, okay?" Moved by their spontaneous act of kindness, the strikers, despite the intense heat, responded with their three-finger salute—a symbol of solidarity. The two young people, who had been strangers moments before, exchanged a glance and shouted the slogans, "Our Revolution," "Our Victory!"

In the eyes of the strikers, there was no trace of anger, hate, or worry—only determination and unity. The scene epitomised the inclusive spirit of the Spring Revolution, transcending age and race, as individuals from all walks of life joined forces to propel the movement forward with unwavering momentum.

"Hey, People! Do you stand united?" "Yeah, United! United we are!"
"Restoring life to Democracy!" "Our Cause! Our Cause!"
"Down with the Military Dictatorship!" "Our Cause! Our Cause!"
"What's the purpose of Our General Aung San's military training?"
"Not to kill our own flesh and blood!"
"The military regime took the coup!" "Get out! Get out!"
"Hey, People! Hey, Students! Do you stand united?" "Yeah, United! United we are!"
"We are protesting the coup!" "Go on strike! Go on strike!"
"Our Revolution," "Our Victory!"

Loud and clear slogans were filling the air over the main roads and streets in the Regions and States, everywhere in the country! The images of the Spring Revolution reflected mostly on local and foreign media pages, online pages and TV screens represented just some parts of the images of Yangon, Mandalay and some cities of the country. Everywhere, the majority of the strikes were joined by hundreds and thousands of protesters, who were given Sa-tu-di-tha, a free of charge treat of breakfasts and lunches, and after the clock struck 5:00 pm, the strikes took a day's break. Amazingly, those crowded places alive and pulsating with the protesters looked clean, not a speck of garbage left by anyone, adding the wow factor to the image of the strikes of the Spring. Lo! The multitudes of the people joining the protests of the Spring are so united, so disciplined! You might even wonder if it is really the Burmese, who used to make a low impression as a whole, and often get snubbed by foreigners for lacking discipline and unity.

When dusk fell, the protesters met those young techies, called the keyboard fighters, they spent their dinner time, checking out the news posts of some leaders of the Spring Revolution, and typing out "like," sharing the posts, and, after reading them, they became motivated, showed their concern, and followed the posts.

The slogans posted from various regions all over the country resounded on the digital platform of the Spring Revolution, "Fly your banner! Cry your heart out! Never turn back! Move forward!", "You, Military, if you don't want the government employees to get involved in politics, attempt no coup!", "The Age of Fear is Over! Turn it Upside Down!", "Students' Strength," "From the Battle to Victory!" The Spring had been on the march in full swing all over the country day in, day out, from day to day.

"Clang! Clang! Clang!"

The clangour and cacophony of pans, tin boxes and iron plates were reverberating in the night air all around! So, the clock struck 8:00 pm. After about fifteen minutes, there rang out in the disconcerting silence of the night some slogans and songs of the protesters everywhere.

"Here we take a blood oath together!
We will fight through the winds and weather!
We'll sacrifice our lives, and we are ready,
We'll fight for our people, our country!
Come what may! We are not afraid of death!
We'll fight till our last breath!
Red is the blood of the Fighting Peacock!
Forward we'll march! Forward!"
"A New History in these critical hours
Written in the blood of ours!
"Respect our votes!" "Respect our votes!"
"Give the people the power of the people!"

As night fell and the Burmese people rested in their homeland rested, the spirit of the Spring Revolution remained alive and well, carried on by their compatriots in countries around the globe. From distant shores, they breathed new life into the movement through various activities: organising Spring fund fairs, rallying in front of Burmese embassies, delivering presentations on the Revolution in bustling city centres, and engaging with local and regional diplomats and parliamentarians to garner support against the military coup. Even online protests resonated with participants overseas. Thus, while the Revolution in Burma may have paused during the night, its flame burned continuously, day and night, across the world, like the relentless ticking of the clock.

Once criticised for internal division and a penchant for asserting authority rather than fostering unity (as the Burmese saying goes, "If there are two Burmese, they would be split into three"), Burmese society has now shattered the barriers of old traditions and culture to stand united against the common enemy of military dictatorship. Today, our people exemplify a boundless unity and strength, transcending borders and boundaries in their noble pursuit of justice and freedom.

Passage:

Forming the Committee of Parliamentarians (CRPH)

February 4, 2021

"Sorry, we have to hurry. Time is running out," said an MP, still dressed in his pyjamas.

"Thankfully, almost every one of our elected MPs has signed the oath certificates, but forming a committee representing the National Assembly is our top priority, as we discussed last night at the hotel."

"Absolutely. Moving to the hotel was a smart move. Now we have more freedom for discussion," replied another representative, busy organising the signed oath certificates from both Upper and Lower Houses.

"Yes, the army officers informed us that we have to leave this Si-pin Yeiktha by the 6th, the last day we're allowed to stay here. Anything can happen after that," cautioned another representative, wearing a fawn-coloured Pinny uniform, the uniform of the winning political party, NLD.

"Well," sighed a representative in a sports jersey, "many of our delegates have already gone back home. Thankfully, most of them signed the oath certificates yesterday. It shows that our NLD party has the mandate to proceed."

"So, we have more responsibilities on our shoulders," responded a young lady in a vibrant voice, known for her decisiveness but always speaking calmly.

Her determination boosted their spirits. "Many senior members of our party have been detained. It's going to be tough to get a CEC agreement for forming a representative committee. But we must not give up."

"The remaining regional chief ministers have also encouraged us to stick to the plan," added another representative, checking her smartphone for updates. "Even the Prime Minister of Kayin state reminded us that we'd be accused of betraying our cause if we simply walked away. Millions of our supporters sent us here to represent them."

"Our constituents are calling us directly now," said another woman representative. "They're urging us to prepare for Parliament. They keep saying, 'We voted for you, you have to fulfil your responsibilities.'"

"But it's impossible to convene Parliament in this courtyard," remarked another.

"You're right...My wife at home gave me an ultimatum," chuckled a representative. "She said, 'Don't come back until you've done something over there.' I can't tell if she's pressuring me as a hen-pecked husband or as a passionate supporter and voter of an MP."

Around 2:00 am on February 1, soldiers and tanks encircled the entire compound, giving all the MPs just 24 hours to evacuate. Among them were representatives of the National League for Democracy Party (NLD), including some members of the Central Working Committee. As anticipated, the party leaders who had directed the elected MPs to convene in Naypyidaw were now being arrested one by one. Faced with this situation, the middle-aged elected MPs decided to convene Parliament and form a representative committee of the National Assembly (Pyidaungu Hluttaw). They understood that the public outcry for respecting the election outcome was not only aimed at the leader of the attempted coup but also at the elected representatives themselves. They were keenly aware of the sentiments and aspirations of voters across the country. Consequently, they had already resolved to do their utmost. However, according to the NLD party's procedural rules, approval for forming this committee must first be obtained from members of the Central Executive Committee.

"The challenge is," said one representative in a Pin-ni uniform, "that those who managed to evade arrest have changed their phone numbers. How are we supposed to contact them now?"

"Well, we're getting out of here," said another representative, hastily changing into travel clothes. His decision seemed sudden, but he wasted no time explaining further. "We'll continue our mission on the way to the 'Liberated Place.' We have two cars to take us out of the capital. First, we'll seek refuge in a safe location in Yangon, where our contacts are waiting.

Meanwhile, we'll try to reach all those CEC members. A young lady from headquarters will facilitate communication."

"Okay," he addressed the other members. "If you need more time, head back to the hotel and leave from there. Everyone, get ready!"

"The army guards will be on high alert," expressed another representative, sounding concerned. "Taking all our people out might pose a challenge. Yesterday, I used a motorcycle to visit the MPs' rooms and blocks to discuss our plans. Luckily, the guards didn't recognize me, especially since I changed my shirt every time I left my room. I've arranged for a friend to provide transportation. We'll also need to switch cars. My friend is waiting now. Who knows when I'll see my car again. It can't be helped."

On that fateful morning of February 1st, some elected members of parliament were jolted awake by news of the coup attempt. Since then, they've been running tirelessly along the Revolutionary Road!

On the Yangon-Mandalay Highway, where there were few signs of private vehicles, military trucks and tanks were driving agitatedly here, there, everywhere.

"Hey, the day will come when we can occupy Naypyidaw, the Capital!"

"Yeah, I'm sure."

Seated in their cars, the representatives were already in motion, some engrossed in paperwork while others lost in thought, leaving little room for conversation. They repeatedly attempted to contact a young woman from the NLD who was their link to the central executives, anxiously awaiting a decision. Despite her frustration and tears, she persisted in reaching out to CEC members for approval. The two cars, packed with passengers, raced down the highway, passing one milepost after another.

"What if the CEC says 'No'?" queried one representative from the corner of the car.

"If we halt our efforts now and do nothing, the voting public will surely erupt in anger," replied another representative, who looked older. He emphasised that the voters' wishes must be prioritised.

"Well," he continued, his expression grave, "we've faced similar challenges in the past. Remember the CRPP (Committee Representing the People's Parliament) formed after the 1990 general election? I think we'll be fine."

"Only God knows. The CEC might view our actions as overly assertive," remarked an older representative familiar with the CEC's mindset.

His tone was tinged with mixed emotions. "We bear responsibility regardless. Even non-voters find this situation unbearable."

"Some people are discontented with the stark reality that, despite the predictability of the coup, the party was unprepared for it. If nothing is done, everything will be lost."

"So, even if they say 'no,' should we continue our mission?"

A variety of comments and opinions ensued. The MP driving, feeling stressed and excited, muttered something harsh into the phone to the young woman at the other end, who served as the sole contact between the representatives and the CEC. "Haven't you received a definitive answer yet? After we reach Yangon, it will be even more difficult as we'll have to disperse. Please, my Sis, you must establish contact as quickly as possible." The car accelerated.

More than an hour before reaching Yangon, the two cars paused at the 63-mile rest area on the highway to Yangon.

Suddenly, a Signal message flashed, proclaiming, "Agreed, Agreed," and amidst the excitement, an eager voice urged, "Do it quick, Bro, do it quick."

"Sister, what if you inform the other congressional representatives that you've obtained agreement from the CEC without any written evidence? It should be in the form of a written letter and a signature. Please obtain it for us."

Shortly thereafter, a letter and a signature arrived, affirming, "We, all members of the CEC, agree and approve the action to be taken for forming the Committee Representing the Pyidaungsu Hluttaw."

Both cars swiftly set off for Yangon. Even the remaining representatives from the other car had to make every effort to convene the National Assembly online. That night, in a vast courtyard in Yangon, they deliberated tirelessly without a moment's rest to establish the Committee Representing Pyidaungsu Hluttaw (CRPH). Empowered by a blank cheque from the CEC, they endeavoured to ensure an adequate number of representatives of the Pyidaungsu Hluttaw (National Assembly of Representatives) were present. Most representatives pledged to carry out the assignment without fail, although some cited poor health as an excuse.

On February 5, 2021, 298 parliamentarians convened the first emergency parliamentary session of the third term of the Hluttaw Session via video conference and formed the "Committee Representing Pyidaungsu Hluttaw (CRPH)." The legitimately and lawfully elected parliament convened virtually, assigning 15 MPs to continue the work of the Pyidaungsu Hluttaw. Several observers, including diplomats from the embassies of Denmark, Sweden, the United States of America, and the Czech Republic, attended. With 63 percent of parliamentarians from the House of Representatives and the House of Nationalities present, it was a quorate meeting. Although some MPs were unable to attend the session, they sent signed letters to support the establishment of the CRPH and the assignment of representatives. The combined number of parliamentarians authorising the formation of the CRPH reached 398 MPs, including both virtual attendees and those who authorised it through signed letters.

Following this, the CRPH issued a statement outlining four requests to the United Nations. It urged the international community to impose economic sanctions solely on military conspirators and their collaborating entrepreneurs, while avoiding comprehensive sanctions that would restrict humanitarian assistance. Drawing on past experiences of the severe impact of comprehensive economic sanctions on the general public, elected representatives made practical and public demands.

On the same day, the National League for Democracy dispatched a letter to the Secretary-General of the United Nations. In it, they implored the United Nations and all global nations to immediately and unconditionally release President U Win Myint, State Counsellor Daw Aung San Suu Kyi, members of the NLD, and activists. They also called for the implementation of the 2020 election results and the preservation of democracy and independence in Burma.

The response to the military coup also came from unexpected sources among our people. The swift wave of the Civil Disobedience Movement (CDM), initiated by medical personnel, expanded to encompass other civil servant groups and even independent private workforces. Young students, workers, farmers, carpenters, and seafarers from all corners of the country joined this resistance movement. Some individuals, dissatisfied with the NLD party, abstained from voting in the 2020 election and also boycotted the military's coup. The wave of the Spring Revolutionary Movement rapidly spread across the nation, characterised not by individual or institutional leadership, but by collective action. Despite facing formidable obstacles, this Revolution has steadily eroded and dismantled the grip of dictatorship.

Passage:

More CDMs and Protests Calling for R2P

On February 5, teaching staff also joined the Civil Disobedience Movement (CDM). In the following days, participation in the CDM swelled among the majority of government employees across various departments, reminiscent of the sudden and uncontrolled release of water from a breached dam.

On February 6, more than 3,000 workers from a garment factory in Yangon staged a demonstration, marching from Bayint Naung Market, the largest wholesale centre in Burma located in Insein Township, to Hledan in Kamayut Township. This journey likely took them over two hours to complete. Hledan is home to the University of Yangon, once renowned as a prestigious institution in Southeast Asia.

In the subsequent days, demonstrations and protests continued in response to the call for citizens to fulfil their duties, occurring regularly in cities, towns, and villages across the country.

On February 7, the momentum of the protesters reached its peak. However, amidst the peaceful demonstrations, there were instances of young people strutting in fancy high-street fashions, akin to catwalk models, seemingly mistaking the serious national campaign for a fashion show. Conversely, there were also daily wage earners, presumably from the underprivileged class, who arrived in a crowded Toyota Dyna, likely pooling their savings for the rental. They played rousing songs at high volumes from a resonating soundbox, singing, "Independence and peace are our goals! This is the ultimate battle we'll fight with our heart and soul!"

That night, a nationwide curfew under Section 144 was announced. However, the following day saw the launch of a voluntary transportation service programme. Protesters returning home were provided free transportation to the townships of Myenigon and Hledan. Thus, the entire operation of the protests could be considered "free of charge," as all involved supported the success of the Revolution by making voluntary contributions of labour, services, and donations of all kinds, including food and refreshments. To provide a pleasant surprise, some packets of meals, packed in Shorea robusta leaves, contained Burmese currency notes slipped inside small plastic bags. These notes served as fares to hire a taxi home, with some taxi drivers even offering them a lift.

"Now that we're liberated, why remain entangled and support the coup? Still eager to go to the office?"

"Why allow your workplace to ensnare you?" "Why endorse the coup?"

These days, slogans of this nature echoed on the roads and in the streets everywhere! The general strike was later joined by students and employees of private businesses. During rush hours, the car engine breakdown strike and the intentionally created traffic jam strike injected new energy into the Civil Disobedience Movement (CDM), and some individuals, including bus drivers, were apprehended for initiating these activities.

One video file went viral:

"Uncle, please help us. Why not join the CDM?" a young boy of pre-school age spoke loudly and clearly to the soldiers and policemen standing within the barricade of barbed wire. In one corner of the barricade stood a stern-looking soldier holding a rifle, already cocked and loaded. On the barbed wire barricade against which the soldier leaned was a printed vinyl sheet bearing the ominous words: "ANYONE PROVOKING INSULT IN ANY WAY WILL BE EXECUTED!"

On February 9th, a police officer from Naypyidaw named Khun Aung Ko Ko joined the mass rally of protesters. It was on that fateful day that, among the protesters in the new capital of Burma, Ma Mya Thwe Thwe Khaing, wearing a safety helmet, stood amid the crowd at a bus stop and was shot in the head, dying on the spot. In response to this brutal act by the military, the protesters chanted the slogan, "Though shot in the head, the Fighting Peacock will never retreat! The Peacock will surely resist the military's madness!" Within minutes, the biodata of the officer responsible for this heinous crime was shared online, and public demands for social punishment grew louder and louder against him. Government officials who had not joined the Civil Disobedience Movement (CDM) were already publicly denounced. Conversely, those who had not hesitated to join the CDM found themselves under increased threat; hundreds of activists, including NLD party leaders, prime ministers of respective regions and divisions, university professors who had joined the CDM Red Ribbon Movement, and Sean Turnell, the Australian economic advisor to the NLD government, were arrested.

Later, the police force and soldiers ruthlessly cracked down on the protesters, using sound bombs and tear gas, causing widespread and indiscriminate harm. As a result, residents in various neighbourhoods had to barricade the roads entering their quarters with sandbags and bamboo matting, while demonstrators had to wear improvised protective gear, such as fibre helmets and shields made of any available hard materials. Their slogans grew more emotional and furious: "We demand retribution for what they owe us from their actions in crushing the 8888 Riot, now in 2021!", "This is 2021! You cannot repeat the atrocities of 1988!" and "Military regime, we will drive you out! It's time for you to settle your debts once and for all!"

On February 10th, forty policemen from the Loikaw Police Force joined the ranks of demonstrators. Nine policemen who were ordered to arrest these officers also joined the protesters. Starting from February 15th, internet access was limited to certain periods of time. Despite this, protesters utilised various means to share the latest news of the strike. The campaign, "Millions to gather, fight together for the Freedom of Mother Suu," was successfully launched at Sule Pagoda Junction in Yangon. While well-known leaders of the 8888 Revolution once again took on leadership roles in the demonstrations in Yangon, young activists known as Generation-Z leaders emerged in many towns and cities across the country.

On February 20th, protesters staging demonstrations in West Sein Pan (Thanlyet-maw) Quarter, Mandalay, were fired upon, resulting in at least two deaths. Following this, cartoons advocating for police to join the protesters were shared as part of a propaganda campaign aimed at persuading the armed forces to join the mass of protesters.

Protest leaders announced in advance that the 22222 Popular Uprising (22-2-2021) would take place in Yangon by February 22nd. Internet connections were cut off throughout the city of Yangon from the evening of the 21st until 12:00 noon the following day. However, at 2:00 pm, hundreds of protesters emerged, marching along main roads, carrying banners bearing Pablo Neruda's motivational line, "You can cut all the flowers, but you cannot keep Spring from coming," with large-scale protests escalating throughout the city. Thus, the 22-2-2021 demonstration staged by all groups of protesters turned out to be a huge success.

The protests continued to gain momentum, with support from prominent people as well. The Pyihtaungsu Hluttaw Representative Committee announced the appointment of Dr. Sasa as the Myanmar Special Envoy to the United Nations. Simultaneously, the State Administrative Council (SAC), or the military regime, arrested celebrities and protest leaders. Myanmar-Athan Television (MRTV) and Myawaddy Television, mouthpieces of the military regime, announced daily lists of individuals issued arrest warrants under Section 505 (A). Additionally, protests against ward administrators newly appointed by the SAC took place, with some administrators resigning from their posts voluntarily. Large-scale protests made stronger demands in response to the UN's expressed deep concern, calling for "civilian protection and guarantees" for the people of Burma. Demonstrations were staged nationwide, with protesters holding placards reading, "We Need R2P" and "Welcome R2P."

Passage:

The Most Important CDMer, the Myanmar Representative to the UN

February 26, 2021

"First and foremost, I would like to reaffirm that I am representing the NLD-led civilian government elected by the people of Myanmar."

These were the words spoken by U Kyaw Moe Tun, Myanmar's Permanent Representative to the UN (and other international organisations) in Geneva, in his opening speech at the UN Assembly in New York. With this statement, he made his position clear. The majority of the people of Burma, watching on their TV and PC screens, assumed that, like the envoys before him representing Burma, he would speak solely for the government currently in power. Consequently, they didn't harbour great expectations that he would voice the concerns of his people. However, the opening lines of his speech—the real surprise—took everyone aback. Were they dreaming? The people of Burma, glued to the bright screen, just like the world leaders attending the UN Assembly, witnessed the unprecedented defiance of a high-ranking Burmese officer in support of the Civil Disobedience Movement (CDM), a rare breakthrough in Burma's political history.

Later, the Myanmar ambassador delivered a message from the Committee Representing Pyidaungsu Hluttaw (CRPH), which was recently formed with members of parliament democratically elected by the people of Burma in the 2020 General Election, deemed free and fair.

"The Burmese military has staged a coup, overthrowing the democratically elected government, resorting to lethal force against peaceful protesters on the streets, committing crimes targeting civilians, attacking ambulances and health workers, and unjustly arresting democratically elected parliamentarians. These actions not only endanger Burma and its people physically and psychologically but also pose serious threats to regional security and the prosperity of the international community. The Committee Representing Pyidaungsu Hluttaw (CRPH) urges the UN, the UN Security Council, and the international community to take necessary action against the Burma military and ensure the safety and security of the people of Burma."

The ambassador emphasised, "At this critical juncture, continued and strong support from the international community is vital for the people of Burma in our struggle against the military regime." He expressed heartfelt gratitude to all countries that have expressed support for the people of Burma, as well as to the Secretary-General, the Special Envoy, and the special reporter for Burma for their assistance. However, he noted, "the people of Burma still feel helpless."

Addressing the President and Excellencies, he continued, "In addition to the existing support, we need further and stronger actions from the international community to immediately end the military coup, cease the oppression of innocent people, restore power to the people, and reinstate democracy." His voice then became calm, firm, and decisive as he made his appeal.

"I appeal to all member states and the United Nations to:
1. Issue public statements strongly condemning the military coup.
2. Refuse to recognize the state administration council and the military regime by any means.
3. Urge the military regime to respect the results of the free and fair 2020 General Elections.
4. Refrain from cooperating with the military until power is returned to the elected government.
5. Take all necessary measures to stop violence and brutal acts by security forces against peaceful demonstrators and immediately end the military regime.
6. Support the CRPH."

These actions, he stressed, are crucial to restoring democracy and protecting the rights and freedoms of the people of Burma.

Civil activists watching the live broadcast were thrilled, pleased to hear the ambassador's speech. Before the conclusion of his address, reactions on Facebook attested to how amazed and supportive the viewers were. Wai Moe Naing, a well-known young protester from Monywa, posted, "Our Hero U Kyaw Moe Tun: 'In fact, this ambassador was appointed, not by CRPH, but by the military regime. So we thought he would speak for the voice of the military, for you see, no ambassador, no diplomat serving the MOFA has ever kicked out the military boots in our history! This evening is the most wonderful evening ever! We all are quite satisfied to hear your speech, H.E U Kyaw Moe Tun. It's quite a tonic for us. Congratulations! Here we throw a challenge in the Ring of Revolution!'"

"Mr President, I believe that our fellow Myanmar people inside and outside the country are following this meeting via webcast with high interest. Please allow me to speak a few words in Burmese," said the ambassador. Then he continued to address the Burmese people in their native language,

"Mingalabar (Auspiciousness to you all). My dear brothers and sisters and our dear members of all national races, I am very grateful to you, all people from all walks of life, for your unity and concerted effort in working towards the immediate end of the military coup, the release of our leader Daw Aung San Suu Kyi, President U Win Myint and others unlawfully detained, the restoration of state power to the people, the reinstatement of democracy, the establishment of a federal democratic Union, and the success of this Revolution. I encourage you all to continue with your noble cause. This Revolution must succeed! It is the people who always play the key role. Our Revolution, Our victory!"

His voice almost faltered. He knew well that as a government employee serving in this prestigious position, he would face great peril for uttering these revolutionary words. Nevertheless, he did not mince his words, but instead spoke what he felt obliged to say.

Following the military coup, government employees initiated the civil disobedience movement (CDM). Initially, doctors, nurses, and health workers took the lead, followed by personnel from various sectors such as education, railway service, general administration, police forces, customs department, agriculture, and the Ministry of Foreign Affairs, joining the movement en masse. When a new minister, formerly a leader of the PPP party and a disgraced election loser, was appointed to a vacant position in the Ministry of Social Welfare, office staff across the board boycotted their duties. The number of those joining the CDM swelled to hundreds of thousands of staff. As the slogan, "No office-going! Liberate yourself!" echoed, measures were taken to halt bus services during rush hours and to gather in front of offices and departments to persuade staff to join the CDM.

Meanwhile, Ambassador U Kyaw Moe Tun's participation in the CDM garnered significant attention worldwide. His commendable decision and courageous action had a profound impact on the Revolution's cause. After his speech, he received congratulations from ambassadors representing various nations attending the meeting. His bravery demonstrated to the world that the primary loyalty and dedication of a government servant should be to the cause of their nation. His heroic act challenged the age-old conventional concept of a government employee's duties, turning it on its head.

Indeed, the Spring Revolution has been gradually dismantling the barriers that have obstructed the citizens of Burma for decades. It has fervently struggled to navigate itself out of the intricate Maze of Burmese politics.

Passage:

Ongoing peaceful revolution with brutal crackdowns

On March 1st, three former UN members, including former UN rapporteur on human rights in Burma Miss Yanghee Lee, established the Special Advisory Council for Myanmar (SAC-M). Just two days later, on March 3rd, poets K Za Win and Kyin Lin Aye were tragically gunned down in the military's brutal crackdown on protests near the Phayani Pagoda on Phidaungsu Road, Monywa.

During a protest in Mandalay, a nineteen-year-old Chinese girl named Kyal Sin, also known as "Bright Star" and alias Deng Jiaxi, was shot in the head. Following her death, authorities hastily exhumed her body, claiming that the bullet lodged in her head was not the one fired by the police force. Kyal Sin was wearing a black T-shirt emblazoned with the words "Everything will be OK" when she was shot. A photo of her went viral both locally and abroad: a young Chinese civil activist in her T-shirt, holding a Coca Cola bottle in her hand as a makeshift shield against tear gas, looking up into the sky to discern the direction from which bullets could come.

Another video went viral as well. In North Okkalapa, Yangon, soldiers brutally assaulted volunteer health workers, striking them on the head with gun butts and kicking them with their military boots. On March 8th, U Khin Maung Latt, a township member of the NLD, tragically died while in custody under interrogation by military intelligence. Following this, numerous cases of human rights violations emerged, with many detainees dying under ruthless interrogation within 24 hours of their arrest. March 8th also marked International Women's Day. Women across Burma, young and old, took to the streets shouting the slogan, "Fly our Htameins ('sarong') as the Banners of our Victory!" They draped their Htameins like flags, hanging them across roads and streets, believing it would deter soldiers, as superstition suggests that passing under a woman's sarong leads to loss of glory. Thus, Burmese women displayed their unwavering strength, power, conviction, and dedication to the Revolution. Interestingly, armed soldiers and police officers merely looked up at the line of Htameins and refrained from advancing, displaying timid behaviour unbecoming of their gender. The sight of fluttering Htameins prevented them from getting closer to the protesters. Although initially met with criticism among protesters, this novel form of protest elicited laughter and gained popularity. Later, as the people matured in their understanding of the Revolution, they recognised the line of Htameins as a bold symbol advocating for women's equal rights.

Since March 8th, in Sanchaung Township, Yangon, soldiers had preemptively blocked the roads before the announcement of the curfew. Consequently, over two hundred protesters, including students and ordinary people, found themselves cornered. In response, residents from other quarters and townships arrived to uplift the spirits of the cornered protesters by banging cans and pans and chanting slogans, breaking the silence of the curfew hours. Frustrated, soldiers fired random shots into the darkness, aiming towards the source of the shouts. Silence momentarily ensued, followed by a unified chant of "Happy New Year!" as a mocking reaction to the armed forces. In the stillness of the night, the following slogans emerged:

"Can't suppress the spirits of Sanchaung!"
"Together we will wage this revolutionary war!"
"The rising tide or the falling tide, nothing
   Can't drown Miss Hyacinth, her flower flourishing!"
"The protests of Yangon bring the good omen of victory!"
"Can't gun down our political beliefs!"

On March 8th, the spokesperson for UN Secretary-General Antonio Guterres confirmed receipt of a letter from Dr. Sasa, proposing action by the UN Security Council against the State Administrative Council to uphold its commitment to R2P (Responsibility to Protect) and the protection of civilians.

The following day, as dawn broke, a heart-wrenching message reached

Ko Zaw Myat Lin's wife. Ko Zaw Myat Lin, an NLD member in charge of the (Amay-Eain) Suu Vocational Institute in Shwe Pyi Thar Township, had been arrested by the military the previous night. His wife was summoned to claim his battered and bruised body, rendered unrecognisable even to her due to unspeakable tortures inflicted upon him. His photo was briefly circulated on Facebook, evoking horror and disgust among viewers who could only imagine the agony he endured.

U Kyaw Htay Oo, in charge of the La-yaung Taw Horticulture Training Academy of Daw Khin Kyi Foundation (Daw Khin Kyi is the mother of Aung San Suu Kyi), shared his harrowing experience upon his release in November 2022. He recounted enduring unspeakable tortures under interrogation, facing threats of imminent death if he didn't comply. Officers showed him a video file on their phone depicting a pointed bamboo piercing through the mouth of school teacher Ko Zaw Myat Lin, followed by the pouring of acid into his mouth. The officers proudly possessed and displayed this horrifying footage, indicative of their lack of remorse or accountability.

Since the early days of the Revolution, people have realised the military's willingness to engage in lawless acts, including random shootings, torture, and unethical conduct, without any sense of responsibility or accountability. Consequently, the people harbour deep-seated resentment not only towards military leaders but also towards members of the security forces such as soldiers and policemen.

On March 10th, the UN Security Council issued a strong urging for the military to end the coup and reinstate the civilian government. Starting on March 14th, mobile phone internet connections were abruptly cut off nationwide. Even on that single day, the crackdown claimed the lives of at least 38 protesters. Martial law was declared to take effect in two townships of Yangon, and in the subsequent days it was extended to other townships, towns, and cities. Beginning on March 18th, the "Myanmarnet" service, which provided internet connections through Wi-Fi technology, was also abruptly cancelled without any limitations.

Tragically, on March 23rd, in Mandalay, a seven-year-old girl named Khin Myo Chit was playing in a compound when her father rushed her inside the house. While sitting on her father's lap indoors, military troops stormed in and opened fire, killing her. They also assaulted and arrested her brother. The inclusion of innocent young victims in the military's violence left the populace bewildered.

March 27th, formerly known as Anti-Fascist Resistance Day, ironically became a red-letter day in the Burmese calendar due to the highest number of casualties and deaths since the military's brutal crackdown on protests began. On that fateful day, the crackdown claimed the lives of at least 114 individuals. Troops set fire to car tires and bamboo barricades erected for the protection of local residents, and gunfire targeted the buildings of the American Center in Yangon. Furthermore, an airstrike was conducted on a Kayin village, located on the Thai-Burma border and serving as a base for the KNU, resulting in the deaths of at least 10 individuals.

On April 1st, the military regime ordered the wireless broadband internet to be cut off indefinitely, with no specified time limit. Two days later, on April 3rd, while celebrating Easter Day, people initiated the Easter Egg Strike by inscribing their desires on the surface of Easter eggs. Subsequently, despite the inability to assemble for traditional protests, various villages, towns, and cities sustained their opposition to the military coup and dictatorship through innovative forms of strikes.

At 5:00 pm on April 5th, synchronised clapping resonated across villages, towns, and cities as people expressed support for the ongoing successful Civil Disobedience Movement (CDM), which they believed would undermine the military regime. Some brave young protesters even risked their lives to conduct demonstrations by burning Chinese national flags as a symbolic gesture.

Credit is due to these courageous individuals who rejected participation in the traditional Water Festival, which marks the Burmese New Year, opting instead to protest against the military. Civil activists engaged in various activities, including spraying red paint on roads and organising the Flower Strike and Rubbish Strike, to demonstrate their opposition to the military regime.

Amidst shouting slogans and brandishing placards with messages like "The People of Mainland Burma and the Hill Tribes Stand Ever United" and "You may not stand on the ground of Truth, but you don't support the Wrongs," the people showcased their innovative spirit by organising a diverse array of strikes. These included the Night Strike, the Diving Strike, the Roly-Poly Strike, the Barbie Doll Strike, among others.

While innovation played a significant role in the Spring Revolution, some aspects of the movement didn't solely rely on innovation but instead emphasised collective leadership as a driving force.

Passage:

The Plight of Medical Personnel

It was 8:05 pm, and amidst the engulfing darkness of the night, stood a young couple dressed in white hospital gowns, each holding a flashlight. Their stethoscopes, glinting in the dim light, hung over their shoulders as they pedalled through the darkness, excitement coursing through their veins. They were headed towards the source of burning flames and billowing smoke that filled the sombre blue night air.

"My dear," one of them began, "we've already handed over our belongings, a few pieces of jewellery, to our parents. Before we depart, there's something I must say. We don't know when we'll have the chance to meet again. We knelt down and paid our last respects to our beloved parents, our benefactors, begging for their forgiveness. And now, we are ready for our mission. We're ready to risk our lives."

"Well, bullets are blind, you know," the other replied. "They don't discriminate between a life-saving doctor and a foe. A blood-thirsty bullet may come from anywhere, and we could be shot at any time. It sends a chill down my spine, of course. But as a medical practitioner, I simply want to live and die with a clear conscience."

Seized by the revolutionary spirit, both young doctors were determined to do something for the victims. As they pedalled along their way, they encountered fellow cyclists who cheered them on, all pedalling their bicycles at breakneck speed. Spotting the two doctors dressed in white gowns, some local residents standing on the roadside began clapping their hands, their applause echoing through the darkness.

Passing by a monastery, they encountered an old monk standing in the shadows. He bestowed his blessings upon them and uttered, "Please take care." Along the roads, burning tires had been piled up as barriers to prevent soldiers from entering residential compounds. Some people swiftly removed the tires to allow the two young doctors, who had come to rescue, to pass through.

"Chin up, son. I'm with you," one of them reassured the other.

"Picture your little son in the eyes of your friends. Don't let yourself down," another urged.

"Dad! Dad! Can you hear me?" echoed the voice of a distressed individual.

Amidst the chaos, dead bodies lay scattered everywhere. Some had been brought here after their demise, while others were dying souls who had arrived just before their final breath.

"I'm a surgeon. I'm at your service, sir," one of the doctors declared, ready to lend aid wherever needed.

"The operating theatre needs you right now. There are so many patients, quite a handful!" exclaimed a distressed voice.

Outside the hospital, gunshots pierced the night air, and emergency ambulances arrived one by one, each carrying gunshot victims – wounds penetrating heads, abdomens, limbs. The smell of blood permeated everywhere, with gunfire echoing through the silence of the night.

"You bloody fools! You bloodthirsty murderers! You keep on taking precious lives, and we keep on saving them. Let's see who wins," shouted one of the doctors in sheer frustration.

"Doc! Take a look...!" exclaimed a horrified nurse.

A patient, with a gunshot wound through the skull, his brain protruding, stumbled out of his hospital bed and collapsed on the floor. Doctors, nurses, and volunteers sprang into action, attending to multiple critical cases simultaneously. There was no discrimination based on seniority or specialisation – everyone pitched in wherever they could. The general practitioner informed patients who had received treatment and post-op patients that he would provide free follow-up care at his clinic for the next few days. Meanwhile, the public health professor, though not involved in clinical treatment, tirelessly worked to prepare operation fields and coordinate with the blood bank for transfusions if needed. Leader doctors and team members were all fully occupied, their foreheads sweating with exertion.

In line with an appeal from healthcare personnel dated February 18, 2021, stating that CDM activities would not interfere with emergency healthcare duties, these dedicated professionals demonstrated that their commitment was more than just words. Without their ethical and loyal service, the number of deaths and casualties on March 14, 2021, would have been even higher.

"I feel a little hurt here," a middle-aged man said, pointing to his bleeding chest where a bullet had lodged.

A teenager with an innocent face, his left arm crushed, calmly addressed the doctor, "Sir, please attend to the more serious cases first."

"Doctor," another patient lying on a hospital bed remarked, "I'm grateful the bullet missed my leg bone."

"I'm OK. Well done," said the left-handed uncle who had to have his left hand cut off.

"Please operate on my back and get the bullet out quickly," said a young man, ardently, "and then please give me a glass of water, and then I'll return to fighting them again."

Families and friends of patients gathered outside the small operating theatre, eagerly awaiting news of their loved ones' turn for treatment. However, the patients themselves were steadfast in their belief that no one held VIP status in such dire circumstances, willingly allowing those in more urgent need to go first. Meanwhile, members of the Red Cross went above and beyond their call of duty, not only attending to patients' needs within the hospital but also providing assistance at the X-ray department and delivering donated food and medicines.

Despite the curfew, local residents braved the dangers to send provisions like eggs, fried rice, coconut noodles, milk, and water to the hospital. This night witnessed the tireless efforts of countless unsung heroes in the hospitals of Yangon.

A Facebook post encapsulated the harrowing realities faced by medical personnel: blocked roads prevented timely treatment for the injured, and soldiers' brutality hindered efforts to transport patients to mobile clinics. Doctors were forced to seek refuge in nearby homes, converting living rooms into makeshift clinics. Tragically, in some cases, treatment came too late, and these generous households provided shelter even to the deceased.

Some doctors risked their lives navigating the darkness to attend to patients, knowing the perilous nature of the task. A poignant anecdote shared on Facebook recounted the heartbreaking conversation between a doctor couple, torn between their duty to their profession and their responsibility to their children. In the face of such adversity, one spouse implored the other to stay home, recognizing the need for at least one of them to survive for the sake of their family. The doctor's words evoke a sense of sacrifice and resilience amid the chaos of revolution.

The heartfelt words penned by Surgeon Dr. Tin Htun in his "Last Will" reflect the deep conviction and dedication he had towards the cause of the people. Despite the inherent dangers and risks involved, he remained resolute in his commitment to fight for the sovereignty and freedom of his fellow citizens.

In his letter, Dr. Tin Htun expresses his profound love and gratitude to his family and loved ones, reassuring them that his sacrifice is made in pursuit of a noble cause. He implores them not to mourn his death excessively but to take pride in his actions, knowing that he gave his life for something greater than himself.

To his comrades, Dr. Tin Htun expresses his admiration and gratitude for their unwavering dedication to the Revolution. He urges them to continue the fight until the people's power is restored and the dictatorship is overthrown. Despite his premature departure, he remains hopeful that his sacrifice will contribute to the eventual downfall of the military regime.

Dr. Tin Htun's tragic death serves as a poignant reminder of the sacrifices made by countless healthcare workers in the aftermath of the coup. Their bravery and selflessness in the face of danger exemplify the unwavering spirit of the people's Revolution.

"Of course, they are the ones who shoot mercilessly! And nobody can guarantee that those reckless killers won't shoot you wherever you are. And nobody can guarantee they won't invade our hospital. You see, they beat health workers to death with the butts of their rifles, saying, 'You are the ones responsible for ensuring that the protestors are helped and treated!' Others might mock us for being afraid of being arrested at the hospital or even being killed there. Our participation in the Civil Disobedience Movement (CDM) isn't driven by reluctance to fulfil our professional duties or by fear. I'm not apprehensive of arrest or death; rather, I'm compelled by an intolerable injustice: the armed oppression of our unarmed citizens. Just yesterday, they callously shot and killed over a hundred people. As a surgeon, how many lives could I save with my skilled scalpel? Perhaps four or five at most per day. It dawned on me that to prevent further loss of innocent lives, we must confront those who have mercilessly taken them. If I wish to safeguard more lives, I must relinquish my surgical tools and take up arms."

These sentiments expressed by the surgeon are grounded in harsh reality. How many others, across various age groups, share his sentiments?

After witnessing the widespread acts of inhumanity, those who had previously viewed peaceful protests as the most effective political strategy against dictatorship have had a change of heart. They have now resolved to "confront bullets with unbowed heads."

Passage:

Role of Youths in Spring

April 15, 2021

"How did it happen?" his friend asked. "Last night, I went to bed late, but I couldn't fall asleep. So, when I woke up this morning, I didn't feel fresh. I've been feeling down these days. We don't know what will happen in the future, you know. I've left my house, but I am not sure if I can get back home. The news of Wai Moe Naing's arrest has made things worse. I had a chance to watch the video showing how he got hit by the police car. Tell me something about the consequences."

The speaker at the other end of the line was talking on the phone. Because his friend was not making a video call, he couldn't see his face, but he could gauge from his friend's tone how angry he was feeling.

"Well," he replied, "Wai Moe Naing is a true activist, you know. You could see him leading demonstrations everywhere every day. Besides, he could sway the audience in Monywa. His speeches even go viral locally. No wonder he must have been the target of the military. Just imagine how the protests have been in full swing on the roads and streets under his active leadership for sixty-eight days, from February 7 to today, April 15. And he had a large number of followers, too. The people of Monywa proved themselves to be good followers. Even the sight of the crowds of protesters following his lead gave me a thrill!" His voice sounded enthusiastic.

"What a despicable act!" he exclaimed. "They appeared out of nowhere in an ordinary vehicle—not even a police car, mind you! Then they sped towards our guy, hit him, and arrested him! I'm worried about him. Those guys are dangerous, you know. I hope he stays safe! And I hope you stay healthy. Take care of yourself, mate. You'll have to adjust to a new environment."

His friend on the other end of the line seemed composed.

"Thank you, my friend," his friend replied. "I'm safe and secure here in the liberated area, but I'm saddened by the fact that many of our youth are getting arrested, and some have even lost their lives. So, I'm struggling with a sense of guilt." His friend's voice grew sombre.

"No, no! Everyone has their own challenges to face. We just have to do what we can, right?" His tone conveyed understanding and forgiveness.

The internet connection was weak, and his voice faded out.

"The internet connection is terrible. Why don't you type on Messenger?" His friend's Messenger notification chimed.

"Well, let's set aside my situation," his friend's message appeared on Messenger. "Let's talk about Wai Moe Naing. He's truly an iconic figure!"

"A writer as well," he typed back on Messenger. "He started writing at the age of thirteen and was an avid reader. It's no surprise he could initiate various campaigns. He was among the protesters who launched the pot-and-pan-striking protest in Monywa."

After the military coup, the people of Burma had to use VPN connections before accessing Facebook and Messenger. Although these applications don't guarantee information security like Signal and WhatsApp, many still use VPN. Moreover, many have developed the habit of deleting files once they're sure the recipient has received their message. People, young and old, are cautious about their information security, often leaving their smartphones at home when going out to public places and opting for keypad mobiles instead.

"Yes, you're right," he responded. "If you check out his posts, you'll see the momentum and impact of the Spring Revolution. I'm currently going through his posts. Just a moment. I'm concerned the internet connection on your end may not be good. I'll send you copies of some of his posts. Check out his daily updates."

"Thanks, friend."

"My dear civil servants," the post read, "As far as I've observed, the military has begun pressuring our respected CDMs, who have bravely defied their unlawful orders so far, in hopes of persuading them to call off their strikes and resume their duties. While CDM staff remain united in defying the military's orders, it's not enough. We all need to take to the streets and join our people's movement. It's crucial for our people and our CDMs to work hand in hand and move forward together. If street protests are strong but the CDM is weak, our campaigns won't succeed. Similarly, if the CDM is strong but people don't protest on the streets, the military could easily pressure the CDMs to comply [...]. I urge you all to stand united. We cannot afford to fail. Neither can I. We must fight until we achieve victory!" (February 13)

While Miss Ei Thinza Maung and Miss Ester Ze Naw, along with factory worker Miss Moe Sandar Myint, led the demonstrations gaining momentum in Yangon, Dr Tayza San took on the leadership role in staging demonstrations in Mandalay, and Wai Moe Naing led the demonstrations in Monywa. What set Wai Moe Naing apart from other leaders was his ability to organise groups for missions: the young supporters didn't just back him up but actively played their own roles. Another strength of his was his daily postings about the movements in Monywa, akin to daily reports submitted to the public.

"Take a look at this post," he typed out on Messenger. "See how tactfully he addressed public opinion on a military staff member who has joined the CDM."

"Today (18-2-2021), while the protesters of Monywa were staging the sit-down strike by the Bronze Statue of Gen. Aung San, a sergeant clerk Than Lwin (Regimental No. 550096) from Light Infantry Battalion No. 16 came and joined our protesters [...]. This sparked off some suspicions among our people over whether he has joined us on his own accord or as a wedge to cleave us apart. What I would like to request of you all is it'd be extremely rash to make an assumption. In fact, he has joined us by sacrificing his life, so Sergeant Than Lwin must be treated equally like the other CDMs. I'd like to request you seriously to have trust in our movement and that all our people may continue to stand united under the leadership of our Boycott Committee for, as we have made our solemn pledges many a time, we will never abuse your trust. We may not breed unnecessary suspicions, but we must be very careful to move forward. Please trust us, trust our movements." (February 18)

"You're right, pal. He's got the situation under control. Without resorting to extremes, he could organise the public."

Day by day, more and more army personnel joined the CDM, but there were scarcely any members of the army forces like Sergeant Than Lwin who stepped up to the stage and addressed the public. The general public's attitude towards army personnel joining the CDM was still fraught with dilemmas. Thus far, activists across the country had continued staging peaceful demonstrations. It was only on September 8, 2021, that the Committee Representing the Pyihtaungsu Hluttaw issued the NUG's Policy for the Tatmadaw and Members of the Police Forces.

"Well, there are so many CDMs in Monywa! Many department offices are now shut down. The State Administrative Council's administration turned upside-down! SAC, now sacked!" he typed out on Messenger. With the high tempo of the CDM, civil servants didn't show up at some offices, creating a vacuum in the administration's mechanism. Monywa deserved credit for its successful strikes that shut down government offices more effectively than any other town or city. On the other hand, the SAC replaced current administrative officers with its stooges. However, residents of respective quarters raised objections at the bottom of the administration hierarchy. The boycotters didn't overlook the residents' role in objecting to the new replacements, further exacerbating the administration vacuum.

"Here you go," he typed, "this one posted a week later. It's about autonomous rule. Other towns and villages, though not in the limelight, have already established their own administrative units and launched their own administrative mechanisms. Their efforts have impressed us a lot!"

"Hello, Monywa, it's time for autonomous rule over your respective quarters and villages! Although the power of the people-elected regional and quarter administrators remains valid until President U Win Myint's term is completed, the SAC has dismissed them from their duties. This completely undermines the quarter/village administration system, which reflects the most fundamental form of democracy. The quarter/village group administrators are representatives of the people, much like the representatives of the Hluttaw. Therefore, the SAC has no right or authority to dismiss these civil servants.

Residents of every village and quarter in Monywa Township are urged to follow these four points:

1. The administrators dismissed by the SAC, who are still entitled to their posts, should defy the orders of the SAC and continue their duties as usual (seeking the strength and support of the public if necessary).
2. Those appointed to new posts as quarter/village administrators should resign from their positions and submit their letters of resignation to the township administrators.
3. Residents of respective quarters and villages should boycott the new administrators by recognizing the role of the former administrators.
4. All administrators are requested to organise local residents and join the main column of demonstrators from all respective quarters/villages at 9:00 am every day.

I urge all administrators to defy the illegitimate SAC and remain loyal to State Counsellor Daw Aung San Suu Kyi and President U Win Myint. Ensure that your autonomy governs your respective village and quarter." (February 20)

Taking measures to fill the vacuum of administration occurred in the early stages of the Spring Revolution. Wai Moe Naing found himself deeply embedded within the network of Revolution leaders: his directives were effectively disseminated among his intended audiences.

"This one," he continued typing, "was posted on the last day of February. Remember? We, the people, were incredibly united. We successfully blocked the Bayintnaung Bridge spanning over the Yangon River with a twelve-wheel truck, dissuading non-CDM office-goers. That was the success of the No Office-going Strike! In another incident, tear gas bombs frightened protesters, causing them to flee barefoot and leaving their slippers behind. However, bystanders collected the ownerless slippers, arranged them neatly, and patiently waited for the owners to reclaim them. Yet another incident involved a car being struck by reckless, enraged chauvinists, but to our surprise workshop owners offered their services free of charge to repair the dents! Such acts are quite rare in our history, you know."

"The following is Wai Moe Naing's experience shared as a protester in Monywa. I urge you to read his writings carefully and thoughtfully. His writings exemplify his exceptional organisational skills!"

"My dear people of Monywa, how united and admirable you are! I am deeply impressed by your solidarity and resilience. Today, we faced unexpected challenges and tensions, but I salute you all for your steadfastness. When I saw the police forces approaching from the other side of the road, I feared that our protest might be dispersed. It's not that I doubted the strength of our people who have endured the pressures of the military regime for decades. However, if the demonstrators at the forefront, especially those near the barricades, had panicked and scattered, it would have been a significant setback. I was worried about how to control the crowd."

"But to my relief, our people followed the instructions of our strike committee diligently and in unison, from the staunchest supporters at the front to those at the back. It was truly inspiring! People were ready to contribute by building makeshift shelters of canvas or vinyl sheets for the protesters, demonstrating an invincible spirit of 'Come what may!' My dear people, you have created a milestone in the history of our town."

"As per our instructions, those at the back of the line, along with vehicles like social welfare cars and motorcycles, stopped their engines to block the way around the Clock Tower. It was a motivating sight indeed. We must preserve this unity at all costs."

"The organisations under the Boycott Committee, such as the Burma Students Strike, the University Students Strike, the NLD, Former Activists of the 8888 Revolution, and the Political Prisoners' Committee, will always be at the forefront. I urge you all to remain united and disciplined. In the days to come, there may be attempts to disrupt our demonstrations, but it's crucial that we respond to such challenges without resorting to violence. We must remain steadfast and resolute in our fight against dictatorship, embodying unwavering determination and conviction."

"Yes," he said, switching on the speaker device in response to the message without continuing to type on the screen, "it's crucial that we avoid resorting to violence. Admittedly, our patience has been wearing thin. If our leader had given the order to 'Charge!', many of our people would have retaliated against the armed forces. You see, when Wai Moe Naing made his post public, the number of victims shot and killed by the military had not yet exceeded twenty. Yet, in just a month and a half, as of today, April 15, the number of victims has surpassed 700! To be precise, 721 victims! You can verify this on the list compiled by the Assistance Association for Political Prisoners (AAPP). Approximately 75 victims are shot and killed every single day, you see. Sorry, pal. I'm just furious right now!"

"How's your internet connection holding up?" his friend typed. Another message beeped on Messenger.

"I am deeply grateful to each and every one of you for your unwavering support, which has enabled us to continue our Revolution. Once we achieve success in the Revolution, there are many people whom I must personally visit and express my humble gratitude to. My heart is heavy with gratitude for your boundless love and dedication to the cause of the Revolution. I am at a loss for words, my dear people, but I solemnly promise that we will persevere in our struggle and emerge victorious through unwavering determination!" (March 12)

"My goodness!" his friend exclaimed over the phone. "Did he mention paying homage to people? He's a Muslim, isn't he?" The phone connection was slightly better now.

"Yeah," he responded. "He's a Burmese-Muslim. You see, we've all grown up in the atmosphere of Burmese society for generations, so it's no surprise that we're quite familiar with Burmese customs and culture. It's just part of who we are."

"The other day, I came across a post someone shared about an upcountry setting. The young Muslims were dressed like our young Shinlaungs entering the novitiation ceremony in the Buddhist Order. They were celebrating their own religious ceremony, but they were doing it in the Burmese traditional way, with young Muslims on decorated carts followed by a long procession with glinting gilded umbrellas. It was something I'd never heard of before, but it makes sense."

"Well, the truth is, we've been censored at the national level and kept in the dark for ages. We've been unaware of the trends in our own history, so the military has kept us under all sorts of illusions."

"You know, Wai Moe Naing wrote about how the military manipulated historical facts, changing and labelling the Anti-Fascist Revolution as Tatmadaw Day. It's a very informative post!"

"Here are some posts expressing his opinions on what could happen in the future. Now we're all quite convinced of the ultimate goal of the Spring Revolution."

"Though we have been striving towards our goal since 1947, we have not yet achieved it—the Federal Union. Yes, this is undoubtedly the ultimate goal of our Spring Revolution. Under the federal system, political authority is divided between two autonomous sets of governments: the national and the subnational, or the autonomy of respective states and divisions. This system benefits not only the minorities but also our Bamars. Its administrative form would help implement reforms faster." (March 20)

"The Anti-Fascist Resistance Day marks the day our Burmese Tatmadaw, led by Gen. Aung San, and the allied forces drove out the Fascist Japanese. During the period of the AFPF government, it was renamed Tatmadaw Day, but in essence it signifies the day when the Fascist devils were driven out of our country. Tomorrow, on March 27, besides the main column, I urge all quarters and villages to march in the columns of demonstrations. I urge you all to close your shops, offices, factories, and mills, and come out onto the streets and roads. It isn't a day to stay indoors! Join any columns of demonstration around you. Be vigilant about your security against all disruptive elements. If confronted with these elements, please follow the instructions of the Defense Team. Last but not least, since information is finding it hard to flow, please do your bit to spread the latest info far and wide among your friends, neighbours, and relatives." (March 26)

"Indeed, the information flow is becoming increasingly restricted. I'm not sure if we'll have the chance to chat again in the future. Take care, my friend. As the well-known writer Bamo Tin Aung said: 'Your opponent might want you to die, but what you should do is be careful not to get killed—this is also part of the Revolution!' Stay healthy. We'll meet again and celebrate when our Revolution is successful, right?"

"Thanks, my friend. I'll read this post."

"We all must exercise extreme caution, remain vigilant, and press forward! We must use every possible means to defy the military dictatorship. Countless individuals have sacrificed their lives and shed their blood. As we march along this path of blood, we must fight and emerge victorious in this battle! While we remember the hardships of our past, we must also apply our prudence, wisdom, and mindfulness as we progress forward." (April 3)

"Well," he said, "people have accepted Wai Moe Naing as their leader. That's good. At first, I thought people would say, 'He's quite young, he's a Muslim,' and so on, and I feared he'd be rejected. Anyway, he's got what he deserves," said his friend, satisfied. The night was silent, providing a favourable atmosphere for the two friends to exchange their conversation. Distance is nothing at all in this digital age.

"Yes, you're right," he said. "He proves himself to be a good leader, dealing with situations calmly. He's brave. So, I'm sure the people all love him, giving him the nickname 'Little Panda.' They are good followers of him." Cooperation, mutual respect, and the acceptance of youth leadership by both young and old people turned out to be the essence of the Spring.

"Yes," his friend replied. "That guy could exploit social media very well for our benefit. He's been treated as their brother. You know, whatever religion you confess, what matters most is adopting a virtuous mind and the right attitude towards your nation. This is the striking feature of the Spring, right?"

"That's right," he said. "Of course, there are extremists in religion spreading hate speech, but we all are now liberal. We no longer react to such hate speech. Now the military are too busy spreading propaganda and false news or fake news or whatever. Besides, Facebook has restricted their page and the pages of many of their supporters. Normally, hate speech has no room among our people, you know, though it's rampant online."

In fact, among those who were arrested early in the morning of February 1 was Ko Mya Aye, the student leader of the 88 Generation. He was criticised for being an old Islamic fellow, and the Chauvinist Buddhist Association named Ma-Ba-Tha launched a campaign against inviting him to give talks in literary events between 2013-2015. Campaigns had been active since 2012, attempting to change the mindset of local people and portray Islamic people as "foreigners or aliens professing a different religion." For decades, the people of Burma had been locked in the Maze of politics founded by the military, exploiting religion as a tool. But in this Spring Revolution, in Monywa, where the majority of the population are Buddhists, the local people willingly followed the leadership of a Muslim youth, Wai Moe Naing, and embraced him as the voice of the Boycott Committee.

The Spring Revolution called for freedom of religion and hammered at the thick concrete wall of the Maze in which religion has been manipulated for the sake of political power.

Passage:

Opening New Pages of Spring: National Unity Government NUG

The headline "CRPH announces the National Union Government has been set up" dominated the front pages of newspapers issued on April 16, 2021. The Committee Representing Pyihtaungsu Hluttaw (CRPH) declared the establishment of the National Union Government (NUG), exercising the political power democratically vested by the people of Burma in the 2020 multi-party General Election. This action was taken in accordance with the Federal Democracy Charter issued on March 31. Through collective leadership and discussions within the National Unity Consultative Council, the NUG was formed with the approval of CRPH.

Led by acting President Duwa Lashi La, with President U Win Myint and State Counsellor Daw Aung San Suu Kyi as patrons, the NUG established 11 ministries initially, including the Ministry of Foreign Affairs (led by Minister Daw Zin Mar Aung), Ministry of Home Affairs and Immigration (led by Minister U Lwin Ko Latt), Ministry of International Relations (led by Minister Dr. Sa Sa), and Ministry of Education and Health (led by Minister Dr. Zaw Wai Soe). By February 2023, the number of ministries had increased to 17, with the addition of new ministries such as the Ministry of Women, Youth and Children Affairs (led by Minister Naw Susana Hla Hla Soe), Ministry of Federal Affairs (led by Minister Dr. Lian Hmung Sakhong), and Ministry of Human Rights (led by Minister U Aung Myo Min). Appointments to these ministries included not only members of the NLD but also representatives from other political parties and national civil organisations.

U Yee Mon, an elected NLD representative, serves as the Minister for Defence Services in the NUG. He reported that measures have been taken to organise the People's Defence Forces (PDF) to oust the illegitimate military government.

The CRPH, established on February 5, swiftly organised the Revolutionary Government within a hundred days of its formation, comprising representatives from various groups, including legitimate elected representatives. This Revolutionary Government, known as the NUG, is presumed to include underground activists and civil activists. On March 10, Mahn Win Khaing Than, one of the initial detainees following the military coup, was appointed as the Union Prime Minister of the NUG. However, just 18 hours later, the SAC discovered that this Kayin leader, who had been under house arrest, had escaped. The whereabouts of other ministers and deputy ministers remain unknown, leading the SAC to derisively liken the NUG to a government existing only in name.

Since March, the CRPH has been tirelessly preparing for the formation of the Revolutionary Government. On March 1, it designated the State Administration Council (SAC) as a terrorist group. Subsequent steps included the appointment of temporary union ministers on March 2, granting additional responsibilities to U Kyaw Moe Tun, Burma's permanent representative to the UN, on March 3, and the appointment of a temporary vice president on March 9. Furthermore, civil administrative organisations established on February 22, as per the interim civil administration plan, were recognised as possessing legitimate regional administrative authority.

In accordance with Order No. 13/2021 issued on March 14, individuals have the right to defend themselves against acts of violence as outlined in the Criminal Law (Crime), Chapter 4: Rights of Defense. Any defensive action taken in accordance with this law is not subject to legal action. Additionally, Order No. 14/2021 issued on March 17 removed all armed ethnic groups from the blacklist of terrorists or unlawful forces. Finally, on March 31, Order No. 20/2021 declared the abolition of the 2008 Constitution.

On that significant day, in accordance with Order No. 19/2021, the CRPH declared the Federal Democracy Charter with the following objectives: to address the conflicts and underlying issues within the Union, to foster collaboration among all national races, to establish a Federal Union that promotes democratic practices and ensures social equity and autonomy, and to foster peaceful coexistence through mutual respect, love, and unity, grounded in freedom, equity, and justice for all citizens.

The impetus behind drafting this Charter stemmed from the National Unity Consultative Council (NUCC), which was established on March 8, 2021. The NUCC comprised 56 representatives from 28 organisations representing various segments of society. These included the CRPH, holding de jure legitimacy from the 2020 General Election; regional autonomy bodies and their administrative structures; armed forces of national races with de facto legitimacy from public support; state/federal unit-based and national ethnic group-based advisory councils; Spring Revolution forces consisting of youth and women's organisations opposing the military dictatorship; workers' unions; civil society associations; CDM participants; boycott committees; and various ethnic group organisations. It was the NUCC that orchestrated the formation of the NUG.

However, within two years, the Kachin Political Interim Coordination Team (KPICT) withdrew from the charter. The first conference, held from January 27-29, 2022, established fundamental guidelines against the military dictatorship, as well as policies, strategies, and transitional measures, albeit under pseudonyms for some figures. Consequently, it is the NUG, rather than the NUCC, that has captured public attention. In the democratic framework, the union government is responsible for administration / executive, legislative, and jurisdicial duties. The CRPH focuses on legislation, while the NUG handles administration/executive functions. However, the full realisation of jurisdiction is pending as the Revolution remains ongoing, and the role of the NUCC remains unclear. Nonetheless, it serves as a platform for political stakeholders, including national ethinic groups, to engage in discussions aimed at building the Federal Democratic Union. Despite this, three organisations have emerged at the forefront of the Revolution following the military coup.

Since mid-April 2021, it appears that new chapters of the Spring Revolution have unfolded one after another. However, it's essential to emphasise that the term "National Unity Government (NUG)" is not a recent creation that emerged solely after the coup. If one delves into the origins of this term, it inevitably leads back to the intricate political landscape of Burma, particularly events that transpired during the final years of the NLD government in 2020.

Wall:

The Walls of Maze: 2020

"There will be the National Unity Government in the post-2020s," says U Zaw Htay. (*Myanmar Times,* November 4, 2020)

During a press conference at the President's House in Nay Pyi Taw, U Zaw Htay, the spokesperson of the President's Office, made a notable statement "on behalf of the government." He mentioned that measures resembling those of a new government, such as the National Unity Government, would be implemented. U Zaw Htay was a prominent figure, having served as a government official and spokesperson during President U Thein Sein's administration. Additionally, he had a military background and was associated with the army-backed party USDP, playing a significant role during the Rakhine conflicts. Despite his affiliations, when the opposition party NLD came to power in 2015, he was reinstated to his former position, causing disappointment among some supporters of the new government. However, his assurances of loyalty to any government helped reassure the public of his stance as a civil servant. It's intriguing to consider why he, "on behalf of the government," would speak about such a significant step on the state's roadmap for the future.

In response to U Zaw Htay's announcement, Dr Myo Nyunt, the spokesperson of the NLD party, expressed ignorance about the matter in an interview with VOA on November 6. He stated, "I'm sorry we don't know anything about it." Dr Myo Nyunt emphasised the party's focus on national reconciliation, encompassing all citizens, including the Tatmadaw and all national ethnic groups. Interestingly, it was a retired senior army staff from the State Counsellor's Office and the President's Office who first introduced the term "National Unity Government," despite the current ruling party's lack of awareness about it.

The term "National Unity Government (NUG)" gained widespread attention and discussion, particularly after its initial mention during the term of the NLD government. While it was introduced before the outcomes of the next election, its use sparked speculation and analysis among political leaders and media commentators.

U Ye Tun, a former Hluttaw representative of the Shan National Democratic Party (SNDP), suggested that the term signalled a potential for collaboration between political parties, including those representing national ethnic groups, to form a government focused on national unity. However, the NLD did not provide detailed plans regarding the implementation of this idea.

In the November 8 General Election, the NLD secured a significant majority with 396 seats, well beyond the required number to form a government independently. This led to speculation that the NLD might not pursue the formation of a government resembling the NUG, especially given its electoral success. U Sai Nyunt Lwin, Vice Chairman of the Shan National League for Democracy (SNLD), suggested that the idea of the NUG might have been considered as a contingency plan before the election results were known.

After the 2020 General Election, the NLD spokesperson, Dr Myo Nyunt, expressed a willingness to share power, stating, "We, the NLD, are not going to monopolise all the seats, nor all the authorities." Meanwhile, Monywa Aung Shin, Secretary of the Party Central Information Committee, emphasised that while the term "National Unity Government" was used, any government akin to the NUG would prioritise national reconciliation, a policy the NLD had been practising throughout its term.

Before the 2015 Election, the NLD cultivated strong relationships with allied ethnic group parties, which later merged into a consolidated power. In September 2019, the NLD Central Committee established the Ethnic Affairs Committee (Central), chaired by Pyithu Hluttaw representative U Htone Kha Naw Sam of Myitkyina. However, a decision taken during an Executive Central Committee meeting on December 26, 2019, ruled out negotiations or collaborations with ethnic parties for the exchange of seats.

A few months before the General Election, on September 8, 2020, a meeting was held with the news media at the Mandalay NLD Division Office. Dr. Zaw Myint Maung, Vice Chairman of the Central Committee and Chief Minister of Mandalay Division, issued a statement, saying, "People may assume that because the ethnic parties have been gaining ground, voting for ethnic parties would ensure the rights of the ethnic races. No. Even if the ethnic parties had won votes, there's no way for them to organise their own government, so what I'd like to urge you all to do is to vote for the NLD, which is the Union Party." His remarks disappointed not only ethnic parties but also those who hoped for strong relationships between the NLD and the national ethnic groups.

In response, U Sai Leik, the spokesperson of the SNLD, stated, "This implies he (Vice Chairman U Zaw Myint Maung) does not grasp the concept of what the Federal Union entails. As a political party committed to building the Federal Union, such a prominent figure should not make such imprudent statements. In other words, if the only parties capable of forming a government in our country are either the NLD or USDP, equilibrium and autonomy, which are our goals, would never be achieved. If votes only go to these parties capable of forming a government on their own, there is no path to building the Union that we all dream of. It means there is no way to restore peace in our country. Never!"

The open letter dated November 12, which the NLD sent to 48 ethnic parties, stated:

"The desires and aspirations of the ethnic groups will be prioritised in the future. We hope you, ethnic parties, will actively cooperate and collaborate with the NLD for the cause of the Federal Democratic Union."

Then, in an interview with *The Standard Times* newspaper, published on November 24, the spokesperson of the NLD, Dr. Myo Nyunt, said:

"The structure or hierarchy of the government will be based on the framework named the National Unity Government, as once mentioned by the spokesperson of the President's Office U Zaw Htay. Saya Zaw Myint Maung, our Vice Chairman, has openly talked about our policy that talented people and qualified people, as well as those who have rich experiences in politics, will be involved in the new government. It is interesting to note that the term 'the NUG' was referred to as 'U Zaw Htay's framework' instead of 'the Policy of the NLD Party'."

On December 12, Chief Minister Dr. Aung Moe Nyo of Magway Division, Chief Minister Nan Khin Htwe Myint of Kayin State, and U Htone Kha Naw Sam of Kachin State from the Ethnic Affairs Central Committee of the NLD Central Committee personally visited ethnic parties. However, no solutions were found from the meetings with the Mon Unity Party (MUP) and the Kayah State Democratic Party (KysDP). In the meeting with the Kachin State People's Party (KSPP), meetings were held only with the representatives of the winning party, and not with those who represent the party.

On January 15, 2021, at the Office of the NILD in Taunggyi, Shan State (South), a meeting was held with representatives of the SNLD. In an interview with Mizzima News Agency, Vice Chairman Sai Nyunt Lwin of the SNLD Party said: "It's high time for giving priority to national unity, isn't it? An issue remains unresolved in Kachin State while there are also issues with the Mon and the Kayah. The Journey of Friendship and Goodwill didn't run smoothly. It would have been better if they hadn't started this journey. When they started this journey, the issues came to the forefront, arresting the public's attention."

"Those representatives involved in this mission," he continued, "have found themselves in a kind of predicament, neither going forward nor backward. They had to follow the instructions from above only. Meetings are beneficial only if there is mutual respect and understanding between the two parties. They should have brought some points for discussions from both sides. What they did during the meetings was they just came to listen to our voices only."

However, in his interview with the Irrawaddy News Agency on January 21, Dr Zaw Myint Maung said that the meetings were a success and that these collaborations signalled a good sign for the Federal Democratic Republic. In the same interview, he also said that the majority of the posts of prime ministers would go to the representatives from the NLD party.

It must be pointed out that a Shan national leader also referred to the term "National Unity Government," which was first introduced by the Spokesperson of the President's Office, U Zaw Htay, and which had since then been widespread as a political catchword of the year. His term might represent the government, as in his words "on behalf of the government," but it was seldom referred to in the legitimate statements of the NLD government or in the media interviews of some top leaders of the party.

At the same time, the NLD Party's efforts to restore "national reconciliation" had come under criticism from various quarters. Even in Sai Nyunt Lwin's interview with the Mizzima News Agency, as mentioned earlier, it was pointed out that there was a discrepancy between the meetings labelled as "national reconciliation" and the content of the NLD's letter, as well as the speech of Daw Aung San Suu Kyi, Chairperson of the National Reconciliation and Peace Council (NRPC). In her New Year Speech, Daw Aung San Suu Kyi said: "We will vigorously develop the post-2020 New Peace Architecture, which will blend the harmony between representation and efficiency." The NLD's open letter to 48 ethnic parties also stated: "In the future, priority will be given to the affairs and desires of the ethnic tribes, our national races."

On November 2, one week before the general election, the military issued a statement entitled "Declaration Statement related to the armed groups with regard to the Election," in which they noted: "During the term of the NLD government, ceasefire agreements were signed only with two armed groups in the peace-making process, and no other significant progress was achieved. The delay in the progress of the peace-making process was caused by the pressures and disturbances of some armed groups, and the citizens of the conflict areas were deprived of their right to vote in the general election due to the pressures and disturbances of those armed groups."

However, the military also made accusations of voter fraud. And during his interview with VOA on November 6, the spokesperson of the NLD government, Dr. Myo Nyunt, said: "We were even criticised for having taken one-sided measures to reconcile with the Tatmadaw, and we have tried our best to cooperate with them. But we could not make significant progress. Finally, the Tatmadaw has now made claims that the government must take responsibility for electoral fraud and that they would have to reconsider the statement of the Union Election Commission. So changes can follow, depending on their Cetana (benevolence), or positive or negative attitude towards the future of our country."

While the term "The National Unity Government" became a widely recognised catchphrase in Burmese politics in the post-2020 era, but it also sparked controversy due to different interpretations among various politicians. U Zaw Htay, who first coined and introduced this term, was not among the detainees after the coup, but he had been under close watch by the military regime. Sadly, he passed away due to a heart attack on May 23, 2022.

Additionally, some top leaders of the NLD were arrested and released, while others passed away. Those who survived have kept a low profile, so nobody has confirmed who was the first politician to coin the term "The National Unity Government," as introduced by U Zaw Htay. Furthermore, whether the National Unity Government, widely known as the NUG, which first came into existence on April 16, 2021, is the same as U Zaw Htay's concept of The National Unity Government or not remains an unresolved puzzle. The extent to which the former is similar or different from the latter remains unclear.

Corner:

Different Stakeholders and Different Perspectives

"DKBA declares no recognition of the NUG"

The Karen Information Center issued this headline on April 23, 2021, reacting to the declaration statement from an educational meeting held on April 22, 2021, which stated, "We will support the NUG." However, the Karen National Union (KNU), the Democratic Karen Buddhist Army (DKBA), and the Karen Education and Culture Department (KECD) clarified that the statement did not accurately reflect their discussions. They emphasised that their meeting focused on education and had nothing to do with supporting the NUG.

Brigadier General Saw Hmu Kho, the spokesman of DKBA, clarified to the Karen Information Center that their organisation had not issued a statement supporting the NUG. He explained that they were closely monitoring the situation and would support whichever party emerged victorious once the new government bodies were established. DKBA later attended a peace conference organised by the military regime in 2022, indicating a possible alignment with the State Administration Council (SAC) after signing a ceasefire agreement.

In her interview with the *Federal Journal*, dated June 14, Vice Chairman Seng Nu Pan of the Kaching State General Strike Committee expressed scepticism regarding the Spring Revolution.

"CRPH has now entered a phase of survival in the international community. It has also been collaborating with local armed groups. Its current status involves working toward Federal Democracy rather than operating under the dictates of the 2008 Constitution. However, we, the national ethnic groups, harbour some doubts. In 2010, Daw Suu (Daw Aung San Suu Kyi) was under house arrest. Upon her release, the NLD's Executive Committee discussed operating under the 2008

Constitution. Despite previous statements indicating the NLD would not participate in elections as long as the 2008 Constitution remained, the party eventually did participate. This raises questions about the leadership of the CRPH. Are these leaders guiding the CRPH because they are the only ones capable under current circumstances?

During the early days of the Spring Revolution, protesters drew strength from the legitimate outcomes of the election, aiming to establish a Hluttaw consisting of their elected representatives and a government formed by those representatives. However, alongside slogans denouncing military dictatorship, there were also negative sentiments toward the election outcomes following the CRPH's declaration of the abolition of the 2008 Constitution. Ethnic groups began clamouring for the establishment of a Federal Union. While the NUG comprises 38 percent of elected NLD representatives, 32 percent are members proposed by ethnic groups. This underscores the need for representation from all national races to truly reflect the country's national unity. Paradoxically, the NUG includes representatives from all national races except the Shan and the Rakhine."

In fact, when considering all-inclusive norms, the Cabinet of the SAC comprises representatives from various national ethnic groups, including not only the 2020 elected representative Daw Aye Nu Sein (Rakhine National Party), Dr. Banya Aung Moe (The Mon Unity Party), and P'dho Mahn Nyein Maung (Kayin People's Party), who resigned from the KNU in July 2020, but also representatives of other national races. On February 26, the Election Commission, newly formed by the SAC, convened with 53 political parties in Naypyidaw, the new capital of Burma. While 21 ethnic parties attended the meeting, there were varying attitudes among them, with criticisms also emerging from people of various national ethnicities. Additionally, the news announced by the International Karen Organization (IKO) on August 10 cited the withdrawal of support from the political leadership by the Karen people, led by Chairman of the Karen National Union (KNU) Gen. Saw Mutu Say Poe, by the Karen people. They called for the resignation of all personnel from their current ranks. Despite discrepancies in actions and attitudes between the two brigades, Saw Mutu Say Poe retained his position as Chairman for a two-year period.

Nevertheless, similar attitudes toward the NLD, CRPH, and the NUG persist. Although the majority of the international community promptly supported the CRPH following the general election results, it took years for the international community to recognise the legitimacy of the NUG. Two years have passed, and, while the international community has engaged with the NUG, recognition of its legitimacy as the government remains elusive. In local politics, the CRPH, expected to serve as the legislative pillar, has gradually receded, primarily confirming and documenting the actions of the NUG and the NUCC. This trend is evident in conferences conducted via video, including the Second Pyithu Hluttaw on June 30, 2021, the Third Pyithu Hluttaw on February 5, 2022, and the Fourth Pyithu Hluttaw on April 18, 2022.

Burmese society has endured not only colonial rule for decades but also years of totalitarian military rule. Perhaps due to this prolonged exposure to repressive regimes, Burmese leaders struggle to divide and exercise the three branches of sovereign power—executive, judicial, and legislative—focusing primarily on executive power and treating legislative and judicial powers as subordinate. Moreover, the society's historical reliance on political symbolism has led to discussions on how to distribute absolute power based on equilibrium among federal units, rather than focusing on the division of the three powers.

Online and social media platforms have become battlegrounds for controversy, stirred by individuals self-identifying as political activists or armed politicians. However, the majority of those on the ground—the boycotters and revolutionary heroes—do not align themselves with any specific groups or objectives. Instead, they courageously sacrifice their lives and shed blood daily, steadfastly advancing the Spring Revolution with unwavering conviction.

I want to be neither a hero
Nor a martyr
Nor a coward

Nor a foolhardy guy
Nor another dilemma-stricken Hamlet
Nor a fellow with a gnawing guilty conscience
Had the days of 'freedom of speech'
When my tongue is cut off,
Had the days of 'human rights'
When I found myself confined,
Had the days of survival
When I was forced to be vasectomized.
Wish the hell we'd been in
Be terminated by our own hand.

I want to be neither an elite politician
Nor a dreamer poet, lost in fantastic imagination,
Nor a supporter of Injustice.

If I had only one minute for my survival,
I'd live, till to my last breath,
with a clear conscience.

The "Testimony of Survival" was presented in stark black and white, embodying the profound sacrifices made by individuals for the Revolution.

Penned by Poet Khet Thi of Pale Township, Sagaing Division, on February 14, 2021, this piece spoke volumes about the unwavering dedication to the cause. However, the poet's own fate took a tragic turn. On the night of May 8, he was apprehended by the military in Shwe Bo. Despite being rushed to Monywa Civil Hospital the following morning, he succumbed to the severe tortures inflicted upon him during interrogation behind bars.

His passing came just four days after the National Unity Government (NUG) announced the establishment of the People's Defence Force (PDF) on May 5.

"They shoot us in the Head,
But those stupid bloody guns do not know
The Revolution lives only in our Hearts!"

His famous verses offer a new perspective on the essence of the Spring Revolution, providing an answer to the intricate puzzle of Burmese politics. The grassroots revolutionaries of the Spring Revolution are not preoccupied with the power struggles between the State Administration Council (SAC) and the National Unity Government (NUG). They are indifferent to the figures leading the Civil Disobedience Movement (CDM) or the NUG, focusing instead on their own role in the Revolution. They wholeheartedly contribute to the Revolution's triumph to the best of their abilities, echoing the sentiments expressed by Poet Khet Thi of wanting to live with a clear conscience. This mindset serves as the driving force behind the Spring Revolution, embodying a soulful movement that transcends differences of race, religion, ethnicity, party affiliation, education, or wealth.

Passage:

Revolution in Non-Bamar Ethnic Regions

*"Those stupid fellows do not know our little fingers
that gave our votes, nor do they know
Why we raise our three-finger salute,
So our index fingers must squeeze the trigger."*

These words were inscribed on a protester's placard, but they came to life in Mindat Town, a charming small town in Chin State. Peaceful demonstrations had been ongoing since February 2021, accompanied by negotiations with regional administrators. However, on April 24, seven protesters who had participated in these negotiations were arrested. They had affixed photos of ministers from the newly formed National Unity Government (NUG) onto pedestals surrounding the bronze statue of Gen. Aung San, along with placards displaying support for the NUG.

Local residents promptly gathered at the police station, demanding the release of the detained young men. However, their appeals fell on deaf ears. The township police officer, feigning negotiation with the people, merely offered empty promises while stalling for time. Frustration mounted among the protesters as evening fell, culminating in the police firing shots at two young men on a motorcycle, fortunately without injury.

Despite administrators' attempts to placate them with excuses and assurances, the seven young men remained in custody as the clock neared nine. Feeling compelled to act, the protesters resolved to take matters into their own hands. With each Chin family possessing flint-lock rifles, the night saw the outbreak of battles at various locations, including the Township Administrative Office, the East Gate of the Town, and the Kan Pet Let Junction to the west.

Empowered by their fighting spirit, familiarity with the terrain, and adeptness in guerrilla tactics, the young Chin protesters transformed into formidable guerrilla fighters. In a stunning turn of events, the soldiers suffered significant losses at the hands of these determined youths.

April 25 passed seemingly unchanged, as if nothing had occurred. However, the anticipated reinforcements from Pakokku and Matupi arrived on April 26, leading to an ambush by local residents. More than 15 soldiers were killed, and army vehicles were destroyed by handmade mines. Additionally, approximately thirty soldiers from Matupi were intercepted en route, prolonging the conflict until nightfall. This news of successful resistance served as an inspiration and renewed vigour for protesters across mainland Burma.

Subsequently, on April 27, the army launched heavy attacks on protester camps using advanced weaponry. Following intense fighting, the army proposed an exchange: the release of the seven young protesters in exchange for the safe exit of the thirty soldiers. A ceasefire was observed during negotiations, ultimately resulting in the release of the detained protesters. which further invigorated the resolve of Spring Revolution fighters.

It is astonishing to note that the Burmese army, ranked 38th in the world's military power and armed with modern weaponry, was defeated by the primitive flint-lock rifles of the Chins.

In Chin State, with the exception of Palet Wa and Tunzan, towns such as Hakha, Mindat, Htantalan, Phalam, Matupi, and Kanpetlet witnessed demonstrations. The Chin Public Movement Coordination Body (CPMCB) was established on March 21, while the Interim Chin National Consultative Council (ICNCC) was formed on April 13, comprising Chin armed forces, political parties, Hluttaw representatives, CDM leaders, local organisations, and international Chin organisations. This model inspired the formation of similar organisations representing ethnic groups in other states.

In Kachin State, demonstrations were held in 15 out of 18 townships. Among the three main political forces—KPICT (Kachin Political Interim Consultative Team), KNC (Kachin National Council), and KPPF (Kachin People Political Front)—KPICT garnered the most support from the Kachin people. The Vice President of the NUG serves as the Chairman of KPICT, which was established during a meeting of Kachin organisations in early March.

In Shan State, demonstrations were held in Taunggyi, Hopone, Si Sai, Tachileik, Lashio, and Muse. Due to the existing Committee for Shan State Unity (CSSU), there was no need for a new political organisation representing the entire state and its diverse ethnic groups.

Throughout Kayah State, the Kayah people organised demonstrations, culminating in the formation of the Kareni State Consultative Council (KSCC) on April 9. The KSCC comprised 2020 elected Hluttaw representatives, political parties, national armed groups, local organisations, youth and women's groups, and intellectuals.

In Mon State, demonstrations were staged by the Mon people in 17 townships. However, the SAC cracked down on the protesters, leading to a decline in the movement's momentum. The Mon National Network (MNN) was established on March 14, but both the Mon Unity Party (MUP) and the New Mon State Party (NMSP), an armed group, chose not to participate.

In other parts of the mainland, people's administrative committees were established in various townships, but no new political groups representing ethnic minorities emerged. In Rakhine State, demonstrations were limited to towns in the southern region, with no significant formation of new political entities. The desire to dismantle the power-hungry Myanmar Tatmadaw led to increased calls for the establishment of a federal army.

On May 5, the NUG declared the establishment of the People's Defense Force (PDF) as the vanguard of the federal army, with three primary objectives: halting the terrorist acts perpetrated by the SAC, ending the decades-long civil war, and implementing comprehensive security reforms.

Padho Saw Taw Nee, Head of the Foreign Affairs Department of KNU, expressed support for the PDF, emphasising the need for collaboration against the common enemy. Meanwhile, U Thein Tun Oo, a former army officer and executive director of Strategy Studies, expressed scepticism in an interview with RFA on May 5, citing a discrepancy between online perceptions and the reality on the ground. He anticipated a gradual calming of the situation.

Interestingly, while the NUG had been steadily gaining international recognition over two years, the PDF's numbers were growing, leading to a loss of ground control for the SAC, which resorted to air attacks. Consequently, the momentum of the Spring Revolution intensified.

By May 13, the Chinland Defense Force (CDF) had already been established in several townships, including Hakha, Htantalan, Matupi, Kan Petlet, Tun Zan, and Paletwa. In Kachin State, although no new defence armies emerged, the existing KIA provided support to PDF soldiers undergoing military training. Additionally, the Taunggyi People's Defense Force was formed in Shan State on May 10.

However, armed conflicts erupted between two Shan armed groups from June 1 to 14. The Rehabilitation Council of Southern Shan (RCSS), headquartered in Southern Shan, came under attack by the Shan State Progress Party (SSPP) / Shan State Army (SSA) based in Northern Shan State. The differing policies of the SSPP and RCSS regarding territorial division and Shan political strategy exacerbated tensions, leading to armed clashes.

The Karenni National Defense Force (KNDF) comprises armed ethnic groups, which include three PDF forces stationed in Karenni State and two PDF forces stationed in Shan State.

Additionally, in Mon State, township defence forces were established in Mawlamyaing, Paung, Kyaikmaraw, and Theinzayat.

> "May no danger ever befall the PDF! Down with the military dictatorship!
> The Spring Revolution must be victorious! Welcome the PDF!"
> "Crutches for the soldiers, and brick houses for the army officers!"

Following the NUG's announcement of the PDF's formation, PDFs sprouted up across the mainland like sturdy bamboo shoots emerging from the ground. Armed with handmade guns and mines, they launched attacks on the troops of the SAC. Meanwhile, peaceful demonstrations persisted, with protesters holding placards urging Tatmadaw members to abandon the group of thugs and stand with the people. Quotes from the Architect of Burma's Independence, General Aung San, were widely circulated: "The Army must not bully or torture its people. The Army must not flaunt its power. The Army must serve its people, not enslave them." These quotes were seen as a warning to the conscience of Tatmadaw members.

However, the SAC aired a program entitled "Stop to Salvage" on state-owned television, aimed at dissuading young Burmese citizens from joining the Revolution. The program's script was alarming, warning youths of the dangers they faced: "Sons and daughters, there's a danger lurking behind you, ready to strike. Learn from the agonising deaths of young souls. Don't be deceived!" This script sheds light on the SAC's negative attitudes and implies the crimes against humanity it has committed.

The ultimate goal of the Spring Revolution is to put an end not only to the State Administration Council (SAC) but also to the current terrorist army. The Revolution has taken on a dual form of attack, both armed and nonviolent, emerging as new facets of the Spring Revolution.

Corner:

International Responses

"A qualified Tatmadaw must adhere to international norms and standards. Simultaneously, it bears the responsibility of safeguarding the people it is sworn to serve, refraining from imposing harm on its citizens."

On March 27, 2021, formerly recognized as the Anti-Fascist Revolution Day and later renamed Tatmadaw Day, a joint declaration was issued by the highest-ranking military officers of Australia, Canada, Germany, Greece, Italy, Denmark, the Netherlands, New Zealand, South Korea, the UK, and the USA. The declaration conveyed a message to the Burmese army led by Senior General Min Aung Hlaing, criticising its deviation from its duty and engaging in terrorist acts against unarmed civilians. In essence, it highlighted the military's unethical conduct, akin to the analogy used by Min Aung Hlaing himself, equating it to "hanging a head of goat in front of the shop and selling the dog meat as though it were mutton."

He used these undiplomatic terms during his speech at the opening of the twenty-first century Pinlong Union Peace Conference on August 19, 2020: "Don't hang a head of goat and sell the dog meat as though it were mutton." His emotional remarks could be viewed in a controversial light. He appeared resentful not only towards the armed ethnic groups but also towards the NLD. It could be inferred that he was suggesting the Tatmadaw had been the true guardians of the state's sovereignty, while accusing ethnic armies of insincerity in their gestures towards peace. However, it is important to emphasise that the senior general's words were likely an attempt to deceive the audience, as it is widely known that his army, the Tatmadaw, has a history of not honouring their commitments. This was why the world's military chiefs emphasised that his army should cease their violent and terrorist acts against the people immediately and return to the path of gaining respect and honour from their citizens.

In the aftermath of the military's attempted coup, nearly all countries in the international community, along with the UN, voiced objections and refused to recognise the SAC. Dr. Sa Sa managed to reach liberated areas and has since tirelessly worked on behalf of the CRPH and the NUG to establish international communication. While he achieved some success in garnering attention from the international community, substantial support remained elusive. Dr. Sa Sa submitted a proposal to the UN Security Council to take action against the SAC under the principle of "Responsibility to Protect (R2P)," which the people of Burma had long hoped for. However, as seen on the placards of young activists, questions arose: "How many lives must we sacrifice to receive aid from the international community?" Despite casualties and the deaths of innocent people, young and old, aid from the international community never materialised. In light of this, activists began to recognise the reality and, relying on their own resources, rallied together, chanting slogans like "Our people are our power," providing mutual support and boosting each other's morale.

On February 23, 2021, a joint declaration was issued by the ministers of foreign affairs at the G7 Summit Meeting:

"We, the G7 Foreign Ministers of Canada, France, Germany, Italy, Japan, the United Kingdom, and the United States of America, along with the High Representative of the European Union, condemn the intimidation and oppression of those opposing the coup. The systematic targeting of protesters, doctors, civil society, and journalists must stop, and the state of emergency must be revoked."

On March 22, the European Union imposed restrictive measures on individuals responsible for the military coup, including some high-ranking officers of the Burmese Armed Forces who were already sanctioned by the United States. It is important to note that the US has occasionally imposed such necessary sanctions. On March 30, Secretary of State Blinken urged international companies to reassess their economic relations with the SAC. Similarly, Kirin Holdings Company, a Japanese beer and beverage holding company, and POSCO Coated & Color Steel, a South Korean steel-making company, severed ties with Burmese companies supporting the military.

On April 1, 75 countries, including the US and the European Union, issued a declaration condemning the Burmese military and calling for the release of illegitimate detainees, including arrested journalists, as well as an end to violence against Burmese citizens. In the US statement on sanctioning Burma, dated April 21, Secretary of State Anthony Blinken said: "We will continue to support the people of Burma in their efforts to reject this coup, and we call on the military regime to cease violence, release all those unjustly detained, and restore Burma's path to democracy."

Among the ASEAN countries, while some like Malaysia and Indonesia do not support the military coup, others like Cambodia and Thailand have remained silent, recalling Plato's dictum that silence gives consent. However, given the Burmese military's alignment with China and Russia, the USA and the European Union urged ASEAN to take the lead in controlling the actions of Min Aung Hlaing's military regime. Consequently, Commander-in-Chief Min Aung Hlaing was invited to attend "the Emergency Myanmar Meeting" held in Jakarta, Indonesia. On April 24, ASEAN announced the peace plan, known as the Five-Point Consensus. This plan included provisions for an immediate cessation of violence, dialogue among all parties, the appointment of a special envoy, humanitarian assistance by ASEAN, and a visit by the regional bloc's special envoy to Burma to meet with all parties.

On April 26, 439 local organisations and 32 individuals issued a declaration statement condemning the Five-Point Consensus. They argued that it failed to reflect the attitudes of Burmese citizens, neglected justice during the transitional period, did not adhere to democratic norms, and did not address the needs of the Burmese people. Additionally, they sent seven points outlining their desires and demands to ASEAN leaders. These points included a solemn pledge by ASEAN to address the grievances of the Burmese people, the implementation of mechanisms for international and local jurisdictions to ensure justice during the transitional period, and calls for the Tatmadaw to consent to the visit of the UN Special Rapporteur on human rights in Burma to monitor human rights violations and report to the world.

On June 3, the Chairman of ASEAN, the Minister of Foreign Affairs of Brunei Darussalam, and the General Secretary of ASEAN visited Naypyidaw to hold discussions with the military. On June 4, SAC-M (Special Advisory Council for Myanmar) stated that since ASEAN had a legitimate responsibility, the meeting should be all-inclusive, including personal visits to the NUG and democratic activists. They warned that biassed decisions by ASEAN could exacerbate the situation in Burma, leading to more casualties and deaths for which ASEAN and the SAC would bear responsibility. Despite this, the situation remained stagnant, with no response from the SAC, and ASEAN patiently waiting.

During the Special ASEAN-China Foreign Ministers' Meeting in Chongqing, People's Republic of China, in early June, H.E. Wang Yi, State Councilor and Minister of Foreign Affairs of China, urged U Wunna Maung Lwin, the Minister of Foreign Affairs appointed by the SAC, to accelerate the construction of the China-Myanmar Economic Corridor. In response, Daw Zin Mar Aung, the Minister of Foreign Affairs of the NUG, sent a letter on June 7 to H.E. Wang Yi, asserting that the SAC did not represent the people of Burma. She highlighted that China's efforts to legitimise the SAC would impact future relations between the people of China and Burma. On June 18, 119 UN member nations condemned the terrorist acts of the military and expressed support for local efforts to resolve conflicts.

On June 20, the Commander-in-Chief embarked on a second overseas trip, this time to Russia for the IX Moscow Conference on International Security. During the visit, he had the opportunity to meet with the Minister of the Russian Ministry of Defense but did not have the privilege of a personal visit with President Putin. While in Russia, he toured the defense industry, where military weaponry and vehicles are manufactured, and the SAC subsequently strengthened its relations with Russia.

On June 21, the European Union and the UK imposed sanctions on holding companies associated with high-ranking officers of the Burmese Armed Forces. Subsequently, on July 2, the US sanctioned mining and technology companies supporting 22 Burmese officers and the military. They also issued a statement indicating that more severe sanctions would be imposed on the SAC and its high-ranking officers until democracy was restored in Burma.

Despite these sanctions, the military persisted in its terrorist acts. In the aftermath of the 2020 General Election, the international community initially congratulated Burma for its apparent transition to democracy without bloodshed. However, they soon realised the military's deception, likened by Min Aung Hlaing to "hanging a head of goat in front of the butcher's shop and selling dog meat as mutton." Their trust in the election results was shattered, leading them to reinstate sanctions they had previously lifted.

The convoluted nature of Burmese politics in 2020 left the international community grappling with the complexities of the situation. Their hopes for swift political reforms were dashed, revealing the intricate web of deception within the Maze of Burmese politics.

Wall:

The Walls of Maze: 2012

The Burmese army, known as the Tatmadaw, has adeptly utilised national media platforms for decades to propagate their agendas and influence public opinion to serve their own interests. They have skillfully crafted narratives through these platforms, never allowing their mask to slip and ensuring that the public remains unaware of their underlying motives.

In early 2012, a wave of anti-China sentiment emerged, fueled by protests against China's energy investment in Kachin state, particularly the Myitsone Hydroelectric Project. This movement escalated to include boycotts of imported Chinese products by local consumers. Concurrently, various logos representing multiple parties engaged in campaigning for the upcoming April by-elections began appearing not only in media outlets but also on the streets, reflecting the vibrancy of civil society.

During the April 1 interim election, the National League for Democracy (NLD) party won 43 out of 45 vacant seats, with the party contesting in 44 of them. This landslide victory dominated not only local but also foreign media coverage. The charismatic presence of Aung San Suu Kyi and the prominence of NLD logos adorned the front pages of newspapers, marking a significant moment as the first political news to receive widespread coverage since President Thein Sein had relaxed media censorship, ostensibly ushering in a semblance of press freedom. Aung San Suu Kyi's successful candidacy in the Kawhmu constituency further amplified her image and that of the township, garnering attention in both local and international newspapers.

In early February of the same year, President Thein Sein announced that foreign observers would be permitted to monitor the by-election closely. Consequently, election monitoring teams from the United States, the European Union, and Asia were dispatched, which led to a more colourful media coverage of the by-election compared to the 2010 general election. Notably, a renowned commercial current affairs journal, previously licensed under a military intelligence sub-battalion, refrained from featuring news and photos of Aung San Suu Kyi and the NLD party on its front page during the previous campaign period in 2012. However, after the by-election, the publication prominently featured news and colourful photos of the public leader on its front page, underscoring the significant role of media research in observing and portraying the nuances of ongoing political events.

As Burma transitions towards media freedom, it remains uncertain what challenges lie ahead. However, this paradigm shift holds promise for breaking free from decades of press scrutiny and propaganda under previous regimes, fostering a more open and transparent media landscape.

Indeed, amidst the campaign period in early 2012, several issues and disputes arose, including a significant ballot error, which could be viewed as a hindrance to a truly free and fair election. However, despite these challenges, the election results in April 2012 injected more optimism into the political landscape, eliciting heightened expectations among citizens. Furthermore, China and certain ASEAN countries, along with the Australian government, called for the removal of economic sanctions imposed on Burma. The Obama administration also bolstered its diplomatic presence by upgrading to ambassadorial level and announced reductions in travel and financial restrictions. Additionally, on April 23rd, the EU relaxed some limitations on government leaders' possessions and lifted nearly all economic sanctions. Both local and international media outlets played a pivotal role in bolstering the democracy movement in Burma, influencing even less experienced social media users in the country.

Reflecting on these changes, an experienced journalist recalled an intriguing incident from 2012. The journalist's office was located downtown, where the local Buddhist community hall was extravagantly decorated towards the end of April. The journalist was puzzled by this elaborate setup and was unaware of the purpose behind it. Soon after, the streets were closed off, preventing access to the area. Later, it was revealed that the ceremony was attended by one of Senior General Than

Shwe's daughters, indicating its significance. Despite initially seeming inconsequential, the organisation, known as Buddha Sasana Nuggaha, gained attention when the General Administrative Office of Yangon Division issued a notification to recruit at least five thousand members monthly from each township in 2013-14. This incident highlighted the intertwined nature of politics and social organisations in Burma during this period.

Four weeks later, a piece of "breaking news" spread, originating not from private news outlets but from state media, specifically the newspapers of the Ministry of Information. The news detailed the rape and murder of a young woman in Rakhine State. While such cases had unfortunately occurred before, including instances of child rape, this particular incident was sensationalised and exaggerated by state media, elevating its status to breaking news and garnering nationwide attention. The newspapers prominently featured the story of "Ma Thida Htwe" being raped and slain by three men in Kyrauk Nimo Village, Rambrai, Arakan (Rakhine) State, accompanied by a shockingly revealing and unethical photograph of the victim.

Reflecting on another incident, an experienced journalist recounted the visit of a well-known ex-revolutionist to their office. This individual had previously joined the student armed forces, the ABSDF, in 1988 before graduating from Harvard and eventually being appointed as one of the directors of the Myanmar Peace Center (MPC). Despite his background and authority in peace-building efforts, when asked about the biassed narratives and inappropriate language used in state media regarding the communal conflict in Rakhine State during Thein Sein's government, the ex-revolutionist showed little interest. Instead, he diverted attention by boasting about his newly issued Burmese passport, courtesy of Thein Sein's government, leaving the editor-in-chief frustrated and perplexed.

These incidents underscored the complexity of Burmese political landscape, with political changes unfolding both in news pages and on the ground, albeit in different ways. The Maze of Burmese politics seemed to have solidified further, with more barriers and chambers shaping its contours.

The state media's decision to sensationalise the case of Ma Thida Htwe, using graphic images and vulgar language, likely stemmed from ulterior motives.

How did a rape report, typically of little interest to readers, become a major news story? Former Colonel Zaw Htay, then serving as director of the Myanmar President's Office, shared the story multiple times on his Facebook account, using the name "Hmu Zaw." His posts included a sensational comment advocating for the immediate execution of the three alleged rapists and murderers, without the need for a proper trial. This post fueled hate speech, which was then widely shared by other accounts. Without critically examining the details of the case, many simply echoed sentiments like, "No! Those three Muslim guys raped and murdered a Buddhist girl. That's too much! Can't let our race, our religion be tarnished!" This kind of hate speech proliferated on social media. On the ground, a mob of protesters gathered outside the police station where the suspects were detained, demanding to take matters into their own hands and exact vigilante justice. Shortly thereafter, the national newspapers reported that one of the detainees in custody had committed suicide.

Towards the end of May, 11 Muslim religious leaders from Yangon, who had travelled to Maungdaw and Bootheedaung, were killed. Once more, state newspapers published a headline that appeared to incite tension, stating, "A group of highly aggressive individuals on motorcycles halted a public express bus on the highway near Taung-gut city, singled out ten Muslim leaders among other passengers, and executed them on the spot."

According to a memoir by retired *New Light of Myanmar (Myanmar Ahlin)* newspaper editor Maung Thu Hlaing, it was on the night of June 4th, just before midnight, when his team received a directive from the Office of the Ministry of Information to publish three headline news pieces. The content, diction, and narrative structure of these reports were already set, and no changes were permitted without prior permission. These reports contained repeated derogatory terms that incited discrimination based on race and religion, such as "Kalar" (black) and "Muslim." The report under the "Hmu Zaw" account was published multiple times in both English and Burmese. Some private media outlets also quoted the same story using the same narrative. These media outlets were owned by individuals with either a background supportive of the military or a supportive community, closely associated with Kyaw San, the Minister of the Ministry of Information at the time.

Kyaw San, a former colonel, was known for his motto "Media versus Media," advocating for media counter attacks against independent media. In response to public demands for more space for independent private media, he issued numerous publishing and distribution licences, in line with the 1962 publishing and distribution law that had not yet been reformed. These licences were granted to businessmen seeking to exert influence on the country's growing economy, as well as to members of the military community, leading to the perception that he was adhering to his motto. Former Minister of Information Ye Htut, who once served in his office, praised him for being the first to initiate media reform in Burma's journalism history.

While "media freedom" became a catchword among political activists who lacked the opportunity or privilege to apply for publishing licences, many military-backed or -supported media outlets recklessly disseminated the horrific news from Rakhine state, both online and offline, without adhering to journalistic ethics, which fueled the flames of hatred ignited by racial and religious discrimination. Take, for instance, the following post:

"On Friday, June 8, 2012, in Maungdaw, where the majority of the population are Muslims, thousands of Bengali Muslims, armed with sticks and rods, came out of the mosque after afternoon worship, and raided the houses of Rakhine Buddhists and some Buddhist religious buildings." This narrative was a script of online posts by the 'Hmu Zaw' account, too. It also appeared in print in state newspapers. The then Deputy Director-General of the Ministry of Information, Ye Htut, also shared similar posts. He later gained public attention as 'Professor Dr. Seik Phwar' (nicknamed 'Professor Bearded Goat'), a popular cartoon character who disparaged members of parliament. Though he denied involvement in scandalising the representatives, the account disappeared after his official hearing at the general assembly.

We were informed that armed members of the Rohingya Solidarity organisation, the Rohingya terrorists, crossed the border, indicating that Rohingyas from outside the country have invaded our land. As our army received this information earlier, we are going to crush them to the end. For this reason, I don't want to hear any talk about humanitarianism or human rights, or about qualities like compassion or empathy. Don't try to teach me. Don't raise your voice if you claim to have high morality.

Visit the Bhootheedaung and Maungdaw Towns of Rakhine state and witness how our indigenous Rakhine people have been driven to desperation, feeling insecure in their own land. This is a heart-rending issue. Don't forget, this is our country—our land.

The above-mentioned words are directed at political parties, parliamentarians, our civil society, and all those who stubbornly oppose, delight in criticising the President and the Government."

The headline of this post reads "This is My Private Opinion," but it must be noted that these posts had a significant influence on public opinion as they were written by an authority representing Thein Sein's administration. On the evening of June 8, 2012, until about one o'clock in the morning of June 9, Ye Htut posted a series of reports about a massive influx of people from Bangladesh into Maungdaw. "The Bengalis are burning this and that village." "The RSOs have crossed the border, armed with weapons." "Our Air Force of Meikhtila have boarded and taken off to the border." "What are the NLD doing? Why don't you speak out?" "You guys are quiet." "National traitors." "If Rakhine falls, all Bamars should be crying." On Facebook, he posted these short sentences throughout the night. Simply stepping into the House of Representatives, members of the NLD party were labelled as a "National Traitor." In April, the social media landscape seemed colourful, but in May and June, it turned into a field of fire burning with hatred. However, in print media, the press scrutiny board still prevailed, as per the 1962 Printing Act. Writers and journalists found it challenging to ignore hate speech and other scandalous writings that incited violence. In other words, censorship became an obstacle in addressing hate speech propaganda.

On August 20, 2012, the pre-printing censorship process for all kinds of manuscripts was suspended. Although so-called freedom of press was introduced, the media and the world of writers did not feel free; they still felt tightly bound by their subconscious minds, given the decades-long state censorship. The pen remained chained to the hand of peer-censorship and self-censorship. Self-censorship was an ingrained act resulting from living under the grip of age-old state censorship, and it took time to find an exit. However, peer-censorship, stemming from newly encountered group pressure, was more sensitive. "The word 'Rohingya'," said an experienced reporter of a reputable journal, "has no way to appear in print. It is not just because state-level officials disfavour its use, but also because religious and ethnic groups have made contacts and threatened us not to use it." "When our journal published news about Aung San Suu Kyi," he continued, "someone from northern Rakhine state called our office and yelled at us, saying, 'Why are you guys promoting that lady? She is the wife of a Kalar.'" Many people posted a Photoshopped image of Aung San Suu Kyi wearing a hijab. Ye Htut, Director-General of the Ministry of Information, was among them, and he eventually apologised for his reckless posting of that Photoshopped image. On the surface of the media landscape, hate speech seemed to sow the seeds of religious or racial conflicts. Only a few people noticed the ulterior motives behind these scenarios.

The Myanmar Peace Center was inaugurated in October 2012, marking the beginning of a historic political process. Instead of negotiating political deals with ethnic armed organisations, Thein Sein's administration prioritised signing the nationwide ceasefire agreement. This process involved ex-exiled revolutionaries and former generals, with General Soe Thein taking the lead. However, following the 2021 coup, his true intentions were revealed in a book secretly distributed among his close acquaintances. He confessed, "I was almost sick with insomnia because I was worried the coup would not happen." Another figure at the Myanmar Peace Center, a former exile, showed more excitement over obtaining his new Burmese passport than addressing potential communal violence in Rakhine state earlier that year. Despite these revelations, the international media and organisations applauded the MPC simply because of its name, "Peace," and provided both financial and political assistance.

However, conflicts erupted again from October 21 to October 27 in various regions including Minpya, Mrauk Oo, Kyauktaw, Kyaukphyu, Yathaetaung, Thandwe, Yambyae, Myaypone, and Pauk. Government newspapers reported on October 29 that 84 people were killed, 129 were injured, and 2,950 homes, 14 religious buildings, and 8 rice mills were burnt down. Despite these grim events, the attention of many foreigners and locals remained focused on the activities of former generals and student activists/revolutionaries at the Myanmar Peace Center.

When people experienced a taste of media freedom for the first time, they tended to overlook propaganda journalism, seemingly forgetting the suffocating censorship of the past. In their perception, this moment felt like a wider corner space in the Maze, unaware that they were still trapped within its confines. The subtle exercise of propaganda journalism and relaxation of censorship were welcomed as signs of newfound freedom by the people.

Former US president Franklin D. Roosevelt once said, "In politics, nothing happens by accident." Thein Sein's government affirmed this sentiment with a statement: "As the unanimous decision made during the meeting on October 24, 2012, we have confirmed the name of our organisation and other details; and on October 30th, we hereby announce the establishment of the Mawlamyaing Gana Vasaka Sangha network." However, this was essentially the precursor to what is now known as the 969 Movement, an anti-Muslim movement led by the religious extremist and chauvinist group Ma-Ba-Tha. Through this organisation, the infamous monk Ven. Wirathu, previously imprisoned in 2003 for inciting religious and ethnic conflict in Kyauksae, found a new platform. He, along with former Military Intelligence Chief General Khin Nyunt, was released on January 13, 2012. Despite being portrayed as a religious movement, 969 exploited media freedom extensively through mass printing and video distribution of hate speech. While the campaign against Chinese products was popular among the Burmese people at the beginning of 2012, it shifted by mid-2012 to a procurement campaign favouring products from individuals of the same religion. The fate of the Sasana Nuggaha organisation following the rise of Ma-Ba-Tha remained a mystery.

It's worth noting that in his Facebook post titled "Looking back to the past," Ye Htut remarked, "Those who have often pointed out the weaknesses of the Ministry of Information are Aung Thaung and Khin Aung Myint." Aung Thaung, known as the principal advisor to former military dictator Senior General Than Shwe, was also the founder of a group of former gangsters dubbed "the Powerful Lords." This group had a reputation for transforming into "the angry mob" at the promise of good daily wages, inciting violence or riots, whether genuine or fabricated. Aung Thaung passed away from a heart attack followed by a stroke roughly four months prior to the 2015 general election.

Since the start of this year (2012), a figure adept at shifting allegiances has risen to prominence in Burma's political landscape, poised to play a significant role for another decade. Former Colonel Zaw Htay served as the presidential spokesperson until the conclusion of Thein Sein's administration in April 2016. Subsequently, he assumed the role of Director-General of the State Counselor Office during the NLD administration. Critics lambasted the NLD for appointing someone like Zaw Htay to such a crucial government position, metaphorically suggesting they were using the wolf to guard the sheep. However, some believed that Aung San Su Kyi and the NLD were sending a clear message to the military: "We have no hidden agenda. Let's pursue national reconciliation through trust-building by including him in our government." With this move, the political Maze grew more complex, with additional twists and turns.

A notable event at the close of the year was the brief visit to Burma by United States President Barack Obama, who was on a trip to Cambodia to meet with regional leaders. On November 19th, he met with Aung San Suu Kyi at her home on University Avenue and declared the opening of a new era of bilateral relations. Subsequently, Aung San Suu Kyi cautioned against the illusion of success in her address: "The United States has been staunch in its support of the democracy movement in Burma, and we are confident that this support will continue through the difficult years that lie ahead. I say difficult because the most difficult time in any transition is when we think that success is in sight. Then we have to be very careful that we are not lured by a mirage of success and that we are working to a genuine success for our people and for the friendship between our two countries."[1] In other words, she expressed concern that the international community might perceive success prematurely, particularly since some opposition figures, including herself, were now able to participate in the House of Representatives.

Following Obama's visit, as anticipated, not only the United States but also other Western countries lifted almost all economic sanctions, hailing Burma's Road to Democracy as a success story without bloodshed. However, nearly a decade later, the international community came to realise that Burmese's democratic journey, portrayed as a mirage in the international media landscape, was far more complex. They had focused only on the success side of the year, overlooking the hatred and tragedy that also occurred. Consequently, some Burmese people, once celebrated for their resilience under pressure, found themselves "grieving under glamorous news coverage."

Nonetheless, Aung San Suu Kyi and the NLD party intentionally and boldly stepped into the Maze (Wingaba) of the 2008 Constitution in response to pressures from all sides.

---

[1] "Remarks by President Obama and Daw Aung San Suu Kyi" (November 19, 2012), https://obamawhitehouse.archives.gov/the-press-office/2012/11/19/remarks-president-obama-and-daw-aung-san-suu-kyi

Corner:

Different Responses in Different Areas

Daw Aung San Suu Kyi to go on Trial at Special Court in Naypyitaw (May 10, 2021, *The Irrawaddy*)

This news was indeed sensational. Following the attempted coup, the detained State Counsellor Daw Aung San Suu Kyi, along with President U Win Myint, faced charges in 19 legal cases, including those under the State Secrets Act and the Anti-Corruption Law. All her previous court appearances had been via video conferences. Throughout her lifetime, Daw Aung San Suu Kyi has consistently practised non-violence, and it seemed that the SAC sought to discern her stance regarding the NUG and the PDF, which were engaged in armed resistance against the military regime. It was anticipated that during her in-person court appearance, she might communicate something to her lawyers, which the SAC could exploit for their own political advantage.

On May 24, a photo emerged showing Daw Aung San Suu Kyi, U Win Myint, and the ousted Chairman of the Naypyitaw Council Dr. Myo Aung on trial at a seemingly makeshift courtroom in Naypyitaw. *Myanmar Now* reported the news with the headline, "Daw Aung San Suu Kyi Says the NLD to Survive Together with the People of Myanmar." On May 21, the SAC's Union Election Commission disbanded the NLD Party and announced that measures were being taken to prosecute party leaders for alleged treason. The ousted leader may have responded with the remark mentioned above to this news. According to lawyers, who had the opportunity to see the detained State Counsellor, Daw Aung San Suu Kyi appeared to be fresh and active, but her exact place of detention remained unknown.

On May 24, the SAC delivered a message to the family of Ko Me Gyi, also known as Ko Soe Moe Hlaing, who was an activist in the students' movement during the 1988 Uprising and had been detained as a political prisoner in Insein Prison and Thayawaddy Prison for six years. The message informed the family that they could come to the Zaung Tu Interrogation Camp to claim his body, as he had been arrested on May 22 while at his house in Zaung Tu, Bago Division. However, when the family arrived at the camp on May 25 to retrieve his body, they were informed that it had already been transferred to Yangon. Subsequently, they had to proceed to Mingaldon Military Hospital, where they were instructed to bury the body immediately, in the presence of only the family members. And so the family had to quickly conduct the burial service at Kyi Su Cemetery in South Dagon.

Ironically, Ko Me Gyi's brother was Lit. General Than Hlaing, who had served as the Deputy Minister of the Ministry of Home Affairs under the SAC. Social media reports suggested that the two brothers had blood ties with the chief leader of the military regime, Min Aung Hlaing's wife, Daw Kyu Kyu Hla. It is shocking to consider that, driven by the lust for power, the military dictators would not hesitate to harm even their own family members. Previously, Than Hlaing had led his battalion in a march to crush the PDF of Sagaing Division, who were known for their high morale and military prowess, but he was wounded and forced to retreat. About one year later, it was reported that he was removed from his position and placed under house arrest.

On June 10, Dr. Htar Htar Lin, the National Immunization Director, was arrested and charged under Section 505 (a) and the Unlawful Associations Act. Her husband, her seven-year-old son, as well as her friend Dr. Aye Aye Nyein and her daughter, were also arrested. The SAC's Anti-Corruption Commission, dating back to April 20, declared that she was sentenced to three years' imprisonment with hard labour according to Section 56 of the Anti-Corruption Law. This was because she had returned a grant of 168 million kyats (US$91,000) from the Global Alliance for Vaccines and Immunization's Health System Strengthening fund, provided by UNICEF and the World Health Organization on February 10, 2021. She was also convicted in a case related to COVID-19 vaccines.

Regarding her case, Dr. Htar Htar Lin stated: "(1) The junta is very low on budget, including foreign currency. They found the funding (75 million in US dollars) paid in advance to the Serum Institute of India (SII), so they want to claim it back by suing the State Counsellor. It seems they do not want to pay another bid (73 million in US dollars). The Ministry of Health and Sports (MOHS) did not grant the loan for purchasing auto-disable (AD) syringes for COVID-19 vaccines from UNICEF for fear of being turned down by the SAC. (2) The Treasury Department under the Ministry of Planning and Finance has kept the funding donated by the people for purchasing the vaccine. On 18-2-2021, the SAC arrested the Union Minister of the Ministry of Planning and Finance, and might be taking measures to get hold of that fund. Our team of expanded programmes on immunisation and vaccine-preventable disease surveillance has left the task of COVID-vaccine and left MOHS, which is why they have a grudge against me. Maybe they want to spread fear by treating my case as an example."

In a Facebook post in February, she explained: "The dictators, using the vaccination program as a weapon, are trying to persuade the CDMs to return to their mother units and are very much keen on putting an end to the CDM." She also explained that it was on February 20 that she had submitted a detailed report together with evidence to the Ministry of Health and Sports, asserting that she was not involved in either the Vaccine Purchase Committee or the Committee of Vaccine Purchase Funding Management, both of which are under the Ministry of Planning, Finance, and Industry. However, her appeal was turned down by the Supreme Court of the Union.

Thus, the SAC's mechanism of suppressing civilians had come to life, operating on a large scale!

"Happy Birthday, Mother Suu! We stand behind you!" (*F... you, any hand that removes this!")

The vinyl poster of the photo of Daw Aung San Suu Kyi was hung on the cable line above the busy main road. That day was June 19, 2021. It marked the 77th birthday of Daw Aung San Suu Kyi.

"We have strong convictions! Our Morale is not the flaming straw, our blood never runs cold, not a second!"

"Metta (loving kindness) can't be won by force. We love you, Mother Suu!"

"Ms Water-hyacinth, gritting her teeth, still wears a flourishing flower!"

Flower boycotts were organised to celebrate the birthday of Daw Aung San Suu Kyi, with hundreds and thousands of Burmese citizens taking photos with flower baskets, vases, garlands, and backdrops displaying their birthday wishes and firm resolutions. According to the BBC, the nationwide celebrations of Daw Aung San Suu Kyi's 77th birthday were more prominent on social networks than usual.

Despite the risks of arrest and ruinous consequences for posting celebratory messages or birthday wishes on Myanmar's social networks, people still took the chance to express their support.

In Kayin, Kayah, Sagaing, and Tanintharyi Divisions, as well as in Yangon and Mandalay, various groups including the PDF, regional guerrilla forces, and the general public celebrated their leader's birthday through donations, poetry recitations, and boycotting the SAC. Additionally, demonstrations were held in the streets and on roads.

Internationally, flower strikes were organised in countries such as South Korea, Malaysia, Australia, and Thailand, as well as in locations like Aung San Suu Kyi Park in Froland, Norway, Parliament Square in London, Dam Square near the Royal Palace of Amsterdam, and Flatiron Public Plaza near the Empire State Building in New York. Well-wishers released white pigeons, prayed for the liberation of all detainees, and gathered with red roses in hand. Even the Minister of Foreign Affairs of Singapore shared his birthday wishes for Daw Aung San Suu Kyi on social media.

The SAC's propaganda claimed that some women who made birthday wishes in Mandalay were arrested. Additionally, in Lone Khin Village and Hmawbon Madayan Village, Phakant Township, Kachin State, where a birthday wish prayer service was held in the morning, three local people were wounded by heavy weaponry in the afternoon. Despite the occasion being her birthday, Daw Aung San Suu Kyi had been convicted under 19 sections of laws such as the Anti-Corruption Law and the State Secrets Act, and had already received an 11 year prison sentence.

A song sung by Kachin singer L. Zai Zi touched the hearts of the Burmese people:

"Here I offer my hands, but who will take my hands?
Here I am waiting for a compassionate heart that would wipe my tears, but when?
I've been going through cruelty so afflicting,
Seeking a healing hand for the innocent victims."

The local circumstances that occurred before June are highlighted by the following newspaper headlines and news summaries:

Ceasefire Agreed between Mindat CDF and the SAC
June 23
   An agreement on the ceasefire between the Chin Defence Front and the SAC troops in Mindat, the Chin State, was declared yesterday, on June 23. The terms of the agreement include: to avoid carrying arms while patrolling; to avoid threatening or pressuring government staff and its administrative duties; to avoid pressuring the CDMs to return to their workplaces, to stop harassing the local people using the Kyaukdu-Mindat-Matupi road and to give permission for vehicles carrying provisions after being check.

Conflicts of Armed Ethnic Groups Going on in Kyauk-Me Township
June 23
   In Tok-sanVillage Group, Kyauk Me Township, Northern Shan State, armed clashes broke out among the SSPP/SSA, TNLA and RCSS/SSA at about 6:00 pm on June 22.

Surprise Checks by the SAC in Some Quarters in Taunggyi
June 24
   The members of the SAC continued their surprise checks in residential areas by using torchlight and making arrests, stopping vehicles at road junctions and conducting searches these days. On the

night of June 23, in North Wapya Village, Kyaung Gyi Su Quarter, the SAC forces fired guns. Information on the casualties is still unknown.

TNLA beats and arrests three villagers in Namatu Township
June 24

Three villagers of Nakho Lyan Village in Pinlong Village Group, Namatu Township, were beaten and arrested by the Taaung (Palaung) National Liberation Army (TNLA) forces.

Six from insecure Mindat die on flight from home
June 24

In Mindat Town, Southern Chin State, the heavy forces of the SAC have made an onslaught on the CDF, driving residents from their homes. The people cannot access healthcare services. According to the reports of the war refugees, there were already six people who died of illness.

KNU to Undertake the Duty of Protecting the People
June 24

The KNU made the following statement: "Since the SAC has been launching heavy onslaughts and engaging in war not only in the countryside but also in some cities in mainland Myanmar, we express a deep concern over the loss of life among local residents. So we will do our best to provide protection for the innocent people."

Families Worried about Having No Chance to see their 5 Paletwa Chin Young Men Arrested to Sittwe
June 24

On June 17, five Chin young men were arrested and handcuffs in Paletwa, Chin State, and sent to Sittwe, and taken inside the military quarters in Sittwe. It was reported that their families have not yet had a chance to visit to their sons.

The War Refugees of Kayah Refuse to Go Home Because of the SAC Troops in the Local Regions
June 24

According to local news sources, the SAC arrived at the war refugee camps in the east of Demoso Township, Kayah State, encouraging them to go back to their homes. Out of fear, however, the refugees had moved to another new site. "They came and told us," said one war refugee, "to go home so that they'd give us protection, they'd keep us safe. About two or three days ago, they visited the camps, and persuaded us to go home. Some of us moved to a new site so as to avoid them. Ya know, we are afraid. They destroyed our homes already, so we have no home, no village to go back to, you know. Bamar soldiers camp there, and stay in a clinic of a war refugee camp. They force us to cook, or fetch water, and so on. So we moved to another place."

KIA Warns against Transport of Guns and Ammunition of the SAC's Army
June 25

Battalion No. 11, Brigade 2 Military Headquarters of the Kachin Independence Army (KIA) issued a warning that no vehicles or buses or non-profit organisation vehicles are to carry or transport the guns and ammunition of the military. If a vehicle carries soldiers, guns and ammunition and gasoline, or if the goods are covered with no necessity, the driver or owner of the car must take responsibility for any ensuing issues.

For Brighter Future Education in Nayun, CDM Teachers Stage Online Boycott
June 25

The CDM teachers of Nanyun under the autonomous administration system of the Naga, Sagaing Division, staged an online boycott with the slogan, "Join the CDM for brighter education in the future."

About 230,000 Myanmar People Flee because of Armed Conflicts and Violence
June 25

On June 24, the Office for the Coordination of the UN Humanitarian Affairs (OCHA) of the UN Secretariat said, "In Burma, about 230,000 have had to leave homes because of armed conflicts and violence this year. They have been in urgent need of aid." Although measures were being taken for supplying aid, the operations had been delayed due to violence, armed clashes and insecurity.

In Kayin State, close to the border of Thailand, about 10,300 people had been internally displaced last month, but the number had increased to about 177,000. In Chin State, close to the border of India, after the clashes between the Chinland Defence Forces (CDF) and Myanmar Armed Forces, more than 20,000 people are being hosted in over 100 displacement sites in five townships.

The Karen National Union (KNU) issued a statement expressing deep concern over the casualties and loss of lives across the country resulting from the increase in violence and the excessively use of force by the military. Since the coup, there were at least 880 people killed and 6,296 arrested by the security forces, as reported by the Assistance Association for Political Prisoners (AAPP).

Solomon Thang's song "Federal Democracy" goes:

"When will it be over? Whats's our goal?
How many more lives do we need to sacrifice, how many souls?
Our people having hard times, we'll fight till the world perishes,
We believe the time will come when our Revolution flourishes.
Don't get discouraged, but be steadfast,
Bravely forward we all will march."
"The time will come for celebrating
Our Federal Democracy Revolution."

His voice carried a vibrant energy, despite singing the song in a soft, melodious tone. The lyrics reflect the direction in which the Spring has been progressing. It has steadily matured, gathering momentum with each passing moment.

Passage:

Unity and Understanding among Diverse Ethnic Communities

A young man stood beside a large poster featuring a photo of Daw Aung San Suu Kyi, clad in the military uniform of the Kachin Independence Army, rifle in hand. A message posted on the Mai Mai Sai Account on July 7, 2021, commemorating Burmese Women's Day and Daw Aung San Suu Kyi's 66th birthday in Laizar Town, read as follows:

"Today I met a friend of mine undergoing military training in this liberated area of Kachin Region. He was accompanied by the other two young men, also trainees. We sat at a shop and exchanged our experiences. 'Hmm…' one guy said, with a sigh, 'I just wonder whether Mother (Suu) knows what is happening outside. Hope she's doing fine.' My friend pinched him. He made a face. He might fear I'd have rows. Well, I poured out my frustrated feelings in black and white, I admit, but this doesn't mean I hate you, Aunty (Suu). I was embarrassed. You know, Aunty (Suu), your 'sons and daughters' are here with me for military training, but they fear they would speak out about you out of their affection. They are mature guys; they know they should be careful in whatever they are going to do or say… I am a charge of these kids, I do not want them to feel timid or insecure under my wings, you know. They are like my bro, my sis, and I must take care of these kids wherever we are. They are quite new to this area, and we hosts must treat them more warmly, more affectionately. We ethnic groups had laid a heap of hope on you, Aunty (Suu), so we suffer a sort of trauma when things went upside down! This picture is proof of our love. We do not hate you. Now your sons and daughters have joined our hands together. They know our trauma and we share mutual love and understanding. I believe we will strive together for a better, brighter future." It is the truth, nothing but the truth that from the Spring Revolution derived the national unity that has never been consolidated in the history of Burma. This unity is the demand of such a crucial national campaign in which we all stand united to topple the common enemy.

On the flip side, there were unpleasant repercussions such as bomb blasts and acts of anarchy, including the targeting and killing of informers and members of the USDP (The Union Solidarity and Development Party, a pro-military political party). Citizens also initiated "Saying No" strikes against the SAC, refusing electricity charges, lottery tickets, taxes, and products from military factories. Instances of cutting off electricity to those who didn't pay their bills and residents being forced to pay were reported. Consequently, offices responsible for electricity metre charges became targets for the PDF and guerrilla fighters. In early July, bomb blasts rocked the Music Zone KTV, associated with the military, and the offices of Mytel Mobile Telecommunications (owned in part by Min Aung Hlaing's son). Following these attacks, some office staff abandoned their duties.

In rural areas of Burma, where the Revolution was in full swing, violence escalated. Gunfire erupted on July 3 and 4 in the bordering regions of West Budalin in Dipeyin Township, Shwe Bo District, Sagaing Division, affecting Kani, Ye Oo, and Dipeyin. Over 50 villagers went missing, with more than 30 found dead. The battle at Satpya Kyin Village was particularly notable.

July 3, Min Aung Hlaing's birthday, is generally considered a dark day in the Burmese calendar. Instead of celebrations, his birthday was met with a barrage of curses from the people. Beginning in late June, the COVID-19 pandemic resurged, spreading rapidly and reaching a critical stage by mid-July. Hundreds of new infections were reported daily across the country, leading to a skyrocketing demand for vaccines and oxygen. *Myanmar Now* reported, based on statistics from July 13, that the mortality rate had exceeded one hundred initially. The four Yangon-based, social welfare organisations had to transport over a hundred dead bodies on a regular basis to four cemeteries in Yangon for cremation, although the rate later increased to over 600. Photos of over 50 dead bodies laid to the right and left and in front of the door of the cremator went viral.

All the cremators at the Ye Way Cemetery crematorium were operating at full capacity, providing twenty-four-hour service. On July 12, during a press conference, Gen. Zaw Min Tun, the spokesperson of the SAC, confirmed that private oxygen factories were prohibited from selling oxygen to the public. The demand for oxygen had reached a record high, causing the prices of oxygen tanks to double. With more than two family members infected, the remaining family members were overwhelmed with the task of queuing for oxygen refills and scheduling appointments at clinics. The mortality rate in Yangon alone rose to approximately one thousand deaths per day. According to RFA, during the 40 days of the third wave of COVID-19, from July 1 to August 10, the music, zat-performance, literature, and film industries suffered losses of 131 artists. Meanwhile, Insecurity Insight, Physicians for Human Rights (PHR), and Johns Hopkins University Center for Public Health and Human Rights (CPHHR) issued a statement reporting that from February 1 to the end of July, the military had raided 86 health service centres and arrested over 190 health workers.

Nonetheless, the Spring Revolution continued to progress. An informal online meeting for Myanmar Affairs, chaired by Britain, a permanent member of the UN Security Council, was held on July 29. Present at the meeting were the Minister of the NUG, Ambassador U Kyaw Moe Tun, Secretary of Kachin Political Interim Co-ordination Team (KPICT) Gun San Nsang, and representatives from eleven countries, all members of the UN Security Council.

In August, Daw Aung San Suu Kyi's lawyer was warned against making any comments to the media. Statements from local defence forces emerged, indicating that SAC soldiers joining the people would be accepted with guaranteed security, and soldiers bringing guns and ammunition would be rewarded. In August, the Sangha Magga Sayadaws and Sangha groups supporting the Revolution and the boycott movement conducted Night Strikes and Day Strikes, spreading Metta (Loving-kindness) to the people and PDFs for their safety and the victory of the Revolution. Around 10:00 pm on August 23, SAC forces stationed inside the Tamadaw Textile Factory in Quarter 7, Hlaing Thayar Township, were attacked with a grenade by the City Guerrilla Force, Hlaing Thayar (CGF HTY).

The main strike force, consisting of villages along the Monywa-Amyint Road in Monywa Township, Sagaing Division, staged a women's strike, chanting slogans like "The Cause for All Suppressed Women – Our Cause! Our Cause!" and "The Glory of Our Women Must Crush the Rapist Army!" During this period, bomb blasts occurred at the houses of local administrators serving the SAC, leading some administrators to resign from their posts due to various pressures. SAC soldiers continued to commit crimes against humanity, launching attacks in regions of Karen, Kachin, Chin, and Northern Shan States. They also stationed forces in Sagaing Division, threatening local populations, resulting in an increasing number of war refugees displaced from their homes and native places.

With the objective of meeting the needs of the PDFs, CRPH-OFP and the Ministry of Defence of the NUG led the campaign called the "5 Million Raffle Ticket Challenge," which commenced on August 12. Within ten days, over three hundred thousand tickets were sold. On August 12, it was announced that the Delta Guerrilla Warfare Collective Forces (DGWCF) had been organised.

In Mandalay, the revered monks of the Sangha Union recited the Mora Sutta (The Discourse on the Golden Peacock's Prayer for Protection and Safety) during the night strikes against the SAC. In Karen State, there were 30 clashes between the SAC and the KNU/KNLA from August 17 to 21. *The Kawthulay News* announced that 20 SAC soldiers were killed. The SAC was busy banning over 40 KBZPay accounts, accusing them of facilitating the Spring Revolution Lottery business.

On September 7, the official announcement of the declaration marked the start of the People's Resistance against the terrorist military group led by Min Aung Hlaing. Duwa Lashi La, the NUG interim government President, signed the declaration, stating that Burma was under a state of emergency covering the entire Union State. The duration of the state of emergency would last until the restoration of the people's administrative power was achieved. The NUG also issued a 7-point order concerning the People's Defence Army, the People's Defence Forces, and the Special Task Forces.

On that day, in Kalay in Sagaing Division, as well as in some villages in Salingyi Township, and Dawei, Long Lon, and Ashe Taw in Taninthayi Division, columns of women's strikes emerged, chanting slogans such as "Women who will Crush the Army, Hold your Salute Fingers even Behind the Bars."

On September 19, Minister for Human Rights of the NUG, U Aung Myo Min, announced that a report on the SAC's massacre in Sagaing Division and Magwe Division had been submitted to the UN Human Rights Council. In Chin State, SAC troops fired heavy weaponry, resulting in over ten houses in Htantlang being destroyed by flames. Pastor Cung Biak Hmun of the Thantlang Centenary Baptist Church (TCBC) was arrested and killed while attempting to help extinguish the fire. His finger was cut off, and his ring was taken away.

In early September, the junta's Vice-Senior General Soe Win travelled to Moscow to attend the closing ceremony of the International Army Games 2021, which was annually held by the Ministry of Defence of the Russian Federation. Surprisingly, Ven. Sitagu Sayadaw accompanied the delegation to Russia, drawing criticism from monks protesting the junta.

Efforts were made to boost mutual respect and understanding among the armed revolution forces, but there was a noticeable shift in attitude towards those who stood decisively on the side of the SAC, despite being of the same religion and race. The people also began to show respect and recognition for the role of women activists. The Spring started to confront the walls of the Maze of Old Burmese Culture.

Wall:

Role of Religious Leaders Before and During the Spring Revolution

"What the people want is a system where the Dhamma (Justice or Righteousness) is enshrined. We are in the cult of the Dhamma, we want the System of Justice, so the people have given their votes. They've got a landslide victory. No one can deny that. On the other hand, you know, those who crave power are shocked, frustrated, and go crazy! So, what did they do? They robbed. They inserted Injustice with their might, their arms! I said, the people gave votes because they dreamed of Justice, for the sake of the person of moral rectitude. When they are disillusioned, when they are confronted with the crude reality, knowing voting didn't work, they pick up the arms, they believe it's only through the power of the might that they could elect their representatives, so our people go for the arms. That's it."

Ven. Sayadaw U Ariyavansābivansa, also known as the Myawaddy Mingyi Sayadaw, died in Mae Sot, Thailand, on October 27, 2022. In an interview with the media after his release from prison, the revered monk spoke about his conviction in September 2019 for "offences against the state" under Section 505 (b). He criticised the military's acts of injustice, including their donation of K. 30,000,000 to a Buddhist organisation known as Ma-Ba-Tha, which was formed on the basis of national chauvinism. After being bailed from the court of justice and attending over thirty hearings of his case, he was arrested two days after the coup for committing an offence "against public tranquillity." He spent six months in confinement before being released on August 2. Following his release, he left the Monastery of Myawaddy Mingyi in Mandalay and sought refuge in a border area, where he passed away in Mae Sot, Thailand.

The revered monk emphasised, "Attacking the militarists means founding the Dhamma (Justice)." Like other revered monks such as Shwe Nya Wah Sayadaw, U Sobita (Alinkar Kyel), and Min Thonnya (Buddhist University), he did not hesitate to criticise the acts of injustice committed by the military. While many monks are displeased with the military's injustices and their use of religion as a propaganda tool, only a few dare to openly confront the military by criticising their actions.

Furthermore, while military leaders and ex-military politicians have historically propagated national and religious chauvinism, it wasn't until 2012 that they achieved significant success in their mission. This success led some individuals to embrace this propaganda wholeheartedly, resulting in a segment of Myanmar society aligning themselves with the pro-military party (USDP) under the belief that it is the sole defender and promoter of Buddhism as the nation's religion. In a country where the majority of the population are Buddhists, the military has effectively weaponized religion for political gain, while some minorities have mistakenly believed that their religious freedoms are under threat simply because they practise a different faith.

Ironically, certain Buddhist monks have contributed to the suffering of minority groups who share the same land and water resources. Under the guise of "Propagation and Promotion of the Buddhist Sāsanā," a term coined by the military to exploit religion for their agenda, tensions have arisen among Buddhists themselves. This division manifests in conflicts between those who support the military and those who advocate for democracy.

The Buddha taught avoiding Mogha Purisa,[2]
The Buddha shunned Tuccapuggala,[3]
The cult of personality,
But those guys talking about the bad things
About the system of sects

---

2 *Mogha Purisa*: A person who brings about no benefits to the dhamma, but is a good-for-nothing.

3 *Tuccapuggala*: A person who has no value.

That came earlier than democracy,
Those guys in a group of only two
Would rather get split into three sects,
Those guys who label themselves heroes,
I won't pay homage to your so-called God of No Right Attitude.

If you have never seen a river in your life,
You'd think the wide Mu Creek as though a river;
If you do not really know what is the teachings of the Buddha,
You'd often mutter to yourself, "O God!"
"O Bikkhus!" "Woo-hoo!"
"My dear virtuous Monkeys and Apes!" "Woo-hoo!"
"No! I will never bow to your Woo-hoo God!"

These lines are from a poem by Poet Kay Za Win, who tragically fell during the crackdown on a demonstration in Monywa on March 3, in the early days of the Spring Revolution. The poem, titled "Thin-do Phaya Ngar Ma-phu" (I Won't Bow My Head to Your God), was written in 2018.

Poets and artists, like the communities practising Consciousness-Mindfulness, do not blindly adhere to religion. Despite efforts to sow seeds of religion-based discrimination and hatred in society, they have largely been unsuccessful. The root of this issue lies in the speeches delivered by influencers or public figures, such as monks who indoctrinate the masses, particularly those Buddhists with blind faith.

Ven. Sitagu Sayadaw has wielded significant influence over the masses for about two decades. He gained prominence for initiating social welfare initiatives, such as bringing foreign ophthalmologists to provide free services, making large-scale donations in disaster-stricken areas during Cyclone Nargis, and managing the distribution of water to nearly 600 monasteries and nunneries on the Sagaing Hill. Sitagu Sayadaw earned respect and reverence among Burmese democrats, especially Buddhist devotees, for preaching raja dhamma, the 10 norms of kingship, during the 1988 democratic movements.

During the 2007 Saffron Revolution, which saw widespread hunger and suffering, Buddhist monks took to the streets reciting the Metta Sutta as a peaceful demonstration against the military regime. Sitagu Sayadaw supported the Revolution and delivered a sermon titled "Lu-maik-to-i-thwar-yar-lan" (The Road the Fools Have Taken), condemning the military's actions against Buddhist disciples as characteristic of fools. His sermons were seen as powerful exhortations to the military on behalf of the people, further increasing his respect and reverence among devotees.

It is crucial to emphasise that in the post-1988 era, during the period of military rule, the relationships between monks and laypeople, or monk-donor relationships, have greatly depended on mutual benefits. Donors provide material support while the Sangha guides them on the path to liberation from suffering. However, merely teaching the noble Dhamma of the Buddha or offering fervent prayers is not sufficient to show the common people a path out of poverty in this mundane world. Therefore, it has become necessary for the Sangha to contribute to community welfare services such as healthcare and monastic education, in addition to providing material support for donors facing hardships.

Paradoxically, while some revered monks offer humanitarian aid with the ultimate aim of attaining Nibbāna, others seem to derive satisfaction from fame and greater influence resulting from such social welfare tasks, known as Parahita. Since only the well-off can afford to make donations necessary for such humanitarian tasks, the donations of these donors can transform the monk's image into that of a revered Parahita Sayadaw, while the fame and influence of the revered monk can enhance the donor's image as a generous and pious promoter of the Buddhist Sāsanā.

Thus, instead of focusing solely on meditation and finding the Path of Liberation from Suffering, devotees are now inclined to make generous, sometimes ostentatious, donations. Such deeds, whether or not they result in merit, undoubtedly elevate them to the status of celebrated devotees promoting and propagating the Buddhist Sāsana. Consequently, the traditional meaning of the monk-donor relationship, based on mutual benefits, has been distorted over the years as military leaders have exploited it for their own gain.

Apparently, military leaders, who have amassed wealth through the abuse of power, have found no recourse to practise Sila (virtue) and have breached their morality. In an attempt to polish their tarnished image, they have resorted to mentorship, approaching monks as their political tools. They select Parahita Sayadaws who can help them earn the prestigious title of "Sāsnā-pyu Min," promoting the government's reputation as a supporter of the Buddhist Sāsanā. Paradoxically, these monks willingly accept sumptuous donations from military leaders who do not hesitate to wield their military power for their own benefit, allowing themselves to be used as mentors. Though the mentors of those with bloody hands, these monks still boldly declare that they are the guardian angels of the Buddhist Sāsanā.

However, the stance of the Ven. Sitagu Sayadaw has been met with scepticism due to some of his sermons. For instance, in a sermon delivered in July 2013, he lamented the replacement of ancient Buddhist temples near the Theingyi Market in Yangon with mosques belonging to Muslims, suggesting this could strain peaceful coexistence between Muslims and Buddhists. Additionally, in a sermon delivered in May 2017, he controversially stated that the killing of someone who does not adhere to the Five Precepts does not constitute a grave unwholesome deed.

Moreover, in 2012, when the controversial monk U Wirathu, known as "the Face of Buddhist Terror," was released from prison, Ven. Sitagu Sayadaw publicly expressed support by addressing him as "my comrade." Furthermore, the Sayadaw delivered controversial sermons at meetings of Ma-Ba-Tha, a pro-military religious extremist organisation, and among military personnel in cantonment areas. He was even associated with providing guidance for a ceremony held on February 9, 2020, in which the Young Men's Buddhist Association conferred the title of Agga Maha Mingala Dhamma Jotikadhaja on Senior General Min Aung Hlaing. This shift in political stance surprised many of his devotees.

On February 4, military leader Min Aung Hlaing, who had detained Myawaddy Sayadaw two days after the coup, paid homage to Ven. Sitagu Sayadaw. Subsequently, on June 22, 2021, the Sayadaw attended the consecration ceremony of the ordination hall at the Moscow Buddhist Centre, where he offered prayers for peace and prosperity in Russia. In

July, he visited towns in Russia like Kaluga and Vladivostok, even posting on his Facebook account about the consecration of the Shwezigon Pagoda replica in ETHOMIR, the world culture city in the Kaluga Region of Moscow, which he viewed as a success for Sitagu and Buddhism as a whole.

"May Peace and Prosperity reign in the Russian Federation!" echoed the sonorous voice of Sitagu Sayadaw U Nyāṇissara (Nyanissara). In response, activists who had emerged during the Spring Revolution expressed their concerns: "But what about your country, Burma? It's all burning in flames, Your Reverend." Another added, "Please don't forget to pray for the health, happiness, and security of our Burmese people. If distinguished, revered Sayadaws remain silent about the ongoing political situation in our country, we citizens carry heavy hearts, Your Reverend."

> "Not at the spot
> Where the Aaram Ganesha statues glittering in royal splendour
> and temples and shrines are located proudly
> never did the Buddha dwell.
> Never do I pay homage to your God of Glory."

In the precincts of the Cinda Muni Minwun Hill Pagoda in Pyinmana, near Naypyidaw, many alabaster images were discovered, purportedly representing the Buddha's image, with "one hand behind the back and the other in front with palms facing outward." Additionally, small pagodas or Cetis were found, labelled as "Ceti for the Stability of Power," "Ceti for the Success of the Hluttaw," "Ceti for the Stability of the Throne," and "Ceti for Promotion," among others. The Ministry of Religious Affairs and Culture under the NLD government issued orders, through the Sangha Maha Nayaka Sayadaws of Naypyidaw, for the removal of these images before July 6, 2020, as they were sculpted according to occult practices contrary to Theravada Buddhism. It was discovered that donations for these peculiar Buddha images had been made since 2010, with public attention drawn to them starting in 2017.

"Your images of occult practices or spirit-worshipping?
Stand for Conception or Ultimate truth? All blurred,
Never do I pay homage to your God
Of Ne'er-do-well!

Whenever a new government seizes power,
They claim, "We'll build a new capital,
We'll move to a new capital,
We'll build a pagoda in occult practices,
In astrological rituals,"
Never do I pay homage to your pagoda
Of wretched, ominous planetary influences!

You label the Buddha the Noble
With all sorts of trash modifiers,
Like "Wish-fulfilling," "Propitiating-the-Bad-Past-Consequences,"
And "The-Malady-of-Madness-Curing,"
And "Your-Lover-Goes-Crazy-About-You"
And "Lottery-Prize-Winning"
And "Attaining-the-Nibbāna,"
Now a new label, "Granting-Peace-to-the-Whole Myanmar"
But never do I pay homage to your Pagoda
Of Christening!

There, look at those wriggling earthworms
That had no chance to pay homage
To the Buddha in person!
So mean! So noisy!
Far from Sammādiṭṭhi, the Right View,
and Sammāsinkappa, the Right Intention!
Never do I pay homage to your God
Of Good-for-nothing!

What is intriguing is the roster of donors for these occult images and Cetis, intended to appease planetary influences and ward off negative consequences, with many contributions originating from the military circle. Donors include former Senior General Than Shwe and his family, former Lieutenant General Maung Bo and his family, Former Lieutenant Sein Aung's daughter Sandar Aung and her family, Lieutenant General Aung Lin Dwe and his family, former Director-General of Food and Drug Administration U Than Htut and his family, Deputy Director-General of Road Transportation Administration U Aung Myint Oo and his family, Police Brigadier General Than Tin Aung and his family, and the family of Gen. Teza Kyaw, South West Command, among others. According to a news article from *Myanmar Now*, personal assistants of former Senior General Than Shwe and Senior General Min Aung Hlaing frequently visited this pagoda platform. In the words of the revered Myawaddy Sayadaw, it is likely that the military recognized that these occult images did not solidify their power and ranks, especially upon learning of the unexpected results of the 2020 General Election, which is likely why the military's last resort must have been a military coup.

Khit Thit Media reported that, according to information from a military source, "The Sitagu Sayadaw named it 'The State Administration Council.' The Senior General met with the monk, discussed the coup plan, and consulted on the regime's name, timing, and astrological rituals. The Wazi-Peik Sayadaw (known for his occult practices) and the Sitagu Sayadaw were informed of the coup in advance by the Senior General. They collaborated and held consultations." It was the former Buddhist monk, the Wazi-Peik Sayadaw, who, after employing occult practices to make calculations, came up with a shocking prophecy, more shocking even than that of the Three Witches in Macbeth, regarding the crackdown on the protesters. "Hail, Bullet, shooting in the head, that shall haul in the new Period hereafter." According to the reports of the Assistance Association of Political Prisoners, as of May 2021, one-fourth of the protesters had been gunned down by the military, who shot them in the head. The complicity of influential Buddhist monks like Sitagu Sayadaw, Sin Chekinda, and the Tahbawa Taya Yeiktha Sayadaw, who maintain close ties with the military, has resulted in their silence regarding the Tatmadaw's brutal actions, which contradict Theravada Buddhism. This silence has caused frustration among the majority of Buddhists, leading to what can be described as "silent anger." Furthermore, members of other religions have begun to question the true essence of Buddhism, particularly in light of the actions of these influential monks. They wonder whether the behaviour of these monks truly reflects the teachings and principles of Buddhism. This situation has led to growing scepticism and criticism of the role of Buddhism in Burmese society.

In fact, in the history of Burmese tradition and customs, blended with the people's belief in superstitions, the practice of propitiating the planetary systems has long been ingrained among the Burmese people, including the governments of successive periods. When the country regained its independence from the British on January 4, 1948, the auspicious time for hoisting the national flag of the Union of Burma was chosen, according to astrological calculations, to start at 4:20 am. On November 6, 2005, mobilising all the departments under various ministries was, according to the dictates of the astrologers, to commence at 6:37 am.

Another obvious instance of superstition is seen after the coup in March 2021; though uprisings broke out all over the country, the military chose to make the most violent crackdowns in townships, towns, and cities bearing names starting with the letter "M," such as Mandalay, Monywa, Myingyan, Myitkyina, Magwe, Mawlamyaing, Myawaddy, Myaung, Myauk (North) Okkalapa, and Myenigon. In February 2022, Senior General Min Aung Hlaing and his wife participated in a ritual to propitiate the planets and dispel imminent dangers by renaming the Thet-Thar Pan Taung Ceti in Pwint Phyu Township as Cekkya Pan Taung Ceti. Photos in the state-owned media depicted the couple spraying scented water from Eugenia springs onto a large slab adorned with cabalistic squares and letters, known as Abaya Jataka. According to astrologers, this ritual was intended to ward off life's dangers. A statue of the legendary Manussiha, reminiscent of the Sphinx, adorned the structure of the Ceti, creating a flamboyant spectacle. All attendees at the event were clad in yellow attire, a peculiar sight indeed. An unusual addition to the festivities was the serving of yellow cheap snacks called Hta-thee Mok, a favourite among children and locally made from the sap of toddy-palm spathe. The pinnacle, or Htee, of the pagoda was raised promptly at 9:45 am after the bronze bell was struck nine times.

One might ask: What role does the State Sangha Maha Nayaka, the highest Buddhist organisation in Burma, play? Throughout Burma's history, various Buddhist sects like Shwekyin, Sudhammaa, Maha Si, and Moe Gok have existed, promoting the study of Buddhist Scriptures (Pariyatti), religious practices (Patipatti), and insight meditation (Paṭiveda). However, apart from the monarchy era, there has never been a position equivalent to the Pope, the head of state for Vatican City. It was in May 1980 when U Ne Win, Chairman of the Myanmar Socialist Lanzin Party, organised the State Sangha Maha Nayaka. This state-level Sangha Society was established with the mission of purifying, propagating, and promoting the Buddhist Sāsanā.

On January 29, 2021, the Sangha Maha Nayaka issued a statement urging both parties—the NLD government and the military—to come together for peaceful dialogue and resolution of the issues stemming from the 2020 General Election. Similarly, the Mandalay Sangha Maha Nayaka made similar requests on February 5 and 10, emphasising the importance of seeking peaceful negotiations to address the ongoing tensions. Additionally, on March 3, 2021, revered Sayadaws with the title of Mandalay Pariyatti Sāsana Dhammā Cariya (Abhivansa) (ME 1336 to ME 1382) issued a statement to the SAC, making three requests: to cease violence and crackdowns on peaceful demonstrations, to release detainees—including the President and the State Counsellor—immediately, and to recognize the results of the 2020 General Election.

On March 16, the Eight 47-member State Sangha Maha Nayaka Committee convened its sixth plenary meeting at Thiri Mingala Kaba Aye Hill in Yangon and announced the suspension of all activities until the country was free from COVID-19 and citizens could move freely. This decision was likened to the Civil Disobedience Movement (CDM). However, the silence of the State Sangha Maha Nayaka Committee did not carry significant weight in the eyes of the public, as individual influential monks were often seen as the face of Buddhism. The SAC continued its actions guided by its own mentor Sayadaws, particularly the Ven. Sitagu Sayadaw.

Despite the military's manipulation of religion as a tool across Burma, all religions, including Buddhism, continue to thrive. While hate speeches have become more pronounced post-2012, peaceful coexistence has been a reality in the past. In the book "Nyein Chan (khe) Thaw Nay Yet Mya" ("Those Peaceful Days"), published by the Myanmar ICT for Development Organization (MIDO) in July 2018, the question of how to foster peaceful coexistence among citizens of different religions was posed to over 180 interviewees in five villages and towns where conflicts between citizens of different religions had arisen in 2016-17. The oral-history stories contained in the book illustrate the strong tradition of social harmony in Burmese history.

One particularly intriguing story features an Islamic lawyer. During his school days, his school would start fifteen minutes late every Friday to accommodate the Islamic students. Additionally, whenever a Buddhist monk from Mandalay, a friend of his father's, visited their town, an Islamic gentleman would graciously host him and offer alms-food. During the 2007 Saffron Revolution, while Buddhist devotees were distributing water and soft drinks to the procession of monks, Muslim Shaikh people left the bystanders, retrieved purified water from a Sunni mosque, and donated it to the Buddhist monks. These anecdotes highlight a time when local residents lived in harmony, love, and understanding, without discrimination based on race or religion.

Another story involves a middle-aged Muslim gentleman living in a hill station. In 1996, amidst rising tensions during protests led by university students against Chief of Military Intelligence Gen. Khin Nyunt, the government deliberately stoked tensions between the Burmese and Muslim communities in a small town, leading to violence that quelled the political unrest. Similarly, an Islamic woman from Mye Lat Town recounts how murder cases involving a Buddhist and a Muslim in Mandalay in 2014 were politically motivated traps.

Young Buddhist monks who have completed an MA in Buddhism at State Pariyatti Sāsana Universities (Yangon/Mandalay), consisting of a two-year course and a three-year thesis, are required to participate in a missionary program in remote highlands or border areas. Interestingly, these areas are predominantly inhabited by Christians. Here, newly graduated young monks offer basic education services to local children. Remarkably, leaders of ethnic armed groups have granted permission for this missionary work.

The local Christians, members of these ethnic armed groups, exhibit a broad-minded approach: they recognize the importance of providing an environment where Buddhist monks can practise their faith freely. They understand that government officials stationed in these regions would not have the opportunity to observe Buddhist traditions and culture without the presence of these monks. This acceptance is rooted in the belief that just as Christians attend church every Sunday, Buddhists should have the opportunity to visit monasteries.

However, the primary objective of sending these young Buddhist monks to remote areas is to propagate and promote Buddhism among the local population, both young and old. Unfortunately, some monks do not prioritise imparting the teachings of the Buddha to local children or persuading them to convert from Christianity to Buddhism. One monk engaged in this missionary work expressed his perspective: he emphasised that the ultimate goal is to preserve the teachings of the Buddha. He believes that as long as children engage in virtuous deeds and refrain from unwholesome behaviour, he is satisfied with his efforts.

Regardless of their religious affiliation, it is crucial for children to receive an education. Teaching them the fundamentals of Buddhism is part of carrying out the Buddhist mission. Many Buddhist monks focus solely on imparting these teachings, exemplified by former Rector Sayadaw Ven. Nanda Marla Biwuntha. Unfortunately, the contributions of these broad-minded leaders and the teachings of revered figures like Sayadaw Ven. Nanda Marla Biwuntha often go unnoticed by both local and international media, and their efforts are underappreciated by the majority of people.

As a result, the public remains unaware of their own situation, unknowingly contributing to the maintenance of the walls of the religious Maze constructed to ensnare them in illusions. Only when these walls are dismantled can the spring of democracy emerge and set the country back on the right path. The towering challenge of breaking down these walls, erected decades ago, awaits the fighters of the Spring Revolution.

Passage:

People's Defense Force (PDF)

"Comrades, do you stand united? United! We stand united!
Comrades, do you stand united? United! We stand united!
Comrades, do you stand united? United! We stand united!
Spring gives birth to the People's Defence Forces under a sunny clime,
The cause of Federal Democracy we all hold high.
Dispel the Darkness, bring the Light of Truth.
The Cult of the Demons must be terminated, forsooth!

Here come the People's Defence Forces!

We will safeguard our people's lives, our people's property!
To the New Nation of Federal Democracy, hail!
We will take you there without fail,

For Justice, For Freedom, our PDF comes,
For the New Union of Equilibrium and Peace, bang the drum!
Let Wisdom take the lead, our policy is pure white,
The Dictatorship we must terminate outright!

Zeya, aged 17, expresses his determination: "Besides those bloody military dictators, we will put an end to their posterity. We will fight until the end of our Revolution. This is the end game. We will continue our Revolution until the end."

A news article dated July 18, 2021, from the *Myanmar Now News Agency*, recounts the story of Ko Zeya, a former social-welfare worker who, despite having no prior interest in political affairs, has now joined the PDF. The article concludes with his ominous declaration, as mentioned above.

He had been a young volunteer in social welfare service at a COVID-19 Centre in Yankin Township, providing healthcare to the patients for three months. However, the military intelligence received false information: a group of young activists, purportedly having undergone military training in the liberation area, had returned and secretly concealed weapons in an apartment. Consequently, one evening in early May, armed troops raided the apartment where Zeya and his friends resided together. They brutally kicked and hit the young men and destroyed everything in the room. The kids were blindfolded and dragged away to the camp for interrogation, where they were tortured ruthlessly. "Stripped stark naked and repeatedly tortured," Zeya replied, "I have no fear of Death!" The news article mentions an account of atrocious torture at the camp. Zeya's head was bloody, but still unbowed. It was the "cruel and barbaric treatment" that transformed him into a PDF, ready to lay down his life and battle for the triumph of the Revolution.

"Beatings day and night to extract information about anti-coup activities took a different turn on the third day. Dissatisfied with my responses, they forced me to stand in the blazing sun for hours. In the evening, they took me to a grove of trees and placed me inside a hole that had already been dug in the ground, with my hands tied behind my back. I could see nothing and couldn't identify who was beating me. Forced to lie face downwards, I was pushed into the hole, while they began to fill it up with lumps of earth, leaving only my head above the ground. Then, one man aimed an axe at my neck, threatening to decapitate me and giving me a chance to pray."

"You know," he said, "immediate death would have been better for me. That was how I felt about it. I prayed fervently that I could have a chance to reincarnate as a member of my family." They didn't let him die, but pulled him out of the hole, saying they had some more questions to ask him. After that, they beat him again and again, grinding on his legs and thighs with a cement pipe, whilst providing him with just enough food and water to keep him alive.

"It'd have been better if they had shot me dead. I hate this. You know the way they torture!" said Zeya.

On the seventh day, his scalp sutures were removed. By the tenth day, he was transferred to Insein Prison, but his underage status led to rejection. He was then sent to the House of Correction, and, following this, he was granted bail and released to return home.

When the third wave of COVID-19 began to hit Burma, Zeya refrained from providing his volunteer service at the quarantine centres. He expressed his frustration on social media, writing, "In my life, the time I will never forget is the time when they put me to the rack, making me writhe like a poor wriggler!" The following day, military troops raided his house, but he had already departed for a liberation area of an ethnic group!

How many young men like Zeya had been arrested and subjected to such atrocious cruelties? Nobody knows. The news of brutal tortures in various regions spread far and wide. In Dawei, a mother posted some words on her social media, prompting soldiers to come and arrest her. Her seven-year-old son retorted to a soldier, saying, "Nobody trusts soldiers like you." Clearly, his immediate reaction reflects the perception of the military as vile and untrustworthy, even among children. Although underage individuals like Zeya were not thrown into jail, many passionate young men in Burma have been arrested. On July 20, the SAC issued an amnesty order that closed criminal cases under trial, but the majority of political prisoners' cases were not included. Uprisings occurred inside Insein Prison, Yangon, due to the high spread of the COVID-19 epidemic and the lack of healthcare services. This led to reports of suppression within the prison walls. On the morning of July 23, some young men took to the streets to support the activities of political prisoners. They marched along Factory Road, Mingala Taung Nyunt Township, Yangon, shouting slogans such as "Don't blame us for staging strikes during the epidemic outbreak. The emergency case is the State itself, so why not come to our rescue?" and "We stand together with the Heroes inside Insein Prison, who are serving imprisonment and nothing more!"

Certainly, one might wonder what the soldiers of the SAC are doing while the fighters of the Spring Revolution have engaged themselves in defying injustice. A news article from *Mizzima News*, dated July 18, provides some insight into this matter. Let's look at some extracts from that article:

"On May 31, commemorating the fourth month of the Spring Revolution, the allied forces AA, TNLA and MMDA attacked and seized a Myanmar junta outpost, No. 123 Light Infantry Battalion, in the large village tract of Nam Hpat Kar, Kutkai Township. Among the seizures were weapons, some drugs and, curiously enough, a few currency notes, featuring the image of General Aung San, now no more in current circulation. Many shared the news on social media: 'Heavy Artillery and One Kyat Old Currency Notes Seized' and 'Eleven of Military Junta, Including Lieutenant Battalion Commander Killed'. The baffling question arose over why those soldiers of the military junta were still keeping the lowest currency notes, K 1, now no longer in circulation."

"At 1 am, May 31, a heavy clash broke out at Nam Hpat Kar. According to the interview with a member of TNLA of Northern Allied Forces, who had been engaged in the recent clash, he replied that heavy artillery, packets of Yaba drug, some flat aluminium pieces and some small currency notes were seized."

"That 'crazy medicine' or Yaba, as well as some rolls of currency notes the cones of which were used to inhale the smoke of the tablet, are also found in the camp we've seized."

"Those Yaba tablets, formerly known as yama (literally 'horse drug' in Thai), can be administered by direct inhaling or indirect inhaling by letting the vapour pass through the water, thus removing the chemicals. To do the direct inhaling, the paraphernalia are: a match, a small flat aluminium piece on which the tablet is placed and heated a little, and a small paper or a currency note, which is rolled into a tube of about two millimetres in size, or a bamboo pipe. This direct inhaling is usually administered by users who move from one place to another. No wonder the rarely used currency notes like K.1, Ks. 20 or Ks. 50 serve well for the purpose of the 'dopers and junkies'."

"Therefore, the currency notes bearing the image of General Aung

San such as K.1, which were found among the seizures at the camp of the soldiers of the SAC, might be useful for collectors and enthusiasts, but except those numismatists, those rare currency notes have been transformed into the paraphernalia for the hopheads!"

"According to the confidential files of the Defence Services Commander-in-Chief's Office, which *Mizzima News* had accessed for preparing this news article, the drug abuse, drug dealing and drug trafficking as a form of commercial business within the Myanmar army have already taken root as a big issue, starting from 2012-2013."

"At the 6/2013 meeting of the Central Committee of the Directorate of Defence Procurement, held at the meeting hall of the Commander-in-Chief's Office (Army) on September 23, 2013, at 9:00 am, the Senior General Min Aung Hlaing, now the military leader of the coup, delivered a speech on the item of drug abuse as follows:

"The issue of drug abuse is, undeniably, making a strong impact on our Tatmadaw, to some extent. It is learned that the kids out there are addicted to glue. The issue of drug abuse is really a big challenge for us. We need to organise and supervise the matter so that the issue will not take root inside our institution. What's wrong with the situation is people talk straight in the presence of the public, but do whatever they like, good or bad, in the absence of others. Supervision is , therefore, very important."

The irony of this speech is that over one year later, on September 17, 2022, in Thailand, one of the cronies of Burma named U Tun Min Latt was arrested by the Thai police force for crimes including drug trafficking, money laundering, and transnational organised crime. Thai police found two Siam Commercial bank books and title deeds to a four-bedroom luxury condominium owned by the junta chief's daughter, Khin Thiri Thet Mon, and her brother Aung Paye Sone among the items seized during the raid. Therefore, one should be sceptical about what this gentleman, who is the "Myanmar Junta Boss," meant by "against the issue of drugs taking root in the Tatmadaw institution" and against "doing whatever they liked in the absence of others" from the Olympian heights.

Some additional extracts from *Mizzima News*:

"According to the responses made by the Northern Allied Forces, most of the seizures from the troops of the SAC were the stimulant yaba and heroin, as well as WY tablet and 88 (1) tablet. The latter has different types, E 88, ML 88, T 88, and H 88, etc. More of these stimulants were seized from the Battalion 77, 88 and 99, especially from the headquarters of No. 88 Division in the clashes with the Northern armed groups."

"Before their men are going to engage themselves in the clashes, they get doped with this sorta stimulant. A few minutes after popping pills, the drug triggers, they get high, they freak out, respond to commands like a blindfolded dog, not afraid of death. When they have run out of pills, they burglarize the houses, they rob, they do all sorts of bad things, you know."

"In the interview with a retired army personnel, who was a lecturer on the subject of military manoeuvres while serving in the Myanmar army, he gave the following comment: 'Our main issue is that of getting new recruits. You know, the state policy has changed, and we can't have child soldiers, or recruiting by force. Besides, our youths have more opportunities for education, as well as more job opportunities, especially during this decade. They have more choices in life. So the military service can't attract them anymore. Well, as the last resort, even a doper or whatever is recruited by force. You know, what a problem maker a doper is! So his parents, willingly, get him to join the army as though a patriot who would sacrifice his life for his mother country. There are drug users in the army. And you see the outcomes. There's almost no ground combat they could beat us. What a shame! this is sort of a civil war, and there should be no Bas, battlefield air strikes, supporting the ground forces."

"On May 18, 2020, the United Nations Office on Drugs and Crimes (UNODC) made a statement that the opiate seizures in the whole history of East Asia and Southeast Asia were made in Northern Shan State."

"According to the recent report, among the ASEAN regions, the

Shan State continues to be the location where amphetamines are mainly manufactured. The traffickers took advantage of the restricted travels due to the COVID-19 epidemic, and extended the large-scale drug production locally in Burma."

Moreover, according to the report issued by UNODC in January 2023, opium cultivation increased by 33 percent, covering 99.09 acres. Taking advantage of the crimes committed by the military, on August 1, Senior General Min Aung Hlaing changed the SAC to a new name, the Caretaker Government, and renewed its term of six months for his rule in Naypyidaw. Thus, the mechanism of atrocities and despotism has continued unabated.

Corner:

Deaths in Despair and Dilemma

"A funeral service without your remains.
No, never say it's your funeral.
Or Mom'll be offended.
"A prayer for her eldest son." That sounds better.
Today, Mom offers a donation to five monks and then shares the merit of the occasion with you. Come, come, come and share the merit!"

The text of the Facebook post above looked weird, but it was not uncommon these days. After the military coup, tragedy befell many innocent people: when evening fell, a troop of armed soldiers and policemen would emerge out of nowhere in FAW trucks, stop at a certain house, arrest a young man for no reason, and the following morning, his dead body was returned to his family.

Very often, the returned bodies, bearing the unspeakable blows of cruel batons and the slashes of merciless bayonets, had lost so many of their human features! Their distorted faces gave the impression of having had acid poured directly into their mouths; some bodies were returned without their internal organs. Some family members were only allowed a brief glance at the face (but not the body) of their son or daughter. Soldiers, like bestial animals, had been committing crimes against humanity with impunity. These days the expression "the corpseless funeral service" doesn't sound strange or unusual. Even if you think it sounds like a striking expression, the people of Burma (alas!) have been going through the deepest tunnel of the darkness.

"Mother returned from the military hospital yesterday. I asked, 'Where's my brother? Why haven't you brought him home, Mom? I haven't seen him in ages!' I know you're no longer alive, Bro, but I wanted to see you one last time. I was hoping to. Guess what Mother told us about you? 'My son,' she said, 'didn't die in an accident. He died while fighting for the country. Everybody knows that!' The truth is, if she wanted her son's body to bring it back home, Mother had to sign an agreement stating, '*** (25 years old), son of Father *** died in a motorcycle accident.' She refused, saying, 'What I want is my naughty, mighty son, not just his body.'"

In its five preceding processes, or the "Roadmap," the military junta, which claimed to have seized power with the lame excuse of voting fraud, included strategic terms for its aims and objectives, such as consolidating nationwide permanent peace and providing the quickest remedy for the economic recession caused by COVID-19. In practice, however, the members of the military's administrative council have been committing crimes against humanity strategically, as though their primary responsibility were imposing a variety of abuses and persecution on many families, including the case of the above-mentioned family. They have taken no measures for restoring temporary peace to the country, and no rule of law has yet been exercised. Instead, they have instilled overwhelming fear by randomly arresting people, confiscating their properties, and extorting money from helpless victims for their own profit. It is no wonder that, in an effort to conceal their criminal actions, they harm innocent families as well.

"Hey, Bro! Remember those mango trees you planted? Now, their leaves are falling in the rough wind and lashing rain of June. Last night, I found myself wandering into your room—I was searching for you, as I always did whenever I needed something. Are you hiding in the big game machine where you spent so much time playing? Or behind the poster of your favourite singer, the American rapper Post Malone? Maybe you're sitting next to the little bookshelf in the corner, crying after a scolding from Dad? Or perhaps you've hidden yourself inside your hollow guitar by the bed? I hope you'll come out when I touch and strum the guitar strings. Can't your soul come out from under the yellow headband you left under your pillow? Come on, Bro! Is that headband too heavy for you to remove and show yourself? Because it says, 'Against Every Form of Injustice.'"

Despite their names, the fallen heroes, beginning with Ma Mya Thwe Thwe Khaing, the first civilian shot dead at the outset of the Spring Revolution, will forever be remembered in immortal glory in the records of the uprising. While not all their names may be remembered individually due to the increasing number of casualties, the families of these fallen heroes will forever carry the endless grief and immortal memories, like deep scars that will never fully heal.

"Last night I woke up in the middle of the night as I heard footsteps in your room. Have you come back home? Come on! Can you please come back, Brother?"

The lovely younger sister uttered not a word of bitterness toward those who cruelly slew her brother and attempted to insult her mother. Her words revealed the extent of the abuse her family endured and the depths of her despair. Some of the leaves of the Spring were blown away by the rough winds, falling to the ground unseen, unknown, and unsung. However, one can only imagine how many of those bereaved families have clung to a shining hope of witnessing the birth of new green sprigs and blooming buds with the gentle breeze after the Storm of the Revolution subsides.

There was another post that began with "My Brother."

"Because he was the eldest among my cousins, I had always treated him as one of my siblings. When we were young, I used to put thanakha paste on his cheeks and shared my pocket money with him. I always loved him as my brother. After his high school finals, he told me that he would join the police force. Having experienced the 2007 Saffron Revolution, I was adamant about not encouraging anyone from our generation to join the Burmese army or serve in the military. But, then again, I wasn't in a position to help him find a job. Instead, I asked him to promise me one thing: 'Be a policeman who adheres to ethical standards and does not engage in any morally wrong activities.'

His decision led to a period of estrangement between us. Later, he became dissatisfied with his service and submitted his resignation letter. Unfortunately, shortly after his resignation, the military coup occurred. As the tide of the Spring Revolution surged, he was transferred to a border station near India. Upon learning this, I immediately called him and urged him to make the right decision, encouraging him to join the liberated area promptly. He expressed concern that he might not be able to see his two young daughters again if he left. However, he assured me that once he was allowed to leave the police force, he would return. He said, 'I'm not going to harm anyone; I'm just going to protect myself and take care of my family.'"

The conclusion of this story was easily predictable. Indeed, after over two years of military dictatorship, the country found itself mired in economic recession due to both economic mismanagement and international sanctions. This inevitably affected the general public in terms of career and professional job opportunities. For some youths, particularly the uneducated, joining the security forces had become a means of supporting their families financially.

"On that fateful day, they were tasked with guarding a bridge, approximately ten feet [1.5 m] long. The two policemen departed from their camp on motorcycles, each armed with an old rifle. As they approached the bridge, they were ambushed and shot by revolutionary students, succumbing to multiple bullet wounds.

On Facebook, the news circulated that two military personnel had been killed in an ambush by armed revolutionary fighters, former students, near the bridge. The news and accompanying videos went viral, referring to the fallen as 'military dogs.' Astonishingly, one of them was my cousin, while the other soldier refrained from joining the Civil Disobedience Movement (CDM) out of fear for his family's safety.

Now, both of you have found liberation for your souls. You died in the line of duty. In death, you received the regime's final decree: 'Now your souls are free to roam wherever they desire.' My dear cousin, I shed many tears, pondering whether it would have been preferable for you both to be captured and taken away instead of being shot. Sadly, you were denied the chance to flee, nor were you afforded the opportunity to be arrested and escape."

Due to the severe and inhumane oppression by the military junta, people's animosity toward soldiers has led to them being likened to four-legged creatures, or canines. This comparison isn't merely a form of hate speech; rather, it reflects the intense anger and resentment felt by the populace towards all members of the security forces, including the police.

"I am crying, my brother," the post continued. "Of course, my tears do not fall for a mere war dog. I keep crying because of your absence, my dear brother, whom I will never see again for the remainder of my days. And I am disheartened by you, who didn't dare to get yourself out although you knew that you were on the wrong path. A generation of innocent souls lost to the tyranny of a corrupt regime! Lives squandered in service to dictatorship. For you, my brother, I can only offer a prayer: 'May you not live a life like this in your samsara [cycles of life].' I will never forget that my brother was counted among those who perished at the hands of a power-hungry and evil dictator."

The loss of a family member while serving under the dictators is undoubtedly a source of profound grief for their bereaved family. It's heart-wrenching to imagine the pain they must endure. Despite experiencing such immense sorrow, this individual chose not to harbour bitterness toward those who harmed their loved one, recognizing the true culprit as the military dictatorship. Though they may not be able to rid themselves of their emotional anguish entirely, they expressed their feelings with a sense of rationality.

However, what about the other family members of fallen soldiers?

Will they find it in their hearts to practise meditation, forgive, and move forward? Or will they be content with identifying the true perpetrator? Can they reconcile with the harsh truth without succumbing to hatred? Or will they remain sworn enemies, seeking opportunities for revenge?

These questions prompt reflection. Beyond the Spring Revolution, how many empty chairs will there be at family dinner tables? While modern medicine can heal physical wounds, the imprints left on the survivors' consciousness may not be easily erased, even with the restoration of justice. Could the people of Burma find themselves trapped in a cycle of political vendettas?

Wall:

Political Parties and their Politics

On August 26, 2021, *Myanmar Now* ran the headline: "Daw Aung San Suu Kyi Rejects the Request of the SAC to Keep the NLD under Control."

"On February 9, 2021, two generals made a visit to No. A 33, Mya Nan Bontha Road, Zeya Theidhi Quarter, Zabu Thiri Township, Naypyidaw, where Daw Aung San Suu Kyi had been kept in house confinement. They told the ousted State Counsellor that there had been some anti-military demonstrations and the strikes against the government servants going to their departments to serve their duties. They made a request to her to issue a statement that such demonstrations and strikes should come to a halt. On January 28, three days before the coup, Min Aung Hlaing wrote a letter sounding like an ultimatum, and sent it to the Hluttaw. The letter read: The Hltuttaw must not commence, which would be vested with legitimacy due to the results of the 2020 General Election, as mentioned in another piece of news from *Myanmar Now News* Agency. This indicates that the Senior General was admitting that the one and only political icon who still has a sway over the public opinion of Myanmar is Daw Aung San Suu Kyi, and not him, who has usurped the Throne of the State Power.

Doesn't it sound absurd? According to the news report, the two generals arrived with a piece of paper already containing a written message. They handed it to Daw Aung San Suu Kyi, expecting her to read it aloud. However, she refused. Later that day, another paper was delivered, containing instructions for the NLD not to make any announcements and asserting that she was in good health. Once again, Daw Aung San Suu Kyi declined to read the letter, stating that she had not been involved in party affairs since November 6, 2020, three days before the 2020 General Election, as she had been focused on government duties. Therefore, she argued, the statement had no relevance to her.

This practice of the military regime, coercing detainees to read prepared statements during live broadcasts, is not uncommon. In another case, detainee U Phyo Min Thein, a member of the NLD and former Chief Minister of Yangon Division, was compelled to read a prepared letter that was later used as evidence against Daw Aung San Suu Kyi, resulting in her sentencing to five years' imprisonment.

In fact, two days before February 9, the NLD issued a statement addressed to nations worldwide, their embassies in Yangon, Burma, the UN, and international organisations, asserting that no relationships should be established with the military junta and that President U Win Myint alone represents the legitimate government of the state. On March 1, 2021, twenty days after she rejected the offer from the two generals, Judge U Maung Maung Lwin of Zabu Thiri Township, Naypyidaw, informed Daw Aung San Suu Kyi via video conferencing that she was charged under Section 505 (a), which criminalises "fake news" and "incitement" against the military.

During her two years of confinement, in addition to the initial two-year imprisonment under Section 505 (a), she was sentenced to a total of 33 years' imprisonment across nineteen cases. On May 23, 2021, Daw Aung San Suu Kyi was transferred to a secret location by the SAC. After more than a year at this undisclosed residence, she was moved to Naypyidaw Prison on July 23, 2022.

At that time, the NLD Party faced various forms of violence: many members were arrested and imprisoned, some were killed shortly after their arrest, and even those who managed to escape were often unable to protect their family members, who were targeted in their absence. The NLD headquarters were raided, documents destroyed, and valuable property looted or set on fire. According to an announcement by the NLD, within two years of the coup, 124 Hluttaw representatives and 1459 members were arrested, with 350 eventually released. Some NLD members' houses and office buildings were sealed by authorities. Despite the passage of time, the party struggled to reorganise its members and resume operations. On July 26, 2021, the SAC declared the results of the 2020 General Election null and void. This decision faced criticism not only from the NLD but also from other political parties, which objected to the annulment and accused the SAC of injustice.

The Shan National League for Democracy (SNLD) declared, "The State Administration Council has violated election laws, bylaws, and provisions outlined in the 2008 Constitution. Their actions deviate from democratic norms and are not free and fair, thus beyond our approval." The Arakan National Party (ANP) expressed concern that Burma's political landscape, already complicated post-2020 elections, was deteriorating further. Annulling the election results, they argued, would worsen the political crisis. U Ko Ko Gyi, Chairman of the People's Party, told the BBC, "Annulling the election results would erode citizens' trust in future elections. This is unacceptable."

In general, not only ordinary citizens but also political party observers often misunderstand that winning an election means defeating the opponent party or candidate. They fail to grasp that an elected representative, having earned the trust of their constituents, is entrusted with the responsibility of serving their country on their behalf. Consequently, there may still be some scepticism among citizens towards the elected party, along with negative attitudes towards its policies (even though their conscious mind knows it shouldn't be so, their subconscious mind may harbour such sentiments). It's not surprising that while some people may not support the State Administration Council (SAC), others may take pleasure in observing how the NLD grapples with unforeseen challenges and speculate about the party's potential downfall. This includes leaders of certain political parties and democracy activists.

In Burmese society, decades of successive military regimes, operating under various grandiose labels, have eroded civic institutions. After enduring 26 years of totalitarian rule, the country transitioned to a multi-party system, but most of these parties were merely in name. Even the NLD, representing the Leagues for Democracy that opposed the Burma Socialist Programme Party (BSPP) during the 8888 Revolution, fell prey to this trend. Throughout these periods, politics centred on the cult of personality proliferated, with many parties founded solely on the fame and influence of their leaders rather than on policy, program, and philosophy. Consequently, it has been overlooked that while the military is an essential institution for a nation, a political party is vital for establishing a democratic society. Similarly, to ensure the success and stability of any institution, it is crucial to recognize and protect all its components for their long-term viability.

As mentioned earlier, when a dominant party faces the prospect of losing power, citizens often believe it is their chosen party's turn to govern. However, they may not fully grasp that attacking one political party poses an indirect threat to the entire political institution. Consequently, efforts to systematically protect the political system may be lacking. Moreover, some have trivialised the Spring Revolution as merely a conflict between the pro-military USDP ("the Green Party") and the NLD ("the Red Party"), or a struggle confined to the Bamars without concern for other ethnic groups. Consequently, some political parties and armed ethnic groups have refrained from openly or covertly collaborating with the armed forces fighting for the Revolution.

Despite the Spring's efforts to dismantle the barriers of the past, a prevailing mindset persists: instead of upholding fundamental democratic principles, people tend to cry foul only when their individual interests are threatened. Even within the Spring movement, a fog of uncertainty clouds the landscape, obscuring the way forward.

Passage:

The Role of the Diaspora

The sky was now clear, devoid of fog or mist. The warm summer sky stretched overhead, unobscured. Against this backdrop, the stirring orchestral strains of the Burmese national anthem filled the air. Slowly but steadily, the flag bearing the emblem of the Fighting Peacock ascended from the bottom of the flagpole. Positioned in front of Buffalo City Hall, a thirty-two-story building in Niagara Square, stood two flagpoles. Atop one fluttered the flag of the United States of America, while atop the other soared the Red Flag bearing the emblem of the Fighting Peacock, its golden yellow streak shooting upwards. This was August 8, marking "Burma Flag Day", commemorating the first hoisting of The Fighting Peacock Flag on September 25, 2010.

"Today, all of you gathered here represent our city's proud Burmese Community, celebrated for its culture, diversity, community involvement, and the significant contributions to the vibrant tapestry of the great City of Buffalo," remarked Mayor Byron W. Brown during his speech at the flag-hoisting ceremony.

"We are immensely proud to have the privilege of raising the Fighting Peacock Flag annually on the anniversary of the 8888 Revolution. It's an honour unique to our city among all the cities of the United States of America. Being a border city, Buffalo has always been supportive. During the ceremony, the Canadian flag is respectfully lowered for a brief moment while we raise our flag. This tradition has been ongoing since around 2009 or 2010, spanning over a decade. It symbolises our legitimate recognition of the struggle for democracy. Buffalo is home to one of the largest communities of immigrants from our country in the USA, and it's only here that we are allowed to celebrate Burmese Flag Day and conduct the flag-hoisting ceremony. I want to acknowledge the efforts of our fellow Burmese residents in Buffalo for making this opportunity possible," expressed a young lady who had settled in the city in the mid-

2000s. She was adorned in a fawn-coloured Pinni costume, the attire of an NLD party member or supporter, and wore a red mask over her mouth and nose.

"This city is a hub for many former Burmese political prisoners. Among them are former Hluttaw representatives, civilian activists with ties to Daw Aung San Suu Kyi, a Buddhist monk who participated in the Saffron Revolution, individuals sentenced to death in absentia, former members of the All Burma Students' Democratic Front (ABSDF), and various ethnic groups. While we used to gather annually for ceremonies like this, it wasn't very frequent. However, since February 1, we've been demonstrating every weekend, providing us with an opportunity to come together more regularly. The Spring Revolution has allowed us, immigrants from Burma who left our beloved country for various reasons, to reunite and embark on a common mission. Perhaps, one unintended positive outcome of the SAC's oppressive rule is that it has brought together all the scattered anti-military forces," shared one of the Burmese immigrants who now call Buffalo City home.

"It's crucial that we maintain our integrity and principles, even in the face of the fascist army," the young Chin leader confided to the woman beside him. "We must resist the temptation to resort to the same tactics as our oppressors. When they resorted to violence and atrocities, we felt powerless without guns in our hands. All we could do was hurl curses at their bloody hands, but we must exercise restraint and not stoop to their level. We mustn't adopt a mindset of seeing anyone different as our enemy. That's something I feel strongly about," he emphasised.

As a prominent activist organising the demonstrators and leading the recital of slogans, he earned the respect of both ethnic groups involved in the movement and former Burmese political prisoners for his unwavering dedication to the Revolution.

David Williams's classification of the Burmese diaspora into seven groups sheds light on the diverse experiences and roles played by individuals living outside of Burma. These groups range from those fleeing conflict and seeking refuge in IDP camps to migrant workers in neighbouring countries, leaders of the democracy movement residing on border areas, and professional activists lobbying internationally.

Of particular interest are the "professional activists" who dedicate their lives solely to political activism. These individuals, often granted asylum in Western countries, engage in lobbying efforts, pressure international bodies like the UN, and communicate with representatives of Western nations. Supported by grants or funds from Western foundations, they work tirelessly to advance the cause of democracy in Burma.

Williams suggests that these professional activists wield significant influence within the Burmese democracy movement, despite their relatively small numbers. Their contributions, both in terms of financial support and advocacy efforts, are essential to the political landscape of Burma and should not be overlooked by observers. Thus, the role of diasporic activists, especially those engaged in professional activism, is a crucial aspect of Burma's political history.

The dynamics of the Burmese diaspora have undergone significant changes, particularly in their activism and focus of funding. During the term of U Thein Sein's government, there was a shift in funding direction from border areas to local areas, altering the nature and focus of diaspora activism.

Some well-known activists among the diaspora have found themselves in a new "material comfort zone" thanks to funding from institutions like the Myanmar Peace Center. Following the coup, these activists may have adapted their roles to align with the military regime or assumed clandestine roles akin to "His Majesty's Secret Service."

Conversely, other activists have remained steadfast in their commitment to the Revolution, joining the Spring Revolution in solidarity with the people of Burma. The influx of diaspora members during this period has led to the emergence of new leaders from diverse backgrounds, including different generations, races, religions, professional and educational backgrounds, and levels of material affluence. This has resulted in a new form of collective leadership, representing a paradigm shift within the diaspora community.

" 'Well,' a former political prisoner said, "even before the NUG and the PDF have come to the political scene, I have always kept myself in contact with the men of my village, the leaders of the strike. So, whatever they need, I could get it done. And every night we always make contact, and exchange the info, you know. We can't let our country slip under the Fascist army once again! Can't take it easy. To tell you the truth, I haven't applied for American citizenship yet. Staying here with the Green Card. I've been here since 2004. For me, Myanmar is my country. This is the country I'm staying in for a while. I was thrown into prison during the 1988 democratic movements. Then in 1999, the uprisings came out again. But I was away in another town, I didn't do anything, but I got the info about an arrest warrant that would send me behind the bars. So, I've left my country. Finally, I was sent to Buffalo as a refugee."

"Me, too," said a young woman, in a voice of confidence. "Myanmar is my country. I still hold on to that belief. I'm already a citizen here, I vote in their election, I serve my duty of citizenship of this country, but Myanmar is, you know, always on my mind. I remember when we heard of the bad news of the coup, we sent words of encouragement to our Myanmar people. You know, the local times are different, so we had a few hours of sleep, getting so much involved in supporting the protests of Myanmar, we nearly lost our jobs! I even got ill.""

The young man nodded, agreeing with the sentiments shared. "That's right! Myanmar has changed a lot, if you compare with the situation when I left my country. Me and my kids, too. My kids have grown up here. Guess what I witnessed! Our Myanmar younger generations are ready for the new changes to come. You know, they are ready for the Open Democratic Society– the way they think, the way they talk. See what they did when the coup broke out. The way they react is quite amazing! One thing for sure is we must continue our fight till we win!"

The conversation continued to gain momentum as the young woman chimed in, "We had a chance to go back to our country. I was quite impressed with the new conditions of road transportation. We donated some cash for the construction of a small school in our village. But the Revolution broke out, and the employees of the school joined the protest against the military, and some young teachers now turned themselves into the PDF. One good thing is because we've already set up connections with the local people a while ago, because we send donations to the school every month, we have no problem sending our aid to the very areas that are in trouble. No need to make donations through the NUG. Maybe, it's because of the frequent connections in and out of our country."

Their discussion highlighted the evolving dynamics and strategies within the diaspora community to support the ongoing struggle for democracy in Burma, despite the challenges posed by the military regime.

Indeed, the diaspora residing in foreign lands often find unity within groups based on their respective races and religions, reminiscent of the camaraderie and understanding they shared back in Burma. However, prior to the eruption of the Spring Revolution, this unity among Burmese people in the diaspora was not readily apparent. For instance, during the flag-hoisting ceremony in Buffalo City, attended by diaspora members from other states of the USA, some diaspora groups settled in Buffalo, particularly those belonging to certain races, chose not to participate. This diaspora encompasses individuals who arrived in foreign lands with varied American Dreams: asylum seekers, business-oriented immigrants seeking greener pastures, war refugees, scholarship students who later opted for permanent residency due to circumstances, among others.

Additionally, observers of Burma include ex-convicts, activists who operated underground, and individuals who resided in refugee camps in Thailand and Malaysia. Depending on their life experiences, some found employment in diverse fields such as sushi restaurants, Uber driving, chicken packaging factories, or highway transportation, leading them to primarily associate with their own cliques, where they shared joys and vented frustrations amongst themselves. However, the Spring Revolution has brought them together under the same sky, fostering broader connections within the diaspora. These gatherings have produced individuals imbued with high morale, strong convictions, and a broad perspective, who now serve as leaders representing their respective cities.

Throughout America, the activities of diaspora members, particularly those of national races gathering in certain cities in support of the Spring Revolution, have garnered more attention than other diaspora groups. Although tension among diaspora groups persists, unity has been restored among themselves for the sake of the Revolution. Previously, political activism was largely confined to the daily routines of political elites, but today, individuals from diverse backgrounds within the diaspora engage in fundraising, dedicate their time to twenty-four-hour service, and actively contribute to the cause of the Revolution, driven not by external influences, but by the dictates of their conscience.

In August 2021, the CRPH-OFP of the CRPH and the Ministry of Defense of the NUG launched a raffle ticket sale for the PDF, priced at $10 each. Initially estimating sales income at $500,000,000, the actual sales exceeded expectations, reaching over $700,000,000. Of this income, 51% was contributed by the local population, comprising over fifty million Burmese residents, while the remaining tickets were purchased by an estimated five million members of the diaspora worldwide. Notably, in Singapore, where public demonstrations are strictly prohibited, the Burmese diaspora accounted for 18.7% of ticket purchases, underscoring their unwavering support for the Revolution.

This remarkable charitable effort by the Burmese people, both locally and abroad, brings to mind Daw Aung San Suu Kyi's remarks on Burmese generosity during the first and second waves of the COVID-19 pandemic. Amid the 2020 pandemic, there was a strong sense of mutual trust and collaboration between the government and the people, as state-owned television and the State Counsellor's Facebook platform appealed for donations to address emergency pandemic-related needs. Remarkably, within hours, millions of kyats in public donations poured in, earning Burma the figurative title of "The Country of Donors on which the Sun Never Sets," according to Daw Aung San Suu Kyi. In contrast, the lack of public trust in the SAC was palpable during the third wave of the pandemic, as state media solicited donations, but it took four days to announce a public donation total of a mere hundred thousand kyats. Rumours circulated that this donation was not genuinely contributed by the public, but rather collected through coercive means.

It is crucial to emphasise that both the charity efforts of the diaspora and the donations from the local people of Burma have continued to uphold the esteemed reputation of being "Donors on which No Sun Sets."

Despite not yet witnessing a unified voice among sons and daughters from around the world, the diaspora has demonstrated unity and collaboration in support of the Spring Revolution, earning the esteemed title of Donors with No Sunset. Through unity and collaboration, both our people and the diaspora from Burma are tirelessly working to dismantle the Wall of the Maze, symbolising the barrier of disunity.

Passage:

Revolutionary Armed Forces

"That darn officer said, 'You like lady shoes, huh? The Lady's lady shoes are now outdated. Take this, my shiny military boots, have a taste!' Then they hit me. And the worst thing is they kicked my loins! I was sorry I had also witnessed them hitting the girls badly! Poor girls! Some even peed, trembling, seized with fear. When night fell, what they did to the poor victims was subject them to electric shock, around thirty to forty times a night. My gosh! When I was thrown into prison, the torture became worse than ever! You see, they hit me until my back skin split like bird wings."

Ko Sai Ko Ko, now serving with the PDF in the liberated area, shared these words with *Myanmar Now*. He was running a construction company in North Okkalapa, Yangon, when the military coup seized power. His criticisms against the coup, citing sections of Myanmar's legal system, led to him enduring nameless tortures during his imprisonment. However, as one of the early detainees arrested in the peaceful protests' early days, he was released relatively early. Subsequently, he headed for the liberated area and has since been serving with the PDF, actively engaged in the Spring Revolution.

Another young man, known for his talent in writing poetry, has joined the PDF after experiencing imprisonment during the early stages of the Revolution. He was part of the initial group of protestors, led by political activist Dr. Tayzar San, who were arrested by the military junta on February 4, 2021, in front of the University of Medicine, Mandalay. While in prison, he witnessed horrifying scenes of soldiers torturing fellow prisoners, including forcing young detainees to crawl like crocodiles and subjecting them to merciless beatings. The sight of bloodstains on the black tar road of the Obo Prison, along with the inhuman acts of torture, motivated him to join the PDF.

A Canadian writer conducted interviews with several members of the

PDF in an emancipation area and compiled their stories in a book titled *The People's Defense Force*. This book features their real-life experiences along with numerous photographs, allowing readers to gain insight into the lives of various PDF members.

"Here," remarked Ko Lay Hnyin, "I am enjoying my life in the PDF; we're like a family. There is no discrimination among us." Previously, he had served in the Tatmadaw, the Myanmar Army, which had long been utilised as a tool of totalitarianism. Raised in an orphanage, he had joined the army not out of patriotic spirit but merely to obtain a national registration card for himself.

During her interview with the Canadian writer, Ma Me-Shar, the younger daughter of a military supervisor, expressed that while she had not offered "one hundred percent" support to the NLD party, she vehemently opposed the military dictatorship. She stated, "Just because the NLD government could provide freedom, if not fully, at least to some extent, for our people."

Another young PDF member highlighted in the interview with the Canadian writer was Ko Yah Yah. He harboured a childhood dream of becoming an astronaut, but like many young people in Burma today, his dream remained unfulfilled. As he matured, he was compelled to pursue a career in medicine. Reflecting on his decision to join the PDF as a physician during the interview, he expressed gratitude to his wife, saying, "I must say I am thankful to my wife. You know, it was because of her encouragement that I decided to join the CDM. She reminded me that I had long been serving the people, not the government. She also assured me that she would not allow me to die of hunger or starvation."

Another interviewee featured in the book was Ko Bo Phyu. He was a former monk, a member of the Sangha in the Buddhist Order, who, bound by the Five Precepts, had taken a vow to abstain from killing or causing harm to any living beings. Despite spending four years in the peaceful life of a monk adorned in yellow robes, he chose to leave the Sangha. Disrobing himself, he joined the PDF and took up a rifle, driven by the growing fear that Burma's totalitarian army, known as the Tatmadaw, posed a grave threat to the future of his country and the promising prospects of its youth.

Another compelling real-life account was that of Ko Poe Te. Despite being newly married, he made the difficult decision to leave his young wife under the loving care of his mother—not because he didn't love her, but because his love for his country surpassed all else. He joined the PDF alongside his three younger brothers.

The following are the real-life stories of the interviewees:

Ko Te Za witnessed the miserable condition of his younger brother, who was released from prison with cuts and bruises. Out of concern and determination, Ko Te Za went underground and joined the PDF.

Ko Phyu Phwe, a former policeman, decided to serve the PDF after closely working with his local community, driven by a deep sense of duty to his people.

Ko Aung Aung, despite being a former farmer, possesses remarkable intelligence and always speaks in a gentle voice. He chose to join the PDF to contribute to his country's cause.

Ko Abraham, a young pastor, made the bold decision to join the PDF without informing his family, driven by a sense of duty and bravery.

Young Khaw Khaw, a well-known YouTuber, abandoned his previous life to serve the PDF, motivated by a desire to make a meaningful contribution.

Ko Pi refused to let his youth go to waste and hoped to make a difference in his country by joining the PDF.

Ko Pyu Saw Htee dreamt of serving in a reformed Myanmar Police Force under a new democratic government, leading him to join the PDF during the Spring Revolution.

Dr. Ralde, a former dentist, left behind his comfortable life to join the PDF and serve his people during turbulent times.

Stoner, despite her mother's objections, was determined to join the PDF and contribute to the cause, showcasing both gentleness and determination.

Ko Gale, leading an ordinary life until now, swiftly transitioned into a full-fledged PDF fighter, inspired by a newfound sense of purpose.

Ko K Pi, a former university student, firmly believed that dictatorship could only be overcome through armed opposition, leading him to join the PDF.

Ko Kelvin, a former seaman, joined the PDF as a member of the medical corps, driven by a desire to serve his country in its time of need.

Ko Jerry's case is particularly interesting: despite his father's former affiliation with the USDP, he later supported the NLD. Following his father's advice, Ko Jerry also became a member of the NLD before ultimately joining the PDF.

These individuals, among tens of thousands of others, young and middle-aged alike, have joined the PDF as new recruits of the Spring Revolution.

Daw Rati Ohn, former head and lecturer of Kalay Technical High School, resigned from her position to establish the Mobile Medical Team (MMT) in the West Division. She has been actively leading the frontline healthcare team, making invaluable contributions to the PDF cause.

Credit is also due to numerous celebrities from the film industry and artists from the performing arts world who have dedicated themselves to their respective PDFs. Renowned figures such as Singer Kyar Pauk, Director Hna Gyi, Film Star Min Maw Kun, and the Har-Nga-Kaung (Five Jokers) have become instrumental in revolutionary fundraising efforts.

Conversely, musician Poe Thagyan, despite winning 19 silver medals in national singing, dancing, songwriting, and music competitions, may not attract widespread public attention. During an interview with *Mizzima News*, he expressed his unwavering revolutionary spirit against the military coup:

"The revolutionary spirit against the military coup has been burning within me from the moment I wake up until bedtime. While I gained recognition as a player of the Myanmar traditional Hsaing Waing Ensemble under military dictatorship, I questioned who truly supported my livelihood. It's my people who have undoubtedly sustained me. The Tatmadaw officials may deliver grand speeches professing love for the countrymen, but they fail to understand true respect and care. I couldn't bear to live under such ungrateful leadership! That's why I decided to join the Five Jokers. Art is a luxury, and amidst turmoil, how can an artist indulge in music? Who would listen to their melodies when the nation is in crisis? When the Spring Revolution concludes, I'll return to the Hsaing Waing ensemble to engage in fundraising for our nation's rebuilding. I won't perform solely for profit at Ahlu ceremonies. We've all been influenced by ideologies and religion throughout our lives, and I refuse to perpetuate negative legacies to the next generation."

The PDF has emerged as an armed force representing a diverse array of individuals with varying experiences, convictions, and backgrounds. Currently, there are 257 armed forces, with the People's Protection Agency (PPA) established in over 250 municipalities, and more than 400 urban guerrilla forces in operation.

Couples, loved ones, siblings, relatives, and friends have joined forces, leaving behind their homes, families, and everything they hold dear to pursue their strong political convictions. However, the suddenness of this operation has left them unprepared, resulting in challenges such as insufficient supply of weapons and ammunition, inadequate accommodation, food shortages, and limited access to medical care.

While victories are achieved in battle, there are also casualties, with fallen heroes mourned by their families and friends. Despite the hardships, the poem "I Love My Country As I Love You" by Kyaw Min

Tun (New York) captures the unwavering patriotism and bravery of those willing to sacrifice their lives for the country, freedom, and democracy.

I love My country Like I Love You, my Man

"You see, Darling,
Wherever I go,
what I always have to carry in my backpack
is my country, lost in curls of smoke everywhere!
Every day is a day of bad luck.
but I love my country,
like I love you, Man.

"If old leaves fall at night,
new sprigs will sprout when the day comes;
When I look up into the night sky,
There are no more shining crystal stars but snipers
watching us from everywhere,
Even the heavenly bodies, engaged in star wars!

"Everyday I'll take a shower
in the rain falling in the spring;
I'll be humming a tune
amid the springtime mist.
Darling, did you hear their comments?
'Her hubby was a PDF soldier,
and she's a PDF, too.
That poor young wife of a PDF,
Now a young widow!
Overhearing their sarcastic gossips,
I had to bite my lips and grind my teeth.
The blade of their sharp words could even cut
my ears bloodied all over!

"You know, I'd rather retort, saying,
'With his strong conviction
of uprooting the Fascist army,
My husband has given up his life!
This is not a myth!
Birds die while flying,
Man dies while planning,
Heroes die in harness.'

"I remember, Darling,
what you said to me,
'A bulletproof coat can protect the body,
but not the Dhamma, or Justice!'
'What is Peace?' you said to me.
'What is Peace Lost?
When there is no peace,
you'd know more about what Peace Lost is.'
'When there is too much of Peace Lost,
Hunger for Peace grows unbearable!
If peaceful protests do not work it out,
What we must do
is fighting for peace!'
Your exact words of truisms
I've strongly nailed it at the Door of my Heart.

"I am a woman with a loving heart, of course.
By the mound, where you lie unseen, unknown,
somewhere in a jungle unseen, unknown,
With a shawl over my shoulder,
with a tear in my eyes,
I do wish to cry over it.
But in my country, my poor country
has to wash her mouth with the smoke of gunpowder,

*and with the smoke of houses in flames_*
*A country where there is no town or village with no bloodshed_*
A country lying helpless, naked,
raped brutally by the powerlust Dictator!

"Because my country is like going through
a night of unwanted marriage,
I must move forward, my man, my darling,
I have to leave your little mound behind.
But I promise
I will come back to you for sure
after the Spring Revolution.
"I love my country
as much as I love you,
So let me go."

The Spring Revolution, now in full swing, could be considered a testament to the endless sacrifices of our people.

Corner:

Injustice in the Tatmadaw

"*My dear Wife,*

Maybe, this is my final note of farewell to you. No tears, please, if I ain't make it home. Afraid I'd get killed in this operation. If I get killed, no blame on PDF. 'Cos this Operation we're engaged in, as far as I've checked it out, is just a death trap for darn fools like us. The bloody dictators going crazy for power is the very object of hatred. If I ain't come back, find a way to earn a living on your own. No cry. Never, ever, get our kid conscripted into the army. Mind!"

"*If I have a chance, I won't mind absconding from the army.*"

"*If I am still alive, I'll come back to see my family, babe, for sure. Now the army's going' haywire! We're fighting just for shit, ma'am! We soldiers have to sacrifice lives, and clear up the tangles of the darn megalomaniac Senior General. Should have listened to your advice. Feeling regret I ain't do nothing but flight from army earlier.*"

This message from a letter went viral on Facebook. The letter was discovered inside the pocket of a SAC soldier's uniform after the soldier was killed in a shoot-out. Its handwriting suggested that it was hastily written on a worn-looking piece of paper, likely intended for his wife. The letter mentioned that he would take a photo of it and send it via Viber, though it's uncertain whether he managed to do so before his death. However, the message provides insight into the current challenges faced by army personnel and their families.

Of particular interest is the soldier's plea to his wife not to blame the young fighters of the PDF who were fighting for the people. This suggests that his wife may have urged him to leave the army earlier. He expressed regret over the untimely deaths of soldiers following orders from the power-hungry Senior General.

What can be inferred from this letter is that it can't be a fake copy because all the army officers, as well as the soldiers, know too well—know much better than an ordinary citizen—how Senior General Min Aung Hlaing has been using his highest rank and authority as a stepping stone, and exploiting every possible means for the benefit of his own family.

The construction company named Sky One was founded in 2013, belonging to Min Aung Hlaing's son, Aung Pyae Sone. According to Yangon Khit Thit Media News, on August 24, 2021, military sources revealed that the Senior General issued a directive to his commanders in the fiscal year 2014-15, stipulating that all construction tenders related to the army must be awarded to Sky One. From 2015 to 2021, spanning the military coup, Sky One won contracts for various construction projects within the army. These projects included the extensions of halls at the Defense Services Technological Academy (DSTA) in Pyin Oo Lwin, the Radiation and Cancer Treatment Ward at the Military 500-Bedded Hospital in Pyin Oo Lwin, the Special Treatment Centre at the No. (1) 1,000-Bedded Military Hospital in Mingaladon, Yangon, the Torpedo Factory and Campus Upgrading Project at Rakhine Chaung Navy in Dala Township, the Myawaddy Media Centre in Yangon, the maintenance of the South Okkalapa Golf Court under the Yangon City Development Committee, aircraft hangars for six Russian Air Fighter Jets in Naypyidaw, air force housing projects nationwide, airfield extension projects, seaport projects under the Kyaukpyu Deep Water Port Project invested by China, and the Sittwe Harbour Project, among others. Rumours suggest that Sky One, owned by Min Aung Hlaing's son, benefited not only from grants for these construction projects but also from acquiring grants for state-owned and military-owned land areas spanning thousands of acres. After the coup, issues concerning fuel and gasoline arose in the country, prompting Min Aung Hlaing to organise a committee for purchasing gasoline from Russia. One of the member companies of that committee is Yetagon Energy Trading, owned by his son Aung Pyae Sone.

What is astonishing is that while the Commander-in-Chief has been plagued by corruption (defined as "the abuse of public power for private benefit," according to Vito Tanzi, 1998) and ego-centeredness, the entire army does not adhere to its responsibility and accountability. They treat their subordinates with a lack of respect, as evidenced by the following piece of news:

"In Demoso, during the clash dated on May 31, 2021, at least ten of the SAC got killed. The Karenni PDF, making a temporary withdrawal from the battlefield, announced that, in accordance with The Law of Armed Conflict: The Conduct of Operations, there would be a temporary ceasefire for the adversary to collect and carry away the dead bodies of their soldiers However, the SAC troops on flight never retraced their steps to the bodies of their comrades. On the second day of the ceasefire, the dead bodies of the SAC soldiers got rotten, smelling intolerable stench, so the Karenni PDFs themselves cremated the bodies. Those soldiers who have "returned to the legal fold" of the people as CDMs confessed that this is a realistic picture of how different ranks of the SAC have always treated their subordinates with no compassion and sense of comradeship.

"Ya know, while in harness, they'd use you to the last ooze of your energy, but let's put it aside your injury or arrest, when you get defeated, you get reprimanded for using the "wrong tactics". That's why I feel disgusted with the army," said CDM Captain Zin Yaw. "Those generals," said CDM soldier Naung Yoe, "would not mind using the army for their personal interests. They know nothing about responsibility and accountability. Never!"

This post explains something about the families of the military personnel.

"A corporal of over twenty years in military service recalled: When the military seized power in a coup, the thought of joining CDM never came to his mind. But his kids said no. When he came back home, his kids struck the cans and drove him away. His sons and daughters are now young adults already, they know what is justice, and what is injustice. They felt humiliated to have a father like theirs. So, when he got back home, almost tired out, his sons and daughters struck the cans and drove him away. They didn't talk to their father any more. The corporal didn't *scold his kids, but he felt sorry, of course. The mother didn't get herself involved in this case. Thus, though he didn't join the CDM, he played the role of informer called "Pha-ye-thee" ("Watermelon," refers to the army combat uniform, in camouflage pattern of black and green but their inner stand is red, the colour of the revolution as the flesh of watermelon), from whom the secret military information of the SAC leaks out to the adversary and the mass media. I collaborated with him, but he had not yet joined the CDM. Then he happened to serve his military service on the frontier. There, he witnessed the air raid on a village. There, he saw the old villagers, of the age of his parents, running helter-skelter, crying in their flight for their life. His heart bled at the moving sight. He, then, made a decision to join the CDM. Because the Pha-ye-thees in the army can't stay secure, he has come over here, to this liberated territory, together with his family.''*

"Yesterday, I said to the little girl, 'How are you feeling since your father has now joined the CDM, and brought you all here, in the liberated territory?' 'Well,' she said, 'to tell you the truth, I'm not happy here, but I'm satisfied with what my dad has done, for himself and for us. You know, clear conscience is important, and we now have this for our whole time.' She said that was enough for her."

It is crucial to emphasise that the current period has witnessed an unprecedented level of desertion and defection from the Burmese army, marking a historic high. The majority of those joining the Civil Disobedience Movement (CDM) are lower-ranking officers, typically aged between 25 and 35, hailing from various branches of the Burmese armed forces, including the army, navy, and air force. These individuals previously served in diverse roles such as information and public relations, ordnance, warfare, intelligence gathering, and medical services, among others. This widespread participation underscores the depth and breadth of military personnel abandoning their posts.

According to interviews conducted with deserters, the Burmese military's recruitment practices bear resemblance to human trafficking. One regulation mandates that officers seeking promotion must recruit a new soldier every six months. This requirement incentivizes officers to resort to various methods, including coercing vagrants or young men with false promises of pay and military benefits, threatening imprisonment for non-compliance, or exerting pressure on their families.

When a diligent soldier secures a new recruit, he often engages in "trading" with a superior officer seeking promotion. These recruits are frequently illiterate but provided with forged documents, such as a Grade 4 Pass, and coached for interviews with officers, undergoing a rehearsal known as a FOC for a viva voce. Consequently, many army personnel are indoctrinated, isolated from current events and global culture, and maintain blind faith in the military as their provider. Thus, these individuals, referred to as "Slaves in the Service of the Military," have long been ensnared in a Maze of ignorance.

The military officers are no longer solely dedicated to serving the people's defence. Instead, they use their military uniforms as a guise, assuming roles in civil service as the "Moe-kya Shwe Kos" (a sarcastic term for the privileged class, literally meaning "Golden Bodies coming from above"). These hypocritical opportunists, driven by unchecked desires, have no qualms about engaging in corruption to expand their socio-economic influence and authority, all to secure a comfortable future. It's hardly surprising that, following the military coup, these Moe-kya Shwe Kos capitalise on the upheaval to enhance their own family's quality of life, despite being fully aware of the military's history of malpractice, injustice, and persecution. Compared to their subordinates' salaries, these officers, with their additional incomes from various sources, have no difficulty maintaining their lavish lifestyles.

One particularly egregious form of corruption that has emerged post-coup involves exploiting well-off detainees, often civil activists. When a detainee hails from a wealthy family, officers reach out to them, offering dubious promises of leniency in exchange for hefty bribes (perhaps MMK. 1,000,000 or MMK. 10,000,000). Additionally, officers falsely accuse affluent businessmen of financially supporting opposition groups, coercing them into greasing the palms of authority figures under threat of property seizure. This pattern of deceit underscores the officers' ulterior motives, as they lay traps with confidence, knowing the military's tendency to turn a blind eye to their transgressions.

Many officers even believe they can secure promotions by fabricating stories surrounding detainee deaths in their reports. These tales often involve suspects allegedly being killed while resisting arrest or during interrogation, a tired excuse for abuse of power.

Even more troubling are the cases of persecution occurring within the ranks of the military, involving both senior-junior relationships and peers, sometimes resulting in fatalities. Yet, no effective measures have been taken against these perpetrators. Consequently, a culture of preemptive and forceful retaliation has taken hold among them. This atmosphere of hostility extends even to families, with both army personnel and their loved ones falling victim to such persecutions.

Female army personnel serving in the Defense Medical Services face barriers to promotion, with their highest rank typically capped at Colonel, and in other branches of the Tatmadaw, women rarely ascend beyond the rank of Major. This limitation breeds disrespect from their male counterparts. Status discrimination, akin to that in an absolute monarchy, has persisted for decades: a soldier's family is expected to live a lifestyle inferior to that of a captain's family, while a captain's family must humble themselves even further in comparison to a major's family.

A Second Lieutenant who defected from the Air Force recounted a harrowing incident from their time in service: "While stationed at Magwe Air Force, I witnessed a disturbing event. A soldier, in a state of intoxication, expressed his inner turmoil through curses. In response, his superior had him bound with rope and ordered fellow soldiers to administer punishment. However, these individuals went beyond the bounds of reason. They subjected him to a brutal beating, even urinating on his body, resulting in his death. Shockingly, no disciplinary action was taken against those responsible. At the time, General Maung Maung Kyaw served as Commander-in-Chief of the Myanmar Air Force. He callously remarked that the soldier's death had no connection to the Defense Services Act. Consequently, the bereaved family received no pension, and their other claims were dismissed. The erosion of the rule of law has reached alarming levels, fueled in part by entrenched power dynamics and a pervasive culture of oppression. Moreover, many soldiers and officers, aware of their own vulnerabilities, refrain from speaking out against the misdeeds of others, opting to suffer in silence. Trapped within the confines of the military, they have lost their moral bearings amidst the injustices and persecutions plaguing their ranks."

Quoting the words of their power-hungry leader, Min Aung Hlaing, who boldly proclaimed that there is nothing on earth the military "does not dare to do," one may wonder if there is any virtue to be found within this institution. They craft their own narratives to conceal their misdeeds, their minds clouded by their own deceitful tales. These same army personnel adamantly assert that electoral fraud occurred during the 2020 General Election. It's difficult to refute this claim, considering the track record of the Burmese military and their political allies, who have a history of committing electoral fraud in every election held in Burma.

There are numerous testimonies corroborating the military's involvement in electoral fraud. One such confession comes from Captain Thu Ta Aung, who has joined the Civil Disobedience Movement (CDM).

"My name is Thu Ta Aung. I had served in the army, my last rank was that of captain. I am a product of the DSTA. I last served at the Security Printing Factory. I have joined the CDM since March 23, 2021."

"I was always proud of myself to be a Tatmadaw man. This was the attitude I had always adopted in my profession throughout my service. Though I did not need to sacrifice my life in my service like those armed staff of light infantry battalions, I always thought I was also contributing my service of defence for my country by serving the important duties of security printing such as the currency notes, lottery tickets and passport."

"I'd like to take this opportunity to explain something about the voting frauds I had witnessed. During the 2015 General Election, I happened to be attending the English Proficiency Course for the Tatmadaw Officers, a three-month training course which has been conducted for some years, there, inside the Royal Palace area, which, as you all know, is a military zone. Then we, trainee officers, got informed that the agents from our respective regiments were coming to see us so that we could cast absentee votes. So I began to do hunting for the background information of the election candidates so as to choose the right Hluttaw representatives. But when our agent came, he didn't bring any absentee votes. 'Bro,' he said, 'I've cast your absentee vote to the USDP Party.' As you know, it's a pro-military party. He had come all the way to give me that info, and that's all. My human rights of voting ended up like that. (Later, I got informed that a suspect for being the source of the leakage of military info was then sent to attend a training so that they could manipulate everything in his absence.)

"But the 2020 General Election was different. Committees were formed and meetings were held so that the junior officers would be assigned duties to check the list of voters and organise the families of army personnel to give votes without fail. In one meeting, the manager of our factory informed us about an instruction from above, which was to be implemented. That instruction for each group was: to perform the duties in respective zones to explain to the families of army personnel about how to check out a particular name in the list of voters. Besides the procedure of casting votes correctly, the instruction also highlighted the following hints: "You may cast votes freely, but any voter should seriously consider voting the parties that would function well in harmony with the Tatmadaw." Well, I suppose many of you know the five guidelines of the Commander-in-Chief on voting. I whispered into our group leader's ear, 'Bro, you might talk about those five guidelines but if somebody has got a video file of your speech, and posted it online, it's you who'll be sued. Then, mind you! nobody would shield you_ that's for sure. You'll be victimised.' So, the officer must have changed his mind, he never mentioned anything about the five guidelines. On the Election Day, all the junior officers were assigned duties in groups to keep the voting polls outside the cantonment under close watch. Some served that duty at their assigned polls, but I was not there because I thought it was all nonsense. Absurd! The local officers were sent back to their respective towns on duty to keep the civilians' voting polls under close watch. In some towns, the local people noticed the presence of the army personnel hanging around in civilian garbs; in others, ironically, the army personnel were held as suspects attempting to disrupt the electoral procedure.

Prior to the 2020 General Election, on July 31st, the Union Election Commission (UEC) made a significant announcement regarding transparency and the freedom of election observation missions (EOM). They declared that 632 voting polls would be established outside cantonment areas specifically for Tatmadawmen voters, alongside 339 polls designated for both civilian voters and Tatmadawmen voters. This announcement caught the military and the pro-military USDP off guard. In comparison, during the 2015 General Election, there were 844 voting polls located within cantonments, with 108 designated for army personnel and their families, and an additional 139 for army personnel and civilians residing in urban and rural areas.

Captain Thu Ta Aung, who has joined the Civil Disobedience Movement (CDM), expressed, "The military exhausted every possible avenue for their ulterior motives, but when the pro-military party faced defeat, their final recourse was the coup. I once took pride in serving my country as a captain, but later, I felt ashamed. You see, the military adamantly clings to the belief that they hold Myanmar's political power. They believe that as long as they are content, they'll allow politicians to govern, but if the civilian government displeases them or triggers their ire, or if the moody military decides, they can seize state power through a coup at any time. They won't hesitate to manipulate elections to suit their agenda, paving the way for eventual coups. It's become somewhat of a tradition: today's commander-in-chief could easily become tomorrow's dictator."

In fact, the military has consistently demonstrated an unwillingness to relinquish state power. This assertion is supported by a news article titled "What did the Former Minister for Home Affairs Maung Oo Talk to the Rakhine Public?" published in the Rakhine Post (No. 9, Vol.4) on July 20, 2011. The excerpt reads as follows:

"I want you all to keep in mind that the USDP will never let go of the state power. Our party will be the one that rules the country forever. The Tatmadaw hands over the power, not to the Hluttaw, but to the USDP. Understand? The USDP is nothing but the one and only party that holds the state power."

"You have to consider the current time and circumstances and then the law must serve the purpose. Everything can't be done in accordance with the law. Now you have the multi-party system, but you have this according to the time and circumstances only. It is the USDP that will take the lead."

(Meeting Minutes of the Union Solidarity and Development Party. The USDP office. Speech delivered by U Mung Oo, the Rakhine State Representative of the USDP and former regional commander of the Rakhine State, in the assembly of local people of Pauk Taw Township on May 14, 2011.)

Over a decade, his speech has still remained valid. On January 26, 2023, the amendment of the law of registration for political parties was enacted. This amendment disclosed that the above-mentioned words of the former representative of the USDP were not just his whims, and that these words really stand for the attitude of the military leaders in line with their long term plan of consolidating a totalitarian government.

The international election observation mission did not fail to witness the military's involvement in voter fraud during the 2020 General Election. Similar practices had been observed during the 2015 General Election. Despite this, the international community had once felt hopeful, believing in the Burmese journey towards democracy, anticipating change. However, one may now question whether the Burmese path to democracy has ultimately led to the intricate Maze of politics.

Wall:

Election and Constitution Challenges

November 9, 2015

Officials at the Carter Center, including former Irish President Mary Robinson, were seated on one side of the shiny ebony table, while on the other side sat political activists and representatives from civil society organisations (CSOs). They were deeply engrossed in a discussion about Myanmar's past and future, with the focal point being the recently completed 2015 general election. Despite the official results not yet being announced, it was evident who the clear winner was and who stood on the losing end. The National League for Democracy (NLD) had secured a landslide victory.

"It's astonishing! There were grossly unfair practices favouring the USDP party, with bags of votes flooding in, and I feared the NLD would barely scrape through!"

The election outcomes took everyone by surprise. Despite many people suspecting covert malpractices during the supposedly free and fair electoral process, they couldn't contain their joy over the results.

"Yes, voters in some states were unable to cast their votes due to security concerns, as they faced threats from local armed forces. Despite these obstacles, the election results are quite remarkable," remarked one participant.

Issues such as voting errors, disenfranchisement, last-minute changes to results due to a flood of pre-election votes, biased campaign restrictions, and the stoking of religious and ethnic tensions were overshadowed by the overwhelming election results. Furthermore, deficiencies in the election law, limitations on eligible representatives, and significant disparities in voter numbers between constituencies were all swept aside in light of the decisive election outcomes.

"Reviewing the election results, it seems our people are saying, 'We reject you, USDP! We demand democracy! We support the NLD!' They've expressed their dissatisfaction through their votes. There's a fear that the USDP could win the election, as well as a fear that even if the NLD emerges victorious, it might struggle to form a government independently, needing to forge a coalition with the USDP and other parties." These were the remarks of a former political prisoner, once involved in the 8888 Students Movement, reflecting on the current sentiments of the public. There was widespread belief that this former political prisoner, exuding confidence, would one day establish his own political party. In 2018, that belief materialised as he indeed founded his political party.

The Carter Center, which had deployed ten experts to monitor the electoral process continuously, received reports indicating that, at various points, the election process fell short of ensuring a free and fair election. However, despite the pressures and challenges, the outcome was remarkable. The National League for Democracy (NLD) could now establish a government with its own representatives.

According to the 2008 Constitution, only 75 percent of the elected representatives in the Pyidaungsu Hluttaw (Union Parliament) are elected by the public, while the remaining 25 percent are appointed from the military. Only a party that secures the majority of votes is eligible to form a government independently. If a party fails to reach this threshold, only the party that collaborates with the military representatives can submit a list of vice-presidential candidates and form a coalition government. The election results now favoured the NLD, eliminating the need to cooperate with any other party or organisation. The NLD would nominate two vice-presidential candidates from the Pyithu Hluttaw (House of Representatives) and Amyotha Hluttaw (House of Nationalities), while the military would nominate one vice-presidential candidate, though the opportunity to nominate the president remains elusive for them. Since the president holds the authority to establish a government, this implies that the NLD would have the autonomy to form an independent government composed of its own representatives.

"But it's important to note that only the Commander-in-Chief of Defence Services holds the authority to appoint the posts of the

Minister of Defence, the Minister for Home Affairs, and the Minister for Border Affairs. In reality, the Police Forces and the Department of General Administration remain under the Ministry of Home Affairs, keeping significant administrative mechanisms under the control of the Commander-in-Chief."

"One of the significant shortcomings of the 2008 Constitution is evident in the fact that approximately thirty sections prioritise the role and authority of the army and the Commander-in-Chief. Regardless of election outcomes, the army and the Commander-in-Chief reap the benefits, solidifying their legitimate power and authority."

"The role of the army has been granted extensive power and authority, essentially monopolising the state's administration and legislation. Section 59 has effectively prevented Daw Aung San Suu Kyi from being eligible for the presidency."

"Furthermore, consider what the 2008 Constitution states: 'The Chief Justice of the Union and Judges of the Supreme Court of the Union shall hold office up to the age of 70 years unless[...]' This means there's no way to dismiss the current Chief Justice, a former army personnel appointed by President U Thein Sein. Since he's around 55 years old, he still has another fifteen years to exert influence over the judiciary. Additionally, the authority over the Police Forces and the army falls under the purview of the Commander-in-Chief."

A heavy sigh, reminiscent of the puff of a steam locomotive, escaped from someone's lips. They exchanged glances, broke into smiles, and erupted into laughter. Despite the mixed emotions, the news of the election's landslide victory was overwhelming, dominating the front pages of all media outlets. While cheerful smiles abounded, there were also audible sighs from those concerned about the challenges ahead.

"The gap between the previous parliament and the new parliament is three months. God forbid! I fear those clinging to the ropes of power might resort to foul manipulation soon," one person remarked. "There was tension between President U Thein Sein and Thura U Shwe Mann, and the speed at which U Thein Sein approved the Race and Religion Protection law, like a trump card, was alarmingly swift. Religion was exploited as a tool during the election. I worry things may worsen in the future."

"I couldn't agree more," another chimed in. "Their ultimate goal is legitimacy. This election won't bring democracy for us, but it will undoubtedly legitimise their power."

"Remember what the NLD did in 2010? They refused to participate in the election until the 2008 Constitution was amended," someone else added. "During the early days of U Thein Sein's presidency, he lifted censorship, leading the world to believe better days were ahead. This softened the local community's stance and warned the NLD that change was coming. If they didn't seize the opportunity to participate in the election, they'd be sidelined."

The conversation quickly escalated into a heated discussion.

"Indeed, amending the 2008 Constitution poses a significant challenge. Section 436 makes it clear that securing a vote from a Tatmadaw representative, let alone from the rest of the elected representatives, is virtually impossible. Those representatives of the USDP Party who resorted to buying votes in the outskirts of Kayah State will certainly not support any proposal to amend the Constitution. That much is certain."

"Do you believe those individuals will welcome peace if it's achieved during the NLD's term, considering they've kept peace at bay during their longstanding rule?"

"Oh, let's not even talk about 'peace.' It's customary for a new government to grant general amnesty to political prisoners, filling them with hope. However, I fear it will be challenging for the NLD to grant amnesty without consulting the National Security and Defense Council, which is firmly under the grip of the Commander-in-Chief. Even if a decision is reached after the meeting, where the Tatmadaw holds six votes and civilians only five, the NLD would come out as the loser."

Sighs replaced smiles as silence descended upon the discussion.

"Complications upon complications! Oh, where has yesterday's joy gone?" one exclaimed.

"Yes, it feels like we're trapped in a Maze," another added solemnly.

The word "MAZE" hung heavily in the air, piercing through the complete silence.

"Oh, our Carter Center is facing tough times," Former President Mary Robinson confessed, looking perplexed. "We know there's a Maze awaiting us, but as a special team of election observers, we must issue a statement tomorrow. I'd appreciate your advice: Should I start by congratulating the Electoral Commission and the government on the astounding election results? Then, I could proceed to report our findings from our close observations of the electoral process. Any suggestions? We're aware of the complications, but should we still extend congratulations to the Electoral Commission and the U Thein Sein government?"

A hush fell over the table for a moment.

"What about congratulating the voters for fulfilling their democratic duties admirably?" suggested one member. "The credit truly belongs to the people of Myanmar. Despite all the malpractices and restrictions, they fulfilled their roles as voters, in-charge at the polling stations, polling station representatives, and observers, both locally and abroad. This decisive outcome was achieved by the people, for the people, and of the people, with each vote cast from the heart."

The response from the female former political prisoner of the 8888 Revolution ignited a spark in everyone's eyes and was met with enthusiastic applause.

"Yes, the people are the true victors! This is their triumph. They have delivered results even seasoned political observers couldn't predict, and they deserve all the praise and victory!"

"Wow! What a brilliant idea!" exclaimed another.

The discussion at the Carter Center concluded, and its statement, dated November 10, 2015, was issued: "*The Carter Center congratulates the people of Myanmar, who have exercised their political rights with pride and enthusiasm. Both on election day and in the preceding months, they participated as voters, observers, political party agents, election officials, and civil society activists. Their empowerment and commitment to the democratic process were not only remarkable but crucial to counterbalancing the considerable structural impediments to fully democratic elections.*"

Indeed, as the thorns and thistles along the Maze loom as high as a hill, the Carter Center itself may or may not know, as a witness, whether our active and responsible people of Burma have been led right into the *Wingaba* (the Maze) or not.

Wall:

The Walls of the Maze, 2016

"Well, to be honest, it seems to me that the Commander-in-Chief holds the fate of the entire country in his hands."

In an interview in January 2016, U Ko Ni, the NLD's Legal Advisor and member of the Central Law Consultants Committee and the Central Committee of the Amendment of the Constitution, commented on the drawbacks of the 2008 Constitution. "When the 2008 Constitution was first enacted," he emphasised, "fifteen committees were formed for the governing bodies. The Central Government operates under the name of the Union Government, while fourteen states and divisions have their own governing bodies. At first glance, it may seem that the Central Government oversees the administration of the entire country, while the states and divisions have been granted their own powers of administration. However, this is merely the surface structure."

He continued, "The police force and the General Administration Department have been tasked with running the administration of the whole country. But both the police force and the GAD are under the control of the Ministry of Home Affairs. And who has the authority to appoint the Minister for Home Affairs? It's the Commander-in-Chief. Therefore, I argue that the Commander-in-Chief holds absolute power, effectively having the entire country under his control." This is U Ko Ni's straightforward assessment of the 2008 Constitution.

Throughout the period leading up to the 2015 General Election, this constitutional expert consistently drew public attention to the incongruities of democracy within the military-drafted 2008 Constitution and the extensive power granted to the commander-in-chief.

"So, who has been entrusted with state power? The 2008 Constitution gives the impression that state power is vested in the people. In the definition of 'The Republic of the Union of Myanmar,' Section 4 states:

'The Sovereign power of the State is derived from the citizens and is in force in the entire country.' However, according to the former constitution drafted by General Aung San, the sovereignty of the Union resides in the people." U Ko Ni drew a comparison between the 2008 Constitution and the 1947 Constitution, which was drafted under the administration of Gen. Aung San, the architect of Burmese independence.

"The Constitution states, 'The legislative power is vested in the Pyidaungsu Hluttaw.' Let's analyse what this means[...]. Only if we have the votes of 120,000 citizens do we have one representative, while 3,200 Tatmadaw personnel have one representative[...]. Who has the authority to appoint the Tatmadaw representatives? It's the Commander-in-Chief." This constitutional expert adeptly explained Sections 109, 141, and 161 of the 2008 Constitution in simple terms.

"According to Section 232, although the President is vested with the power to appoint ministers, the sole authority to appoint ministers for defence, home affairs, and border areas affairs lies with the Commander-in-Chief. This means neither the Hluttaw nor even the President has the authority to reject this decision. So, who appoints the Commander-in-Chief? The President has no authority in this matter. Surprise-surprise! Section 342 states, 'The President shall appoint the Commander-in-Chief of the Defence Services with the proposal and approval of the National Defence and Security Council.' This implies that the President simply signs the Order as proposed by the National Defence and Security Council. But who controls the NDSC? It's in the hands of the Commander-in-Chief. So, who appoints the Commander-in-Chief?"

"Who is truly in charge of state administration? The President or the Commander-in-Chief? Think about it. Section 343 states: 'In the adjudication of Military justice: the decision of the Commander-in-Chief of the Defence Services is final and conclusive.' U Ko Ni's explanations about the Executive power and judiciary were always concise and to the point, which garnered him a large audience every time he spoke."

On March 30, 2016, the National League for Democracy gained legitimacy in government for the first time. The most intriguing question on the minds of the people was: Who would become the President of the new government? According to the constraints of Section 59 (a) of the 2008 Constitution, Daw Aung San Suu Kyi was entitled to be the President of the Republic of the Union of Myanmar. Her supporters were anxious about her role in the new government. They worried that despite the President being elected by the NLD or being proposed by Daw Aung San Suu Kyi, the constraints of the Constitution could limit her leadership. At the time, she held positions as the Union Minister of the Ministry of Foreign Affairs, the Ministry of the President's Office, the Ministry of Electricity and Energy, and the Ministry of Education. U Htin Kyaw, who was not an elected representative, served as the President.

However, during an interview with more than 400 foreign and Burmese journalists in November 2015, she made a remark in English, seemingly in jest, "I will be above the president." What did she mean? Only God and Daw Aung San Suu Kyi knew at that time.

On March 31, 2016, NLD representative U Aung Kyi Nyunt, a member of the Amyotha Hluttaw Draft Law Committee, submitted the State Counsellor Bill at the Amyotha Hluttaw. This move came as a shock to Tatmadaw lawmakers and the USDP, the opposition party. Not surprisingly, they vehemently objected, almost voting with their feet in the Assembly. However, on April 6, 2016, the State Counsellor Law, signed by President U Htin Kyaw, came into effect as Pyidaungsu Hluttaw Law No. 26/2016-State Counsellor of Myanmar was enacted. The statement included read: "Daw Aung San Suu Kyi, the Chairperson of the National League for Democracy, who has won overwhelmingly strong public support during the 2015 multiparty democracy general election, is accordingly appointed to the post of the State Counsellor by the Pyidaungsu Hluttaw."

In accordance with this Law, despite the military-drafted 2008 Constitution barring Daw Aung San Suu Kyi from becoming the President, the Law is included under the provisions of the Constitution in accordance with Section 217, granting the Lady, the figurehead of democracy, executive power to lead her nation. As she had hinted in the interview with foreign and Burmese journalists, she was now "above the president."

According to Section 217 of the 2008 Constitution: "Subject to the provisions of the Constitution, the executive power of the Union shall be vested in the President. Nothing in this Section shall prevent the Phyidaungsu Hluttaw from conferring functions and powers upon any authoritative body or person, or be deemed to transfer to the President functions and powers vested in any authoritative body or person concerned under the existing laws."

Formerly, political observers were concerned about the ominous prospect that Senior General Than Shwe, the former dictator, might reappear on the political scene, having been vested with the executive powers of the country's leader. The 2008 Constitution, drafted over a prolonged period by the military and pro-military parties, was intended to secure military-centred privileges. It led political observers to wonder whether Section 217 might have been included for Than Shwe, known as "The Old Reader," to return (as reported by one of his loyalists, stating that the former leader, no longer involved in political affairs, spent his leisurely hours reading—reading what?).

However, from 2010 to 2015, during U Thein Sein's "good governance and clean government" period, that clause remained inactive. On the other hand, the NLD government acted swiftly: immediately upon gaining legitimacy in government, they enacted the State Counsellor Law within seven days, positioning their charismatic leader, Daw Aung San Suu Kyi, "above the president." Imagine the helplessness and frustration felt by the pro-military USDP and the military, as the Burmese saying goes: "You feel like getting gored by a wild buffalo."

The political community believed that there was no constitutional expert quite like U Ko Ni, who could thoroughly examine the 2008 Constitution, highlight its shortcomings, and effectively and beneficially exploit it. It's likely that even the military circle had recognized his expertise. Four years after U Ko Ni's assassination, evidence and confessions presented in court, as described in a Myanmar Now news story dated 2021, revealed that it was this advocate for constitutional reform who had capitalised on the Constitution's loopholes. Lawyer U Khin Maung Htay remarked, "If we can't reform the Constitution, we must do something within its provisions."

He went on to explain, "After the 2015 General Election, in which the NLD won a landslide victory, U Ko Ni had intense discussions with his colleagues at the Laurel Law Firm, including myself. Eventually, we arrived at a solution—a new administrative position for Daw Aung San Suu Kyi." *Myanmar Now* provided further details: "In his book, 'Than-tha-yar Ta-gwe' ("A Turning Point in the Saṃsarā") (pp. 759-760), U Win Htein, the Patron of the NLD, recounted the same story of how the State Counsellor position came to be. On January 29, 2017, at 5:07 pm, upon returning from a study tour to Indonesia, U Ko Ni was assassinated at the exit of Yangon International Airport. He was shot dead at close range by the murderer named Kyi Lin. Despite the political assassination looming over her, the State Counsellor continued her service in accordance with the Constitution."

The press conference held by Police Major General Zaw Win at the Ministry of Home Affairs revealed shocking details about the assassination of U Ko Ni. It was reported that former army officers Zeya Phyo and Absconder Aung Win Khaing harboured resentment towards U Ko Ni and conspired to assassinate him, spending over ten million Burmese currency in the process. Former Lieutenant Aung Win Zaw and his brother Aung Win Khaing, a former lieutenant-colonel, had been seeking a hitman or a gangster as early as May 2016, coinciding with the enactment of the State Counsellor Law. In 2019, two defendants were convicted and sentenced to death, while two others were jailed. However, the alleged mastermind, Aung Win Khaing, remains at large, with the last sighting near the National Herbal Park of Naypyitaw, country's new capital, which is heavily surveilled.

Despite these revelations, questions linger about whether Aung Win Khaing and Zeyar Phyo truly harboured intense hatred towards U Ko Ni and desired his assassination. U Ko Ni was seen as the architect behind the creation of the State Counsellor position for Daw Aung San Suu Kyi, but tragically paid with his life for his contributions. In light of his instrumental role in reshaping the political landscape, his assassination left many wondering about the sinister motives behind his murder.

The 2015 General Election presented a potential opportunity for President U Thein Sein to secure a second term if the USDP emerged victorious. However, he made an unexpected offer to Senior-General Min Aung Hlaing: to serve only half of the presidential term, with the Senior-General assuming the presidency for the remaining period. This offer seemed to ignite ambitions within Senior-General Min Aung Hlaing, who began to entertain the idea of becoming the President himself.

However, the USDP's hopes for success in the 2015 General Election were dashed, leading to their defeat and the transfer of power to the NLD party, led by Daw Aung San Suu Kyi. Despite attempts by the USDP to contest the election results, their efforts were rejected by Rtd. General U Tin Aye, the Chairman of the General Election Commission. Ultimately, former Senior General Than Shwe intervened, advising them to accept the outcome and hand over power to the NLD. As a result, the NLD assumed control of the state, with Daw Aung San Suu Kyi at its helm.

There is an extract from The Irrawaddy News Agency, issued on February 1, 2022, under the headline: "The Military Coup Leader's Dream of Presidency: Is it Close Enough?" U Thein Sein and his comrades were displeased with the ongoing good relationship between Daw Aung San Suu Kyi, who entered the Hluttaw after the 2012 Interim Election, and Thura U Shwe Hman, the then Chairman of the Pyidaungsu Hluttaw. Formerly, Commander-in-Chief Min Aung Hlaing had been on good terms with Thura Shwe Hman. According to the feature article in The Irrawaddy, "Since he has established good relationships with the figurehead who had won overwhelming public support and the chief of the armed institution, Thura U Shwe Hman is more likely to be appointed to the post of President in 2020. But U Thein Sein and his comrades did not want the existence of such good relationships," as mentioned by one Union Minister who served his duties as a representative during President U Thein Sein's government. According to the article, U Thein Sein and his comrades invited the Commander-in-Chief and some generals for a meeting. In this meeting, U Thein Sein warned that if Thura Shwe Hman became the President, he would join hands with Daw Aung San Suu Kyi and confiscate their property. These words were uttered by a retired general in his interview with the correspondent. Of U Thein Sein's comrades, U Soe Thein played a key role. He often muttered to himself, "No! Can't let Shwe Hman be the President." He also took measures for amending the Civil Service Law so that the Commander-in-Chief Min Aung Hlaing could legitimately continue his service until the age of sixty-three, i.e., until 2018. If you check the BBC News article titled "Support the Coup: Confessions of a Retired General," dated January 29, 2022, you can see U Soe Thein's uncontroversial stance, as well as his true colours.

However, U Ko Ni was made a scapegoat, disrupting the grand plans of the USDP and the military in 2015. His loss was deeply felt not only by the NLD but also by Burma as a whole. The influence of this strategic legal advisor could have extended far beyond the enactment of the State Counsellor Law.

As the NLD transitioned from opposition to leadership, former comrades, or erstwhile "fellow sufferers," looked towards the party with hope for political reforms. On April 5, 2016, the Democratic Party for a New Society (DPNS) called for amnesty as the first step towards change, urging the release of all political prisoners and the repatriation of revolutionary forces scattered across the international community, engaged in diaspora politics. Subsequently, on April 7, 2016, during its brief tenure in government, the State Counsellor Office issued Declaration Statement (Notification No. 1/2016), signed by Daw Aung San Suu Kyi:

> (a) According to Section 204 (a) of the Constitution, "The President has (a) the power to grant a pardon." His Excellency has the power to grant a pardon to either an individual detainee or many or a group serving his term of penalty. According to Section 401 (1) of Criminal Procedure, the Burma Code, "When any person has been sentenced to punishment for an offence, the President of the Union may at any time, without conditions or upon any conditions which the person sentenced accepts, suspend the execution of his sentence or remit the whole or any part of the punishment to which he has been sentenced."
>
> (b) According to Section 204 (b) of the Constitution, "The President has (b) the power to grant amnesty in accord with the recommendation of

the National Defence and Security Council. Accordingly, all persons serving the term of punishment and the accused subject to the ongoing legal proceedings are all inclusive under the general amnesty.

(c) According to Section 494 of Criminal Procedure, the Burma Code, "Any Public Prosecutor may, with the consent of the Court, in cases tried by jury before the return of the verdict, and in other cases before judgement is pronounced, withdraw from the prosecution of any person either generally or in respect of any one or more of the offences for which he is tried;

(d) The declaration statement also included a detailed account: "On the auspicious occasion of the New Year, the pardon granted for prisoners of conscience, political activists and students, subject to legal proceedings for having been involved in political affairs, coming under Paragraph 1 (a) and (c), measures are being taken." In other words, the statement implies that Paragraph 1 (b): "with the recommendation of the National Defence and Security Council," i.e., the recommendation of the Commander-in-Chief, shall not be referred to. According to the 2008 Constitution, the National Defence and Security Council (NDSC), composed of six high-ranking military personnel and five civilians, is the Political Crown Council with the highest sovereign power. Hence, it is apparent that the military-civilian ratio of the Council is unbalanced. No wonder, during its five-year term of service, the NLD government, a civilian government, never called a meeting with the NDSC, starting from its first and foremost action of granting amnesty to the prisoners of conscience, as mentioned above.

(e) On April 8, in accord with Section 494, Criminal Procedure, the Burma Code, 199 prisoners of conscience were acquitted. On April 17, in accordance with Section 401 (1), Criminal Procedure, the Burma Code, the President granted amnesty to 83 prisoners of conscience. Before the end of April, in accord with Section 494, another 48 political prisoners were acquitted.

It should be noted that the NLD government attempted to address political issues to the best of its abilities without involving the National

Defence and Security Council (NDSC). Consequently, no steps were successfully taken towards granting a general amnesty. This meant that no amnesty was extended to Burmese democratic forces in the international community or to the Burmese diaspora. Only select individuals returning from abroad were granted permission to reenter Burma after complying with the rules and regulations of the relevant ministries. This failure to grant amnesty sparked resentment among activists.

Meanwhile, the military felt that the NLD government was sidelining their role and making unilateral decisions for political gain. The opposition USDP party appeared to have been marginalised as well. Exploiting the loopholes in existing laws, the new government seized power and opportunities, seemingly disregarding the military and holding them in contempt. Consequently, the Maze of Burmese politics deepened even further.

Passage:

The Undercurrents of the Spring

A lawyer recounted the statement that President U Win Myint made in the court on October 12: "At about 5:00 am, on February 1, the day that military made a declaration statement about the coup, two army officers came to the House of the President. They forced me to resign from the position of presidency, threatening me that if I was not going to collaborate with them, my personal life would be in danger. I said nothing on earth could force me to resign from my present position, and I was ready to sacrifice my life. I also told them to do things in accordance with the law. I questioned, 'Did you say something about the coup?' 'No way!' I said." (Source: Myanmar Now)

This was the most sensational news of the week, blended with a tone of satisfaction and elation, "How bravely our President reacted! He said, 'Kill me, if you want.' See." The news went viral not only on social media but also in the streets. Though the military made a statement that they had orchestrated the coup for the sake of "safeguarding the power" in accordance with the 2008 Constitution, this news had disclosed the truth, nothing but the truth! According to Section 417, "If there arises or if there is sufficient reason for a state of emergency to arise that may disintegrate the Union or disintegrate the national solidarity or that may cause the loss of sovereignty, due to acts or attempts to take over the sovereignty of the Union by insurgency, violence or wrongful forcible means, the President, after coordinating with the National Defence and Security Council, shall promulgate an ordinance and declare a state of emergency." Then, according to Section 418 (a), "In the matter concerning the state of emergency according to Section 417, the President shall declare the transferring of legislative, executive, and judicial power of the Union to the Commander-in-Chief of the Defence Services to enable him to carry out necessary measures to speedily restore the original situation of the Union." So what the SAC had done was merely an act of breaching Section 417 and Section 418 (a) of the 2008 Constitution. In other words, it is obvious that because the SAC's coup came down from no "sufficient reason," what they have committed is treason!

It was due to the impact of this news that Brunei, then holding the Chairmanship of ASEAN, as well as other member states, reacted to the coup as an illegitimate attempt, or "disgust," and did not invite Min Aung Hlaing to the annual summit on 26 October 2021. The SAC's response to the ASEAN's impact was to impose a "gagging order" on the lawyer to ex-President U Win Myint, barring him from speaking about the ex-president's testimony and his message to the media.

"In fact, the 2008 Constitution has vested crooked power and authority to the C-in-C, as well as to the army, but why the coup? Gak! Do these dudes want more than enough?" said a young man, setting aside the newspaper, to a middle-aged man, seated beside.

"Well," the middle-aged man said, "the military have been going beyond the authorities and protections vested by the Constitution, of course. As I've checked out, nearly 30 sections in total included in the 2008 Constitution give priority to the C-in-C and the military. This might bring a frown to your face, 'Why the coup? They want more than enough?' Well, the C-in-C might want more than enough because he has to draw a superannuation pension sooner or later. When his privileges and his power vanish, then it's game over. So he needs to hold on to that power for some time, you know." Listening to his words, everyone engaged in the 'roundtable discussion' agreed.

"But isn't it too much if he's motivated solely by self-interest with no care about whatever might happen to his country?"

"Mind you, this is one of the personality traits of a dictator."

"Since January 28, before the coup, the military approached the NLD for give and take for sure, but the details were not plain as day. Daw Suu might have suspected about the coup, but she had remained unprepared. This took me by surprise! Well, we all have to grit our teeth and bear all the consequences!"

They got more spirited in their discussion. They all talked freely, exchanging their views. If the topic had not been that of the "Spring Revolution," these men, young and middle-aged, might not have gathered here because each came from a different background, and there was a sort of generation gap among themselves. But they happened to meet one another at a column of protest, shared the same views and decided to continue the protest in their own ways, and always keep in touch. Sometimes, they would meet at their favourite haunt and discuss the present, as well as future plans.

"Hmm, the silver lining out of these disappointing circumstances is it's crystal clear to all of us that the 2008 Constitution is more complicated than you might suppose, and that the military have never wanted to let go of the power. Otherwise, the military would have continued to hold the legitimacy of persecuting everyone under the umbrella term, 'national reconciliation'!"

"In fact," said the young man, getting into a bit of argy-bargy, "we've been cornered by this Constitution!"

"That's right! That's why the NLD didn't enter the 2010 General Election," said the middle-aged man, weighing his words. "Well, the tight predicament was that if the NLD had hidden its light under a bushel, the military and the pro-military USDP would have had the legitimate government, and the NLD would later find it hard to stand as a political party in the future, let alone standing as an opposition. You know, the people have been rather fed up with the Revolution since it's been so long-drawn-out from 1988 till 2010. The international community just expects a sort of improvement rather than a real change. That's where the Maze of 2008 has begun." His words sounded more or less mature.

"Hmm, it's like walking on and on, with no trace of the destination!"

"Well, after 2008, we all got lost in the Maze!"

"Yes, it's the real Maze!"

"Kaboom!"

"No! On the floor! Run!"

The sound of an explosion set all the people running helter-skelter, finding a place to hide, all in a commotion! It had been a long time since urban life had lost security and the atmosphere of freedom. Those were the days you had been blessed with the exercise of mindfulness about every step you took, everywhere you went, everything you did. Now you could hear the wail siren of a police car coming from a distance. Silence fell. The tea party now broke up unexpectedly, leaving the stools scattered here and there. Dead silence.

Passage:

From the Spring to the International Community

On August 6, 2021, the US attorney of the Southern District of New York made a statement that the FBI had arrested two Burmese citizens over conspiracy to "seriously injure or kill" Myanmar's ambassador to the United Nations, U Kyaw Moe Tun. Later, *Myanmar Now* disclosed the information that these two young men came from the military circle, and they had the backing of a master-minded Burmese arms dealer in Thailand, referred to as CC-1 in the case, The United States of America vs. Phyo Hein Htut. This arms dealer had enjoyed the privilege of being granted construction and hotel projects at minimum bids during the terms of the former Senior General Than Shwe and former President U Thein Sein. However, he turned out to be a money grubber, with his projects becoming disasters. He was also a confidant trusted by successive Burmese military attaches in Thailand.

In fact, on February 27, the military had made an attempt to "remove the Ambassador from the post" ("for betraying the country," *The Irrawaddy*, August 5, 2021), and issued an arrest warrant for Myanmar's ambassador to the UN. In July 2021, the military proposed that U Kyaw Moe Tun be replaced by Colonel Aung Thurein, who had served in the military for 26 years. However, the UN rejected the proposal. Hence, no representative of the SAC had a chance to be present in the UN Assembly that commenced on September 14.

On August 11, at a press conference held in New York, Miss Schraner-Burgener, the Special Envoy of the Secretary-General on Burma, expressed her concern that the NLD party could "soon be forcibly disbanded." She referred to the words of the Chairman of the Union Election Commission, who had stated in the army-appointed UEC's meeting with political parties in July that the NLD party must be abolished. However, on August 12, during the online meeting of the SAC-appointed Minister for Foreign Affairs U Wunna Maung Lwin and H.E. Mr. Chen Hai, the

Chinese Ambassador to Myanmar, Mr. Chen Hai expressed disapproval to the SAC, as quoted in *The Irrawaddy*.

On the other hand, China promised 6 million US dollars for 21 Chinese projects invested in Burma, covering areas such as animal vaccination, culture, agriculture, science, tourism, and prevention of natural disasters within the framework of Lancang-Mekong Cooperation (LMC). On July 21, on the centenary of the founding of the Communist Party of China (CPC), the NLD sent a message of "warm congratulations" to the CPC, which responded with an official letter of gratitude to the NLD. Minister for Foreign Affairs Wang Yi stated on July 3 that China would stick to a friendly policy toward Burma, emphasising that it was for all the people of Burma and expecting "all parties in Burma to prioritise the big picture and the interests of the people, adhere to rational consultation, and realise political reconciliation."

The steps taken by China in the domestic affairs of Burma have drawn the attention of many nations to the stance and role of Burma's neighbouring superpower. Not only the USA and Western European countries, but also ASEAN countries, are closely monitoring China's actions. Many political analysts view that China continues its relationships with the NLD as one of the political parties of Burma to evade contact with the NUG and the PDF, to exercise its veto power in the UN to stop interference from the international community, and to attempt to insert the Burma affair into the hands of ASEAN, which China has now begun to influence.

On the other hand, India, now apprehensive of Burma falling under China's influence, has continued to sell arms to the junta. Despite this, it remains a member of the Quadrilateral Security Dialogue (Quad), comprising the USA, Australia, Japan, and India. India's policy has shown flexibility: sometimes exerting pressure on the Government of Manipur, which has been providing aid to refugees, including CDMs, and sometimes ignoring the issue altogether. Additionally, the Defense Minister of India has initiated relations with the PDF.

"Myanmar," stated the Commander-in-Chief Min Aung Hlaing, "is not isolated. We cooperate, yes. And we collaborate with Russia, yes. And you know, China, etc." In his interview with *RIA News* of Russia, he emphasised having good relationships with all nations, including neighbouring countries. Major General Zaw Min Tun, the spokesman for the Burmese Army, known popularly as "Mr. Dark-skinned Roly Poly," asserted, "We have strong ties with Russia. So you might say, concerning the Air Defence System of Myanmar, Russia is the key. Then, you might say, China stands second. We have even greater cooperation and collaboration. So you might say, the Air Forces of the two countries are forging stronger ties than ever. Therefore, you might say, 'Make Myanmar great again!'"

Chief of the General Staff (Army, Navy, and Air), General Maung Maung Aye, attended the Army 2021 and the International Army Games, held from August 22 to 28. Alexander Fomin, in charge of foreign military relations, stated, "The parties positively assessed their rapidly developing mutually beneficial relations in the military sphere and reaffirmed their intention to make the most of the existing potential in order to enhance military and military-technical cooperation in the spirit of strategic partnership." Thus, Burma has become Russia's most trusted "strategic partner" in the Asia-Pacific Region and Southeast Asian Region.

During this trip, the Burmese delegation visited the war memorial and museum of Russia, as well as factories manufacturing SU 30 SME fighter jets, Orlan 10 E UAVs surveillance drones and radar equipment, and Pantsir-S1 surface-to-air missile systems for the Burma Army. Meanwhile, ASEAN nations, having adopted the 5-point consensus on the Burma crisis, have reacted differently to the impudent SAC, which signed the agreement but implemented none of its points. Commander-in-Chief Min Aung Hlaing missed the chance to be invited to attend the 38th and 39th ASEAN Summits held on October 26, 2021. He was also not invited to the 24th ASEAN-China Summit held in November. This sheds light on ASEAN's stance and pressures on the SAC. The totalitarian leader of Cambodia, Hun Sen, who would chair ASEAN by 2022, misconceived that he could exert his influence on the SAC. At the same time, Thailand was facing its own political turmoil and had to deal with Burmese refugees in the border areas due to pressure from the USA.

However, the SAC frequently exerted pressure on the Thai police forces, forcing Burmese refugees to timidly cower under the corrupted Thai security forces and members of the national intelligence agency. Despite their inability to support the coup and the SAC's reckless rejection of the people's votes, other nations continued to engage with the SAC, enticed by the promise of economic benefits.

Nevertheless, as Burma has become geopolitically entwined with China not only at the government level but also among the public, the Burma Affair has come under consideration not only on its own merits but also in light of China's stance and reactions. In other words, countries wishing to keep China at arm's length, as well as those threatened by China, are dealing with the Burma Affair based on their individual reactions. Moreover, the military relationships established with Russia over decades have intensified, making it harder for the UN to find a practical resolution to the Burma issue. Consequently, Burma's complicated politics remain like a Maze with no clear exit, even among members of the international community.

Passage:

CDM Participants: Pearl of the Spring

The heat of the forge intensified, with bright blue tongues flickering and shooting out, and red flames twisting and leaping. The iron rods in the crackling orange flames had lost their original hue, now covered with shining, red crispy crusts. As a burning iron rod was placed firm and steady on the cold, hard anvil by the blacksmith's assistant, the middle-aged blacksmith began to strike it hard with a heavy hammer, his dark-skinned, broad back shiny and wet with beads of sweat. The owner of the blacksmith shop watched the scene, seated by the generator.

A young woman approached. "Why not take a break?" she said, stopping at a distance since the blazing forge was intolerably hot.

"Umm!" the man responded, tilting his chin up at the burning iron rods in the forge, "I have to finish up these. They ordered many knives, you know."

"Have some pickled tea, my man. We have some leftover rice from this morning, so let's satisfy our starving tummies for this afternoon. You can continue after this. We have time, right?"

"Yes, you're right, girlie. My spirit's going spunky, but I'm starving already."

Leaving the forge behind, the couple moved over to the wooden bedstead underneath a big shady rain tree in the wide compound. On the bark-skinned trunk of a tamarind tree growing by the makeshift bamboo door was hung a small plywood board, reading the colourful chalk letters, "'Lovers of Justice.' Knives for Sale." The clangs of the strikes at the forge continued, as though claiming for justice over and over again.

"Wow! Yummy, yummy." The owner of the blacksmith shop looked at his wife, then swiped his spoon at the steel bowl of cold rice mixed with pickled tea, and gobbled up.

"Mm! After we've finished with this batch of orders," the young wife said, "I thought of cooking a special meal, uh, a special meal for our kids, you know." Though she tried to speak casually, her voice sounded a bit hesitant.

"Well, my dear wife," he replied, "I must thank you. You and our kids allowed me to make the decisions, and didn't hesitate to accept my choices, follow wherever I go, and lend a helping hand to me in my new jobs. You may cook any appetising meal for our kids. Do as you please, as long as we can make both ends meet." He gulped down the hot plain tea.

"Yes," the young wife said, "we must think about making both ends meet. Nobody knows when our life will return to normal again—" She paused, a thought crossing her mind.

"Let's hope it won't last long," said the man. "If we all keep our resolution firm and strong, the time will come sooner or later, for sure."

"But I've heard that some have resumed their duties as Non-CDMs."

Silence fell. The forge had fallen silent since the blacksmith's assistants took a break from their work.

"Please don't misunderstand me," said the young wife. "I don't have great expectations of returning to our row house, and I don't want to rely on a government servant's salary like we did before. I just don't want to see you struggling with your new life plan. But I also don't want to see you become a government servant serving under their administration. Our kids may not go to school anymore, but that's okay. We can teach them through formal or informal education. The problem is, not many people are sticking together. Some, bless their hearts, are risking their lives or sacrificing themselves, even though they could be arrested at any moment. But others, without a guilty conscience, carry on as if nothing is wrong with the world, returning to their offices, going to pagodas, and attending school. Without unified action, progress is slower than expected." His young wife let out her pent-up feelings.

"How I miss Ko Chit Min Thu from Yangon!" the man sighed. "I remember what he said. He feared there would be many like him, who would stay indoors and not join the protests, which would hinder Myanmar's path to democracy. So he joined the protest, and he was hit—a fallen hero! I joined the CDM because I never want to serve the SAC. You know how much I love the train whistle, toot-toot. I miss my little station.

I never had a house of my own, but I still feel homesick."

A wrenching moment of silence passed. "But," his voice thundered, "I remind myself, 'This is our end game!' We cannot allow the dictator to extend his lifespan to the lifetime of younger generations. We must be decisive! Believe me. Believe us! Only after the Revolution is over will we have a chance to achieve full human status, enjoying our full human rights." He hadn't finished his meal but set the bowl of rice down on the bedstead and strode over to the forge, where his assistant was hammering and beveling the edge of a knife.

His wife followed him. "I understand your feelings, dear," she said calmly. "We've all heard about how the NUG has been reaching out to provide aid. But the NUG doesn't have direct access to the public and doesn't see the full picture of what's happening here. They just send the message, 'Buckle up! Buckle up!' but how? We don't know the details. Warnings are issued about actions against those who have resumed their service without joining the CDM, but it doesn't seem to work. Some of our friends have cut ties with us, resumed their service, and even been promoted—they're doing well. This can really dampen the spirits of those who lack strong convictions."

"Saya," his assistant said to him, after a few puffs of his cheroot, "Can I interrupt you?" The owner of the blacksmith shop nodded at him.

"I must say what your wife was saying is all true," said the assistant. "I've befriended a couple much like yourselves. They are CDMs, and indeed, they are facing hardships. Their lives have taken a turn for the worse since they fled to the countryside in search of a safe haven. The wife used to run a Burmese cuisine shop on the university campus where her husband worked. Those were the good old days, of course. But life isn't easy anymore. Sometimes, they have to take up masonry jobs, sometimes odd jobs. Eventually, they've become a waiter and a maid washing dishes. Many graduates have had to resort to selling what you might call 'fashion waste,' or second-hand clothes, or making snacks to make ends meet while remaining committed to the CDM cause. The harsh reality is that every CDM must find some way to survive. Some receive financial support, but not everyone. Even those who do receive regular financial support find it difficult to cope with the high cost of living. My question is: How much does the NUG really understand about the harsh realities faced by the CDMs?" As a CDM himself, the assistant was expressing his doubts and frustrations about his own situation.

"Well," said the owner of the blacksmith shop, "we've made our own decisions to join the CDM, without any prompting from others, but according to the dictates of our own conscience. So I won't blame anybody, you know. Perhaps the NUG could understand what we CDMs are going through. Some CDMs were forced to leave the country as part of the diaspora, and if compared with their lives, ours is comparatively better because we just miss our homes, while those abroad surely miss their homes as well as their country. They might be going through cultural shock, feeling out of place with foreign food, climates, and languages. Things may be going well for them, but homesickness can't be easily healed. The people working for the NUG must have similar feelings. They'd wish the Revolution could be finished off soon." With a deep sigh, he fell silent, lost in thought.

The majority of CDMs, especially former staff from the Ministry of Education and the Ministry of Health, have had the opportunity to join the Revolution and support the NUG. The Ministry of Education under the NUG has been conducting offline education programs in regions where the PDFs have control, and online schools and universities in other regions. Successful School Family Day celebrations have been held in some upcountry regions, with student performances, as reported in online news. The Ministry's website has also posted video files covering all grades and subjects of basic education for students to access. Additionally, students can enrol in undergraduate and post-graduate courses offered through joint ventures with international universities. Revolution Supportive Groups have conducted short courses on foreign languages, democracy, and federation. Despite boycotting schools run by the SAC, CDM teachers have continued to promote lifelong learning initiatives.

Similarly, it is important to note that nearly eighty percent of healthcare service employees in the Ministry of Health under the NUG are CDM medical officers, nurses, and other healthcare workers. The number of hospitals in frontier areas reaches nearly 200, with approximately 250 mobile clinics. It should be emphasised that, although not under the Ministry of Health, some CDM doctors have continued their healthcare services in regions inhabited by ethnic groups, where they have relocated for safety reasons. The Ministry of Health launched the telehealth program on June 19, 2021, providing online consultations with health experts. This program actively involves not only CDM healthcare personnel but also doctors and nurses who have resettled abroad. Health education programs for the public are also conducted through both offline and online services.

During the Revolution, some CDMs have been unable to continue their professions in their daily lives and have resorted to odd jobs such as blacksmiths and online shopkeepers for survival. Determined never to serve the SAC, the majority of CDMs even contribute financially to the Revolution. They have shifted their mindset from being "government servants" to "civil servants" carrying out their duties for the country. The depth and breadth of their resolution is one of the admirable characteristics of the Spring Revolution. Despite being indoctrinated for decades with the idea that a government servant serves the current ruling government, these CDMs have rejected this notion. They have cleansed their suppressed souls and spirits with their resolution to never become trapped in the Maze. They are committed to shaping a new federal democratic Union of the future as civil servants and responsible citizens. Therefore, the commendable role of the CDMs should be regarded as the brightest and most beautiful dimension of the Spring Revolution.

Passage:

Aiming for the New Spring Army

"In our KIA, Kachin Independence Army, the young men who have passed the matriculation exam join the officer cadet military training. Many attend the Salang Kaba Chief Civil Administrator Training Course (run by the Department of General Administration, the civil administration department of the KIO). But quite a few join the officer cadet training programmes under the military academy, so we have to send a notice to our people, all the Kachin families of the local regions, to come and serve our KIA. Warning: young people of a Kachin family refusing to join our army would otherwise be arrested. Well, I must admit that there are quite a few who have joined the KIA out of their duty of conscience or out of their love of safeguarding their own ethnic group. The majority of the KIA soldiers are the sons and daughters of the civil war refugees. I'm telling the truth.

"However, during the Spring Revolution, something astonishing happened. Into our army flooded in a considerable number of new young recruits from the mainland of Burma: young men from the well-off, educated families, Gen Z, who came down from ordinary families, many young Burmese people from all walks of life, but equipped spiritually with the same resolution and goal, and with high morale, too. I was quite impressed with these young Burmese. They've come all the way over, they've come to take military training under the armed ethnic groups they could reach out for their laudable aim of annihilating the military dictatorship. For their achievements, these young people could have made such a claim from the Olympian heights, but mind you, they are quite mature and humble enough!"

These are the words of Gen. Gwan Maw of KIA, which have gone viral on Facebook, the Messenger Platform of the Spring Revolution. His words resonate with sincerity. Furthermore, his message implies the need for unity among the citizens of Burma living in hilly regions and the mainland. As a result, his post has been liked and shared by many viewers.

"We KIA, it must be stressed, did not send a message inviting the Gen Z from the mainland with the promise that we would provide them with the service of military training. I got informed that some Gen Zs had come over here after borrowing some money for the transportation charges. Some young Gen Z guys look so smart, you know, like K Pop stars! I interviewed one guy, and he said he was a second-year medical student!

"Some Gen Zs came in groups. They said, 'This is all we've brought_ dry foodstuff to prepare for meals. And this is all we've got the money we've pooled together. Please accept. And give us good military training. We promise we won't go back home until we've successfully completed our mission, I mean, the Revolution.

"I am so sorry. These young guys should be studying in the classrooms, you know. But they've come all the way to an unfamiliar region. Casting aside their pride, they've come with strong expectations to take military training from our resource persons. This has reminded our KIA comrades of behaving ourselves in their presence so that we would appear to their eyes as good models of a disciplined military institution. I must admit many of our KIA soldiers had been down in morale, but after they have met these young, active new faces from the mainland for the first time, the morale and the fighting spirit of our young Kachin comrades has been, indeed, boosted up once again!

"I am really grateful to you, Gen Zs from the mainland!"

The words of Gen. Gwan Maw of KIA, who has a passion for music, echo the sentiment expressed by Mao Zedong, the de facto leader of the Communist Party of China, who famously stated, "Politics is war without bloodshed while war is politics with bloodshed" (Lecture, 1938). This quote illustrates Gen. Gwan Maw's approach to politics amidst the ongoing conflicts.

"My salute to the Chin PDFs of Kalay Town and the Kayah PDFs! You have had no previous training in military strategies, but your onslaughts on the first battle in your lifetime, guided by your morale, impressed me very much. Many of you picked up their home-made percussion lock firearms, fought for their race and region, and sacrificed their lives. You stand as the model of all PDFs forever. My deep respect from the bottom of my heart to you, Comrades!

"Never will we forget you. My dear PDFs who have come from ordinary lives, though not equipped with good formal education, you are Sayagyis, the Big Boss of the Revolution! You have cut off all ties of attachment, family attachment or whatever, and prove yourselves as true-blue brave warriors, take the initiative in the battles, dare to fight, dare to sacrifice your lives. As far as I know, because of your acts of valour, the morale of the other PDFs has got boosted up. My dear PDFs of ordinary backgrounds, I love you! Though not equipped with schooling, you are the heroes of the Revolution. I believe you will continue to take the lead."

The Canadian writer Margaret Atwood once said, "War is what happens when language fails." These profound words serve as a poignant reminder of the critical need for unity among all citizens of Burma, whether they reside in the mainland or the hilly regions. Atwood's statement serves as a call to action, urging individuals to come together and demonstrate their solidarity.

In 2011, the pro-military U Thein Sein government proposed a nationwide ceasefire agreement, a central component of the peacemaking process. However, the Kachin Independence Army (KIA) did not sign this agreement, signalling a breakdown in communication and a failure of language between the KIA and the junta.

Following the attempted coup, the State Administration Council (SAC) initiated "peace talks" with certain armed ethnic groups, seemingly attempting to engage in dialogue despite the language barrier. After years of using revolutionary rhetoric, some armed ethnic groups now find themselves at a loss for words. Conversely, individuals like Kachin

General Gwan Maw have worked to bridge the linguistic gap between mainland and Kachin State, offering words of friendship and goodwill to prevent future conflicts that could disrupt harmony and understanding among the oppressed.

"My dear PDFs, my dear brothers, my comrades, you are now engaged in combat despite your low battle experience. Be careful.

"You could get killed anytime, anywhere. Take advantage on the attack. All security matters, including information security, are very important. It's important to be good followers strictly following the strategy of the leaders. You must restrain your impulsive desire to get popular on the media by leaking out the information. I'm worried about you, Bros.

"You have the support of the whole population of 50 million. You have the blessings of God and the loving kindness of your people. Never will your revolution fail. Finally, Justice always wins! You people love you as their sons and daughters no matter who your biological fathers and mothers are.

"Well, we are engaged in our fights in different locations, but our targeted foe, our common enemy, is one. I'd like to apologise some of you who have already gone back to the mainland to carry out for their mission. Please forgive us if we had not been hospitable enough. Hope we shall meet again with the laurels of victory.

"You must live till you have reached your goal. You are the very assets for our new nation."

Best regards,

@gwanmaw

"What you did in 1988, don't repeat it in 2021!" This resounding slogan from the Gen Z generation serves as a stern warning to the military dictators, a reminder of past failures and the determination to avoid repeating them. The younger generation holds little respect for the older political activists, known as the 88 Generations, who were unable to achieve their goals in the 1988 revolution.

However, there are concerns among some members of the older generation regarding the lifestyle and behaviour of the new, more outspoken younger generation. There is a fear that their lack of discretion could lead to the leakage of revolutionary and military secrets. Indeed, these fears are not unfounded. This is why figures like Gen. Gwan Maw express concern about the conduct of the Revolution.

Despite not holding the highest rank in the Kachin Independence Organization (KIO), Gen. Gwan Maw's name is widely recognized among the people of the mainland and other ethnic groups. His example underscores the importance of military leaders possessing strong communication skills, political knowledge, and experience. In contrast, the Commander-in-Chief of the SAC appears ill-equipped in these regards, rendering him somewhat of a laughingstock as he clings desperately to power. The attempted coup on February 1, 2021, was seen as a desperate bid to prolong his military rule and extend his own tenure.

The Spring Revolution has underscored the crucial role of military leadership in the fight against military dictatorship, emphasising the importance of military leaders with a solid understanding of politics. The slogan "Uproot the Fascist Army!" coined by the Gen Z activists reflects a nuanced approach that targets the oppressive actions of the military under fascist dictators rather than condemning the institution of the army itself.

The goal is not to dismantle the army entirely but to end its role as enforcers of fascist rule and disruptors of the political process. Instead, there is a need to transform the military into a professional force that fulfils its duty of protecting the state rather than acting as a barrier to political progress.

The aspiration to establish a genuine federal army represents an attempt to break through the barriers imposed by the military's interference in politics, symbolised by the metaphorical "Wall of the Maze of Politics." This endeavour signifies a collective determination to overcome the entrenched power dynamics perpetuated by the military dictatorship and pave the way for a more democratic and inclusive political landscape.

Passage:

Heroes of the Spring

"Upcountry fellows we are,
Deprived of the inborn human rights,
You know what I mean
If you share the same experiences of our life.

There, on the roadside, a middle-aged man was reciting these lines of poetry, standing by the flickering, shooting tongues of fire on the bare ground, the fire devouring the crackling dry twigs. There, a young man sat on a wooden bench, playing guitar to the accompaniment of his partner's poetry recitation. Their exact whereabouts remained unknown. Both faces of the poet and the guitar player were blurred. But the poet's calm tone could be heard distinctly in the silence of the evening.

"Though at the school-going age,
our children spend their childhood, tending
grazing cattle and goats on the pastures,
then grow older, live unseen, unknown,
No chance to dream
the Big Dream of Worldwide Fame,
And finally, their life ends up
in a full stop. Period.

Who would eulogise the beauty
of a dark-skinned upcountry damsel
wearing rough pastes of Thanaka on her cheeks?
No! I don't want a country bumpkin's life,
so simple, so innocent, any more.

Madame Naw Mar, you said you'd be happy to see
the blooming Let-pan, the red silk cotton flowers.
Keep that in mind
This upcountry lad is ready to sacrifice everything,
his blood as red as the Let-pan flowers!

It was a lengthy free verse, rich with vivid imagery depicting the challenges faced by the upcountry regions. The lack of rainfall, coupled with recurring droughts, has been a persistent issue in these areas. The inhabitants, often derogatorily referred to as A-nyar-tha, endure hardships such as drinking unclean lake water and consuming meagre diets of dry grasses. In some villages, the luxury of electricity remains elusive, leaving them engulfed in darkness when night descends upon their hamlets.

In stark contrast to the more favourable conditions in hilly regions, the Dry Zone yields scant harvests of crops and fruits, perpetuating the cycle of poverty for its residents. Many struggle to access public education due to language barriers, with Burmese serving as the primary medium of instruction. Additionally, numerous Bamars from upcountry areas face challenges accessing the Free Primary Education System due to transportation difficulties and personal survival concerns.

While international schools and universities prioritise scholarships for minority groups, Bamars in rural areas, belonging to the majority, are unable to afford selling their assets like cattle or paddy fields to access these opportunities. Consequently, children in upcountry regions, labelled as "stupid blockheads," are trapped in a cycle of ignorance, reminiscent of "mute inglorious Milton."

"Here's low-value upcountry men!\
We dare to kill,
So we dare die!
To kill those vile, merciless demons,
Our dauntless peasants
sell their paddy fields and buy guns
for the sake of justice!

The poet's voice carried a subtle undertone of emotion, yet his words resonated deeply with the audience. While it's common knowledge that a morsel of rice can sustain life, the harsh reality facing these upcountry people is the need to confront bullets with bullets. In a cruel twist, it's not rice but guns, known by the code name "Lipsticks," that now ensure their survival. They must trade their paddy fields, once sources of sustenance, for weapons that offer protection.

Paradoxically, they have become known as expendable individuals, whose lives hold little value in the eyes of the state.

"Low value upcountry men we are!
The little herdsman got killed at the village gate cottage,
Gunshots from the hedges at the edge of the village,
Mortar shots, the deep scars on the trunks,
On the boughs of neem trees and toddy palms,
 Poor fellows, poor country bumpkins
Who took to heels through the flying bullets,
Poor wrinkled old women, who have to find a hiding place
At the bad news, "Soldiers coming!",

How I missed you, Madame Naw Mar,
while taking refuge
In the camouflage of darkness of the night!
How I missed all sorts of things!

Alas, the unfortunate fate of Burma! Despite regaining independence, the country has been plagued by political and social instability, as well as racial discrimination among its citizens. This has led to significant tension between the Bamars, the majority ethnic group, and the various minority groups. These tensions have erupted in the form of armed ethnic groups, predominantly non-Bamar, that have proliferated in recent decades.

A handful of military dictators have seized control of the Burma Army, using propaganda to justify their actions under the guise of promoting and perpetuating the Bamar race, religion, and Buddhist Sāsanā. However, this propaganda ignores the true essence of nationality and religion. Consequently, the majority of Bamars have become the backbone of the Burma Army.

In contrast to regions inhabited by other ethnic groups, the upcountry regions have long been considered areas of peace and political stability, where guns rarely fired. However, these upcountry inhabitants, who had been living in a world of illusionary peace, are now beginning to see the true troublemakers who have deprived them of social and mental security. They are now witnessing gunshots disturbing the once-quiet landscape and tragic incidents, such as the killing of a young herdsman while tending his cattle on a pasture.

"Well, we are now immersed in the Revolution. Initially, my hands trembled when I first grasped a rifle. But then my younger brother, a PDF member, was killed. The Military Hounds also took the lives of both my father and mother and burned down our house. Now, I am left alone, with no possessions. What choice did I have? I took up my brother's rifle and joined the PDF. I will only pick up the chalk again when this revolution is over, when I can return to my teaching job," said a young man from the upcountry, formerly a schoolteacher. His voice remained calm, but his story was profoundly tragic. How many more young upcountry men have already sacrificed their lives? The SAC has set fire to villages and residential houses, predominantly in Sagaing Division and Magwe Division, the upcountry regions of Burma.

"At first," said a nineteen-year-old girl, "since I livin' from hand to mouth, I thought de revolution was nothin' to do wit' me. Every day I us'd to spend my life pluckin' beans, weedin', harvestin' de sesame n herdin' de goats. Oh, how I miss dose days! When I saw de military torturin' dose simple people n killin' de innocent lives, I, then, realiz'd what is Justice. I am an eye witness of de military's horrors. We afraid of dem just because dey have de arms n we ain't, so I thought of joinin' de forces of defence 'cos, ya know, fight fire with fire. Now I feel vely active to join de forces manufacturin' de landmine n de heavy weaponry. I wish more n more deads dose SAC fellas, 'cos many of our people has lost de lives already. I us'd to hold a goad n herd de goats togeder wit' my friends, hold a sickle n harvest de sesame, n at lunch time, we sat togeder in a circle n ate happily. I miss dose days! When de revolution over, I'll hav my family togeder, herd de goats n harvest de sesame n beans, as before. Yep."

This girl's dream of the Revolution is simple and naive. She does not aspire to become a parliamentary representative, a village/quarter administrative officer, or a diaspora Bamar settled abroad. All she desires is to return to her former simple lifestyle, the life of a herd girl, which others may dismiss as lacking prospects. Yet, she has chosen this perilous path, risking her limbs and even her life during the Revolution. Her goal in life may seem modest, but it is to live the quiet existence of a simple herd girl, unseen and unknown.

"If Life is easy once again, if things are back to normal,
I wish to take you, my dear Madame Naw Mar,
To the village where I don't want to live anymore."

The concluding lines of the poem shed light on the prevailing situation in the remote areas of the upcountry regions of Burma. Nowadays, the idea of embarking on a pilgrimage to the renowned pagodas of these regions seems almost unimaginable. The poet behind these verses is Nyan Nyan, and the title of the poem is "Have You Ever Been to Yinmabin, Madame Naw Mar?"

Credit must be given to the upcountry people who have joined the revolutionary forces in large numbers. These individuals deserve recognition for their significant contributions to the Revolution: they have transformed themselves into weaponsmiths, utilising their creativity to manufacture firearms made in Burma using whatever raw materials they could acquire! They dismantled the Mytel Cell Towers, which are owned by the military, and repurposed the aluminium poles and beams into heavy weapons. In a short span of time, they have developed a diverse range of battery-ignited Qassam-type rockets, handmade mines, handmade drones capable of dropping homemade bombs, and handmade guns and firearms. Many Bamar youths, including those from upcountry Burma, who were committed to fighting against the military dictatorship, sought refuge in the liberated regions of non-Bamar armed ethnic groups and willingly underwent rigorous military training. Surprisingly, the number of these young, active revolutionary Bamar comrades recruited within a few months nearly matched the number of military soldiers recruited within a decade! Impressed by their dedication and ingenuity, some leaders of the armed ethnic groups publicly acknowledged these new young revolutionary comrades, stating, "These young Bamars' revolutionary spirit and innovative ideas truly deserve recognition!" However, other leaders expressed their concerns.

"The thrill of the touch of firearms and the discovery of the exhilarating power of 'Mr. Kurtz's thunderbolts' might one day transform them into the outlaws or military dictators."

Ironically, these words were spoken by an armed ethnic group leader who has taken up arms for nearly five decades and has continued to do so under the banner of the nationwide ceasefire. It is evident from documentaries, interviews, and reports that the post-revolution aspirations of the majority of young upcountry PDFs, including the upcountry herd girl, are simply to return to their former lifestyles. There is no record yet of how these young revolutionaries have responded to the negative perception of them expressed by the armed ethnic group leader.

In fact, the majority of young and middle-aged new recruits themselves, or at least one member of their family, had been subjected to the tortures of the military. This is why they chose to join the PDFs, convinced that they could not treat the soldiers of the SAC, who have been brainwashed and trapped in the chain of command, with gentleness. They believed that the only language these soldiers could understand is the language of frontal assault. When the post-revolution day comes and the country begins to enjoy peace and political stability, these PDFs will leave their firearms behind and return to their former lifestyles and professions. The military's propaganda, spreading among the barracks, labels these PDFs as stooges of western countries. However, these young revolutionary fighters, expecting no further support from countries expressing "deep concern" for Burma, are focused on tirelessly innovating on their own, surpassing the military's pace.

Passage:

Rohingya Contribution and Responses

"The Day of A-ku-dhou (evil) in Myanmar Calendar"
1st February saw the rise of the merciless Tower
Of the military coup over the State Power
Year 2021 flung the country deep
In the mire, making the people weep.

Out flowed thousands of people in protest,
demonstrating their detest
Of the coup, no dilemmas
to show their three fingers.

And their protests spread
North and south, the east and west.
Agitated pictures of our country bare
all over the world, here and there.

Soldiers' bullets fly low and high,
Hundreds of our poor people die.
The dictator's bullets hitting the target
of the poor victims, hitting on the head.
Beaten, tortured, those arrested
Inside a cruel prison, go almost dead.

"Come on, anybody who wants to die!"
Brandishing their guns low and high.
Fling open the military camp's doors
scaring the people lying on the floor.
Time will never make a pause,

But the Day of A-ku-dhou (evil) shall not be forgotten.
Our people's cause! Our cause!.

The young teacher, clad in a white shirt and a white sarong, led the singing of the poem with strongly rhythmic beats, joined by his schoolchildren. They were not wearing the school uniform but rather shabby clothes of various colours and designs. Both the teacher and the students recited the poem with reverence, akin to reciting a religious verse. Their accent suggested they were pronouncing the lyrics of a language that was not their mother tongue.

Among the emotionally charged poems that emerged from the heartbeats of the Spring Revolution, this children's poem stood out as unusual. It addressed contemporary issues garnering international attention and was intended to be included as a prescribed poem in the school textbook. What's more, the scene unfolded at the Kayafuri Rohingya Refugee School in the Rohingya refugee camp in Cox's Bazar, Bangladesh. This self-established high school (Kayafuri) was teaching the poem, marking the unwelcome anniversary of the military coup.

For generations, the majority of Burmese citizens have unwittingly accepted the military regime's propaganda, which labels certain people as illegal immigrants rather than citizens. When the Revolutionary Council seized state power in 1962, they deliberately manipulated public perception. Their long-term strategy aimed to cultivate a generation of unquestioning followers who would adhere steadfastly to their totalitarian directives. This plan operated under the guise of the 1962 Publishing and Distribution Act, officially known as the Press Scrutiny and Registration Division under the Ministry of Information. This division played a central role in censoring mass media and promoting government propaganda activities.

The Burmese Socialist Program Party also enforced oppressive measures aimed at suppressing the languages of indigenous minority groups, designating the Myanmar language as the sole official language. One particularly damaging action was the removal of the "Rohingya" language from the official Burmese Broadcasting Service channel. Furthermore, starting in the 1970s, the term "Rohingya" was systematically erased from printed materials and broadcasting channels. Through these measures, successive military governments successfully propagated the idea that "Rohingya" were foreign to the land of Burma in the eyes of future generations.

Therefore, this poetry video serves as a poignant tribute to the anniversary of the Spring Revolution. Despite enduring displacement from Burma for over half a decade and facing numerous hardships, it highlights their enduring sense of unease and insecurity. Credit is certainly due for the decision to incorporate this poem into the curriculum for teaching. After viewing this video, a Burmese citizen may find themselves questioning whether they can continue to view these victims of racial discrimination as strangers, thus acknowledging their plight as Rohingya.

"Time will never pause,
But the Day of A-ku-dhou [evil] shall not be forgotten.
Our people's cause! Our cause!"

The significance of the text is profound. By using the term "Our people," it encompasses all persecuted citizens of Burma, including the Rohingya. Additionally, the phrase "Day of A-ku-dhou (evil)" carries implications that even though they identify as Muslims, they are familiar with the concepts and beliefs of the Buddhists. The creativity in coining such a phrase and composing a poem like this raises questions about the depth of their understanding and the universality of human suffering and resilience. Despite being marginalised and oppressed, they demonstrate a remarkable ability to express their experiences and emotions through art and language, challenging preconceived notions and stereotypes.

It cannot be denied that there have been instances of illegal immigration from Bangladesh into Burma, particularly under the label of "Rohingya." This phenomenon has occurred due to the porous border between the two countries and corruption among officials on both sides. However, it would be incorrect to assume that people from Bangladesh, with a higher

GDP, would not immigrate into Burma, an undeveloped country. Such assumptions are based on prejudices and fail to consider factors such as Bangladesh's overcrowding and Burma's vast, fertile agricultural lands.

Nonetheless, it is a fact that there are Rohingyas and Muslims who have been born and raised in Burma for more than three generations. In a statement on Rohingya policy dated June 3, the National Unity Government announced that it does not accept any discrimination and is committed to ending human rights abuses against the Rohingya. The NUG believes that its policies will address the issues related to the Rohingya people in Rakhine State while considering attitudes, background events, domestic and international laws to find solutions that respect everyone's human rights. Regarding recent events in Rakhine State, the Government of National Unity has expressed concern about the acts of violence committed by the military junta against the Rohingya people, leading tens of thousands to flee their homes due to fear of impending dangers and threats, and subjected to the atrocities and violence of the terrorist military.

It is stated in the NUG's Policies:

"The whole population of Myanmar, now sharing the same plight in the present time and circumstances, are sympathetic to the tragedy of the Rohingya people, and it is fair to take legal action against those who have committed such atrocities and violence. It is adopted as a priority in the Polices because it is not only a precautionary measure but also a precaution against such an event in the future. Special action is taken against the military junta who are guilty of crimes against humanity so that every victim must receive compensation for justice. It ensures that the future Federal Democratic Constitution includes rehabilitation and justice. It is to reform and revise all oppressive laws, including the 1982 Citizenship Law, to complete the drafting of the Constitution. According to this new Myanmar citizenship Act must 'base citizenship on birth in Myanmar or birth anywhere as a child of Myanmar citizens.' Implementation of National Identification Card/ citizenship scrutiny card that cause human rights violations against Rohingya and other peoples will be abolished. Every citizen must have full access to equal

civil rights with other citizens, according to laws consistent with norms of the federal democratic principles. Rohingya residents, who have been evacuated from the Rakhine State (Armenia) to neighbouring countries because of terrorist attacks, will come back dignified. Resettlement is an important issue, and we shall continue to agree on binding agreements with neighbouring countries for the purpose. We would like to firmly say that Rohingya people will be resettled as soon as there are such situations as could afford a dignified resettlement to them as their homes."

The Multi-Religious Network of the Spring Revolution also stated on August 25th: "The Rohingyas have suffered genocide in Rakhine state, along with ethnic brothers and sisters from all over the country who have been abused for generations. We apologise to all, including minority ethnic groups such as the Hindus, Mro, Thet, Khami, Mrama, Dat, and the Kaman, for our failure to effectively deliver justice."

On the anniversary of August 25th, the Rohingya community demanded an apology from the National Unity Government. While some ministers of the NUG expressed sympathy, the word "apology" was not explicitly mentioned.

On August 26th, Deputy Minister of The Ministry of Women, Youth, and Children, Daw Ei Thinza Maung, wrote a letter addressed "To My Rohingya Sisters":

"Long time no see, dear Sisters. I'm writing this letter to you because I know you all are missing your homes. I do understand your feelings of homesickness because I've been away from home for a long time, and only when our revolution has successfully come to an end, only if the dictatorship collapses will we all be able to go back home. So let me tell you that we're fighting for all of us, dear sisters.

"Now it's good to hear that the people who hated you, those who didn't know anything about 'Rohingya' now express words of apologies to you, dear sisters. They also regret their unwarranted hatred and racism. They have been fighting for you, dear sisters. As you know, military supporters, till today, keep saying 'there is no Rohingya.'

When those wretched war criminals are eventually tried in the public tribunal, let's see whether they will deny their merciless acts.

"These years, dear sisters, you must have been very tired, and I can't put my sorrows into words. But I myself had to run for my life, and I don't know when I will have a chance to go home. I am not putting my sufferings on equal footing to yours, as there is nothing to compare to your sufferings. One thing I can say with certainty, dear sisters, is that I understand your feelings."

On August 27th, the Minister of the Ministry of Human Rights, U Aung Myo Min, announced the inclusion of two Rohingyas as members of the Advisory Committee.

The Spring Revolution has undoubtedly been making efforts, although it has not yet dismantled the Maze of the Past.

Wall:

The Walls of the Maze, 2017

Starting from 2012, the Rakhine State, formerly known as Arakan, became a focal point for both local and international attention due to escalating tensions and a decline in peace and political stability. Interestingly, this region drew more attention than even the long-standing civil conflicts in Kachin and Shan states.

According to the history of Burma, the Burmese monarch invaded the kingdom of Rakhine on December 31, 1784. It's no surprise that the notion of "Rakhine-Burmese goodwill and friendship" was merely propaganda during the Socialist Period. Starting from May 15, 1961, during the tenure of Prime Minister U Nu's government, the Rohingya language, representing one of the minority ethnic groups of the Rakhines, was allowed to be broadcast on the Burmese Broadcasting Service. However, in October 1965, following a military coup, programs in Rohingya and other ethnic languages such as Mon, Pa-O, and Lahu were discontinued. The term "Rohingya" was subsequently banned from appearing in print or any form of mass media. Consequently, by 2012, many Burmese citizens were influenced by the military junta's propaganda, which denied the existence of any ethnic group in Burma like the Rohingya, instead referring to them as illegal immigrants known as Bengali.

Meanwhile, over time, the Rakhines developed a negative attitude towards the Burmese people, perceiving Burmese national chauvinism as detrimental to Rakhine language, literary culture, and natural resources. From the Burmese perspective, the Rakhines are also known for their strong national spirit, but the Rakhines argue that the term "Rakhine" itself signifies "the guardian of one's own race." One area of agreement between the two groups was the army's propaganda, which denied the existence of any ethnic group named Rohingya within Burma.

It wasn't until after the 1990 election that the Rohingya, who still survive today, began to notice the existence of racial discrimination against them in the Rakhine State. During the election, some Rohingyas were elected as representatives to the Hluttaw (House of Representatives). However, the State Law and Order Restoration Council (SLORC) failed to convene the House of Representatives. Furthermore, in the Rakhine State, travel and transportation for Rohingyas between cities were banned. Any Rohingya wishing to travel had to report to the State Immigration Supervisory Office and fill out Immigration Application Form No. (4). This made it very difficult for the majority of Muslim students in the region to pursue their studies in other towns or cities.

It should also be noted that new military manoeuvres in the Rakhine State were initiated in the 1990s. Between 1992 and 1993, a significant number of forces continued to pour into northern Rakhine. Over two hundred thousand indigenous people, including Rohingya from Butheetaung and Maung Taw, were forcibly displaced to Bangladesh. According to a notification signed by Secretary General Khin Nyunt, criminals, including many non-Muslim prisoners still serving sentences in mainland prisons, were compelled to sign agreements under amnesty to relocate with their families to northern Rakhine. They were provided with cattle and carts to establish settlements in the region.

Since then, conditions in northern Rakhine remained notably stable. In 2012, under President U Thein Sein's government, violence erupted in southern Rakhine, specifically in Kyauk Ni Maw-Thandwe, where no military outposts were stationed. Despite this unrest, northern Rakhine remained unaffected. Meanwhile, conflicts escalated between the Arakan Army (AA), established in 2009, and the State army, with increased armed clashes occurring in 2011.

During the 2012 by-election, Hmu Zaw, the government spokesperson, introduced the motto, "Only tears to the Bamar if Rakhine falls." Concurrently, from June 2013 to 2015, in mainland Burma, the Union Solidarity and Development Party (USDP) promoted the enactment of the Race and Religion Protection Law. This law comprised four parts: the Health Care Act for Population Growth Control, the Act on Religious Conversion, the Special Act on Myanmar Buddhist Women's Marriage, and the Monogamy Law. During this period, the Rakhita Lanzin gained popularity throughout Rakhine.

The Rakhine National Assembly took place in Kyauk Phyu from April 27 to May 1, 2014. Attendees included AA leaders Brigadier General Nyo Tun Aung and Colonel Kyaw Han, who had never before been invited to meetings at the Myanmar Peace Center in Yangon (the Arakan Army has been denounced as outlaws). Also present were Prime Minister of the Rakhine State, Chairman of the Union Parliament Thura Shwe Man, U Soe Thein and U Aung Min of the Peace Center/President's Office, and General Maung Maung Oo of the Ministry of Defense.

Under the slogan "Towards Security, Peace, and Development: Goals of the Rakhine National Assembly," unanimous consensus was reached on four sectors: the political sector, the sector of peace and stability, the socio-economic sector, and the sector of natural resource allocation and environmental management. Sixteen sub-topics and 91 key points were established for consideration in policy-making. A press conference was held in Chiang Mai City, Thailand in February to provide an overview of this Assembly.

In 2015, President U Thein Sein's government, which had introduced country's peace-making process to the world, pressured the TNLA, MNDAA, and AA to renounce armed revolution. Furthermore, before the 2015 general election, the Parliamentary Assembly Commission refused to nominate Muslim candidates, including Rohingya candidates. Although the Democratic and Human Rights Party proposed 18 Rohingya candidates, the Electoral Commission only authorised three. Across the entire country, Muslims were vastly underrepresented, with only 28 candidates compared to 5,130 Buddhists and 903 Christians. Even within the USDP party, there were three Muslim representatives; two decided not to participate in the 2015 election, while the last one, Bhu Thee Taung representative U Shwe Maung, resigned from the USDP and applied to establish an independent representative party. However, after a protest by the Arakan National Party (ANP), his application was rejected by the Electoral Commission.

In the 2015 general election, the Arakan National Party secured 45 seats nationwide. However, despite forming the Union government, the

NLD party did not collaborate with the ANP for administrative authority in Rakhine State. Consequently, the appointment of Prime Minister U Nyi Pu, chosen by the NLD, was met with disapproval from Rakhine residents. This sentiment was compounded by the appointment of U Aye Thar Aung of the Arakan National Party as vice-chairman of the National Hluttaw, a position without administrative power to benefit the Rakhines. As a result, the Rakhine people were deeply disillusioned with the NLD's governance. Subsequently, on October 10, 2016, an anonymous group launched raids on three police stations in the townships of Maung Taw and Yathe Taung, leading to increased political instability in northern Rakhine.

The military's largest operation followed the killing of several indigenous people in the Mayu Mountains of Rakhine in early August 2017. At the time, the Commander-in-Chief was abroad on national duty in Japan. Upon his return, he convened a meeting with leaders of the Arakan National Party, including Dr. Aye Maung, on August 9. Measures were then initiated for what was termed as the "Operation for the Cleansing of the Region." Following the meeting, Commander-in-Chief Min Aung Hlaing posted on his Facebook page about a gathering focused on "Peace and Development in Rakhine." Speaking to journalists, Dr. Aye Maung revealed, "We had prepared a proposal regarding the security situation in Rakhine to be presented to the House of Representatives and the National Hluttaw. However, our proposal statement was rejected, leaving us no option but to seek assistance from the Tatmadaw. We have accepted the security measures implemented by the army." He further confirmed that the Commander-in-Chief had provided them with detailed explanations about the Operation.

After meeting with Rakhine politicians, Commander-in-Chief Min Aung Hlaing dispatched Vice Commander-in-Chief General Soe Win and Minister for Defence General Sein Win to brief State Counsellor Daw Aung San Suu Kyi on the Operation. State Counsellor Office spokesman U Zaw Htay informed journalists that the meeting included discussions on designating the Arakan Rohingya Salvation Army (ARSA) as a terrorist organisation. Subsequently, on August 11, the State Counsellor's Office issued a statement outlining measures to safeguard innocent civilians in the region, including the enactment of Emergency Law Section 144 as necessary. The government also affirmed its collaboration with military security forces to counter the escalating terrorist activities.

Indeed, the Ministry of Defence's Facebook pages displayed photo news of two fully equipped regiments (Regiments 33 and 99) being dispatched to northern Rakhine on August 10, the same day as the meeting between Commander-in-Chief Min Aung Hlaing and the Arakan National Party (ANP). This was one day prior to the government's declaration statement. Notably, the troops were mobilised by aircraft, a departure from previous ground-based mobilisation methods. While the State Counsellor's Office had just released the Section 144 statement, 70 troops were already deployed across Rakhine in towns such as Um, Sittwe, Taung Gok, and Kyauk Taw. Additionally, at least three military vessels had arrived in northern Rakhine by that time.

According to journalist *Wai Moe of the Thi-Sat Myin-hnant (Independent Journal of Burmese Scholarship)*, when the Commander-in-Chief sent two representatives, coordination was intended with the government to declare the "Martial Law" in Rakhine. However, the State Counsellor Daw Aung San Suu Kyi did not give the green light. As a result, the Curfew Order Section 144 was issued, and special authority was granted only for stationing troops in the region.

On August 24, the NLD government accepted a report by the Rakhine State Advisory Committee, led by former United Nations Secretary-General Kofi Annan. According to the report, drug trafficking had increased in recent years, with a rise in cases of cross-border drug trafficking from Bangladesh in 2017. It was reported that the ARSA raided an army headquarters and more than 30 police stations simultaneously on the night of August 24 until the morning of August 25. In response to this attack, an operation was launched for 10 days. In the weeks following, Rohingyas fled en masse. The Bangladesh government and the United Nations reported about 700,000 refugees, while the Myanmar government reported more than 500,000.

During this period, Facebook pages were inundated with news of anti-Rohingya, anti-democracy, and military support campaigns. While the army had dispatched military personnel to Russia, China, India, and North Korea since the late 1990s to acquire communication technologies, political observers noted that the technique of spreading hate speech propaganda on social media in 2017, employed by the army, bore similarities to tactics used by Russia.

Meanwhile, international media primarily focused on Daw Aung San Suu Kyi's response to the Rohingya issue, neglecting to examine the gradual divergence of views and responses among the people of Burma. They overlooked the extent of collaboration between the army and the government. However, they did highlight the existence of two rivalling governments in Burma: civilian and military. With accurate information about the government and the military, including historical evidence, lacking, supporters of Daw Aung San Suu Kyi continued to back the charismatic NLD leader, as did supporters of the military junta.

Nevertheless, human rights activists utilised the freedom of the press and media to demand greater transparency, accountability, and responsibility from both the NLD government and the military junta.

For generations, the Western Gate of Burma has remained insecure, with hordes of people living along the border between Bangladesh and Burma making illegal migrations in and out. When it was announced that the refugee camps would open to those migrants, local people grew worried about a potential influx, fearing an increase in the number of people coming from Bangladesh. However, the military community and chauvinists supporting the army, steadfast in their belief that all who had fled were merely illegal migrants, pressured against welcoming them back. To the army, the term "Rohingya" was utterly unacceptable, and the Rakhine people shared this negative attitude. Daw Aung San Suu Kyi herself referred to them as "the Muslims from the Rakhine region." In national news media statements, the term "Bengali" was widely used to refer to this ethnic group, much to the satisfaction of the majority of Rakhines.

The fear among Rakhines is that the term "Rohingya" would imply legitimate acceptance of them as an indigenous group. While it's possible that some of those who have fled might be eligible for citizenship,

Rakhines believe that only those who meet the criteria outlined in the 1982 Citizenship Act should be welcomed back. According to this law, only individuals who were well-established in the land of Burma before British colonisation, including in the Rakhine region, or those who have lived on this land for three consecutive generations, should be granted citizenship rights.

There is a significant number of inhabitants who, being humanists, believe that regardless of citizenship, responsibility and accountability must be taken for the loss of human rights and violence. Both the army and the NLD government, prioritising the citizenship issue, argued that the ARSA deserved a similar response to their acts of violence. It's worth noting that the ARSA had planned an assault even before August 24. They had also sent audio recordings via WhatsApp to young members and cells of their organisation to carry out attacks. According to CNN, which aired in January 2018, up to 150 foreign fighters were involved in the campaign, led by a Pakistani terrorist.

Nevertheless, it's undeniable that the military's counterattack operation violated the human rights of the local people, leaving those who value human rights and the international community deeply disappointed. However, the international community failed to investigate the army's detailed activities and remained unaware that, according to the 2008 Constitution, only the Commander-in-Chief has the authority to make decisions and launch ground operations. Consequently, the reputation of Daw Aung San Suu Kyi and the NLD government suffered both domestically and internationally.

Even more troubling was Daw Aung San Suu Kyi's silence throughout the outbreak of the incidents. Despite the Commander-in-Chief and the army bearing sole responsibility, both local and international communities felt that as the leader of the existing government, Daw Aung San Suu Kyi should have responded appropriately by expressing sympathy for the victims in Rakhine State. Internationally, the Rohingyas, as ethnic and religious minorities, were seen as oppressed and unjustly treated, while domestically, the Rakhines viewed them as illegal immigrants. Simultaneously, local Muslims, who share the same religion as the

Rohingyas, believed that during the operation, the local Rakhine people assisted the army in committing massacres and arson in the region. Furthermore, there was a widespread belief that the issue stemmed from the conflict between the majority and minority groups, namely the Rakhine versus Rohingya, and Buddhist versus Muslim.

On September 19, 2017, State Counsellor Daw Aung San Suu Kyi delivered a 30-minute speech in English addressing the country's issues. She acknowledged that the NLD government had been in power for less than 18 months when the incident occurred, emphasising the need for time to unravel the events. Daw Aung San Suu Kyi attributed responsibility for the acts of terrorism to the ARSA and stressed the importance of engaging with both those who fled and those who remained, including Rohingyas, Rakhines, Dai, Mro, Thet, Maramagyi, and Hindus. However, her delayed speech disappointed the international community, particularly due to discrepancies in reported numbers of destroyed Rohingya villages and her assertion that there was no racial discrimination in accessing education and health services in Rakhine State.

The situation was further exacerbated by Daw Aung San Suu Kyi's comments regarding two Reuters journalists sentenced to prison under the Law on Protection of Confidential Information for their reporting on murders in 'Indin' village. In September 2018, when questioned by a foreign journalist, Daw Aung San Suu Kyi responded that the journalists were imprisoned not because of their profession, but because they had violated the confidentiality law. This response, however, disappointed freedom of expression activists and led to increased criticism of the NLD leader.

On the other hand, the NLD government established approximately 10 committees and commissions to address the issue. However, the Arakan National Party (ANP), the dominant local political party, was excluded from participation, leading to a lack of coordination between the Rakhine people and the government. Despite this, negotiations facilitated by China allowed the Arakan Army (AA) to attend the Third Pinlong Peace Conference in July 2018, albeit without participation in formal discussions. Instead, the AA held informal meetings with the State Counsellor and the

Vice-Senior General.

However, in December of the same year, while the military declared a ceasefire in the Kachin & Shan regions, it escalated military operations in Rakhine. During this period, the AA achieved significant victories, leading the Rakhine people to view the AA's armed approach more favourably than the political path pursued by the ANP.

During this period, on June 13, 2009, the chairman of the Asia-Pacific Committee of the Foreign Affairs Committee in the U.S. House of Representatives stated that the Rohingyas should be welcomed back unconditionally. He went further than advocating for the establishment of a safe zone, proposing that if the Rohingyas were not protected as citizens, the northern Rakhine regions should be ceded to Bangladesh. Such remarks intensified the propaganda efforts of local chauvinists. State and army-backed media swiftly responded to these comments, accusing the international community of excessive interference in local affairs, neglecting Burmese history, and encroaching on the territory and sovereignty of Rakhine state and the country as a whole, rather than prioritising human rights in the Rohingya issue.

These incitements propagated by national and military media permeated informal conversations, even in settings as casual as tea shops. Consequently, individuals from all walks of life, including some Burmese expatriates, rallied behind Daw Aung San Suu Kyi for representing her country at the International Court of Justice (ICJ), declaring, "We stand with Mother Suu."

At the ICJ, Daw Aung San Suu Kyi acknowledged that the civilian judiciary lacked the legal authority to prosecute the military in court. This admission was seen as a betrayal by the military, who believed she should not have attended the ICJ trial and viewed her actions as a political manoeuvre to bolster her chances in the 2020 election. The military argued that despite international criticism, she should have avoided appearing in court altogether.

Meanwhile, the international community criticised Daw Aung San Suu Kyi for prioritising national reconciliation with the military over defending human rights on the international stage. She was condemned for assuming a political role rather than championing human rights. Consequently, some countries and organisations rescinded the awards and honours previously bestowed upon her, marking a significant shift in her international standing.

A well-known retired army officer wrote a satirical post remarking, "Daw Suu's face no longer garners favour from the international community." This post resonated with many military personnel who harboured resentment towards the NLD leader.

Local political parties and non-Bamar indigenous groups felt that their hopes for equality were being compromised, and they perceived Daw Aung San Suu Kyi as aligning more closely with the military, betraying those who had stood together in the struggle for democracy. However, the majority of ordinary citizens believed that the ICJ had not sued a particular party or the army, but rather the state as a whole. Despite the risk of damaging her reputation, Daw Aung San Suu Kyi chose to sacrifice it and attend the ICJ trial for the sake of her country and its people. In response, the people of Burma strongly supported her decision, recognizing that if any action were to be taken, the most responsible defendants would be the Commander-in-Chief and his associates.

During the 2015 election, the USDP, a party backed by the military, attempted to win the election through various means but ended up facing a disastrous defeat. In contrast, the NLD party secured a landslide victory and formed its government with its members in early 2016. Despite this success, the USDP spread rumours that the NLD government, composed of inexperienced individuals, would fail within six months. However, during its first year in office, the NLD government adhered to the motto "Time to Change!" and demonstrated its capabilities. Despite these achievements, the USDP and the military underestimated the NLD's potential, predicting its downfall within two years. Coincidentally, as the NLD government reached the two-year mark and adopted the motto "We Stand with the People!", it faced intense local and international pressures from all sides. The issue of the Rakhine state emerged as a significant challenge, causing complications in Burma's political landscape and trapping Daw Aung San Suu Kyi and the NLD in a complex Maze.

Passage:

The Spring Faces the Tatmadaw's Cruelty

The following pieces of patchwork news may give you a flashback on the then political situations in Burma.

The SAC's Controversial Report on the Tragedy of 44th Street

Concerning the tragedy of 44th Street, Botahtaung Township, Yangon, in which some young activists jumped off the high apartment, evading the arrest and violence of the SAC armed forces, the SAC's report made glaring differences from the eyewitnesses' reports.

According to the eyewitnesses' reports, the SAC armed forces blocked the exits on both sides of 44th Street and stormed in. Then they fired on the young men who managed to make an escape by jumping from one roof of the four-storeyed apartment to the roof of another. Of the five young men who jumped off the roof into the back alley, one got killed by a gunshot.

On the other hand, the SAC reported that, based on the information received, the police forces raided Room No. 16, Level 4 of an apartment, and caught two men and one woman red-handed with 16 hand-made grenades and explosives, including soft gun powder and firecrackers.

The National Unity Government of the Republic of the Union of Myanmar Accepts the Jurisdiction of the International Criminal Court (August 20, 2021)

Acting President of the National Unity Government Duwa Lashi La submitted to the Registration Officer of the International Criminal Court the Declaration that the jurisdiction of the International Criminal Court on the crimes that the State Army had committed in Burma was accepted. July 1, 2002 marks the earliest date valid in the Rome Statue of the International Criminal Court, and so the cases submitted on the days onwards were submitted for the jurisdiction of the Court.

The NUG submitted the Declaration to the Court in accord with Article 12 (3) of the ICC Statute. This enabled the ICC to make jurisdiction on the nation that has not signed the Agreement of the Roman Statue. The Declaration was transferred on July 17, 2021, to the Office of the ICC Prosecutor to be considered.

Two Young Activists Among 100 Most Influential People of 2021 (28 September 2021)

Burma's anti-coup movement women activists Ei Thinza Maung and Esther Ze Naw Bamvo were recently listed among the World's 100 Most Influential People of 2021, according to Time Magazine.

"We've just focused on drawing the attention of the international community to the needs of our nation rather than seeking the world's recognition of our performances. However, getting our names as the two comrades listed in Time Magazine as the world's 100 Most Influential People of 2021 means the international community's recognizing and respecting the issues of Myanmar today," wrote Esther Ze Naw on her social network page. She is a Kachin activist who has been engaged in political movements starting from the Setback of the Kachin War to the present Spring Revolution.

Ko Jimmy Arrested in North Dagon (October 24, 2021)

"The SAC forces raided a house in North Dagon last night, and arrested the 88 Generation Student Leader Ko Jimmy," wrote Ma Nilar Tein, Ko Jimmie's wife on her Facebook. She also wrote that she was worried about his life and that the SAC must take the responsibility for the ensuing actions. In her interview with BBC News, Ma Nilar Thein said: "Contact with him broke down last night. We made enquiries, and found out that he had been arrested in North Dagon. Why? We don't know. Where he's been taken to, we don't know, either. An arrest warrant in accord with Section 505 (a) had been issued for the arrest of Ko Jimmy for taking the lead in the anti-dictatorship movements after the coup. The residents of the Pinlong Hninzi Estate also informed the BBC that the SAC armed forces raided the Estate, and conducted overnight guest checks, and that they heard the gunshots on the early morning of October 20. Ko Jimmy, a well-noted leader of the 88 Generation Students Movements, had served a long-term imprisonment.

AAPP's Statement on the Status of the Correspondents (October 2021)

It was reported by the Assistance Association for Political Prisoners, that the number of the journalists detained till October 25 is 98, while 46 are serving imprisonment; six journalists were judged guilty; five were sentenced to imprisonment for breaching Section 505 (a).

"Whoever publishes or circulates any statement or report containing rumour or alarming news … can be charged under Section 505 (a)." The definition of what is "rumour" depends on which kind of information the military wants to hide from the public eye. On May 24, the managing editor of Frontier Myanmar Danny Fenster, who is an American citizen, was arrested and charged for incitement, also known as sedition. On November 12, he was sentenced to 11 years' imprisonment. But on November 15, he was released from jail and was given a grant for leaving Burma.

Clashes in Myaung Township (October 25, 2021)

Celebrations in Support of the Tatmadaw in Some Cities, Including Naypyidaw (October 25, 2021)

24th ASEAN-China Summit, the Myanmar Military Leader Uninvited (October 26, 2021)

The ASEAN leaders in ASEAN Summit Claim for Implementing the Exact Measures for Myanmar Crisis (October 26, 2021)

ASEAN Parliamentarians for Human Rights (APHR) urges ASEAN to formulate "effective policy recommendations for courses of action" during the Summit held this week, and make urgent contacts with the National Unity Government (NUG).

The UN Secretary-General Announces the New Special Envoy on Myanmar (October 26, 2021)

Secretary-General of the United Nations Antonio Guterres Appointed Ms. Noeleen Heyzer, a Singaporean, Senior Diplomat and UN official, as his New Special Envoy on Myanmar.

Daw Nan Khin Htwe Myint Sentenced to 75 Years' Imprisonment (November 9, 2021)

The Special Court of Justice, Hpa-an Prison, sentenced the Prime Minister of Kayin State Nan Khin Htwe Myint to 75 years' imprisonment, charged with five cases, including a case of breaching Section 55 of Anti-Corruption Law. (May 2021, two years' imprisonment, charged with 505 (a): "Whoever makes, publishes or circulates an statement, rumour or report_ with the intent to cause, or which is likely to cause, any officer, sailor or airman, in the Army, Navy or Air Force, to mutiny"; sentenced to three years' imprisonment, under Article 130(a) of the Penal Code, which "relates to violations of certain provisions in the 2008 military-drafted Constitution and Acts of Parliament". 80 years' imprisonment in total)

Nine Women Members of Kalay PDF Medical Corps Arrested (November 16, 2021)

On November 6, 2021, the SAC armed forces raided a PDF camp to the southwest of Kalay, and arrested the members of the medical corps, age ranging from 20 to 28, namely Ma Zam Zoe Zam, Ma Man Lun Dein, Ma Nyaun Dut Kyin, Ma Mal Sam Daung Eit, Ma Mal Tan Lwe Ei, Ma Lal Lun San Ei and Ma Mal Pyan Hpe E. (They were sentenced to 12 years' imprisonment.)

First Press Conference of the National Unity Consultative Council (November 16, 2021)

The SAC Announces U Phyo Zeya Thaw is Arrested with Firearms (November 19, 2021)

The SAC announced that the member of the NLD Central Committee U Phyo Zeyar Thaw was arrested on November 18, 2021, at Yadanar Hninzi Estate, Dagon Seikkan Township, Yangon. It was informed that three men, whose faces were covered with shirts, were arrested by the SAC armed forces. But the Press Conference mentioned only one name: U Phyo Zeyar Thaw.

In November, several town, village, and quarter administrative officers were killed, leading to many resignations from administrative posts. The People's Defense Forces (PDFs) have shifted their focus to targeting the administrative pillar of the State Administration Council (SAC). In response, the National Unity Government (NUG) has expanded civil administrative committees (CACs) to strengthen and stabilise the administrative structure. Elected representatives from 2020 typically assume patron roles within these CACs, which are established in various townships. The NUG has emphasised prioritising healthcare services and local security, recognising their critical roles in the regional administrative framework. As clashes persist nationwide, there has been a surge in strikes and military movements by civilian guerrilla forces, exacerbating the spread and intensity of the civil war.

Passage:

The Silent Strike

"Do you remember that day,
It was a morning drenched with dewdrops,
Dull and ponderous
Silence reigned over the streets, on the main roads, everywhere,
Looking so cold and lifeless,
Did you see the Presence, the Massive Power,
Did you feel it,
Deep in the Silence?

"That day" referred to December 10, 2021, which marked Human Rights Day. With the rallying cry of "Reclaiming long-denied human rights through the Revolution!", the Burmese people initiated a Silent Strike from 10:00 am to 4:00 pm. The Silent Strike was first launched on March 24 of that year and had a remarkable nationwide impact. However, amidst ongoing brutal suppression, there was uncertainty about whether the entire country would participate in the strike for the second time.

On December 7, a tragic incident occurred in Don Taw Village, Salingyi Township, Sagaing Division. Approximately 100 soldiers stormed the village, arrested residents, tied them with ropes, and burned them alive, as depicted in viral evidence photos. On December 8, four more charred bodies were discovered. This horrifying event stirred deep sympathy and righteous indignation among the Burmese populace, prompting them to express their outrage. However, the pervasive threat of violence made it perilous to stage protests or voice dissent in the streets, where the military's brutal crackdown continued to claim innocent lives.

Do you remember that day?
I heard the loudest Voice of Protest

On the silent streets and roads!
Did you hear that?
The Shadows of the Spring!
The Voice of the Silence, the Voice of the Spring!

Look over there!
Did you see that?
The Blood overflowing in the Depth of the Silence!
Look,
And see!
See Htan Tlang writhing in pain,
Poor lives on the Road of War refugees,
See Pan Pin Gyi Village, a tragic plight,
And Don Taw Village, more tragic,
And young men moving so active,
There, in the Depth of Silence.

The idea for the Silent Strike stemmed from the notion that "Silence is the Loudest Scream!" With this principle in mind, the movement was designed to minimise risks to the safety of participants. Preparation for the Silent Strike began on the night of December 9, as people shared food and money, particularly among those who relied on daily wages, ensuring everyone could participate. Shopkeepers unanimously agreed to keep their shops closed, while Facebook users actively promoted the movement by sharing posts and expressing solidarity.

Despite attempts by the State Administration Council (SAC) to discourage the anti-coup movement through tactics such as promoting COVID-19 vaccination and warning against shop closures, over two hundred towns and villages across the country remained silent and motionless, successfully staging the Silent Strike. Streets were deserted, shops remained shuttered, and the Voice of Silence resonated from within homes. Burmese nationals residing abroad also joined in by donning black T-shirts, raising the three-finger salute, taking selfies, and sharing their support on social media platforms.

"Clap! Clap! Clap! Clap!"

The success of the Silent Strike was fueled by a resolute mindset embodied in the sentiment, "Ours is the town we've monopolised! We may move or stand still, as we like." This unwavering determination led to the strike's triumph. At 4:00 pm, representing the Fifth Pillar of Democracy, working people emerged from their homes, stood at their thresholds, and thunderously clapped their hands—a resounding tribute to their own morale, signalling, "We did it!"

On that day,
I caught a glimpse of a dazzling streak of light
Out of the tangible darkness,
There, in the Depth of Silence.

The lines of Poet Lu Kha Kha's poem, "The Voice of Silence," served as undeniable proof of the unity among the people, surprising even some diplomats from Western countries. The collective silence, which resonated as the unified Voice of Protest among Burmese citizens, dealt a sudden and unexpected blow to the SAC, akin to a surprise attack.

However, some shops faced consequences for closing down on the day of the Silent Strike. While these shops reopened the following morning, in certain townships, such as those in Yangon Division and Bago Division, SAC forces compelled shops to remain closed. Stickers were affixed to these shops until permission was granted by the City Development Committee. Additionally, instructions were issued to shut down markets and bazaars for seven days due to false reports of a COVID-19 epidemic.

Then, on December 14, tragic news spread widely about Freelance Journalist Ko Soe Naing: he was arrested while taking news photos in Latha Township and subsequently died under brutal interrogation by military intelligence. It was also reported that inmates who had participated in the silent strike inside Insein Prison were subjected to severe beatings, while the leaders were placed in solitary confinement.

"We stayed inside our cells the entire day and participated in the Silent Strike. We refrained from talking or chatting throughout the day. Only in the evening, after four o'clock, did we gather outside our cells and clap our hands. However, the wardens and their staff rounded us up before the main jail and beat us severely, about 93 inmates in total. Many inmates from Special Ward, Ward No. 2, were arrested. Some from the Meditation Camp were also subjected to torture, resulting in severe injuries, including bloodshed from the mouth and ears," detailed one inmate.

As the impact of the Silent Strike reverberated across the country, another Silent Strike was planned for the anniversary of the February 1 coup in 2022. The SAC, gripped with fear and concern, made efforts to prevent it. The General Strike Coordination Body (GSCB) initiated a campaign to commence on January 22. On January 25, the SAC issued a warning, citing legal provisions such as Section 52 (a) under the Counter Terrorism Law, and Penal Law 124 for expressing disapproval of government measures, as well as 505 (a) criminalising fake news and incitement against the military. Additionally, Section 33 (a) under the Electronic Transactions Law was mentioned, which could lead to imprisonment ranging from 10 years to a life sentence, along with the threat of confiscating one's property as state assets.

The second Silent Strike proved to be another success. Even though some shops were coerced into opening, they displayed only a fraction of their goods. Customers entering would be greeted with red stickers boldly proclaiming, "Come and buy, if You Dare." A chicken vendor opened her shop but presented only a chicken with three toes, the claws deliberately removed, resembling a Three-Finger Salute. Other shops remained open but displayed empty bowls with labels bearing the names of goods, mocking any potential customers. Metaphorically, the SAC received a significant blow to its vulnerable position.

Newspapers published by the SAC from January 29 to February 1 reported actions taken against shops participating in the Silent Strike and its organisers. A total of 40 shops from Yangon Division, 10 from Mandalay Division, 4 each from Ayeyarwady Division, Tanintharyi Division, Kayin State, and Shan State, 3 from Sagaing Division, and 1 each from Magwe and Bago Divisions were targeted. It was evident that the SAC was immobilised by fear and uncertainty.

Passage:

Spring All Across the Country

As towns and villages across the country engaged in non-violent anti-military movements, armed clashes in various states began to erode the resources of the SAC. According to reports from the *Federal Journal*, issued every three months from February 2022 to April, a summary of the clashes in non-Bamar ethnic regions indicated that the SAC faced strong resistance in the Greater Bamar upcountry regions. Engaging in attacks on numerous well-defended locations, the SAC forces were described as fighting blindly and desperately, akin to a mad bull, according to Sun Tzu's principles.

Kachin State: In townships such as Puta-O, Sunprabon, Moe Nyin, Shwe Ku, Mam Si, Myitkyina, Tanaing, Hopin, Hso Lao, Bhamo, and Pha-Kant, there have been over 30 clashes between the KIA and the SAC, and more than 20 clashes between the SAC and the combined forces of the KIA and the PDF. Additionally, there have been at least 10 air attacks as reinforcement within a span of three months.

Kayah (Karenni) State: Fierce clashes erupted in Dimawhso, Pharoso, Pekon, and Loikaw, as well as in Pasaung, Mobye, Bawlake, and Pinlaung. Over 150 skirmishes occurred between the SAC and the combined forces of the Karenni Nationalities Defence Force (KNDF) and the Karenni Army (KA). The SAC conducted at least 80 air attacks within three months. The KNDF issued a statement declaring that the administrative mechanism of the SAC has ceased to function in about 90 percent of Kayah State.

Chin State: In townships such as Mintat, Hakha, Phalam, Ma Tu Pi, and Kanpetlet, there were more than 60 clashes between the Chin National Army (CNA) and the SAC, along with one clash between the CNA and the Zomi Revolutionary Army (ZRA). The third regular committee meeting of the Chinland Joint Defence Committee (CJDC) took place at the CJDC headquarters office, the Victoria Camp of the Chin National Front (CNF), from April 7 to 12, 2022.

Karen/Kayin State: More than 1,443 clashes broke out between the combined forces of the Karen National Liberation Army (KNLA) and the Karen National Defence Organization (KNDO) and the combined forces of the SAC and the pro-military Border Guard Forces (BGF). The SAC conducted more than 20 aerial attacks and over 400 artillery attacks. Within three months of the clashes, 1,184 SAC soldiers were killed and 767 were wounded. Conversely, 44 soldiers of the KNLA and KNDO were killed and 94 were wounded.

Mon State: In such townships as Mawlamyaing, Ye, Thahton, Bilin, Kyaikmaraw, and Kyaik Hto, more than 32 clashes occurred between the combined forces of the KNLA and the PDF and the SAC. There had not been any clashes between the National Mon State Party (NMSP), an armed ethnic group of the Mon State, and the SAC.

Shan State: Within three months, about 18 clashes occurred between the SAC and the Myanmar National Democratic Alliance Army (MNDAA), and approximately 15 clashes between the SAC and the Kachin Independence Army (KIA). On the other hand, there were 2 clashes between the armed ethnic groups, the RCSS/SSA and the UWSA, and 4 clashes between the RCSS/SSA and the SSPP/SSA. The seven armed forces of the Southern Shan State People's Defence Forces were combined as allied forces.

Rakhine State: Within one week of February 2, clashes broke out: 1 between the SAC and the ARSA, and 1 between the SAC and the AA. The Commander-in-Chief of the Arakan Army wrote a warning on his social media network that the SAC had meddled with the sectors of administration and jurisdiction of the AA.

The emergence of gangs like Thway-Thauk ("Blood Comrades") targeting members of the NLD and committing murders has heightened tensions in mainland Burma. On April 25, 2022, six members of the NLD party in Patheingyi Township, Mandalay Division, including an executive member, were arrested at their homes. The following day, on April 26, a dead body was discovered near Thingazar Creek, with a message from the Thway-Thauk gang claiming responsibility. This marked the beginning of a series of killings, with at least five NLD members losing their lives within a short period, each body tagged with a Thway-Thauk Gang insignia.

Adding to the turmoil, another group named the Yangon Castigate Group-YCS emerged on Telegram, issuing threats against NLD members, People's Defence Forces, news media, and individuals involved in social activism, as well as their families, properties, and businesses. On April 27, this pro-junta militia escalated tensions by publishing the names and addresses of journalists and artists critical of the coup, posing a direct threat to their security.

According to a news article from *The Irrawaddy* dated June 13, titled "Who's Involved in Thway-Thwauk Gang?," the gang is said to comprise several pro-military political leaders, organisers supporting the military, and graduates of the Defence Services Academy (DSA). The idea to form this organisation allegedly originated from a Facebook account under the name Min Yaung, which is associated with Michael Kyaw Myint, the former chairman of the United Democratic Party (UDP) and leader of The Proletariats' Welfare Party. A member of the gang disclosed to *The Irrawaddy* that the head of the Mandalay Region branch of the gang is Kyaw Tun Thein, while Lieutenant Gen. Moe Myint Tun, ranked fourth in the State Administration Council (SAC), and U Chit Ko, both graduates of the DSA Badge 30, serve as mediators between civilian members of the gang and the military.

The military's violence against villages and communities has been ongoing since 2022. On February 9 and 10, in response to military assaults on villages along the east bank of the Chindwin River in Kani Township, Sagaing Division, thousands of local residents from 24 villages in the Inpaung Village Group were forced to flee their homes. Additionally, from February 8 to 11, SAC planes conducted air attacks on civilians in Sagaing and Bago Regions. In retaliation, the People's Defense Forces (PDFs) targeted the residential homes of Air Force pilots in Yangon, sparking ground combat. These attacks resulted in the deaths of 85 SAC soldiers. On February 26, army helicopters fired on participants attending the closing ceremony of a PDF military training near Chin Pon Village, Yinmabin Township, Sagaing Division.

On March 2, several celebrities, including Lu Min, Pyay Ti Oo, Eaindra Kyaw Zin, and Paing Takhoun, who had been sentenced to three years' imprisonment for incitement, were released after nearly one year of detention under the Amnesty Law. However, on March 5, armed pro-military thugs known as Pyusaw-hti brutally killed a young girl and her parents in In-nge dauk Village, Paul Township, Magwe Division. Eight family members, including a twelve-year-old girl, were abducted, and several houses were set on fire.

On April 14, clashes erupted in Loikaw, Kayah State, followed by fierce clashes on April 15 in Lae Kay Kaw Town, a restricted area of the Karen National Union (KNU) in Kayin State. More than 30 soldiers of the SAC were killed in these clashes, and one NLD representative who had sought refuge in the town was arrested. As a result, local residents and refugees were displaced and forced to seek refuge in Thailand.

On April 17, Burmese New Year's Day, the SAC released 1,619 inmates under the Amnesty Law, but political prisoners were not granted release.

The data provided by Data for Burma indicates that from February 2021 to the end of April 2022, the SAC forces and its subordinate organisations set fire to at least 11,417 residential houses and buildings. The Sagaing Division, predominantly inhabited by Buddhist-Bamars, suffered the most from these man-made calamities. However, it's important to note that there may be shortcomings in data collection, suggesting that the actual situation on the ground could be even more dire than the reported numbers of victims. Thus, the spring season has taken on a sombre image of bloodshed and flames, seemingly without an end in sight.

Passage:

Preserving Culture during Revolution

"We are the Shwe Nwe Thway Strike Group from Sagaing Division. We've been active, staging anti-coup protests every day for over 350 days. Our Troupe welcomes the New Year with our Than-gyat verses."

The music troupe comprised thirty young individuals, each wearing a black mask. The men were dressed in white shirts and reddish-brown Paso (a men's wrapping sarong), while the women wore white blouses and red Htamein (women's wrapping sarongs). Led by a young woman, the troupe's leader, whose voice was loud and clear, they engaged in antiphonal chanting of Than-gyat verses. Accompanying them was a young man playing the solo drum. The performance involved the leader initiating the lead vocals while the rest of the troupe responded in a satirical chorus. Adorned with red cotton armbands around their arms, all the performers looked smart and composed in their new uniforms, with fresh and active eyes.

"Justice must live and grow!" "So Injustice must vanish for sure!"
"Yes, Injustice must vanish for sure!" "Justice must live and grow!"
"Let the Truth prevail." "So, get the wrongdoers back off!"
"Yes, get the wrongdoers back off!" "Let the Truth prevail."
"The good and the noble must live and grow." "So the crooked must be a good riddance."
"Yes, the crooked must be a good riddance." "The good and the noble must live and grow."
"Stop the so-called Race, so-called Religion, so-called Sāsanā." "No more double-dealing twisters."
"Yes, no more double-dealing twisters." "Stop the so-called Race, so-called Relgion, so-called Sāsanā."

The scene was both vibrant and poignant, as the dancers moved gracefully to the rhythmic beats, their voices carrying the hopes and aspirations of the people. Against the backdrop of nature's beauty and the symbolic banner, their performance echoed the resilience and determination of the Burmese people in the face of adversity. Each step, each word, was a testament to their unwavering spirit and their commitment to seeking justice and freedom. They also had a large cotton backdrop: "Ever Active Shwe Nwe Thway (Golden Blood)," the red banner with the insignia of the yellow Fighting Peacock, fluttering in the breeze.

"Don't use Religion to blind our people." "No racial discrimination."
"Yes, no racial discrimination." "Don't use Religion to blind our people."
"The Streams of Blood stained on the tar road," "Can't get wiped out by the Thingyan water."
"Can't get wiped out by Thingyan water" "The Streams of Blood stained on the tar road."
"Oh, we have the Army, the glorious Army," "But fighting mighty against which nation?"
"Yeah, fighting mighty against which nation?" "We have the army, the glorious Army."
"Who looted our belongings? Who ever plunders?" "You loot our belongings, you ever plunder."
"You loot our belongings, you ever plunder." "Who looted our belongings? Who ever plunders?"
"What tricks does the Army know, the Army know?" "All criminal tricks the Army knows"
"Yes, all criminal tricks the Army knows" "What tricks does the Army know, the Army knows?"
"What did they learn from Daw Sein Aye?" "How to torch the villages, the villages."
"Yes, how to torch the villages, the villages." "What did they learn from Daw Sein Aye?"

The acronym of the Defence Service Academy is DSA, but it is affectionately nicknamed as Daw Sein Aye (Madame Cold Diamond). Hence, the army officers and personnel who have undergone military training at the DSA have been colloquially referred to as the products of Daw Sein Aye for years. The tragedy of the flaming villages, still being set on fire by SAC forces today, could be linked to a rumour: After the attempted coup, the Commander-in-Chief, perhaps overwhelmed with apprehension, allegedly remarked in a meeting, in an ominous tone, "If we fail, the whole country must remain in ashes!"

The antiphonal chanting of the Than-gyat verses is a cherished part of Burmese traditional culture. Originally, it was a song-like piece sung in an antiphonal manner, traditionally nestled within Nat-chins (songs propitiating the Spirits) and Yein-chin (songs for synchronised group dance). However, its role has evolved over time: it now consists of a series of couplets of satirical verses sung in a light-hearted tone, poking fun at the foibles of society or government. This satire is not meant as an insult, but rather as a tantalising commentary aimed at promoting social reform. The subjects of Thangyat satire would ideally reflect on their behaviour, while the audience would smile and take the Thangyat verse in jest. It is no surprise that Thangyat has been a beloved aspect of Burmese culture for decades: Thangyat, the Song of Social Reforms, always accompanies Thingyan, the Water Festival, which symbolises cleansing away the old year's troubles and welcoming the new year in the Burmese calendar.

"We 5/ Citizenship Card holders, no water throwing, no water splash," "During the Thingyan Festival, the Water Festival."

"Yes, during the Thingyan Festival, the Water Festival," "We 5/ Citizenship Card holders, no water throwing, no water splash."

In terms of administrative regions, Burma is divided into seven regions and seven states. When citizenship cards were issued to citizens, these regions were identified with serial numbers. For instance, Yangon Division is identified as No. 12, and Sagaing Division as No. 5. The phrase "5/ Citizenship Card holders" refers to natives of Sagaing Division. In other words, as part of an anti-coup campaign, even though the Thingyan Festival, or Water Festival, had traditionally been a time for fun, the people of Sagaing Division boycotted the festival because they believed it was not an appropriate time for celebration. "When we build our new nation," they declared, "no privileged class should be exempt."

"No privileged class must join," "when we build our new nation."
"We've launched a campaign, we're going to uproot," "No timid blood, but a brave heart only"
"No timid blood, but a brave heart only" "We've launched a campaign, we're going to uproot."
"This is our country, this is ours," "The Spring Revolution must be a success."
"The Spring Revolution must be a success" "This is our country, this is ours."

The Water Festival traditionally falls in mid-April, marking the transition from the old year to the new year. However, in the years 2021 and 2022, it took on added significance as part of an anti-coup campaign known as the "No-Water-Splash Strike" during this Burmese traditional festival. Despite the circumstances, efforts were made to maintain tradition by sharing Thangyat chanting videos on social media networks.

In addition to the Shwe Nwe Thway Troupe, several other troupes participated in the Thangyat Strike, including Shwe Let Nyoe, Ha-Nga-Kaung, Monywa Chindwin Doe, Daung-to-Myo-set, Yangon Lunge Tawlan Thangyat, Khut-Daung Pyo, Pha-kant Tawlan Thagyan, The Netherlands Thagyan, and Do-yebaw Thangyat. Even the Linyon Squadron of the Cobra Column, engaged in combat in southern regions of Burma, joined in the Thangyat chanting under the motto, "The Revolution Thingyan, the Voice of the Contemporary Times." Their satire targeted the military leaders who abused their power: "This Thangyat Verse shall break the Sceptre!"

The Thangyat verses operate on the principle of subtle and sometimes poignant satire, akin to Swift's "biting satire and unflinching criticism of his times." Therefore, these verses, chanted during the ushering in of a new year, typically highlight the foibles and shortcomings of both society and the ruling party. As such, it is a commendable tradition passed down through generations in Burmese society.

The Spring Revolution seeks to eradicate military dictatorship through both armed and non-violent means. The participation of the new generation in Thangyat chanting, aligned with traditional culture, demonstrates their appreciation for the cultural heritage of their society.

Corner:

Handling News and Information under Pressure

"If I have to tell you a story,
About the upcountry regions, full of glory,
We're driving the anti-dictator revolution
Sooner or later we're having celebrations
'Cos united we stand, we believe the people have the power
To the Fascist Revolution far superior,
The pioneer of the Federal Union on the way
We'll hold the federal unit system in our sway.
This is the end of a true story
Of the upcountry regions, full of glory."

It was a lively song, concluding with the gentle melody of a sweet flute, echoing the ambiance of the upcountry regions.

"Welcome to the programme, All Stories about the Upcountry Regions". This week, we'll entertain you with a story, based on the on-the-ground-news, 'Darn Good Army Turns into Dung'. Hey you! Here we go …," said the announcer Thant Wai Kyaw, dressed like a woman from an upcountry region. She was a member of the NLD and former representative of Sagaing Region Hluttaw.

"Well, to begin with, I hope you all know Aya-taw Town in the upcountry region is famous for Thanakha, don't you? Unlike cosmetics, you apply the paste of Thanakha rough on your cheeks. I mean, our guys at Aya-taw were rough and tough enough, of course. The SAC, doggedly marching along the jungle path between Naung Gyi Ai and Aya-Taw. Needless to say these darn stupid fellows always blindly follow the commands from 'bove. Ya know that. Well, our Aya-taw comrades give them a treat of Jackfruits, our home-made landmines! How the darn stupid guys took it with relish!"

This was the first broadcast of the program, and the presentation of the news was outstanding! The background featured an aerial photograph of the battle scene, captured by a drone. "Well, on May 18, more than three SAC fellows, including a captain, bit the dust in a flash," she remarked sarcastically. The script included some slang terms such as "Candy" (Sweet and sour), "local-made Banana Bud" (handmade mortar bomb), "All sorts of Crops" (all types of firearms), "Parachuting with water and electric supply" (A mission with full facilities).

"The SAC forces came to Nyaung Kar-yah Village, and were about to destroy the village, when there were explosions!" said the announcer. Then, quite absurdly, she picked up a line from a melancholy heartbreak song, singing its distorted version, "Alas, now I know, Mom, I was wrong. I'd rather meddle myself in a hundred love affairs. 'Cause the duty of fighting in a battle I can't bear."

The broadcasting program of Public Voice TV (PVTV), which began on May 26, 2022, has consistently captured public attention and gone viral. Following the attempted coup, the military intensified its efforts to pressure and dismantle the media. Many professional journalists and correspondents were arrested, while others were forced to flee the country. Families of media personnel began viewing the profession as unsafe, urging them to change careers. Numerous news agencies, including 7Days, Mizzima, DVB, Khit Thit, Myikyina, Delta News, Tachileik News, Zeyar Times, Kandayawaddy News, and Independent Mon News Agency, had their publication licences revoked. Additionally, offices of Kamayut Media, Mizzima, and The Irrawaddy News were raided. Consequently, The Irrawaddy, Mizzima, DVB, and Myanmar Now relocated their offices abroad. Correspondents who fled to liberated areas faced challenges in settling into new locations and redirecting their operations. Limited internet connectivity and irregular electricity supply made short news programs and entertainment shows more appealing to viewers. Having personally experienced harsh realities, audiences sought news that could offer relief from the burdens of reality, rather than focusing solely on shocking or distressing content. However, journalists and news writers adhering to mainstream journalistic ethics found it difficult to accommodate these preferences. Some adapted their presentations to meet the demands of the changing public taste. It is important to note that shifts in media consumption behaviours have influenced media production to some extent.

In addition, as many young individuals opted to join the armed revolution, correspondents found themselves compelled to devise new terminology and repurpose existing words in order to report on clashes and fundraising efforts without violating social media platform restrictions. Code names were utilised for description purposes, such as "Lipstick" for bullets and "Pineapple" for hand grenades, among others. Some pages displayed news, opinions, and reactions in a highly creative manner, with satirical content targeting the State Administration Council (SAC) being particularly popular. At times, news agencies faced challenges in obtaining information from within the military for broadcasting. Consequently, some agencies resorted to presenting partially informative and partially malicious news using a blend of code words, aimed at boosting morale among comrades.

"Their own armed forces trampled underfoot, and their own territory breached more and more. That darn bombastic Than Hlaing now kicked out. Doesn't take time for Nemesis to play on a stone-hearted guy for getting his own brother crushed to death, in the process of interrogation. Poor Lieutenant General! Lost his biological brother, and met his own tragedy under the grudge of the Dictator! Quite a commotion in the inner circle of the army, you know. Of course. This is the modern version of the tale of the two baby birds, the Two Parrots, blown apart by a storm. His story throws light on the essence of Life and Death. His brother proved himself to represent Life worth living before he died, saying, 'This is an answer to why we live in this world'_ the Hero standing for the Truth, who had sacrificed even his life. That Lt. General is a symbol of living dead after strutting about on the Stage of Life just to please the Dictator. The two brothers, but representing two different values in

terms of humaneness and integrity. A gaping gap between the characters of the two brothers, like Heaven and the Earth. In the world history, six million Jews were murdered_ Hitler's 'final solution', which turned out to be a historic genocide, the Holocaust, the Crime against Humanity! But Adolf Eichmann 'simply followed orders'. So d'u think he was freed? Definitely not. Lo! Followers of Kyin-Soe, see the tragedy of Eichmann! The Buddha says, 'Asevna ca balanam. Not to associate with fools!' Avoid being followers of Min Aung Hlaing. Now! So that you won't have the same plight as that of Than Hlaing."

The satirical piece was initially posted on the Facebook page "Kyu-li Paung News" on June 5, 2022. Remarkably, this post predated the broadcast of the news by established agencies like Thanlwin Time and The Irrawaddy Time News Agency, which reported on June 6, 2022, that Lt. General Than Hlaing had been relieved of his positions as Deputy Minister of the Ministry of Home Affairs and Chief of the Myanmar Police Force under the State Administration Council (SAC). Instead, he was reassigned to resume his duties as Chief of DOS-6 (No. 6 Operation Special Task Force, Office of Headquarters of Defence Service - Infantry).

In the past, Lt. General Than Hlaing had been involved in operations to suppress the upcountry revolution, including the Alaungmintaya Operation in Sagaing Division and the Yaw Region, as well as the Anawratha Operation in Chin State. Rumours circulated that during these operations, he sustained injuries while facing fierce resistance from local fighters of the Spring Revolution, compelling him to retreat to his main unit. These rumours were later confirmed.

It's noteworthy that Kyu-li Paung News, despite not being a traditional news agency, had posted this information a day earlier than other outlets. This page, known for blending news with rational deductions from real-life events and using code names for characters, often includes coined and distorted words and phrases. For instance, Min Aung Hlaing, the Commander-in-Chief, is referred to as "Kyin Soe", which is a play on "Kyo-Sin" (Gallows), suggesting a grim fate. Additionally, members of the SAC are depicted using various derogatory code names such as "Four-foot kid,"

"Shortie," "Aung Net the Dog," "Laphet-Chauk (Mr. Tea)," "Khit Dwe," and "Zaw Me Lone." The headlines are designed to be attention-grabbing, like "Let's Hit Mr. Shortie's Forehead with the Mortar of Education" and "The Sitagu War Refugees Camp of Wives." Despite the scandalous tone, Kyu-li Paung News has garnered a substantial following, with readers being avid fans of this social media page.

The public now has access not only to the news from traditional news agencies but also to occasional or regular updates on platforms like YouTube and Facebook. With the focus squarely on the downfall of the SAC and the oppressive military regime, public resentment has reached new heights. Consequently, news presentations have diversified in both style and content. While some professional news agencies persist, others prioritise the latest updates on the ongoing revolution.

Burmese society, having endured half a century under the restrictive Press Security and Registration Division, has long struggled with low levels of information and media literacy. The distinction between censorship and editorial discretion remained murky, blurring the lines between activism and journalism. The lifting of press censorship on August 20, 2011, marked a pivotal moment, leading to the proliferation of media outlets. However, this media landscape resembles mushrooms—some nourishing, others toxic.

Inexperienced readers, both local and abroad, find it challenging to discern between reliable and biased news. They lack the critical thinking skills necessary to evaluate the integrity, accuracy, and impartiality of media coverage. Fed up with the military's propaganda and lies, these individuals readily embrace anti-military narratives, regardless of their professionalism or credibility. They become followers of such narratives, eagerly anticipating the military's downfall, no matter how unrefined the presentation may be.

Despite potential shortcomings in the presentation of news by agencies reporting on leaked information from the military, the public tends to overlook these weaknesses because they perceive these agencies as aligning with their interests. Additionally, numerous Facebook pages affiliated with the People's Defense Forces (PDFs) have emerged. These pages not only disseminate information but also pressure or urge action on sensational topics, purportedly on behalf of the people.

During the early stages of the Spring Revolution, writers refrained from attaching their names to posts to avoid potential repercussions. Instead, they encouraged viewers to spread the information without attribution, stating, "No need to give credit to the original post, but share." Unfortunately, this practice has fostered a culture of plagiarism, where content from original posts is copied and posted without acknowledgment. Viewers, lacking assurance of reliability, nonetheless react to this information, both positively and negatively.

On the flip side, the SAC, akin to a stalker, constantly monitors the posts shared among the comrades of the Spring Revolution, taking swift action against the writers. Instances have occurred where individuals were apprehended within an hour of posting information. Consequently, no pages or accounts are posted on Facebook anymore. However, unethical accounts on platforms like Telegram, such as Han Nyein Oo's, have emerged. These channels are used to disseminate propaganda and false news. Notably, Han Nyein Oo's account is suspected to have a coordinated network with the ruthless enforcers of the SAC. Consequently, there is no longer a safe and secure environment for press freedom or freedom of expression. Present circumstances do not require adherence to professionalism or ethics. Thus, after lying dormant for some time, the inertia of the Maze now resurfaces, bubbling up to the surface once again.

Passage:

The Role and Impact of Reporters in the Spring Revolution

"We call for Strikes! Strikes!"
"Power to the People!"
"Free Our Leaders! Now!"
"Free Our People! Now!"
"Who are We? Yangon People on Strike"

The bold white words were written on a long black cotton cloth. Above the white slogan on the black cotton piece, "Never Bows Madame Hyacinth, Her Blue Flowers Ever Flourishing" ("Her Head is Bloody, But Unbowed") was the white line art, portraying Daw Aung San Suu Kyi. "The only real prison is Fear and the only Freedom is Freedom from Fear" The white words written on a red cotton piece. Young men wearing black masks, holding Eugenia sprigs in their hands, shouting this slogan.

Honk! A car horn blared. Then the protesters scattered in all directions. No more figures on the chaotic screen. Just frantic shouts and fleeing. The camera shot of a young man with a backpack looked shaky and distorted shades.

Another video clip.

"No! The car hit the kid! Another kid!"

A shout from the veranda of an apartment. The scene on the road. An olive-green Double Cab military car drove from behind the line of the protesters and crashed into the crowd at furious speed.

What the Burmese people learned from this video clip was evidence of how the SAC dispersed the strikes "in accord with the procedure." It was estimated that at least five lives were lost, while more than ten people were injured. This incident occurred on December 5, 2021. While taking news photos of the protests on Pan Pin Gyi Road, Alon Township, Yangon, the correspondents of Myanmar Press Photo Agency (MPA), Ma Hmu Yadanar Khet Moe Moe Tun and Ko Kaung Set Lin, were severely injured. The former, a young woman, sustained critical injuries to the scalp, right eye, and thigh. At first, her condition was deemed hopeless, beyond management. However, according to a news article issued in April 2022, her health had improved. (However, in December 2022, in accordance with Section 50 (e) of the Counter-Terrorism Law, she faced legal action and was subject to a potential life sentence or a minimum of ten years' imprisonment.) Ko Kaung Set Lin, who was arrested alongside her, suffered injuries to the waist and other parts of his body and faced legal action under Section 505 (a).

"We were ordered to issue our correspondent card. Well, the circumstances compelled us to tell lies. We said the card was not with us, and they took us to the camp. On the way they threatened us, saying all sorts of things."

"As soon as we got there, we were forced to take off our clothes, then squat down on the cement floor. We were blindfolded. Then the torture began. Strike, hit."

"They'd say, 'Are you a correspondent? Are you sure?', then they'd strike and kick our heads with their military boots and kick us in the ribs, you know."

These are extracts from an interview with Freelance Correspondent of Myanmar Now, Ma Myat Moe Thu, conducted by VOA News on March 5, 2022. DVB Senior Correspondent Ko Kun Kyaw Oo and Freelance Correspondent of Myanmar Now, Ma Myat Moe Thu, along with three matriculation pass girls who had fled as war refugees, were arrested not by the SAC but by a small armed group named Karenni Generation Z (KGZ). On February 20, 2022, they were accused of being decoys for the SAC and were subsequently arrested and robbed of their cash and belongings. In response to this incident, the Karenni Nationalities Defence Force (KNDF) expressed deep concern over the violence against civilians, correspondents, and women, as well as the violation of human rights. They clarified that the KGZ is a separate armed group operating independently, beyond the command of both the KNDF and the Karenni Army (KA).

Hence, when encountering any armed group, the on-the-ground security of correspondents becomes uncertain. While there may have been occasional conflicts between revolutionary forces and correspondents over the past two years, only the incident mentioned above garnered public attention. Nevertheless, this incident deeply affected the young female correspondent. When asked whether correspondents today find it harder to survive, Ma Myat Moe Thu responded, "Did you say 'harder to survive'? Well, I might say it's quite impossible to survive. On one side, we were cornered by the SAC, fearing arrest, so we sought refuge in liberated areas, states where the anti-military revolution is in full swing. But here, while many armed groups are well organised and disciplined, there are also a few militant groups filled with pride over the power of firearms. I am now quite scared of what you might call 'Ralph E. Lapp's weapons culture.' Where is the place for us? Should we simply give up the profession of correspondent? But I can't. This profession has brought me trouble, made me suffer, but I don't want to give it up."

In fact, Ma Myat Moe Thu has been a war news correspondent in northern Shan State since 2019. Today, she continues her profession as a war news correspondent in the Karenni Region. She is responsible for a ten-minute news broadcast program at the Do-Athan ("Our Voice") News Agency.

"Well, my profession could get me arrested, and even killed."

"My family and my profession … Hmm, I feel I have given more time to my profession."

"I've heard of cases like making a surprise check of the overnight guest's list and arresting a guy whose profession turns out to be that of a correspondent. So, every night I can't fall asleep."

"The present condition is I have no more guarantee for my tomorrow. How long will I continue to be a correspondent? Well, until I get arrested."

"You know, human rights have been violated more and more these days. So I feel a correspondent is more responsible for that."

"My profession as a correspondent has now become sorta illegitimate. Only those guys working for the news agencies are granted permission by the SAC, they come and go, out under the sun freely and boldly."

"As far as I know, there are some correspondents who now live the lives of poor, disabled persons."

"The duty and responsibility of a correspondent is to speak out all about the hardships of the public, so I continue to live locally."

"Hmm … I have to risk my life and my security to live the life of a correspondent."

"I have to make contact with either the CDMs or the PDFs, so I'm worried about the security of mine, as well as theirs."

"I can't stick to only one spot, I also have to change my phone numbers, off and on."

"Can't fall asleep every night. When I have to interview a family who has lost a member, when they sob and talk about the tragedy of their family member, I don't know how to say comforting words. Feel so miserable."

"When somebody says, 'How do you make a living?', I have to keep mum. How I hate this kind of life!"

"I'll be a correspondent as long as the SAC exists."

The information about these correspondents reflects the current state of human rights and press freedom in Burma. Over the past two years, 154 correspondents have been arrested. Only 92 have been released, while 58 remain incarcerated, with 26 serving prison sentences and four killed. According to a report by the Committee to Protect Journalists (CPJ), Burma ranks second only to China in the number of journalists and correspondents arrested and detained. With the majority of mainstream news agencies shut down, most media outlets now operate online. Consequently, journalists and correspondents have become primary targets, as the military intensifies efforts to suppress the flow of information.

The majority of correspondents and journalists faced legal action under Section 505 (a) of the Burmese Penal Code. Others had their cases referred to court under Section 52 (a) and Section 50 of the Counter Terrorism Law, or sometimes Section 33 (a) of the Electronic Transactions Law. On March 9, 2021, military forces raided the office of Kamayut Media, resulting in the arrest of Chief Editor U Nay Than Maung and founder U Han Thar Nyein. They were charged under Section 505 (a). Subsequently, U Nay Than Maung, an American citizen, was released, while U Han Thar Nyein faced additional charges under the Electronic Transactions Law in addition to Section 505 (a). Editor Ma Htet Htet of Thingankyun Post News Media and journalist Ko Wai Lin Yu were charged under Section 5 of the Explosive Substances Act. In some cases, individuals were released only to be re-arrested weeks later. Freelance Correspondent Ko Soe Yarzar Tun, who provided information to Mizzima News Agency, was arrested during anti-coup protests in March 2021. After spending 122 days in detention, he was released from Insein Prison under the Amnesty Law on June 30. However, on March 10, 2022, he was arrested again while evading authorities at a monastery in the Phaung Gyi-Minkon wilderness near Bago Yoma.

Due to the political turmoil, some mainstream journalists and correspondents have chosen to abandon their profession, which is rooted in "finding the truth and seeking justice in all matters." However, in response to local needs, new individuals have emerged in this field. Witnessing acts of injustice, some local journalists urgently contact news agencies to report on events. However, lacking formal training in journalism, their information often fails to be presented as a cohesive news story. Occasionally, their information is incorporated into more comprehensive news reports by others. These new journalists, unfamiliar with copyright laws, regulations, and ethics, may send their information and news photos to multiple news agencies, only to feel frustrated when their contributions go unrecognised by the public.

While a correspondent or journalist may avoid arrest, they face another challenge: even after well-established local and foreign mainstream media outlets risk their lives to collect information, plagiarists may casually appropriate their work without giving credit or compensation. Furthermore, information from non-professional media sources does not contribute positively to the media landscape. Given the paramount importance of accuracy, this situation has led to physical and psychological harm. Part of the problem arises from local journalists' unfamiliarity with this practice, compounded by their lack of knowledge regarding digital security and legal protections.

While local correspondents and journalists, residing in their respective regions and disseminating the latest news to the public, endure a dismal plight, those in liberated areas are tasked with compiling the military's propaganda narratives and language. Simultaneously, the SAC dispatches intelligence agents to border towns in Thailand in an attempt to locate mainstream correspondents and journalists seeking refuge there. Some correspondents are aware of these efforts. While some journalists continue to adhere to journalistic ethics, others living abroad leverage their media skills to satisfy themselves or provide an outlet for their mental well-being. Some journalists, citing current circumstances, obtain information from nearby sources and offer commentary. However, when it comes to on-the-ground news, they rely solely on the latest updates from social media.

Amidst these developments within the private news media sector, the information warfare, largely concealed from public view, persists from the past into the present.

Wall:

Media, Misinformation and Disinformation

In November 2021, Reuters published a report on the military's ongoing propaganda efforts following the coup attempt, titled "Information Warfare." Thousands of army personnel were tasked with special duties for this "information warfare," aimed at disseminating the SAC's propaganda among the populace. Those who had deserted the army were to be branded as traitors. Captain Nyi Thuta, who had previously crafted speeches for Commander-in-Chief Min Aung Hlaing and had been involved in the military's propaganda campaigns, revealed, "Soldiers were instructed to create fake accounts, and the information and propaganda they were required to post were provided from higher authorities."

Details of the project can also be found in online discussions joined by Captain Nyi Thuta. The propaganda campaign employs three distinct methods: white, brown, and black.

The White Method involves sharing seemingly trivial information. While this information may appear ridiculous to viewers with critical thinking skills, it garners significant attention and reactions, ultimately achieving the mission of brainwashing with over 100 million views.

The Brown Method entails shaping true news and sharing it. Viewers anticipate the news to be verified eventually, but it never materialises, leading to disillusionment with the revolution.

The Black Method revolves around disseminating false news exclusively. Its goal is to sow discord among comrades, fostering suspicion and spreading fabricated information and comments. These three methods continue to be effective, with some revolutionary comrades unwittingly aiding in the dissemination of military propaganda due to their lack of suspicion regarding the military's motives.

According to Reuters' analysis of social media posts in 2021, approximately 200 soldiers regularly distributed propaganda alleging electoral fraud and branding protesters against the dictatorship as traitors.

These efforts are overseen by the "Ka-Ka Kun" unit of the Defence Service Network (DSN) within the Public Relations and Psychological Operations Department in Naypyitaw, where hundreds of soldiers are employed.

In response to their hate-spreading behaviour, military accounts have been banned from Facebook due to their involvement in collective activities. Additionally, YouTube and TikTok have restricted channels and accounts affiliated with the military supporting violence. However, the military's information warfare, supported by the DSN, continues its mission of violence through the arrest, surveillance, and harassment of individuals and their families.

The initial measures taken by the Military Council after February 1, 2021, included banning the use of Facebook in the country. Consequently, the 28 million Facebook users in the country had to resort to VPNs. However, when they ventured outdoors, the SAC forces and police frequently violated citizens' privacy by inspecting their mobile phones and arresting suspects or extorting money from them. Consequently, people had to leave their phones at home and carry basic keypad phones when going out.

Furthermore, long before the election, soldiers and their family members were ordered to register their own Facebook accounts with the authorities, subjecting them to constant surveillance. This left them unaware of events beyond military propaganda and placed them in a difficult position if they wished to participate in the Civil Disobedience Movement (CDM). Consequently, members of the SAC forces were already at a disadvantage, both on the ground and in information warfare, before they engaged in combat.

Indeed, according to The New York Times dated October 15, 2018, the Offices of the Military Psychological Operations Branch in Naypyitaw, Yangon, and Pyin Oo Lwin have employed approximately 700 personnel. These individuals serve on day and night shifts, tasked with creating fake online news stories, posting propaganda, establishing fake news pages, and disseminating provocative comments using numerous fake accounts.

Shortly after this report, hundreds of people gathered in front of Yangon City Hall, chanting slogans in support of the Commander-in-

Chief and condemning Facebook for interfering in the affairs of another country. Approximately six months prior to this incident, some civil activists had applied for permission to stage a peace demonstration in the space in front of City Hall. However, their application was rejected by the General Administration Department under the Ministry of Home Affairs, a department solely monopolised by the Commander-in-Chief.

It is possible that the people's reliance on social media without exercising critical thinking contributed to the military's focus on spreading propaganda on these platforms. In mid-2012, Burma had only 2.1 million mobile SIM card users, but by 2018, this number had surged to 56.9 million. By 2019, there were 21 million Facebook users in Burma. The government at the time also utilised Facebook to disseminate current news, ranging from power outages and water supply issues to important state-level notifications. Consequently, Facebook became an indispensable part of daily life for the Burmese people and a crucial medium for correspondents and journalists.

Following conflicts in Meiktila and several towns in the West Bago Region in March 2013, the chauvinistic organisation known as Ma-Ba-Tha, formed on June 26, began providing training in posting news, shooting news videos, and online communication from mid-2014 to 2017 under the program "The Buddhist Sāsanā Upgrading Course." Ma-Ba-Tha members and supporters, using multiple accounts, disseminated false news and made random comments labelling dissenting posts as "terrorist." This concerted effort aimed to report original posts that disagreed with them, effectively launching an operation to have the posts restricted or temporarily deactivated by Facebook. One disadvantage of Facebook is the insufficient number of content moderators proficient in the Burmese language, and there have been controversies surrounding the critical thinking and decision-making of Facebook staff. Consequently, the Facebook platform has further complicated the political Maze of Burma.

According to Aiden Moe's article, "A Study of Spreading Systematically Linked Propaganda Using Facebook," published in December 2021 in the *Thi-Sat-Myin-Hnant (IJBS)* Journal, despite Facebook deactivating pages, groups, and accounts associated with the military in 2018, there were still 34 pages promoting military news and spreading false information. Interestingly, the admin location of 14 of these pages is listed as "foreign countries," including Russia, Vietnam, Thailand, Indonesia, and the Philippines. Frequently, two accounts from the same location would post fake news pages, along with four or five groups. There were attempts to purchase popular pages and groups, followed by efforts to exploit these platforms. Often, a single post would be sent to multiple accounts, or many accounts would be used to post a single, pre-prepared propaganda comment under news agency posts.

On February 14, 2021, the Law Amending the Penal Code, signed by the Commander-in-Chief, was announced. Section 121 of this law states: "Whoever wages war against the Union of Myanmar or any constituent unit thereof, or assists any State or person, or incites or conspires with any person within or outside the Union to wage war against the Union or any constituent unit thereof, or attempts or prepares by unconstitutional means or any other means to overthrow the organs of the Union[...] shall be guilty of the offence of High Treason." Additionally, according to sub-Section 124 A, action would be taken against individuals who "by words, either spoken or written, or by signs, or by visible representation, or otherwise, brings or attempts to bring into hatred or contempt, or excites or attempts to excite disaffection towards the Government established by law for the Union or for the constituent units or the Defence Services or Defence Services Personnel [...]."

Furthermore, a sub-Section 505 A was added to Penal Code Section 505, allowing action to be taken against individuals who "cause or intend to cause fear to a group of citizens or to the public [...] (or) cause or intend to spread false news [...] (or) cause or intend to commit or to agitate directly or indirectly criminal offences against a Government employee [...]." On February 15, an amending law on the electronic transactions law was promulgated, along with the announcement of a cyber security draft. The Ministry of Transportation, responsible for implementing the latter law, was joined by the Ministry of Home Affairs and the Ministry of Defence. Consequently, the police force was granted legitimacy for intercepting the use of phones, emails, and the Internet. Action could be taken against foreigners as well. Anyone who breaches Section 505 A and posts false news, fake news, or pornography could face imprisonment, a fine, or both. Online services subjected to action could be temporarily suspended or permanently abolished.

Another amendment was the Law for Protection of Personal Privacy and Personal Security of Citizens, which abolished Section 7: "No one shall be detained in custody without permission of the court for more than 24 hours except in cases permitted under any existing laws." Consequently, other political activists, including the 88 Generation leader Ko Mya Aye, writers Than Myint Aung, Maung Thar Cho, Htin Lin Oo, and Monywa Aung Shin, were detained for months before any charges were brought against them under any section.

According to Section 21 B of the 2008 Constitution, "No citizen shall be placed in custody for more than 23 hours without the permission of a Court," yet the SAC flagrantly violated this section, while always claiming to be following the laws, revealing the true colours of the SAC.

This was not all that the SAC had done. Convinced of the negative responses from the majority of the people, the SAC resorted to deceiving itself by believing the fabricated stories it created. The policy "To Fight the Media with the Media" still seemed valid, leading them to legitimately permit media outlets that would help spread their propaganda.

The online channels of news agencies that regularly attended the press conferences of the SAC included 22 Facebook pages, 11 Telegram Channels, 10 YouTube Channels, 6 websites, and 2 VK accounts, as mentioned in the article of Khit Thit Media, titled "Sit-tat Alo-kya Ludu-ko Lein-le-yan Kyosa-ne-thi media amyi-khan-mya, Asun-yauk Ma-Ba-Tha nint Amyotha-Lobby-mya, Sit-Oke-su-i- Nauk-myee Swe-mya-ko Phaw-htoke-chin" ("On Pro-military Groups, Chauvinists, Organizations, and the Stooges of the Military").

These media outlets could be categorised as follows: the media under the chauvinists Ma-Ba-Tha (e.g., *Myanmar National Post*); the pro-military media openly spreading the propaganda of the military, founded after February 2021 (e.g., the so-called national-beneficial journalist agency, telegram channel); the so-called misinformation scrutinization media that spread only misinformation distorting revolutionary news (e.g., Fact Check's Facebook page, Telegram Channel); so-called media that appeared neutral on the surface but worked closely with the military for economic benefits (e.g., Trend News Journal).

The article contains the names of other media outlets, the date of establishment, detailed dates of broadcasting, as well as permission from which ministry and the names of the shareholders.

In fact, transparency in media investment is virtually non-existent, leaving the majority of viewers unaware of how media outlets are perceived as a burgeoning market and how they can wield political influence or wreak havoc in politics if things don't go as planned.

For example, established in 1999 and co-founded by Australian citizen Ross Dunkley as the chief editor, *The Myanmar Times* was a propaganda project of Military Intelligence Chief General Khin-Nyunt, effectively exploiting social media as a weapon aimed at the international community. Major Thein Swe, head of the International Relations Department of Military Intelligence, and his son Sonny Swe, owned 51 percent of the shares. Founded during the tenure of the Press Scrutiny and Registration Division, publication permissions came not from the Ministry of Information but from the Ministry of Home Affairs, often bypassing the Division, colloquially known as the "Literary Kempeitai" in derogatory terms. Permission for publication was swiftly granted if requested by the Military Intelligence Department.

Initially published in English and later in Burmese, *The Myanmar Times* was originally intended to disseminate propaganda among foreigners, resulting in more liberal news and articles in English than in Burmese. Intriguing articles with flexible attitudes expressed in critical tones captivated not only foreigners but also Burmese entrepreneurs who viewed politics as a marketplace for economic gain, as well as scholars seeking access to the international community. Despite subsequent changes in policies, investors, and the editorial board, *The Myanmar Times* quickly gained attention, with Thein Swe, a shareholder, later promoted to Brigadier General and appointed Chief of the International

Relations Department of Military Intelligence.

Unfortunately, in 2004, Military Intelligence was disbanded, and both Thein Swe and Sonny Swe were imprisoned on charges related to press scrutiny and registration. Upon release, Sonny Swe founded the *Frontier Myanmar* news agency, which continued news programs such as Do-Athan, Mye-lat A-than, and *Delta News*, funded by international media foundations. In an article published by *Irrawaddy News* on November 15, 2022, Min Aung Hlaing of the SAC requested former intelligence officers for intelligence information to suppress the Spring Revolution and sought their advice. Sonny Swe's father, U Thein Swe, a former intelligence officer, had to visit Naypyitaw to meet the Commander-in-Chief.

Accessing funding from the international community posed a significant challenge for Burmese journalists. While some editors adhered to fossilised practices in the conventional news industry and could present news and articles in line with ethics, they also had to align themselves with modern tastes and market changes. Then, unexpectedly, the coup occurred, bringing forth many new challenges. Naturally, journalists were compelled to write proposals to international foundations to ensure the survival and long-term functioning of their news agencies and newspapers.

However, opportunities for media funding tended to favour political activists familiar with international knowledge, adept at writing impressive proposals, and experienced in propaganda tactics with high proficiency in language skills. Consequently, journalists whose advantage lay solely in their journalism experience found it difficult to survive due to financial problems. Thus, the role of investors in the media business remained controversial in Burma's mainstream media scene.

The situation became even more challenging due to the stark reality that local investors offering the highest bids for investment were often former military officials and their families, relatives, and friends. Furthermore, the younger generations of military officers, with their international experience, language fluency, and understanding of international corporate socio-economic culture, could amass wealth and exert financial power. They were like winners who took it all, building financial empires through their connections to power.

In contrast, ordinary journalists found themselves at a disadvantage in such unfavourable circumstances. They had limited choices in their careers and were often compelled to work for crony-owned media or media owned by the offspring of military officers or media headed by the military itself. While news presented without constraints may appear more interesting in terms of public interest and long-term survival, the influence of wealthy investors on news editors and newsrooms could not be ignored.

Even when different media outlets reported the same news, the reaction from the State Administration Council (SAC) was intriguing. For instance, in October 2022, gunfire erupted at the foot of the hill leading to the famous Kyaikhtiyo Pagoda in Mon State. Several local news agencies reported on this incident. However, the SAC filed a case against the BBC and *The Irrawaddy*. While the case against the BBC was dismissed, only *The Irrawaddy* faced legal action. Its office was raided, and journalists, staff, and even the publisher were arrested.

Despite these challenges, mainstream media outlets like the BBC, VOA, and RFA managed to survive locally. However, the public perception has shifted, with many considering VOA as a media outlet that often presents news favourable to the SAC.

The Spring Revolution is often seen as a moment when all masks were removed, revealing the true intentions of political parties and media outlets. People began to discern which parties genuinely respected public opinion and which ones were solely driven by a thirst for power. Similarly, in the realm of media, particularly among mainstream news agencies, observers noted which outlets prioritised ethics and the public interest, and which ones manipulated data and information.

While press scrutiny and censorship, products of the 1962 Printers and Publishers Law, were effective, the State Administration Council (SAC) employed even more relentless propaganda tactics through various channels. This created a prevailing mindset in the local community reminiscent of "The Wizard of Oz" by L. Frank Baum, where every citizen of the Emerald City had to wear green-tinted spectacles, metaphorically representing a skewed perception imposed by the military.

Furthermore, the country's education system lacked quality education, further perpetuating a state of blindness among the people. Many believed that access to information was crucial for societal change. Efforts were made during the rule of the National League for Democracy (NLD) government to enact a Right to Information (RTI) law, but these efforts were unsuccessful. Unfortunately, even some mainstream journalists failed to grasp the essence and concept of the right to information.

There was a push for a society that valued direct access to primary sources of information over information disseminated through social media, which often involved distorted narratives. However, the coup disrupted these efforts. Today, the media is viewed as a mass destructive weapon, with information warfare raging day and night.

Indeed, the Spring Revolution found itself ensnared in a complex web of challenges, grappling with the swirling currents of inertia within the Maze.

Corner:

Identity Politics

"Hey, Sis, are you still awake?" A message popped up on the screen.
"Oh, hi! Good morning! Are you already up? Isn't it a bit early?" came the reply.
"Well, it's a bit chilly on my end of the world. I felt quite sluggish. I thought I fell asleep last night."
"Take care, Sis. How's everything in Burma? Hot and humid nights here. Power cuts every night. Can't get a good night's sleep."
"That's too bad. Been a long time since we last had a chat. Is it OK to talk to you on the phone?"
"Good idea. Ring me on Signal."
"OK."
"Hello. Can you hear me, Sis?"
"Hi. Anything new?"
"Well, where shall I begin? Don't know. The situation here is all messed up."
"Why?"
"Hmm, I stumbled upon an old video clip. You know, there's this Karen girl who's fuming because the PDF, the Gen Z, CRPH, and NUG have all crowded the Karen region. She's bitterly criticising these Bamar groups for seeking refuge in the liberated areas of the KNU. It's just too much! Racial discrimination and hate speech and all that. People criticise the Bamar people's chauvinism not because they don't want us to change our mindset, but because they just want to condemn us. So disappointing."

During the Spring Revolution, Bamar people's chauvinism came under criticism, mostly targeting the NLD. Some criticisms sounded positive, while others often mixed personal feelings into their comments.

"Well, you feel affected by those criticisms because your nationality is

Bamar, but what about a mixed-blood like me? I think you might have heard of the new policy of the Eight States. If I come back to Burma, I'm afraid I wouldn't have space to set foot on the land where I was brought up," said the young lady, who was staying abroad. It was already morning, so the Bamar lady, talking on the other end of the line, could hear the sounds of chirping birds and car honks. She could hear the sigh too.

There are quite a considerable number of minority groups living for ages in Burma, but if the government implements the policy of establishing the Eight States according to the eight nationalities in terms of equality to found the federal system, controversies could ensue from this kind of paradigm shift because the Chinese, the Indians, and other mixed-blood individuals who have been settled in the country for ages would be left out from the considerations. Hence, proposals were made thus: the social life-oriented federal system be taken into account, which would enable the citizens, individually or in minority groups, to enjoy justice, equality, and freedom as human rights.

"Hey, Sis, why are you keeping silent?" said the Bamar lady. "Take it easy. I'm really sorry for you. We Bamars are the majority, but we're standing small because of the consequences of the mistakes made by the military leaders and senior politicians throughout successive periods in history. So we Bamars now find ourselves as the target of scathing criticism in the international community. Actually, we ordinary Bamars have also suffered the same plight together with the minorities under the successive governments. You've been settled here for ages, but you were criticised for being mixed blood of different religions, and I am sorry we didn't show empathy to you, citizens of Burma holding the FRC, the Foreigner Registration Certificate. On behalf of our Bamar people, I apologise. I also regret how you've been ill-treated. Now I understand your feelings much better."

It must be pointed out that the majority of the middle-class and low-class Burmese citizens have been quite unfamiliar with political philosophy. Thus, justice and equality have often been viewed not from the perspective of nationality, but in terms of discrimination based on a person's position, wealth, and profession. The majority who understand the true conditions of their country's administrative system do not support the army because they believe that throughout successive periods, the military themselves have always discriminated between ordinary civilians and military personnel.

"It's okay, Sis. Empathy grows in you only when you yourself go through the same experiences. But I am rather worried about these controversies, you know, the eight nationalities and the armed ethnic groups talking about the division of power and natural resources. So, what about us, both racial and religious minorities? You receive criticism because you are Bamars. The international community expresses deep concern over the Rohingyas and the Muslims, but there's nobody who would speak out about our case. Which state should we move to? Which state would accept us as citizens? Could we choose an ethnic group to be under its rule?"

There came the sound of flushing the toilet in the Signal app, which finally faded out. Among the non-Bamar, non-Buddhist minorities are the Hindus, the citizens who profess Bahá'í and the Jews, as well as the Chinese, the Indians, and the European descendants. The Rakhine crisis has recently drawn the attention of the international community to speak out for the cases of the Rohingyas and the Muslims, but the rights of the above-mentioned citizens of Burma have long been ignored.

"Well, I also feel concerned about the way they divide the territories. You know, they claim for the former size of their territories as before the colonial period. But some even go crazy — excuse my expression — holding the crumpled map dated before the 18th century in their hands and claiming for their old kingdom back! Crazy! These guys have covered their territory through meetings with the media."

There came the sound of brushing teeth with a toothbrush, and the voices sandwiched with laughter. The trouble with the people living in mainland Burma was the lack of regular power supply and the Internet, so they find it hard to join online conferences. They neither had a chance to join the discussions nor dared to do so. Thus, only the majority of the people and the media, now settled in the liberated areas, could join in these discussions while others remained as the audience, like a third party.

"Well, I am not the type of national chauvinist or racialist, you might say. I always wanted to be a humanist. You know, if you take the view of those elite politicians on the territory of the Bamars, we'd remain in a landlocked, inland dry zone only. According to their discussions, Yangon would become the territory of common property. And both the Mons and the Karens claim the Irrawaddy delta as their own territory, so there's no Bamar making such a claim. Why doesn't anyone representing the Bamars join in discussions like that? Phew, it's so embarrassing!"

"Oh ha ha, there's a pop-up of your national chauvinistic spirit! We have the mighty BPLA. Right?" said the lady from abroad, with the sound of mouthwash after brushing her teeth.

"Did you say, BPLA? The Bamar People's Liberation Army? It's an army, not a representative of the Bamar people joining in political discussions. People say, The NLD is a Bamar party. No, it's wrong because the NLD does not think so. Some leaders are non-Bamars. So, there's no representative of the Bamar nationality. Well, let's drop this subject. Another issue is the armed ethnic groups declare they represent their particular race, but we have two or three armies of the same ethnicity. Isn't it the irony of Fate that the Shan ethnicity has two armies, engaged in the Shan vs Shan conflicts? No Shan political party could stop them. In the case of the KNU, the Karen National Union, even one organisation has the armed wings, KNLA and KNDO, and a splinter group, the Kawthoolei Army, in terms of brigade structure. One single organisation or party still cannot represent one whole ethnicity, you know. In fact, I have no interest in the cases of the nationalities, let alone nationalism or chauvinism. My blood happens to be that of a Bamar, so I've been categorised in the group of Bamar. Is that the reason I should take the blame? Then, with the feelings of being a degraded subject of racial discrimination, that chauvinism arises in me. That's an awful thing, indeed."

Although there were online controversies and pressures among political activists, it was uncertain to what extent these pressures manifested in on-the-ground conditions. However, young people who spent hours online truly felt these pressures.

"In that video clip, the young Karen lady was venting her feelings; she must have been holding them in for who knows how long. The same goes for us. Each of us has individually been politically abused. We've done nothing wrong, yet we've been degraded. As a result, we become victims, mentally wounded, harbouring hatred in our hearts. Each of us may react differently because some people can handle this change in mentality while others cannot. Now I understand what you're going through, and I'm deeply concerned for you because I know you inside out. You've been against the military dictatorship for so long. Now you witness the military killing countless Bamar people. Isn't it time we showed empathy? Shouldn't we stop saying, 'You Bamars, you deserve it for all your racialism'? I know, Sis, your heart is pure, free from any sort of racial discrimination, but when you're blamed by other ethnicities, even you may feel a surge of national chauvinism, don't you? I fear that if other Bamar people were to be overwhelmed by this sort of racialism, it would spoil everything, it would affect our Revolution because the Bamar people are the majority. That spirit of strong national chauvinism might be brewing even among some leaders. Things would all go wrong if the whole Bamar population were tainted by that spirit."

Silence fell. Both ladies could hear their breathing on the phone. Their voices remained calm.

"I just wonder why the NLD and the NUG could not fulfil the promises made to the ethnic groups. I fear this could lead to trouble brewing among the PDFs! You know, those armed ethnic groups have been fighting for sixty or seventy years, and they've become divided into many factions. Naturally, clashes often occur among themselves at the slightest provocation!"

"Well, you just mentioned that there's still controversy over whether the NLD represents the entire Bamar nationality or not. From my perspective, it's clear that the NUG and the NLD are not the same organisation. It was the NUCC that took the lead in organising the NUG by bringing together representatives from all ethnic groups. This implies that the NUG is not solely composed of NLD members. Perhaps the NUG has a stronger presence from the NLD, but it doesn't have absolute authority to represent the Bamar nationality or any other ethnic group."

The issue of representation for a group or ethnicity remains unresolved. It's important to emphasise that even a representative elected from a specific region represents that region alone. However, there are misconceptions that a political or armed group garnering public support for an extended period automatically represents its people.

"In fact, the largest population in the country is Bamar," said the young Bamar lady. "Even in prison, the Bamar people might take pride in being the majority. Just a joke! Isn't it an oversimplification to say that Bamar dominates simply because they are the majority in many aspects? Those armed ethnic groups have been waging the revolutionary war against the military regime for ages, but it seems to have gained momentum only when the Bamar people joined the Spring Revolution. Right? So, I think it might be risky to mobilise the majority without a positive motive." Some people interpret acts of adopting racial hatred and considering the majority as an issue as a sign of foresightedness.

"Yep, you're right. Today, people talk about federal democracy and autonomy, the right of autonomous enactment, autonomous armed forces, and autonomous territory, but the concept of 'The Union Spirit' has been toned down, you know. It's no wonder some foreign political analysts have said that if the military meets its downfall, the civil war could worsen. That would be a disaster for minorities like us. Sorry to say that," said the young lady of minority background, with a tone of despair. Sometimes, people tend to prioritise their individual dreams over collective ones. This is the reality, of course.

"I understand, Sis. I've been feeling a bit down lately too. I'm just an ordinary guy, and those older folks who have been mentally wounded must have needed to let out their feelings for sure. The top priority is the downfall of the SAC. Hopefully, we can argue, negotiate, and sort things out after that. Fortunately, our young Gen-Z's on our side have kept racial prejudices at bay so far. They are very liberal, you know. They don't confine themselves to narrow-minded ideas. They hope for the best, too."

Their tones were becoming lighter. Nevertheless, the young people, not burdened by the bitter grudges of the past, are expected to make more liberal and rational decisions.

"Sis, I'm going to send you a quote from Mandela on racial issues that impresses me a lot," said the young lady from abroad. "Enjoy. But it's getting late. Go to bed. Sleep well. Sweet dreams."

"Okay. Enjoy your breakfast. Since you're all alone staying abroad, please take good care of your health, Sis. Remember, staying healthy means staying engaged with the revolution. Take care."

"Thank you. We've been arguing like this for a lifetime, haven't we? Well, let's keep arguing, keep searching for a path, and keep working towards a solution, I suppose. Actually, I feel like we seem more disorganised when discussing things online. On the ground, there seems to be more understanding among those standing back-to-back, working hand in hand."

"I agree, Sis. Alright, I'm going to hang up. Our Revolution, Our Victory!"

"Our Revolution, Our Victory!"

At the end of their conversation, a message popped up on Signal.

"We have never really accepted multiracialism. Our demand is for a non-racial society, because when you talk of multiracialism, you are saying that you have in this country so many races. This is in a way to perpetuate the concept of 'race' and we prefer to say we want a non-racial society. We discussed and said exactly what we were saying, that we are not multi-racialist(s), we are non-racialist (s). We are fighting for a society where people will cease thinking in terms of colour ... It is not a question of race; it is a question of ideas."

(Nelson Mandela: Conversation with Myself, 2010)

The Age of Anxiety, experienced by Europeans from 1914 to 1950, now permeates the hearts of both local Burmese citizens and the Burmese diaspora, burdened with overwhelming anxiety. With the exception of the SAC and its supporters, both the majority and the minority endure psychological or physical torture. Controversies arise over critical decisions concerning the future of Burma: The mission of the Spring is not solely focused on overthrowing the military dictatorship but also involves addressing fundamental issues necessary for the nation's future.

Thus, the Spring deserves credit for its efforts to dismantle the military regime and for undertaking constructive measures for rehabilitation. In essence, it is a revolution that confronts unresolved sensitive issues from the past and seeks solutions. Clearly, the Spring, struggling within the Maze but making progress by breaking barriers, brings not only hopeful news but also subjects of melancholy and despair.

Wall:

Inter-Ethnic Conflicts and Remnants of Colonialism

"Down with Chauvinism! Martyrs number more than nine!"

This new slogan emerged among the chants of protesters during the Spring Revolution, sparking numerous discussions and writings against chauvinism and racial discrimination. The slogan was primarily propagated by the General Strike Committee of Nationalities (GSCN). In Burmese history, July 19, 1947 marked the assassination of nine martyrs, including Gen. Aung San, the Architect of Burmese Independence. Every year, on July 19, Martyrs Day is observed in Burma to honour these fallen heroes. Importantly, these martyrs hailed from diverse backgrounds, encompassing both Bamars and non-Bamars, as well as non-Buddhists. The entrenched notion that only Bamars and Buddhists dominated the political landscape needed to be dispelled. Thus, the slogan "Martyrs number more than nine" was disseminated nationwide to remind people of the numerous heroes throughout Burma's history who sacrificed their lives for the cause of freedom and deserve recognition and respect.

Although U Aung San was assassinated while serving as the Prime Minister, not as the Commander-in-Chief, of the Interim Government in 1947, persistent propaganda has ensured that society refers to him as "Bogyoke Aung San" (General Aung San) or simply "Bogyoke." This portrayal emphasises his image as a sacrificial and iconic political figure in Burma, representing not just a civilian leader but the epitome of military leadership. Notably, Captain Ne Win, who planted the seeds of the coup in Burmese history, was one of the thirty comrades who fought for the country's independence. This group, known as "The Origin of the Tatmadaw," played a pivotal role in driving out British colonialists and Fascist Japanese forces.

Even though Aung San was not actively serving in the military at the time of his assassination, his widespread recognition as General Aung

San transcended his earlier identity as Thakhin Aung San ("Thakhin" being a term adopted by civil activists against the British colonialists). Consequently, the image of General Aung San became more deeply ingrained in people's memories than that of Thakhin Aung San, the civilian politician. Over time, this mindset led to the proliferation of army personnel holding the rank of general, leading to the perception of "cheap generals." In 1988, the title of "Senior-General" was introduced for the highest-ranking military officials, yet the public, particularly within the military, continued to regard the title of "Commander-in-Chief" as the ultimate position of authority.

This perception of the Commander-in-Chief as the pinnacle of power became so deeply entrenched that even figures like film star Kyaw Thu, known for his social welfare work and opposition to the military, humorously titled his autobiography *The Commander-in-Chief of Social Welfare Missions*. This choice of title may have been satirical, reflecting the inflated image associated with the position. (In 2016, according to existing protocol, the rank of Commander-in-Chief was supposed to hold the eighth position. This lower ranking was met with disapproval from Commander-in-Chief Min Aung Hlaing, who viewed it as a slight to his perceived importance.)

General Ne Win's military regime, which seized power in a coup amidst Burma's political turmoil in 1962, introduced a new ideological framework. This regime asserted that only the military had played a significant role in securing the country's independence and that it was the sole institution capable of safeguarding the state. To solidify its power, the military regime took steps to dismantle the 1947 Constitution drafted by U Aung San and his colleagues. Additionally, it sought to marginalise other patriotic figures from non-Bamar ethnic backgrounds who had contributed to liberating the country from colonial rule. Press censorship and registration, propaganda campaigns, and Socialist Education programs were deployed to achieve these aims.

Throughout this period, Daw Aung San Suu Kyi, the daughter of U Aung San, made efforts to foster a relationship with the military institution founded by her father. She often reiterated the sentiment, "The

Tatmadaw is the one founded by my dad," in an attempt to bridge the gap between the military establishment and her own leadership. During the Let-ba-taung Crisis in 20212, she delivered a speech: "Some people would snub me if I say, 'I love the Tatmadaw.' Can't help it. Yes, I'm telling the truth, I love this institution because I was brought up as a daughter of a soldier, I had been inculcated with a love of the Tatmadaw since I was a kid. Of course, there are things that the army has done that I don't like. I don't like what they have done to me, I don't like what they have done to our people, but I still love the Tatmadaw as an essential institution of our country."

However, through the successive periods after the BSPP (Burma Socialist Programme Party), the military took measures to erase Aung San's logo from stock photos, stamps, and currency notes. Even a person wearing a military uniform resembling that of Gen. Aung San, with an Aung San logo badge, was arrested and thrown into jail. What a mean ulterior motive! Daw Aung San Suu Kyi was repeatedly referred to as Daw Suu Kyi to dissociate her name from Aung San. The military might have been embarrassed by her cherished words, "The Tatmadaw is the one founded by my dad." From their perspective, she sounded, as a Burmese saying goes, "like climbing up the flagpole of a decorative pavilion and claiming the banner" of the original ownership. By attempting to dissociate the image of the Father of the Tatmadaw from his daughter, the military aimed to instil in Burmese citizens the concept that only military leaders are entitled to the heritage of state leadership, being honoured as the offspring of the Tatmadaw. Thus, Aung San and her daughter, the targets of personal grudges of the military leaders, found themselves in a tight predicament, like a poor little gourd locked up with arrogant thorns from all sides.

The history of a country devoid of peace and political stability, coupled with the racial and religious divides that hinder the establishment of a unified and truly independent nation, alongside the looming presence of the military and its peace-making efforts post-2011, wearing civilian attire after shedding the old military uniform, adds layers of complexity to Burma's narrative. Burma fell under British colonial rule in 1885. Among the notable confrontations against the British government was the 1920 first university students' boycott, led by the majority Bamar people and educated youths. For decades, other ethnic regions remained politically inactive until instigations stemming from national and religious causes, primarily led by the Dobamar A-si-ayone, prompted the Bamar majority to join the movements, significantly contributing to the struggle for independence. Thus, Burma's political history is synonymous with movements spearheaded by Bamar youths. In addressing the concept of chauvinism or national racialism, an excerpt from an article by Thi-ha Thway is pertinent. *"Bamar-lu-myo-gyi-wada-ne-myet-mauk-federal-ti-sauk-ye-kyo-pan-hmu-pati-pakkha"* ("Conflict between the Bamar Chauvinism and the Struggles for Building the Federal System"):

"According to the data in the history of Burma, the Burmese representatives went over to India to get separated from the Indian administration and claim for equal autonomy like India. The Karen ethnics also joined the mission, but submitted a report to the British government that it was too early to hand over the autonomy to the Bamar mainland and that the Karen ethnics preferred the option of remaining under British rule. To take an overall view, the British colonial rule had more or less helped breed the Bamar ethnics racialism. However, it was this growing ethnics racialism that led to the anti-British movements, then reaching the climax of the armed revolution. Therefore, the Bamar ethnics racialism and the independence of Burma were intertwining strands of a strong rope. On the other hand, the British government was tactful in its administration: The ethnics were misled to adopt the mindset that, excluding the Bamar from the map of independence, they had their own right to decide, "To be, or not to be"; and the independence of the Bamar mainland and that of the ethnics, as well as their future dream, were separate things. In other words, the independence of the ethnics was a matter to be settled between the ethnics and the British. The Burmese political leaders began to doubt that under the divide and rule system of the colonist British, the ethnics did not want to come under the banner of the Burmese leaders.

Another issue was the mentality of the 'conservative' Bamar people: the majority were proud of themselves for being the "Descendants of the God of the Sun", building the empire of might and glory even over the Asian continent."

Another intriguing aspect highlighted in *In Search of the Panglong Spirit: The Role of Federalism in Myanmar's Peace Discourse* (p. 81) by Michael Siegner follows:

"...the British were increasingly concerned about growing Bamar nationalism; they were reluctant to recruit Bamar soldiers into the armed forces, formally banning the ethnic-majority Bamar from entering the army in 1925. The result of this policy was that by 1931, the Karen, Kachin and Chin ethnic groups, representing approximately 13 percent of the colony's population at that time, accounted for 83 percent of the indigenous portion of the armed forces in Burma. Popular Bamar rebellions against the British colonisers, such as the famous Saya San rebellion in the early 1930s of the 1936 student strikes, were predominantly crushed by ethnic nationality troops, particularly by Karen forces................It is therefore argued by several scholars that ethno-linguistic identities undoubtedly already in pre-colonial Burma, but that colonial geographical-administrative divisions and British policies provided the basis for solidifying ethnic identities while also sowing the seeds for inter-ethnic conflict."

In fact, reflecting on the past, ordinary people living in countries under feudal systems, with kings and lords, rarely entertained the idea of taking up arms against their monarchs until their nations fell under colonial rule. However, as colonisation occurred, people became enraged at being subjugated and losing their sovereignty and rulership. The entire ruling system underwent a transformation, and locals, who had long been obedient subjects under absolute monarchies, had to adapt to the laws of a new order. Moreover, the history of Burma is marked by bloodshed, with instances of invasion and occupation of regions belonging to various ethnic groups such as the Mon, Bamar, Shan, and Rakhine, among others. As Michael Siegner noted in his book (p. 79), some ethnic groups did not view the British colonists unfavourably, as colonial rule helped preserve their national domains and identities.

> .... most Shans were thankful for the 'British Umbrella' as it not only rid the Shan fiefdoms of intrusions by the Bamar soldiery but also ended the ceaseless fighting among the various Shan Sawbwas. Chao-Tzang Yawnghwe therefore observed that many Shans remember the colonial era as a 'Golden Age'.

On the other hand, the Bamars often had nostalgia over the monarchical days of their own sovereignty as the Periods Under the Golden Umbrella, referring to the periods before it became a British colony.

When the narrow-minded, or blind, concept of living in a small feudal kingdom in peace and contentment had been replaced with the fate of surviving in a domain or territory with its own identity, both the Bamars and the non-Bamars had to go through a kind of dormant psycho, plagued with a desire of time-travelling back to the Golden Era. These people wanted to escape from the fate of 'enslavement,' but what their mind was obsessed with was to rebuild the former feudal kingdom and gather reinforcements so as to safeguard that kingdom. What's going on out in the world? They didn't care. What new philosophy of politics, what new ruling systems have taken place in the modern world? Only a few cared. As a result, almost every race began to see that the role of generals and war leaders play a more important role than the intelligentsia and the artists. Moreover, since a political party or an armed ethnic group is more bent on the cult of personality and power than the democratic practices, in the social environment of both the Bamars and the non-Bamar nationals, a leader still remains through the course of time, despite the wind of change.

Under the British administration, the country was divided into Ministerial Burma, or "Burma proper," and Scheduled Areas: under the former came some regions of the Mon, the Karen, and the Rakhine, together with the Bamar, while the latter areas included the regions of the Shan, the Chin, the Kachin, and the Karenni. Hence, the present administrative domain divisions, namely the Bamar divisions and the states of the nationals, originated from British rule. When the Panglong Agreement was signed on February 12, 1947, Aung San, a Bamar representing mainland Burma, took the lead, and the chiefs of the Shan, the Kachin, the Chin, and the Kayah signed as representatives of the hilly regions. According to the above-mentioned article by Thi-ha Thway: "To review the historical consequences, with the ultimate goals of autonomy and equality, the nationals waged war against the British colonists (and the Japanese Fascists), their missions were founded on different historical consequences: While the Mon, the Karen, and the Rakhine claimed separate existence, the Shan, the Kachin, the Chin, and the Kayah (Karenni) wanted to follow the pledges outlined in the Panglong Agreement."

Concerning the issue of when the terms of the Panglong Agreement were first breached, Michael Siegner wrote in his book (p. 99):

"Within two months, Chan Htun and U Nu changed several clauses of Aung San's draft constitution - particularly relating to federalism. On 24th September 1937, the Constitutional Convention adopted this modified constitution without debate. Chan Htun later admitted that the final 1947 Constitution, 'though in theory federal, is in practice unitary.

However, those lacking extensive knowledge of the country's history often place blame on Gen. Aung San and Daw Aung San Suu Kyi, criticising these two figures of great integrity, claiming, "Aung San and his daughter never keep their promises." A notable flaw in Burmese society, which tends to be conservative, is the tradition of categorising the government as one of the Five Enemies . Moreover, it is a society that, perhaps due to a lack of political maturity, tends to criticise and scandalise the "ruling party" or "the superior one." Although the generations of both U Nu and U Chan Tun remain active in Burma's current political landscape, they generally avoid criticism from the School for Scandal, likely because they lack the fame and power of others.

During the tenure of Thein Sein's government in 2011, it was not until 2014 that the military ceased its stubbornness and first accepted the term "federal." However, they continued to argue that the 2008 Constitution was the foundation of federalism. Subsequently, during the NLD government's term, although the federal process was framed under the title "The Panglong Conference," the military maintained its stance and approach, opting for direct negotiations over mediation-based negotiations. Under Thein Sein's government, known derogatorily as "Baung-bi Chuk" (a term denoting a government composed of retired military personnel no longer in uniform), peace negotiators—comprising retired military personnel and those who had retired from armed conflict—managed to establish mutual respect and understanding between the military and armed ethnic groups, facilitating smooth direct negotiations. However, during the NLD government's term, a new institution was established: The National Reconciliation and Peace Centre. A civilian doctor was appointed as the leader of peace negotiators, but the process did not proceed smoothly. The NLD's shortfall perhaps lies in the fact that only Daw Aung San Suu Kyi seemed to have the authority to make critical decisions, resulting in a lack of understanding of the views and sentiments of armed groups by civilians.

According to Siegner, "Bertil Lintner called the peace process 'a farce' and argues that the NLD and Aung San Suu Kyi have lost control over the process while the Tatmadaw is dictating its momentum and direction." He also wrote thus: "Padoh Mahn Nyein Maung, a senior leader of the Karen National Union KNU publicly stated that he did not think the conference would help the peace process because the Tatmadaw did not allow the meaningful discussion of political issues." Ironically, Mahn Nyein Maung later became a member of the cabinet of the SAC, likely because he had now adopted a blind faith in the military.

The peace-making process has remained a failure due to several factors:
1. Lack of equality: Those in power and their affiliated groups or parties, often of the same race and religion, assert their superior status of

authority and rights. This includes neglecting the recognition of non-Bamar languages, literature, national days, flags, territorial terms, red-letter days, and cultural affairs. Attempts to legitimise proposals favouring the state religion and directives to play songs of the Tatmadaw during traditional Bamar festivals, such as Thingyan, further exacerbate the issue.

2. Limited rights and opportunities for collective national identity-building: Political clashes have led ethnic groups to take up arms, but these forces are often formed based solely on race rather than political philosophy. Political parties have failed to convince their members of the importance of collective identity. Additionally, militarization has strained social harmony between civilians and the military. For example, the military's slogan changed from "Our People, Our Guardians" to "The Tatmadaw, Our Guardian" after the 1988 uprising.

3. Poor management and administration: Successive military governments have centralised power excessively, neglecting the development of states and remote areas. The dictatorship governments focused solely on executive power, leading to severe racial discrimination and further centralization. Additionally, according to the 2008 Constitution, elected representatives and the civilian government cannot unilaterally declare a ceasefire but must collaborate with the military, which holds practical control over this aspect.

In October 2015, the Nationwide Ceasefire Agreement (NCA) was signed, with 8 small ethnic armed organisations (EAOs) initially joining, followed by two more in February 2018. However, the majority of significant armed forces, including the Wa, Kachin, Ta-aung, Koe-kant, and Rakhine, have not signed the NCA, representing around 80 percent of the EAO population. Controversies persist regarding the effectiveness of the NCA.

During the Peace Summit Conference in October 2018, Min Aung Hlaing emphasised that only guarantees of non-secession and integration into the Union could ensure lasting peace in the country. Conversely, the leader of the Restoration Council of the Shan State, Yawd Serk, suggested that the Tatmadaw's insistence on non-secession stemmed from their desire to maintain state power and hinder the success of the civilian NLD government led by Daw Aung San Suu Kyi.

While the Thein Sein government made efforts to advance the peace process, it remained incomplete. Military leaders may have been reluctant to see the NLD government succeed in achieving what they had failed to accomplish for decades. Despite substantial international funding, the third 21st Century Panglong Conference (21CPC) yielded only 51 agreements, lacking political significance. Furthermore, disagreements between the Tatmadaw and various EAOs on security sector issues halted the peace process.

Following the 2021 coup, the SAC claimed to continue the peace process, although its focus may have shifted towards suppressing the People's Defense Forces (PDFs) amid the Spring Revolution. Consequently, the SAC's priority appeared to be securing ceasefire agreements with EAOs such as the RCSS, possibly for manipulation rather than genuine peace-building efforts.

Concerning the peace-making process during the term of the NLD government, Michael Siegner wrote the following:

"The NLD and Aung San Suu Kyi have been cautious in the negotiations about federal reforms, obviously attempting to play the role as a mediator between the EAOs and the Tatmadaw. In an interesting move during the Peace Summit in October 2018 however, Aung San Suu Kyi tried to break the current deadlock over the non-secession clause in the Pyidaungsu Accord by suggesting that it should be referred to the National Parliament to decide. While this suggestion was categorically dismissed by both the Tatmadaw and the EAOs, it nevertheless represented a bold attempt to assert more NLD control over the negotiation process. Arguably the most important reason why the Tatmadaw as well as the EAOs are suspicious of the NLD's intentions is that they do not know where the NLD stands with regards to federalism."

He also discussed how controversies arise among the ethnic groups over the interpretation of the concept of "federalism":

"The bigger groups such as Shan, Kachin or Karen envision federalism as being first and foremost about increasing powers held by the existing ethnic-based states. Smaller groups that mostly form second-order minorities such as Pa-O, Taáng, Wa or Danu on the other hand view federalism as a way to decentralise significant powers to lower levels of government like Self Administrative Areas SAAs or even for the creation of new states."

Indeed, as part of the peace-making process, measures were taken to hold political talks among various ethnic groups. However, it was the Tatmadaw that raised objections to these region-based activities. In the first half of 2017, national-level political seminars were successfully held for the Pa-O, the Chin, and the Kren. Yet, the Mon national-level political seminar faced numerous restraints imposed by the South-East Division Command. Similarly, the military did not approve the Shan national-level political seminars led by the RCSS. Furthermore, using security concerns as an excuse, the Tatmadaw prevented the Rakhine national-level political seminars from occurring in the Rakhine State.

Many Ethnic Armed Organizations (EAOs) were misled into believing that both the NLD and the military shared the same stance. Consequently, they came to believe that not only the military but also the NLD was responsible for providing no opportunity to discuss federal issues. Like the military, the NLD was criticised for adopting an attitude of strong national racialism.

It was also pointed out that throughout successive historical periods, every nationality and race has encountered issues related to social classes and the lack of materialistic equality. Therefore, these issues should be taken into account in political seminars. Stephen Campbell and Elliott Prasse-Freeman also emphasised that discussions should address these issues to address deeply-rooted Bamar national racialism ("Burman Chauvinism") and the pressures stemming from class and status. They suggested the following approach:

> "Ultimately, however, the failure of pre-coup liberal politics to deal with material inequality in Myanmar hurt not only ethnic minority upland villagers, but poor Burmans in the lowlands as well. For this reason, a serious project of political economic restructuring_ involving land reform, nationalisation of military holding companies, and significant redistribution of wealth, for example_ has the potential to address the material structures upending inequality, both between the lowlands and uplands, and between the elite and marginalised populations within the lowlands. While such policies will not ineluctably lead to improved inter-ethnic relations a politics _building on Burma's rich leftist tradition _ that stresses how average Burmese subjects of every race and religion have more in common among themselves than with economic elites_ even those of their own ethnicity _ that have raided the country for decades, just may."

Thus, the Maze, involving the NLD, the military, Burman Chauvinism, Bamar and non-Bamar nationals, federal outlook, the Golden Age of the feudal nation, democratic rules of conduct, unarmed civilians and armed military, the haves and the have-nots, still prevails to this day, even during the Spring.

Wall:

Maze 2017, 2018, 2019 and 2020

Mon

Tensions between the NLD and the non-Bamar nationals had been simmering since the post-2017 period. The racial discriminations were now being viewed more sensitively than ever, exacerbated by the Rakhine crisis. Another incident added fuel to the fire: the naming of the bridge connecting Mawlamyaing City and Chaung Sone Township, formerly known as Balu-Kyun, or "The Island of the Ogres." On February 13, 2017, the Mon State government organised a celebration for the opening ceremony of the sign-board bearing the name "Bogyoke Aung San Bridge." However, objections were raised by local parties and nationals, prompting a change in the name to "The ThanLwin Bridge (Chaung Sone)." The issue originated from the Pyihtaungsu Hluttaw, where on February 15, the NLD Pyihtaungsu Hluttaw of Paung Township, led by Mi Kun Chan, proposed to the Union Government that the bridge be named Bogyoke Aung San Bridge in honour of the national leader, sparking objections.

Local people expressed their discontent, stating that the name "Bogyoke Aung San Bridge" seemed to disregard the interests of the local Mon community. Protests erupted in Mawlmyaing and Kanyaw Village, Chaung Sone Township (Balu-Kyun). However, despite objections, the opening ceremony of the Bogyoke Aung San Bridge (Balu-Kyun) proceeded on May 9. Present at the event were Chairman of the Pyithu Hluttaw U Win Myint, Union Minister of the Ministry of Construction U Win Khaing, prime ministers and ministers from Mon State, Kayin State, Tanintharyi Region, and Bagon Region, as well as chairmen of states and regions and Hluttaw representatives. Construction of the bridge had commenced in February 2015, leading some to suggest that the NLD took advantage of the project to promote their party during their term in government. Even non-Bamar members of the NLD faced criticism for failing to address the desires of local ethnic groups and instead prioritising loyalty to the party leader.

One peculiar development regarding the bridge occurred on May 31, 2021, following the attempted coup, when the military once again changed its name to "The Thanlwin Bridge (Chaung Sone)." Present at the "reopening" ceremony were Commander-in-Chief Min Aung Hlaing and SAC members, including Dr. Banyar Aung Moe, a central executive member of the Mon Unity Party (MUP). According to The Irrawaddy, Dr. Banyar Aung Moe paid MMK 20,000 to each participant and "hired" local individuals to dress in traditional Mon attire and attend the ceremony.

In an interview with a young Mon man, he expressed his dismay, stating, "What a disgrace! Being 'hired' to attend a ceremony? Isn't it strange to 'reopen' a bridge that already had an opening ceremony and has been in service? From my perspective, both the NLD and the SAC were wrong in naming the bridge. The SAC is attempting to portray respect for the desires of local people, but the act of 'hiring' is shameful to our Mon community!"

The extent to which a political party genuinely respects the desires of an ethnic group remains a challenging question in contemporary Burmese politics.

Kayah

In 2018, another issue related to Bogyoke Aung San arose when plans were made to erect a bronze statue of him in the park of the Kayah State Hall at a cost of MMK 800 lakhs. This initiative was spearheaded by the Kayah State government. However, local residents voiced objections, arguing that Bogyoke Aung San was perceived as a hero of independence only by the majority Bamar population, not by the Kayahs.

Notably, during the term of the pro-military USDP government in July 2012, Kayah youths, despite close military surveillance, distributed pamphlets about Bogyoke Aung San and Martyrs' Day. They also cleaned the park where a column was erected in memory of the martyrs and organised a parade on Martyrs' Day. These youths were instrumental in campaigning for the NLD party in the 2015 General Election. However, they were the same individuals who objected to the proposed bronze statue of Bogyoke Aung San.

As a consequence, four of these individuals faced repercussions for their objections to the memorial bronze statue, while 20 Kayahs were sued for distributing propaganda pamphlets detailing the history of Karenni under Section 505(a).

"I suppose," said U Thaung Htay, the Chairman of the NLD in Kayah State, during an interview with RFA, "this is not the opportune time to implement such a project for the moment. We should listen to the voices of the local people."

On the other hand, Chief Minister of Kayah State L. Paung Sho stated in an interview with Myanmar Now News Agency: "Concerning the project, we invited all the village/quarter group administrators in the whole Kayah State, and all the members of the National Literature and Culture Committee, as well. Only after we've got their approval, we commenced to implement the project." (News article, "Politics of the Kayah State behind the Bronze Statue of Bogyoke Aung San," *Myanmar Now*)

The NLD party, along with its government, issued a statement affirming that the project of erecting the bronze statue of Bogyoke Aung San did not deviate from their policy. According to the article, the number of supporters and objectors to the project were found to be nearly equal.

"Just a memorial, you know. It doesn't cause grievance to those who object," remarked a 21-year-old Kayah woman. Another local Kayah man, who was sentenced to 32 years' imprisonment in 2008 for breaching the 2008 Constitution, told *Myanmar Now*, "Those (NLD) guys and their supporters do not have a knack in politics. They've taken the shortcut in politics. They want to build an image of their own, but not purely out of the proof of their performance. They just want to exert their political influence under the shadow of a public figure." (*Myanmar Now*)

More importantly, the Karenni National Progressive Party (KNPP), which remained an armed ethnic group until 2012, sent a letter to State Counsellor Daw Aung San Suu Kyi expressing deep concern about the arrests of local people who objected to the bronze statue project. Simultaneously, some local political forces demanded that the KNPP boycott the 21st Century Panglong Conference scheduled to be held in Naypyitaw. The article provided background information on the prime minister of Kayah State and the NLD in Kayah State.

The article detailed the history of Kayah State, highlighting events such as the 1990 General Election where half of the eight constituencies were won by the pro-military USDP. Subsequently, the military declared Kayah State as an NLD-free zone, exerting pressure on NLD members. In 1994, the NLD representative of Sha-taw constituency, U Aung Tin, resigned from his membership due to the challenges faced by the party. In 2011, when the NLD registered for the election, two factions emerged: the old-member NLD was not recognized by the Yangon headquarters. These old members formed the Kayah Ethnic Group Democratic Party, but it was unsuccessful in the election. They later merged with a local Kayah party, renaming themselves "The Kayah State Democratic Party." In the previous general election, young Kayan (Karenni) activists mobilised support for the NLD to defeat USDP prime ministers of the pro-military party, U Aung Min and U Soe Thein. No wonder the NLD won three-fourths of all constituencies in the state.

However, after assuming power, the NLD government faced challenges in maintaining relationships with its allies, and imposed restrictions on local organisations' movements. For instance, obtaining permission for cultural celebrations required recommendations from various departments. As a result, local activists began to believe that rebuilding trust was no longer easy, and that the NLD government and the Kayah people were moving in different directions.

Chief Minister L Paung Sho of Kayah State held a Bachelor of Education degree from The University for the Development of National Races of the Union (Ywathit-gyi, Sagaing), established by the military dictator U Ne Win. Admission to this university required candidates to pledge adherence to the Three Causes and refrain from involvement in party politics. Prior to his political career, L Paung Sho served as an Assistant Township Education Officer (ATEO) in Me-Sè Township, Kayah Township. He resigned from this position a few months before the 2015 General Election, joined the NLD, and was subsequently elected as a representative in the election.

Following the NLD's assumption of power, Dr. Aung Kyaw Htay, a former assistant doctor at Loikaw State Hospital, emerged as a popular candidate for the post of prime minister of the state. However, some youths and armed ethnic groups in the state advocated for a local Kayah national to hold this position. As a result, Dr. Aung Kyaw Htay, who belonged to the Karen nationality and hailed from Kaw-Hmu Township, Yangon, was disqualified from the role. The decision was communicated to Daw Aung San Suu Kyi through state NLD leaders. Ultimately, L Paung Sho, another eligible candidate for the position, was appointed as chief minister.

Thirty-year-old political activist Khun A-than, who had been involved in Kayah State politics for over a decade, expressed his perspective on the matter: "From my viewpoint, the NLD had no alternative; L Paung Sho was the sole choice, whether one favoured him or not."

One intriguing aspect is the notion held by local people: "Only the local national is entitled to the post of chief minister." In a democratic system, the separation of powers into legislative, executive, and judicial branches is fundamental, with each branch playing an equally crucial role. However, a flaw in the 2008 Constitution is that civil politicians face more constraints in exercising authority over legislative and judicial matters, while there is a strong desire for executive power among all concerned authorities.

According to *Myanmar Now*, the emphasis on selecting a prime minister based on local nationality resulted in the appointment of L Paung Sho, of Shan-Kayah descent and a Christian, to the position. However, issues such as his perceived lack of political acumen left local nationals disillusioned with the NLD. Similarly, in Rakhine State, although the Arakan National Party secured votes in the majority of constituencies, the positions of Chairman and Vice-Chairman of the Rakhine State Hluttaw were filled by party members U San Kyaw Hla and U Phone

Min. Yet, the post of state prime minister was awarded to U Nyi Pu, from southern Rakhine State, elected by the NLD. This decision sparked anger among local Rakhines.

One weakness of the NLD lies in its failure to select the right person for the right position. A case in point is the chief minister of Kayah State, whose tenure came under scrutiny in early September 2020. President U Win Myint revoked L Paung Sho's appointment following accusations levelled against him during a session of the Kayah State Hluttaw. He was accused of leasing land designated for celebrating Kayah State Day to a private businessman, a plot previously approved by the Pyithu Hluttaw. Additionally, concerns were raised about the lack of transparency in machinery procurement.

The Hluttaw conducted a vote to determine whether L Paung Sho was fit to continue in his role, ultimately finding him unfit. This decision was endorsed by the President, making him the second chief minister to face action during the NLD government's term. The first was Chief Minister of Taninthayi Region, Dr. Le Le Maw, who faced legal action in March 2019. She was charged under Section 55 of the Anti-Corruption Law with multiple counts of corruption, including abusing her position to clear bushes at the airport compound. In May 2020, she was sentenced to thirty years imprisonment, and her property, including her residence in Thayet Chaung, was confiscated as state assets. Notably, she only became an NLD member in 2012, as evidenced by her biography.

In contrast to these representatives, the NLD members who endured years of arrest and torture under the military regime and subsequently became chief ministers of their states or regions included U Win Myint, Dr. Zaw Myint Maung, Dr. Myint Naing, Dr. Aung Moe Nyo, and Nan Khin Htwe Myint. Following the coup in 2021, these chief ministers were arrested and imprisoned. However, in line with the NLD's policy of "national reconciliation" and Daw Aung San Suu Kyi's directive to "Give priority to the Sculptors rather than the Woodcutters," many individuals retained their positions or were transferred to other departments.

Among these individuals were U Zaw Htay (Hmu Zaw), a former director and spokesperson under Thein Sein's government who actively promoted chauvinistic propaganda, and U Ti Khun Myat, known as the "opium king" and a member of the 2008 Constitution drafting commission. Others included retired Major Henry Van Htee Yu, retired Colonel Min Thu, U Kyaw Tint Swe, Dr. Thaung Tun, retired Colonel U Thein Swe, U Hla Maung Shwe, and their associates at the Union Peace Centre. Many perceived the NLD government's association with these figures, who were once adversaries, as akin to befriending a foe that ultimately betrays, like a serpent or adder.

The revelation that these former military personnel, ill-suited for their roles under the NLD government, remained in positions of influence further disappointed the Burmese people. The NLD's failure to appoint suitable individuals to key positions only compounded public disillusionment.

Karen/ Kayin

Another point of contention between the non-Bamar nationals and the NLD government emerged when the latter prohibited the celebration of Karen Martyrs' Day. An article from *Irrawaddy News*, dated September 29, 2019, highlighted that "Starting from 2018, tensions between the NLD government and non-Bamar nationals, particularly the Kayins, over the definition of the word 'martyrs' escalated significantly. The conflict stemmed notably from the annual ceremony commemorating the fallen Kayin leaders who perished while fighting for Karen State's autonomy. While the Karen nationals consider these fallen leaders as martyrs, the NLD government disapproved of such terminology."

On August 12, 2019, the Kayin Martyrs' Day was observed to honour fallen leaders, including Saw Ba Oo Gyi, the founder of the Karen National Union (KNU). However, Naw Ohn Hla, Saw Albert Cho, and Sa Thein Zaw Min, the organisers of this event, faced legal action by the Kyauktada Police Station for violating the Peaceful Assembly and Peaceful Procession Law. Notably, similar ceremonies had taken place in Yangon in 2014 and in Pha-An and other KNU-controlled territories in 2015. In 2019, the Minister for Kayin National Affairs, Ga Moe Myat Myat Thu (NLD) of the Ayeyawaddy Division Governing Body, issued a notification through the Kayin Literature and Culture Promotion Committee, banning the term "Kayin Martyrs' Day." Consequently, no memorial ceremonies were permitted at the column erected in honour of Saw Ba Oo Gyi in his native village, Bè Ga-yet, Pathein Township. Only tree-planting ceremonies were permitted as a form of commemoration. Requests for permission to hold similar ceremonies in Kamayut Township and Dagon New Town (East) Township in Yangon Division were denied by the Township General Administration Department. Another request to assemble and celebrate the ceremony in Bandoola Park, in front of Yangon City Hall, was granted on the condition that the term "The Karen Martyrs' Day" not be used. In contrast, ceremonies held in Pa-An and KNU-controlled territories proceeded smoothly without interference or disruption, as reported by *The Federal Journal*.

Ga Moe Myat Myat Thu clarified to *The Irrawaddy* that the phrase was banned to avoid confusion with independence heroes like Bogyoke Aung San, Mahn Ba Khaing, and the other seven martyrs. In a press conference dated September 13, U Zaw Htay, spokesman for the President's Office, stated that the protesters were arrested not for commemorating the Karen Martyrs' Day, but for violating the Peaceful Assembly and Peaceful Procession Law.

The social-based groups and national political parties, along with their allies, demanded the dismissal of the case and the release of the detainees. The KNU-Concerned, led by former KNU Vice-Chairperson Naw Ci Pora Sein, issued a warning: if the government did not comply with the demand, the entire Karen social community would launch a national campaign, holding the government responsible for the ensuing consequences. General Secretary Padoh Saw Tardo Hmu, in an interview with The Irrawaddy, emphasised that the Burmese government and the majority Bamar population should recognize the national identities, cultures, and literatures of ethnic minorities, or at the very least show an interest in their concerns. The columnist of the article also noted that other armed ethnic groups, observing the treatment of the Karens, would be cautious, as any inequality or attempts to erase their history could lead to hesitation in signing the Nationwide Ceasefire Agreement (NCA).

One intriguing observation is the contrasting reactions among government departments regarding the celebration of the Karen Martyrs' Day. The Minister for Kayin National Affairs, a Karen woman, expressed concern over the use of a particular term. While the Township General Administration Department in Yangon Division granted permission for a peaceful assembly, it also restricted the use of that term and took legal action for its breach. Conversely, the Karen State Governing Body, led by Nan Khin Htway Myint, also a Karen woman and a member of the NLD, authorised the celebration of Karen Martyrs' Day, with the cooperation of the Pha-An General Administration Department. This discrepancy in responses within the same government ministry highlighted a lack of clear policy regarding non-Bamar national affairs by the NLD. Consequently, both the Karen people and political activists were left disappointed with the NLD's handling of the situation.

Altogether, it can be assumed that since there were quite a number of non-Bamars as members of the NLD, the party believed it had already embodied the concept of a union party. Consequently, it failed to regard other political parties formed by ethnic groups as representing their respective communities. The trouble with these ethnic group parties was that one group often had three or four factions, mirroring the armed ethnic groups that harboured multiple armies within a single ethnic group, each with its own policies and procedures based on battalions and brigades. Naturally, the NLD came to conceive of itself as the sole party comprising various nationals and representing the interests of all communities.

Meanwhile, those advocating for the causes of their respective communities, including parties and armed ethnic groups, were weak in assessing the role of ethnic groups within the NLD. Instead, they attempted to emphasise their own roles as representatives of entire ethnic groups. In this situation, the military continued to mutter, likely driven by some ulterior motive: "The political parties and organisations of the national races represent only their supporters, while the Tatmadaw represents the people of the whole country." Nevertheless, it showed no sign of relinquishing its political leadership role.

Hence, it must be emphasised that civilian organisations paid more attention to topics such as the spirit of unity and the identity of the nation, while politicians were primarily concerned with the triangle of race, territory, and power. It is no wonder that to ordinary people, the concept of politics, as labyrinthine as a Maze, has remained a constant throughout history.

Wall:

The Walls of Maze 2019-2020

Rakhine

On the morning of January 4, 2019, approximately 100 soldiers of the Arakan Army launched a coordinated attack on four police outpost stations in Butheetaung Township. This sparked a new armed conflict that spread to Kyauk Taw, Mrauk Oo, Min Pya, Ponna-kyun, Butheetaung, Yathe Taung, and Mye Pon Townships, as well as Paletwa Township in the Chin State. Border guard forces, including the Maung Taw border guard police outpost, Than Taung Police Station, Yoe-tayoke Police Station, Okkpho and Nyaung Chaung police stations, and Lay Nyin Taung temporary police station, were targeted. Policemen were assassinated, and fatalities resulted from bomb blasts. Additionally, the AA detained local administrators, members of the fire brigades, and office staff.

According to the state-owned Kye Mon newspaper issued on November 1, 2019, the AA arrested 82 civilians. Conversely, the military also detained local civilians, including the Commander-in-Chief of the AA, Gen. Tun Myat Naing's wife, two children, brother, sister, and brother-in-law. Shells from heavy artillery exploded in villages where no clashes had occurred, resulting in numerous casualties and injuries. However, neither the military nor the AA admitted responsibility for these incidents.

The clashes resulted in the cancellation of several regional projects, including the Kaladan Multi-modal Transit Transport project, a US $484 million initiative slated for completion by 2020. This project encompassed the construction of the Kaladan Bridge in Palwetwa Town, Chin State, an area largely under the control of the AA. The disruption caused distress among local Chins, leading to the near suspension of the project.

However, the state's second special economic zone, part of the One Belt One Road (OBOR) initiative, also known as China's Modern Silk Road, remained unaffected by the clashes. The Kyaukphyu Special Economic Zone (Kyaukphyu SEZ) continued without interruption, as it did not fall within the conflict zone. China proceeded with its project in this area. The Commander-in-Chief of the AA stated, "We have no objections to the projects of China at all."

Among the detainees abducted by the AA on November 3, 2019, were Chin State Upper House lawmaker U Whei Tin of the NLD, a representative of No. 11 election region in Paletwa Township, and five Indians. Sadly, one Indian engineer died of a heart attack, while the others were eventually released. U Whei Tin regained freedom on January 21, 2020. Tensions between the NLD and the AA had been escalating since early 2019.

In Yathetaung, a literary talk ceremony was held commemorating the Fall of the Sovereignty of the Rakhine State. During this event, Representative of Un Township Dr. Aye Maung and Writer Wai Hin Aung expressed support for the armed revolution. Consequently, they faced legal action under Section 112 (Offences against the State: High Treason) and Section 505 (b) (Statements conducing to public mischief) and were sentenced to twenty years' imprisonment by the Sittwe District Court on March 19, 2019. While political prisoner activists argued for their classification as political prisoners, Dr. Myo Nyunt, the NLD spokesman, stated, "Since these two speakers advocated for confederate-status Arakan State, if they are punished, they will not be considered political prisoners but criminals breaching the penal code," as reported in the article "2019 khu-nit a-twet A-htoochar-son Rakhine Pyi-ne" by *Mizzima News*.

Starting from June 1, 2019, internet connections were severed in nine townships spanning the Rakhine State and the Chin State. Although connections were eventually restored in most areas, four townships remained disconnected for over a year. Since November 2018, the NLD government had established a social media monitoring team, allocating a budget of MMK 600 million. Consequently, civilian organisations began to perceive the internet shutdown as an act of digital totalitarianism.

On November 11, 2019, the UN's International Court of Justice (ICJ) informed the Myanmar government that it "has jurisdiction under the Genocide Convention to hear the application filed by The Gambia against Myanmar." In response, Daw Aung San Suu Kyi declared her intention to appear at the ICJ in The Hague. This announcement drew both supporters and dissenters. NLD offices organised gatherings to express support for Daw Aung San Suu Kyi's decision. However, amidst preparations for one such assembly, U Yè Thein, Chairman of the NLD in Butheetaung Township, was abducted by the AA on December 11, 2019, amid a dispute between the AA and the military.

On December 25, the AA released a statement claiming that U Yè Thein had been killed in a clash with the military. A *Mizzima News* article reported on the dispute that arose between the AA and the military regarding the death of the NLD Chairman. The AA stated to the media, "The Tatmadaw fired heavy artillery, and U Yè Thein was killed. His body was mutilated, so we buried him. No photos of his body will be released." Conversely, Brigadier General Zaw Min Tun, Secretary of the Tatmadaw True News Information Team, informed the media on the same day, "We have received information from local sources indicating that U Yè Thein was killed not by the Tatmadaw's heavy artillery explosion, but rather, as a detainee of the AA, he was tortured and killed."

In her defence of Myanmar at the ICJ, Daw Aung San Suu Kyi's stance was perceived by civilian activists as aligning with the military. This perception was shared by many local Rakhines, who believed that the NLD government and the military were closely linked. During the General Election held in November 2020, the majority of votes in Rakhine State were cancelled under the pretext of security concerns. Even during the ceasefire period in Rakhine State, elections were not reinstated. Just before the election, three NLD representatives were abducted by the AA.

Regarding the AA's position on the General Election, the Commander-in-Chief of the AA stated in an interview with *The Irrawaddy*: "The Myanmar government should engage in negotiations with us. Our people want the General Election, so if the Government genuinely wants it to happen, they should negotiate with us." He also expressed the AA's goals, saying, "Like the Wa State, we prefer a confederation where state power is distributed among the states because it aligns with the needs, history, and expectations of the Rakhine people." Regarding economic plans in Rakhine State and Chin (Paletwa) State, he stated, "They must pay taxes to our ULA (United League of Arakan). This is non-negotiable. No tax, no permission, to be frank. While we haven't established the Arakan Government yet, we are going to establish the Arakan People's Governing Body."

Shortly after the military's attempted coup in 2021, the Commander-in-Chief remarked on the NLD and the military, stating, "Formerly, our foes were united. Now they are two distinct hostile parties fighting against each other. Both sides expect us to join their ranks."

A closer examination of these events reveals that the Rakhine crisis extends beyond the interests of the Rakhine people; it has become intertwined with China's economic interests. The NLD Government's failure to comprehend the longstanding complexities, disputes, and animosities between the Rakhine and the Bamar, as well as between the military and the Arakan Army, has exacerbated the situation. Instead of addressing the underlying issues, the NLD government focused solely on addressing immediate causes. Thus, the Rakhine crisis has remained a convoluted issue in the Maze of country's political landscape for decades.

Corner:

"The Horror! The Horror!"

"I've slay'd twenty-six guys!"
"How?"
"What d'you say?"
"You says you've kill'd twenty-six fellas, but how? By gun?"
"Nope. I pull'd de trigger, ya know. Not with my hands."
"Me? I cut de throat!"
"Cut de throat? Yep, I also done dat, man. A lot."
"Me? Just five in number. Just five, man."
"Me? I ain't done nothing like that."
"I'm scar'd!" (mimicking a timid voice of a girl) "I'm scar'd!" "Ha… ha… ha…"
"Eight. Ya know dat? Eight already, man."
"I'm tellin' de truth. I ever kill'd, but not as many as you done, Big Brother. I am disgust'd with de blood. I kill, but I hate to see de blood, dat smelly blood!"
"Chopp'd into three parts. Then … over there. The battalion commander says…"
"Yep, you're right. I said I'm disgust'd"
"Yesterday I whack'd dose guys. I whack'd de guys I caught hold of. De battalion commander in wildin says, 'Sergeant, wud you care to chop three parts n bury in the ground right away, will you?' Yep, dat's what he says."
"What happen'd when you chopp'd? Flesh slippin' out? Why not sell 'em for de pork offal skewers?"
"Something yellowish? Yep, yellowish."
"You means you never seen dat before?"
"Yep. Never seen dat before."
"Chop, chop, chop, chop. Four, five or six chops. Then I buri'd 'em in

de ground."

"His head blown up, ya know. When I took off his Paso, even de flesh got peel'd off. What a charred body! Very disappoint' Flesh all torn out, ya know."

"Well, if ya need this, why not raid the houses in the village? I hope ya hav this."

"I'll slaughter a pig if ya want to eat pork. Or I ain't mind havin' a slingshot catch of the villagers' fowls."

"Ya don't believe me? Come n see. I am a killer expert, ya know. Since I was a boy, I had the killer spirit, killin' others. But, mind, I ain't want a prickin' of my flesh."

Disgusting oily faces. Quite sickening to hear the way they were talking to each other. This would remind you of the famous quote from *Gregory David Roberts' Shantaram*: "Cruelty is a kind of cowardice. Cruel laughter is the way cowards cry…" It is a video clip of nearly 10 minutes. In the video, three SAC soldiers were sitting by a building, taking a live selfie video, having a chat in a leisurely manner: the fair-complexioned guy, with a cropped haircut, taking the selfie video, wearing a bulletproof vest; the one with a moustache, also with a cropped haircut, sitting in the middle, dressed in an ordinary, long-sleeved shirt; and the dark-skinned soldier wearing the military uniform, with a corporal badge on his arm.

The armed SAC forces have committed, and continue to commit, atrocious cruelties and violence in the upcountry regions. A local man from A-yadaw Township accidentally picked up the mobile phone belonging to one of those three soldiers. In the gallery, 144 photos were found, including a video file taken by the phone's owner. Among the photos were selfies taken by the owner with other soldiers. The local man sent the video file and the photos to the RFA. The RFA news announced the information about one photo showing "a group of about thirty villagers, hands tied behind their backs, forced to gather underneath a teak monastery with wooden poles." A closer look at one photo shows two SAC soldiers standing by the bodies of five blindfolded locals, who are dressed in ordinary clothes with their hands tied behind their back, shot dead in the back of the head, all lying in pools of blood.

An examination of the badge on the military uniform and the headstamp on the stock of their rifles, which were standing against the wall of the building, shows that these soldiers served in battalion No. 708 Light Infantry troop under the Sagaing Division-based North West Division Command and the Yangon-based No. 4 Operation Supervision Headquarters. The photos depicting scenes of stark atrocities provide evidence that they were taken between April 13 and June 3, capturing the ruthless interrogations and tortures by the military.

In Mon Taing Pin Village, Ye Oo Township, a massacre of thirteen local villagers took place between May 10 and 13. While it cannot be conclusively proven that these photos provide evidence of the terrible tragedy, some local people have confirmed that the monastery depicted in the photos is indeed the Mon Taing Pin Monastery. What the photos and the video file reveal is that the SAC soldiers have recorded their acts of violence with unsatiating pleasure and in a cowardly manner! Previously, the hearts of the Burmese people were filled with empathy toward the soldiers, viewing them as poor stooges forced to commit war crimes under the commands of the megalomaniac SAC generals. Consequently, efforts were made to persuade the soldiers to prioritise the interests of the public over their military service. However, after witnessing their true colours and other evidence of the harsh realities, the people have become thoroughly disgusted with all soldiers, as well as the police force. They now refer to them as "the Military Dogs" and "the Police Dog." The Burmese people, along with other nationals, are resolute in their belief that only by dismantling the military can the injustices and tortures inflicted upon the people of Burma come to an end. They envision a future federal democratic Union where only a federal Tatmadaw exists, one that abides by rules of conduct inclusive of all nationals and safeguards the interests and security of its citizens.

Firearms indeed have the capacity to erode the virtues of humanity. While the people support the People's Defense Forces (PDFs), who are fighting against the military with the aim of dismantling it, it is true that, due to misinformation and potentially other factors, there have been instances where some PDF members have made mistakes by killing innocent individuals in certain regions, whom they accused of being decoys or informants for the military. On June 21, 2022, the National Unity Government (NUG) announced in a press conference that several complaints had been received regarding PDFs targeting the wrong individuals (over 50 cases submitted to the Ministry of Judicial Affairs and over a hundred cases submitted to the Ministry of Home Affairs under the NUG), and that action was being taken against the defendants. This has sparked apprehension among some members of the public. While the public understands that the NUG is endeavouring to integrate all the various armed revolutionary forces that have emerged independently, without a systematic network of connections and coordination, many still believe that military informers should not be murdered, but instead dealt with through legal channels. They express deep concern that such extrajudicial killings of adversaries could tarnish the reputation of the Spring Revolution.

The atrocities committed by the SAC forces had become increasingly intolerable. It became evident to the people that there were individuals acting as decoys or informants for the SAC forces, and their identities had been exposed. These decoys, through leaked information, enabled the SAC to launch attacks, make arrests, and subject revolutionary comrades to torture and execution, resulting in the loss of hundreds of innocent lives. This sparked a shift in mindset among the people, who recognized the urgent need to halt the ruthless actions of the SAC forces, likened to unleashed hounds, and to retaliate against the SAC's decoys and their staunch supporters in order to safeguard the safety and security of the populace. Ultimately, akin to eradicating lice that feed on human blood, the campaign to eliminate the decoys was initiated. Consequently, in certain areas, local residents lived in fear due to threats from both sides of the armed conflict.

The NUG announced that, in order to address cases involving accusations against certain PDFs for unlawful killings, a judicial board of judges had been established in 15 townships in Sagaing Division, which are now under the rule of law. This board was formed on May 19, and preparations were being made, including the construction of prisons, for detaining defendants during the interrogation process. The Ministry of Judicial Affairs of the NUG issued a statement declaring that action would be taken against certain members of the group led by Bo Thanmani, also known as U Sopāka, of Yinmabin Township, for the murder of their fellow warriors. However, there were criticisms directed at the NUG for the delay in addressing this case.

Currently, there are local people's defence forces, or allied forces, operating in coordination with the NUG. However, there have also been reports of armed groups claiming to be PDFs engaging in robbery and looting against civilians. In response, the NUG has announced the establishment of a warrior code for PDFs under its system to adhere to. Additionally, rules have been enacted to safeguard innocent civilians, who are not intended targets. The NUG has stated that action will be taken against those who violate the code and rules. Furthermore, should any armed groups outside of its system breach the warrior code and civilian protection rules, they will also be subject to prosecution under the NUG's judicial system.

However, there are also individuals who support the assassination of SAC decoys, members of the USDP, and local administrators whom they believe to be collaborating with the SAC. Consequently, a prevailing narrative emerged: the armed revolution, purportedly in defence of the Spring Revolution, is merely a cycle of violence where both sides seize any opportunity to eliminate each other. Particularly concerning is the targeting of well-known peace advocates with international experience, who have been vocal in the international community. These advocates issued a statement to the SAC demanding increased security measures, seemingly presenting it as evidence to the international community that the Spring Revolution, NUG, and PDF have resorted to revolutionary terrorism.

However, this statement has its flaws: it lacks concrete evidence and fails to mention any acts of violence perpetrated by the SAC, which has not adhered to the rule of law. Consequently, many supporters of the Spring Revolution were astonished by the political stance and judgement of these experienced peace advocates. In some countries, especially in Asia, there was a misinterpretation that the NUG's decision to launch the armed revolution signalled an abandonment of nonviolent revolution. Meanwhile, unlawful killings continue to occur unchecked. On June 30, the NUG clarified that there is no sanctioned scheme for assassination against those who hold differing views.

From the public's perspective, the brutal killings committed by the SAC forces, as depicted in the video clip aired by the RFA, have gone unpunished because those responsible know they will not face consequences, but rather be rewarded for their actions. Essentially, the message trickling down from the military dictator to every level of the military hierarchy was: "The more heinous the act, the more commendable." This message, supported by evidence, has reached the ears of international journalists and many foreign governments. However, as the SAC has managed to sway the international community to some extent, the focus has shifted towards portraying the comrades of the Spring Revolution as disregarding the norms of the warrior code, rather than addressing the ongoing war crimes committed by the SAC.

AK Moeller, a doctoral student in the Department of Geography at the National University of Singapore, penned an article on June 17, 2022, titled "The International Community Needs to Prepare for a Post-Tatmadaw Myanmar." In the article, Moeller advocated for proactive planning for a scenario where the military no longer holds dominant political power in Burma. This would involve deeper engagement with democratic opposition forces, building diplomatic coalitions supporting a new federal charter, and increasing humanitarian aid.

This pragmatic approach to Burma's political crisis resonated with the people, offering a glimmer of hope. They desire empathy and kindness from the international community, regardless of whether aid is provided.

Despite enduring acts of violence and political manoeuvring, the people of Burma remain resilient, steadfastly preserving their human dignity to the best of their abilities.

Corner:

Executions and the Deaths of Heroes

"Only the player who plays a fair game must win the game."

This was the message sent from Jimmy to the military dictators who, always following the practices of injustice, could snatch the Flower of Victory only with the abuse of power.

"He says everything happens in the chain of cause of effect, he does meditation, and his Dhamma is with him always. He also says, 'Don't worry about me whatever news you hear. Take good care of your health.' This is a message from him."

Jimmy delivered this message during a Zoom meeting with his family on July 22, 2022, just one day before news broke that he had been executed by hanging.

So, what is his Dhamma? What did he mean?

"My sweetheart Nya Yee Hnin and I
Always avoid the Games, 'The Flying Fish' and 'The Fish Traps'
But move along calmly, like the Water Hyacinths.
No desire to cause wounds,
But display our archery skills just to hit the target.
Everything is free from pains,
It's a happy night with the smiling Moon.
May the miserable Past be forgotten,
May the Blessings descend on the Present,
And the Future."
Jimmy

This excerpt is from his poem "A Prayer on a Moonlit Night." Jimmy and his wife Nilar Thein, who goes by the pen name Nya Yee Hnin, collaborated on a book of poems titled *Hnalone-thway Gita Chit-thu nè Kyama* (*Poems: Of Me and the Lover of Heartblood Music*). The line "No desire to cause wounds" reflects his "Dhamma," or his moral principles. The following line also suggests his belief in archery skills that hit the target without causing harm. Despite having been wounded himself, he must have relied on his archery skills. He attempted to banish the painful past from his memory, but it has resurfaced, haunting the people of Burma, including himself. "You know, my dear," he then said to his wife, his lifelong companion, "my heart ached to see young people, the age of our son and daughter, marching at the forefront and getting shot in the head. I am past fifty. Happy to die. I'll stay AG, instead of UG, and escalate my actions, doing whatever I could. I am happy to die in my boots."

Since the evening of June 24, rumours circulated that Jimmy and Phyo Zeyar Thaw were slated for execution by hanging. During an early June press conference, General Zaw Min Tun, the SAC spokesperson nicknamed "Mr. Black Rolly-Polly," mentioned that action would be taken "according to the decree already made" (by the judge or the Commander-in-Chief?). However, according to existing rules and regulations, the process of executing an inmate by hanging involves several steps: first, the President must grant permission to proceed with legal proceedings, followed by a last-minute opportunity for the inmate to see their family and say prayers in the presence of a Buddhist monk, obtaining a health certificate, and various other procedural steps. Often, circumstances arise where the punishment of death is commuted to life imprisonment for the majority of criminals. Some people believe that the execution of Jimmy and Phyo Zeyar Thaw by hanging has not yet occurred.

During a Zoom meeting with his family on July 22, which lasted about twenty minutes, Phyo Zeyar Thaw even asked his mother to bring him some necessary personal items on her next prison visit. However, the families involved were not informed of the exact date when the execution by hanging would take place. Furthermore, if the executions had indeed occurred, the bodies of these two activists were not returned to their families.

"The decree confirms the death penalty," Phyo Zeyar Thaw's mother calmly informed a young female journalist. "As for when? Well, they said it may be either Saturday or Sunday. They claim they can't disclose the exact date. I asked the authorities to inform me of the exact date so that our family could have monks say prayers and share merit for the departed. But they rejected my request. They said returning a dead body to the bereaved family was not part of the plan. Well, I gave up. It was his destiny. He was meant to meet his end like that, I suppose. You know the situation, don't you?"

Phyo Zeyar Thaw's mother, a doctor, impressed the public with her resilience in the face of her son's tragedy. Her calm demeanour during the interview revealed the SAC's deep animosity towards the two activists, highlighting the public's fear as authorities refused to disclose the execution details. The old lady exemplifies support for justice, her courage and stoic determination garnering empathy and admiration.

The news sent shockwaves through the international community, eliciting deep concern and objections. With Jimmy's family denied his body for a proper burial and provided no details of his death, they declared they would not hold any merit-sharing ceremony, essentially refusing to acknowledge Jimmy's death.

"What I love is the Truth;
What I hate is war;
What I am hungry for is Peace;
What I've been journeying
is through the War of Morale;
What I breathe in is Veracity."
Nya Yee Hnin

In her poem "My Agony in My Lover's Arms," Jimmy's wife Nilar Thein (pen name Nya Yee Hnin) highlighted her "Dhamma." She entrusted her ten-year-old daughter to her parents' care, while she herself, situated in a liberated area, engaged in battles of both physical and mental prowess. Here, she fought for the truth she cherished and the sustainable, genuine peace she fervently desired.

On July 23, 2022, Jimmy, known as Ko Kyaw Min Yu, Zeyar Thaw, known as Ko Phyo Zeyar Thaw, Ko Hla Myo Aung, and Ko Aung Thura, were executed by hanging on charges of "terrorism." Among these men, the former two were celebrities, prompting news agencies to conduct interviews with their grieving families. The tragic news reverberated both locally and abroad.

Yet, this does not mark the culmination of the injustice perpetrated by the SAC and its cohorts.

Around 1:15 pm on July 27, a group of thugs associated with the SAC, disguised in civilian attire, congregated in front of the residences of Jimmy and Zeyar Thaw in Insein Township and Kyauktada Township. These individuals, known colloquially as "nga-htaung-sar" or paid hooligans, engaged in a barrage of misconduct: hurling curses, crafting slingshots, and pelting the houses with stones and rotten eggs. They arrived purposefully in light trucks, causing damage not only to the targeted residences but also to neighbouring buildings, including the windows of an adjacent apartment and a bank, which were shattered. This wanton violence was carried out under the pretext of "Down with the Terrorists!" Yet no measures were taken against these perpetrators. In essence, those responsible for inflicting grave injustice upon the populace have abused their authority and undermined the rule of law. It is no wonder that the sentiment expressed in Jimmy's poem, "Only the player who plays a fair game must win the Game," continues to reverberate, haunting the SAC's memory.

"Did you say, 'Whoever wins the game
Has played the game fair and square'?
Do you think bullets can write history?
Mind, you'll get your so-called Justice
Only when the Student Generations have run out.

"Did you say, 'Whoever wins the game

Has played the game fair and square'?
Do you think cannons can write history?
Mind, you'll get your so-called History
Only when the raindrops from the sky have gone dry.

"No! Only the player who plays a fair game
Must win the Game!"

Passage:

Youths and Armed Forces

"You know, even the King of Celestials can't stop us from fighting back the army, for if the King of Celestials should abet the army, we'd shoot him down!," remarked a dark-skinned girl who had not yet reached the age of sixteen. Hailing from an upcountry town, she sported a ponytail and was clad in a blue tracksuit, black jacket, cap, and a mask covering her mouth, with dangling ear drops. A photograph on the Public Spring Web page captured a moment where a PDF officer awarded the Most Outstanding Trainee Award to this young girl. Referred to as "95" in an article detailing her life, this designation was her enrollment serial number. Her modest home, constructed in the upcountry architectural style, appeared rather dilapidated, featuring a spacious platform and minimal furnishings—a single bedroom for the entire family and a small cupboard inside. Despite earning the Most Outstanding Trainee Award from the PDF, "95" is presently not engaged in warfare but lives a civilian life at home, sustaining herself through traditional loom weaving.

At the training completion ceremony, she strode across the training ground, saluted the PDF flag, and accepted the award, displaying all the manners of a true military woman. "This girl is outstanding in all aspects of the training," remarked a veteran who conducted the military training. "You see, she ranks first in obeying orders, possesses the best stamina, and when it comes to shooting practice, nobody can beat her. Imagine how strong her enthusiasm is! This training is typically for young men with strong builds, but I was so impressed by this girl! She truly deserves the award!"

Regarding the recruitment process for the armed forces, the National Unity Government issued a statement emphasising that children under the age of 18 should not be enlisted as revolutionary soldiers. However, the trainer raised a pertinent question, stating, "Do you think those 'Fascist forces' would show compassion to kids under 18 when they enter a village?" He argued that young women require military training to protect their communities, as obedience to commands enables them to defend villages and relocate to safer areas if necessary. Guidelines for protecting children during armed conflicts were issued on March 4, 2022. Nevertheless, villagers remained concerned about the irrational violence perpetrated by military council members. Having experienced a raid on her village by soldiers, the girl nicknamed "95" decided to undergo military training to defend herself and protect the elderly. When she received information about the military training to be conducted in her village while holding a sickle to cut peanut beds, she made the decision to enrol immediately. In fact, she was the only person at home capable of providing protection to her family.

The end of the article is fascinating.

"I was lost in gazing at the little girl, Comrade 95, working at her loom in a small compound in the upcountry region. In our interview, she said, full of enthusiasm, that the military training was not as much exhausting as transplanting in the paddy fields, that she would not mind carrying out the duties of intelligence corps or the duties of the department of supply and transport and that if she had reached the age eligible for recruitment, she would join the armed revolutionary force, known as PDF (People Defense Force). To my question, 'What have you got for the most outstanding award?', she smiled and said, 'It's a torch light.'"

*

"I wish my parents would never have to endure the pain of having a son like me in the afterlife," said Maung San Min Paing, his voice heavy with sorrow and grief.

As the youngest son of the family, he had fled his home to join the armed revolution. However, he was apprehended in August 2021 and, due to his age of seventeen, was sent to the Thanlyin Boys' Training School, a facility designated for rehabilitating juvenile delinquents. During his detention, his mother managed to visit him in prison, while his father was taken to an army interrogation centre and subsequently fell ill, becoming practically bedridden.

On September 23, 2022, a group of fourteen detainees, all charged with active involvement in political movements, successfully executed a prison break. Among them was seventeen-year-old San Min Paing. "That day, members of the state administration council combed through the entire town of Thanlyin, going door to door and showing photos of the detainees to the public in their hunt for the escaped convicts," reported BBC News.

Fortunately, they managed to reach the "Liberated Area." In an interview with BBC News, San Min Paing recounted the tragic events: "On September 29, 2000, a friend from my neighbourhood called to deliver devastating news about my parents. 'Don't panic, buddy,' he said over the phone. 'A few cars arrived, carrying those brutal soldiers and Pyu Saw Htees (military supporters). They stormed into your house and opened fire. When they left, the neighbours checked and found your mom and dad lying dead in pools of blood.'"

Explaining further, he added, "They shouted, 'This is revenge!' It happened to coincide with the murder of the quarter administrator and his wife in South Dagon Quarter No. 25 that morning. They falsely implicated me in that case." His parents, U San Myint and Daw Thi Thi Soe, both aged 58, were fatally shot. Due to the oppressive military presence, their funeral was conducted discreetly, devoid of any ceremony.

It is crucial to highlight that during the people's armed revolution, the military itself has been responsible for such heinous crimes across the country. Until the state administration council ceases its indiscriminate killing of innocent civilians, how can we hope to achieve community peace?

"About a month before I made the prison break, I lost contact with my family, and I was deeply traumatised," expressed Maung San Min Paing, his voice heavy with sorrow. "Having run away from home to join the revolution, I now have no place to return to. My father and mother were killed because of me, and I'm too afraid to face my brother and sister. I fear I may never see them again in my lifetime."

"I deeply regret shattering my father's dreams," he continued, his heart heavy with guilt. "I wish they had not given birth to a son like me. They should have had a daughter like my sister, who dutifully honoured our parents, or a son like my brother, who excels academically. I pray that in their afterlife, they may be blessed with better children."

His words serve as a stark warning, revealing the mental wounds inflicted upon Myanmar's youth as they march towards an uncertain future. Their hearts are burdened with sorrow and regret.

"Our enemies are revealing their true colours, but we must persevere," declared Maung San Min Paing with conviction. "Despite the loss of my parents and the ruin of my life, my determination to fight against military dictatorship remains unwavering!" Now in the Liberation Territory, his resolve burns brighter than ever.

As the news concludes, the echoes of resentment, bitterness, and fury reverberate throughout Myanmar's society, a testament to the enduring struggles faced by its people.

*

"My name is Sarah. I graduated from the University of Monywa in 2012, with a major in Chemistry. In 2014, I began my career as a school teacher. However, when the military coup occurred in 2021, I made the decision not to continue my service under the military regime and joined the Civil Disobedience Movement (CDM)."

"My brother is currently serving in the army. From a young age, due to our family's financial struggles, he enlisted to support our family. He now holds the position of corporal in Thayawaddy Light Infantry Battalion 35, based in Bago Division. I owe him a debt of gratitude for his sacrifices as a soldier, which allowed me to pursue a university education and become a teacher."

"It's a painful truth that the military has ruthlessly set fire to many villages, including ours. On that tragic day, our village was engulfed in flames, and we lost our home. I hoped this news would change my brother's perspective, so I shared it with him. However, he responded, 'There's nothing we can do! Why are the houses being set on fire? It's your fault!'"

"He believes, 'We're just doing our job, and those who interfere have chosen the wrong side.' That's what he said."

"Currently, as far as I know, he's engaged in operations around Myaung Town, so I can still reach him and speak to him over the phone. During our conversation, he told me, 'Mind your own business, Sis. Don't involve yourself in matters that don't concern you.' I responded, 'I've chosen to get involved because I believe this is a matter of great concern to me and everyone else. You're following your path because you believe it's the right one. If our forces ever clash (God forbid it!), shoot me if you're quick enough, Bro. And I'll have to shoot at you if I'm quick enough. From that point on, our relationship as siblings is gone.' He stubbornly continues on his chosen path, breaking our parents' hearts. It's agonising to imagine the pain our parents must endure, powerless to steer their son away from the wrong path."

"Their behaviour is utterly rude and leaves one speechless. If they were truly brave, they wouldn't destroy or even touch the property of innocent people. Their fighting strength is dwindling, relying solely on their air force and heavy artillery for destructive power. What a foolish notion! They persistently believe they'll win by setting fire to people's property. In contrast, our people are focused solely on achieving victory in this revolution. They're undeterred by personal losses or property damage. That's the difference."

Yes, indeed, there are countless divided narratives in the upcountry regions of Myanmar, such as the divisions within families, between siblings, and between generations who have chosen divergent paths–some in support of the SAC and others in opposition to it. The SAC's military, formerly known as the army of the Bamars or the Myanmar army, historically recruited heavily from the youth in these upcountry regions. The personal account of Sara, a teacher involved in the CDM movement, illustrates how her brother serves as living proof of the SAC's powerful influence, which has effectively brainwashed many young soldiers and led to the ruin of their once-innocent hearts.

*

Daw Yati Ohn, the former head and lecturer of Kalay Technical High School, recounted a deeply sorrowful incident during an interview with BBC News. She described attending the funeral of one of her students, a young boy who had not yet reached the age of eighteen. She expressed profound grief over his untimely death, noting that he died as a fallen hero. Despite her efforts to reach him in time, she arrived too late, and there was no medic available for immediate treatment. She emphasised the heartbreak of witnessing his funeral and the loss of such a promising young life.

In response to the challenges faced in the frontline regions, Daw Yati Ohn established a healthcare organisation called the Mobile Medical Team West Division. This team focuses on providing first aid, arranging transportation to advanced medical facilities, and conducting health checks at sentry posts. Before the military coup, Daw Yati Ohn volunteered at a COVID-19 quarantine centre in Kalay, after obtaining permission from the Ministry of Health. She also led health education campaigns during peaceful protests, emphasising the importance of measures like handwashing and mask-wearing.

As the situation escalated and defence posts were established, Daw Yati Ohn continued her humanitarian efforts by visiting these posts at night, flying a Red Cross flag. She provided medical services, distributed food, and offered spiritual support to the sentrymen, demonstrating unwavering dedication to the well-being of her community amidst challenging circumstances.

Despite facing immense challenges, including shortages of funds and resources, the young people were determined to fight against the SAC and attempted to invent gunpowder weapons on their own. Tragically, some lost their lives in accidents caused by explosions during this process. Daw Yati Ohn attributed these incidents to the lack of financial resources, which forced them to use poor-quality materials for their inventions.

She also recounted a particularly harrowing experience during the Kyauk Pyoke Battle, which took place on a full moon night during the Thadingyut season. The Myit Thar River was swollen due to high floodwaters, complicating efforts to transport a severely wounded patient to safety. Despite the challenges, they managed to save the patient's life, albeit with the loss of one of his legs due to severe injuries.

Throughout her interview, Daw Yati Ohn remained composed and articulate, providing a detailed depiction of the harsh realities faced by revolutionary soldiers. Despite being cornered by some interview questions, she maintained a polite demeanour, highlighting the resilience and determination of those fighting against the SAC despite the adversities they encountered.

*

Dr. Kaung Htet, a young man in his early 30s, expressed his firm resolve to never return to his previous life and to continue his underground activities as a guerrilla fighter for the PDF. Despite his youthful vigour, he displayed a maturity beyond his years as he discussed his motivations and principles.

Rejecting the notion that being armed with a gun grants one the right to do as they please, Dr. Kaung Htet invoked Hammurabi's code, emphasising a principle of proportional retaliation: "If you hit me, I'll hit you." He was adamant about protecting the lives of innocent unarmed people and vowed not to let their lives be destroyed in vain.

Dr. Kaung Htet hailed from a middle-class family in Yangon, with his father being a retired Major from the Directorate of Military Engineers (Field). Tragically, his father was arrested by the military and subsequently died under interrogation. The military's callous response, offering a perfunctory apology and denying the family the opportunity to claim his father's body, added to Dr. Kaung Htet's determination to continue his resistance against the oppressive regime.

Despite facing personal loss and adversity, Dr. Kaung Htet remained resolute in his commitment to the cause of the PDF and the fight for justice and freedom in Myanmar.

In 2022, the SAC learned that Dr. Kaung Htet had joined Operation

Cobra. Subsequently, the military took his mother to an interrogation centre, blaming her for failing to control her son. Unfortunately, she died during interrogation on May 1. Dr. Kaung Htet was informed of her death the following day. The military reported that she died from a blood clot in the brain.

"I received a picture of her dead body. My younger brother is also active as a UG. He got the news, but they didn't return our mother's body. Now my grandma is sick, bedridden," Dr. Kaung Htet said calmly. His real-life stories are heartrending and may seem unbelievable if not recounted in an interview or in black and white.

"I had the chance to see my mom when she visited Myawaddy, a border town between Burma and Mae Sot in Thailand," he recalled. "She said, 'Take care, Son.' She was pleased to see me again, saying, 'You are my eldest son, and you are a doc. I'm proud of you, Son.' And we exchanged smiles. Before she passed away, we sometimes spoke on the phone. In our conversations, she always wished me good health." His voice carried a sense of pathos. It is a universal truth that no matter how strong one's spirit is, the loving kindness of parents can soften the heart like the petals of a flower.

"My brother is a major serving in the military, stationed at the headquarters of the Yangon Division. His wife is the niece of a VIP in Naypyidaw. When our parents died, I had a conversation with my brother. He accused me of being the cause of our parents' death. And that was the end of the relationship between the two brothers," he said, his tone casual but revealing the underlying tension and coldness of the dialogue.

"On the first day of being employed as a doctor, I was so happy, you know. I thought I could save lives. I was appointed to May Dha Wi Hospital, not far from my home, so it was convenient for me," said the young man, who had previously lived in North Okkalapa, Yangon.

"In my early days in the jungle, I suffered from food poisoning because, you know, you could find no proper food in the jungle. You have to eat whatever you can find, without knowing what's safe to eat. I slung my medicine bag over my shoulder, held a rifle in one hand, and continued to engage myself in the Revolution. I was wounded in the Lay Kay Kaw

Battle and had to starve for about seven days. In the Taung Soon Battle, a bullet from an enemy's gun cut off two veins in my temple. I needed four blood bottles for intravenous therapy."

Undoubtedly, he has been carrying out his duty in the Revolution without orders from any authority, but in line with the dictates of his own soul. He once questioned himself, "If you don't continue this Revolution, who will?" He rubbed his gun with unnamed affection. There, he's a true soldier joining the forces of the Spring Revolution.

The pain inflicted upon hundreds of Burmese people who have sacrificed their families for the cause of the Revolution, like the girl known as 'Comrade 95,' 'San Min Paing,' 'Sara,' 'Daw Rati Ohn,' and 'Dr. Kaung Htet,' has pierced their hearts deeply. However, the Spring Revolution has transformed the bitterness of their feelings into mature compassion, turning their agonies into acts of loving-kindness. They have risen above the bonds of blood relations, demonstrating their noble love for the innocent unarmed people by sacrificing their lives, blood, and families.

Unable to tolerate the rule of the state administration council and the military any longer, they harbour such bitter hatred for "the war dogs at large" that they have resolved to establish the Federal Army. These decisions of the Spring Revolution forces show that they are not mere dreamers. Nevertheless, the message conveyed by the spring, "An Eye for an Eye, a Life for a Life," has revealed itself as a bitter truth.

Passage:

Rebuilding Society

On July 28, 2022, amidst the turmoil of the Karenni Region, where hospitals and clinics had become targets of heavy artillery and fighter jet bombings by the SAC, a beacon of hope emerged in the form of a mobile operation vehicle belonging to an on-the-ground healthcare service group. This vehicle marked the debut of the RAY Medical Movement's innovative approach to healthcare delivery, as reported in the *Federal Journal*.

In a declarative statement, the RAY Medical Movement addressed the challenges faced in providing medical services due to the frequent attacks in the vicinity of existing medical centres. The movement's doctors and nurses found themselves constantly on the move, encountering various difficulties in their operations. To address this issue, they conceived the idea of an improvised mobile operation vehicle, dubbed Rx622.

The Rx622 is designed to facilitate medical services in conflict-ridden areas, eliminating the need to transport wounded individuals to hospitals for surgery. Instead, the vehicle is equipped to provide treatments and perform operations on-site for local residents, comrades, and war refugees. Additionally, the movement aims to offer first aid training tailored to the needs of the Karenni/Kayah Region.

The name "Rx 622" is derived from the English term "treatment," symbolised by "Rx," and signifies that the mission was completed in June 2022. The primary objective of the mobile operation vehicle is to conduct emergency surgeries and provide critical medical care in the midst of conflict.

From February 1 to July 31, 2022, a total of 220 clashes occurred between the SAC forces and the Allied Forces under the Chin Joint Defence Committee in nine townships across Chin State, including Kalay Township in Sagaing Division. According to a statement issued by the CJDC on August 11, 927 soldiers of the SAC were killed during these clashes, while the CJDC forces lost 53 fallen heroes.

On August 23, 2022, tragedy struck in Chan Aye Tharzan Township, Mandalay, when a couple riding a motorbike was mistakenly shot dead between 56th and 57th streets on 30th Road. They were wrongly identified as police majors from the Criminal Investigation Department (CID). In response to this incident, the Tiger Force Mandalay issued a statement expressing deep regret for their mistake.

Subsequently, on August 27, a prayer for the deceased couple and an anti-violence protest took place at the corner of 30th Road and 57th Street in Chan Aye Tharzan Township, Mandalay. During the protest, demonstrators chanted slogans denouncing the PDF as terrorists and condemning the murders of innocent citizens. Despite armed groups admitting responsibility for the mistaken shooting, no further action was taken, and the case was closed with a statement expressing concern about the deaths.

The public's reaction to the incident was primarily limited to comments on social media, often accompanied by sad emojis. Many local residents were surprised by the anti-PDF campaign's smooth execution, considering the SAC's harsh crackdown on any form of protest at the time.

On September 12, 2022, in Yinmabin, a tragic incident occurred where ten individuals, including some members of the PDF, were mistakenly killed as wrong targets. Responsibility for the crime primarily fell on the Saya San Group and Ko Aung Zaw, also known as RPG. In response, the NUG issued a statement declaring that the perpetrators would face court-martial proceedings and pledged to provide necessary assistance to the families of the victims.

The incident stemmed from actions taken by Bo Taik Kaung, also known as Bo Phone Htet, and his group on November 16, 2021. They arrested and subsequently killed four men, including two firefighters, and five members of the Hero Tiger PDF, including Bo Htaik Maung, from the La Po Village Base. Despite being summoned for interrogation three times, Bo Taik Kaung failed to appear, leading to further suspicion. The victims were rightfully recognized as comrades of the PDF, and the guilty individuals, whether affiliated with the PDF or other defence groups, were declared illegitimate under the NUG's Ministry of Defense. Measures were implemented to disarm them under close supervision.

Ven. U Vājama, representing the Spring Revolution Network of Religions, raised concerns about the handling of the case, noting that while 21 people were killed in Yinmabin, only ten were acknowledged in the NUG's statement. Complaints from bereaved families regarding the oversight of other victims were disregarded. Additionally, there was criticism over the lack of action against Bo Thanmani and his group, as blame was predominantly placed on the Saya San Group. Despite the NUG's statement, no further action appeared to have been taken against Bo Thanmani and his associates following the investigation.

In the Federal News Journal, dated September 14, 2022, it was reported that two camps of the Burmese army, situated in the Naung Htao Region of Si Sai Township, within the Pa-o Autonomy Region of Southern Shan State, came under attack by the combined forces of the United Southern Shan Federal Brigade on September 12. The assault resulted in the deaths of over 20 soldiers from the Burmese Army. The Brigade comprised five allied battalions: No. 1005 Battalion, No. 1008 Battalion (SSRY), No. 1009 Battalion (formerly the Inlay Region People Defence Force/IPDF), one battalion under the NUG, and the Pa-o National Defence Force (PNDF). These battalions had been active since the outset of the Spring Revolution, marking the first instance of their offensive action in Southern Shan State.

Despite Shan State being considered a region with a significant presence of armed ethnic groups, clashes against the SAC forces had been relatively infrequent following the attempted coup. Instead, conflicts often arose over territory between the Shan armed forces, specifically SSPP/SSA versus RCSS/SSA, with the TNLA and UWSA potentially aligning with the former. The RCSS/SSA had signed the Nationwide Ceasefire Agreement (NCA) and sought to maintain positive relations with the SAC. Efforts by the influential SNLD Party in Shan State to facilitate peace negotiations between the armed factions proved unsuccessful, exacerbating the plight of displaced refugees caught in the crossfire.

This situation provided the SAC with an advantage, as it could refrain from deploying reinforcements to regions where clashes occurred between armed forces of the same ethnicity. Consequently, SAC battalions could focus their efforts on combating resistance fighters of the Spring Revolution in other areas. Although the movement of the Southern Shan Federal Brigade was significant, it did not immediately register as a pressing threat to the SAC forces.

In the *Federal News* on September 19, 2022, it was reported that during his meeting with Prime Minister of Central India Narendra Modi in New Delhi, the Chief Minister of Mizoram, Pu Zoramthanga, urged the Indian Prime Minister to play an active role in the rehabilitation process aimed at addressing political conflicts in neighbouring Burma and restoring peace and stability in the country. However, it was noted that India has continued to be a supplier of arms to the junta, raising concerns about its stance on the matter.

On October 3, 2022, the Ministry of Judicial Affairs under the NUG issued a statement announcing the imminent establishment of military tribunals to address cases related to war crimes committed by revolutionary forces under the Ministry of Defence of the NUG. According to reports from *Mizzima News*, based on information from Permanent Secretary U Min Naing Khaing of the Ministry of Judicial Affairs, these military tribunals will be organised by the Ministry of Defence and are expected to commence operations by October. The tribunals, comprising legal experts, will adjudicate on cases of war crimes.

It was further disclosed that jurisdiction over cases in Sagaing and Magwe Divisions has already been established under the Ministry of Judicial Affairs of the NUG. Additionally, local jurisdiction boards, composed of lawyers and respected community members, have been tasked with handling civilian cases, reflecting the civilian jurisdiction system. Prisons have been constructed to detain defendants found guilty of committing crimes.

On October 4, 2022, during the online Cabinet Meeting, Acting President Duwa Lashi La of the National Unity Government delivered a speech emphasising the pivotal role of the people in the Spring Revolution. He urged NUG ministers to prioritise close contact with the people, even if such opportunities were limited, emphasising the importance of understanding and empathising with their experiences. He cautioned against detachment from the realities faced by the people and called for unity and diligence among NUG members. Additionally, he condemned the air strikes carried out by the SAC, which targeted civilians outside of conflict zones, resulting in casualties. He stressed the need for the NUG to be prepared for on-the-ground resistance and to take measures to protect civilians from further attacks to the best of their abilities.

As of October 4, 2022, the Arakan Army reported that the number of displaced war refugees in Rakhine State had risen to 82,419. Despite a temporary ceasefire between the SAC and the AA following the 2020 General Election, clashes intensified starting in August 2022. This led to a surge in displaced families seeking refuge, with over 20,000 now housed in 150 refugee camps. These camps faced food shortages exacerbated by the Ministry of Social Welfare, Rescue, and Rehabilitation under the SAC failing to supply rice for over four months. Additionally, the SAC imposed strict bans on humanitarian aid from international NGOs and social organisations to the war refugees of Rakhine Region, pressuring them to return to their conflict-affected villages. By the end of November, news had spread that the ceasefire between the SAC and the AA had ended.

During the first week of January 2022, information leaked regarding an online meeting between the Arakan Army (AA) and the National Unity Government (NUG), leading to discussions. As a result, *The Irrawaddy* reported, citing the community administration of the State Administration Council (SAC), that local residents engaged in woodcutting, charcoal production, and farming in the Rakhine Yoma region were instructed to vacate the area by January 16 at the latest. This announcement hinted at imminent SAC assaults on areas near the Rakhine Yoma, suggesting potential armed conflicts in the Rakhine Region. In 2019, armed conflicts persisted for months, punctuated by a three- or four-month ceasefire believed by some political critics to have afforded the SAC a temporary respite amid its widespread engagements across the country, likely influenced by external factors, particularly those involving China.

On October 10, 2022, the Restoration Council of Shan State (RCSS) issued a statement proposing a meeting with Ethnic Armed Organizations (EAOs) within the Union to address political and military conflicts in Shan State and the broader Union, with the aim of establishing a Federal Union. The RCSS set a deadline for responses to the proposal between October 10, 2022, and February 10, 2023, according to the *Federal News Journal*. However, as of the end of 2022, no organisations had responded to the proposal.

From November 9 to 10, 2022, the State Peace Talks Team (SPTT) engaged in discussions with a delegation from the New Mon State Party (NMSP) in Nay Pyi Taw. The talks centred on assessing whether certain agreements outlined in the Union Agreement were in accordance with the Constitution and existing laws. However, in September 2022, several Mon civil organisations jointly declared, via an open letter to the NMSP, their decision to halt further meetings with the State Administration Council (SAC). Subsequently, on December 16, 2022, local revolutionary forces in Ye-Balu launched an attack on SAC artillery forces stationed in Ye Township.

On November 16, 2022, the *Federal News* conducted an interview with Padoh Saw Tar Ni regarding the gathering of the Kayin people at Ta-kaw Village, Hlaing Bwe township. Padoh Saw Tar Ni stated, "During the peace-making process, the armed Kayin groups among ourselves have tried many times to find a way for reconciliation for nearly ten years. This is the very first time we have had this kind of formal gathering after the coup. I believe this is the opportune time to draw the attention of our people to the changes in the political situation. I'd like to take this opportunity to tell all our different Kayin organisations—it's not a new idea, of course—it is time we stopped having conflicts and tensions among ourselves because today we must stand united to annihilate the military dictatorship. So, I urge our people to rebuild unity among ourselves so that we can continue our mission."

He continued, "Well, there's no agreement of great significance to be made from the assembly. We just meet, we talk. We haven't met for a year. We have a chance to talk to our people about our political objectives. Yes, that's it. We're now facing the worst period of the military dictatorship, and we must drive it out, we must overcome it. Here, understanding is the most crucial thing among ourselves."

On February 12, 2022, Padoh Saw Tar Ni attended the 75th Diamond Jubilee Union Day celebration, hosted by the SAC, along with the Chairman of Duplaya District, KNU, Padoh Saw Shwe Maung, and Saw Chit Hla. The KNU issued a statement clarifying that their presence at the celebration did not represent the KNU. However, in an interview with the CNI News Agency, Padoh Saw Shwe Maung stated that their attendance did not represent the KNU and that he and his companions were attending the celebration as special guests. He mentioned that he would be carrying a letter from the Chairman of the KNU to Senior-General Min Aung Hlaing.

The *Federal News*, issued on November 25, 2022, reported that after the Foreign Secretary of India's visit to Myanmar on November 20th and 21st, the SAC began to decrease its operations' tempo in Kachin and Sagaing while increasing it in the Chin State. On the Kayin New Year Day, falling on December 22, 2022, the SAC launched assaults in Kawkareik township using heavy artillery and air strikes. The number of armed conflicts between the SAC and the KNLA had been increasing in Kawkareik township.

Passage:

The Prison of the Spring

"A Piece of Abstract Art"

"Be the Foul Air made.
And the Foul Air made."
In this magnet field so strong
Ego, malice and slanders
Have taken too much space.

Scolds so rough, so rude
Her baton has no tongue
And her hand holding the baton
Has got biting canine teeth only…

Here, cacophonous sounds of clanks echoed as the furious baton struck the iron bars with undisciplined force. It was a nightly ritual, akin to a clock chiming "goodnight." "Bitch! F*… ya all! Ya makin' lousy noises! Shut up!" shouted the harsh voice of the warden. The iron rod of the prison shutdown struck nine, breaking the silence of the night. Inside the cell, a group of women inmates struggled to find space, rolling out scanty sheets on the cold cement floor and unfolding their thin blankets, tossing and turning, whimpering and muttering to themselves. Their whimpers were all too familiar, as was the foul air that emanated from the foul-mouthed female wardens, wielding their batons like "biting canine teeth," as described by the late Poetess Ma Sein Pin, who herself had spent months and years in the women's ward inside the Insein Prison.

"It's high time, Bros, Blood Brotherhood. Stand together, be united.
The history of ours written in the blood of ours, the Pledge in blood we have sworn!

It's high time, Bros, Blood Brotherhood. Stand together, be united.
The history of ours written in the blood of ours, the Pledge in blood we have sworn!"

Amidst the sombre silence, a soft voice emerged from the darkness. Female inmates, both young and old, lifted their heads, smiled quietly to themselves, and offered silent encouragement.

"Shh...Thamee," whispered a female inmate from the neighbouring cell, once a comrade in an urban guerrilla force. "Look! Those ogresses over there! They could run wild any time!"

The large, round eyes peering through the darkness conveyed understanding. "I know. Let it be, ma'am." Those eyes belonged to Suu Myat Zaw. She lowered her voice, singing a revolutionary hit song with a gentle lisp. At barely three years old, she was considered a political prisoner, detained alongside her mother who lay beside her. The female inmate resting at her mother's feet was her grandmother—all political prisoners. They were accused of the crime of having familial ties to Suu Myat Zaw's father, a political prisoner who had evaded capture by the SAC. No law exists in the world to punish individuals solely based on familial connections, yet these female inmates were charged with violating Penal Code Section 505(a).

A closer examination of the case reveals that the actions taken were not in accordance with the law: Little Suu Myat Zaw's father worked as a public service employee in the Department of Sanitation under the Yangon City Development Committee. He, along with a group of colleagues, was tasked with removing posters of the coup leader, Senior-General Min Aung Hlaing, which anti-coup protesters had affixed to the roads. Instead of carrying out the assigned task, however, the group, including Suu Myat Zaw's father, decided to join the Civil Disobedience Movement (CDM).

"One evening, around 8:00 pm, a troop of soldiers stormed into our staff housing estate," her mother recounted to her fellow inmates. "We were just about to leave. It was too late. I urged my husband to flee alone, hoping they wouldn't harm the families. Unfortunately, they apprehended us—my sixty-four-year-old mother-in-law, my two-year-and-four-month-old daughter Suu Myat Zaw, named after Daw Aung San Suu Kyi, and myself." They have been imprisoned since March 2021, as the father remains at large. The family consists of six children, the eldest being a ten-year-old boy with autism who cannot speak. His mother and grandmother are deeply concerned about his well-being.

The family was later informed that all staff who had joined the CDM were to vacate their living quarters. The fate of the five children without their mother and grandmother remains uncertain. While several prisoners were granted amnesty between June and October 2021, the little girl, her mother, and her grandmother were ultimately sentenced to three years' imprisonment.

"Here,
A cup of cool water,
A bite of a fresh fruit,
A white rose to take a breath,
A smile
that would not impose a burden on the Future,
a whistle not infested by suffering,
steps in countless number,
Hours to talk about with longing,
A wall where delicate rays of sunshine fall,
A kite with a dangling ribbon,
Flower beds of a pen seized with mood
All got lost in the deep yearning,
All drop their heads amid the tuneless silence.
Fall asleep to the iron rod's monotonous strikes
One, two …
How long has it been going on,
With the morning beauty turned into a hump of flesh
That a dog's teeth have clutched?

Every morning, as the iron doors of the ward swung open, a female warden would enter. Anticipating the command for the squatting position with arms raised, known as Pon-Zan, Suu Myat Zaw, the youngest inmate, would be the first to call out, "Pon-Zan!" Once the warden had confirmed the presence of all inmates, she might engage in conversation with Tan-si, a senior inmate acting as an in-charge, forgetting to give the command, "At ease." It was then Suu Myat Zaw who would issue the order, "At ease," before assuming the position herself, her little legs apart and hands tucked behind her back. Her demeanour endeared her to the entire ward, her presence akin to a sweet-sounding bell to all.

Despite her tender age, Suu Myat Zaw sometimes spoke with the maturity of an adult. Although she should have been attending nursery school, she was condemned to spend another two years behind bars in a prison devoid of basic human values or regard for reputation. It's difficult not to feel a pang of sorrow witnessing the world's youngest inmate endure her childhood in such miserably confined circumstances.

In fact, it is difficult to fathom the lasting impact of the gloomy days spent in prison on a delicate young girl like Suu Myat Zaw. For every prison stint leaves behind haunting memories and recurring nightmares. Suu Myat Zaw's tragic tale serves as a stark reminder that any citizen of Myanmar, regardless of age, could find themselves incarcerated at any moment, perhaps on dubious charges, as Sean Turnell aptly puts it.

"Here,
No clock, but the Calendar
Be careful, be careful!
To preserve the reputation of a fruit
Get it soaked
In bitter, salty water
The heart-blood throbbing
Beneath the thin skin,
Now the pulse going slow, now racing fast
The beats of the African drums
The curling, dancing cigarette smoke
In the precious centre of light and shade

Ashes dropping!
This is not Pride, this is not Life,
The waning days Ahosikan
everything is going down the drain!"

The sentiments expressed in these lines can be applied to the case of the Australian economist Sean Turnell. Despite being a "mild-mannered economics professor" with a deep understanding of economics, particularly Burma's economy, his expertise and experiences were disregarded, if not completely disregarded, by the military regime. These lines also capture Sean's own experience of spending 650 days in prison in Burma.

"The physical environment was horrible. It was a concrete cell with old rusty iron bars, completely exposed to the elements. Being in Yangon meant enduring monsoon rains, incredible heat, insects, rats, and the horrifying presence of big scorpions that would enter the cell...

"I was treated quite badly, and I witnessed and heard torture taking place all around me. Although I wasn't subjected to physical torture myself, except psychologically, I endured months of solitary confinement without anything to read. I would describe it as psychological torture, but my Myanmar friends who were caught experienced physical torture. They had electrodes attached to them and were electrocuted. People were beaten.

"The worst physical moment was being in a van and driven to a nearby court just outside the prison for a remand hearing.

"This van, meant to hold around 20 people, had 50 of us crammed inside. We were all chained together, packed into the back of the van. The heat was unbearable, sweat was pouring down, people were vomiting around me, and fainting."

"The conditions were pretty terrible. The food was bad, and it was very easy to catch diseases, so I got COVID five times while I was there.

"In Insein prison, it was a proper bucket. In Naypyidaw, Myanmar's capital where I was shifted up for the trial, it wasn't even that. They were dirty old construction buckets that had been full of paint, and the paint stains remained on the outside. This very thin bean soup was sort of put in, and another bucket would have rice in it."

After being detained for nearly two years, in September 2022, Sean Turnell was sentenced to three years' imprisonment. However, on November 17, he was released, one of the prisoners granted mass amnesty by the SAC, and deported directly back to Australia. (He was released together with the former British ambassador Vicky Bowman and the documentary film director Toru Kubota.) Soon after, he often talked to the media about his horrible experiences of his prison life in Burma, as well as about the time he spent having a conversation with Daw Aung San Suu Kyi. This prompted the SAC to issue a statement in January, revoking its pardon of Sean Turnell and requesting his arrest.

The Assistance Association for Political Prisoners (AAPP) made a statement that the total number of political prisoners detained in all prisons and jails in the territory of Burma had reached 11,743. The AAPP also shared information leaked on July 20, 2022, that two comrades supporting the League for All Burma Students' Union were tortured by the wardens for making an official request to be permitted to pay tribute to the Fallen Leaders on Martyr's Day. One was severely injured and is receiving oxygen administration treatment at the prison hospital.

The news also stated: "On July 7, which marks the military government's suppression of a student demonstration at Rangoon University and the arrest of more than 6,000 students, the prisoners of conscience in Insein Prison, Yangon, paid silent tribute from 12:00 noon to 12:07:07 pm commemorating the 60th anniversary of the 7 July Movement under the motto: 'Wage Wars with the Undying Spirit of July 7.' An inmate gave a talk on the history of 'July 7' in honour of the role of student politics over successive periods, and a program with seven items, including poetry recitation, was carried out."

Throughout the history of Burma, there have been numerous cases of violence behind bars. For instance, as quoted by Radio Free Asia (RFA), Sean Turnell mentioned Khin Maung Shwe, also known as Ya Kut Bai, who was "killed after trying to mediate in a fight in Yangon's notorious Insein Prison."

"My dear friend Khin Maung Shwe," Turnell wrote in a post on his Facebook account.

"He stood up for me. He kept me healthy. He kept me sane. He saved my life." "He was beaten and kicked to death by prison guards in Insein, a month after I was transferred up to Naypyidaw."

Since 2016, Khin Maung Shwe had been serving a 65-year prison sentence. A fight erupted between Kyi Lin and Aung Win Zaw, who were convicted of murdering Lawyer U Ko Ni, and other inmates recently imprisoned on charges of 505(a). Khin Maung Shwe attempted to mediate but ended up in a fight with Kyi Lin and Aung Win Zaw. Tragically, he became the sole victim, beaten and kicked to death with batons and iron rods by wardens and other prison guards. The incident occurred on November 17, 2021, and Khin Maung Shwe passed away the following day. There are no official records documenting brutal deaths in prison like that of Khin Maung Shwe, but it is likely that there have been at least dozens of similar incidents.

The paradox within the jurisdiction under the SAC lies in the exemption of prison department staff, much like soldiers and policemen, from facing repercussions for any unlawful acts or crimes committed within the penal institution. In reality, there are few instances where prison department staff are held accountable for the deaths of inmates or detainees.

"Here,
The neighs of some Souls
getting the tedium to explode
Roll like the rumble of earthquake
There's a Ghost, untouchable …
Drops a stone
the tranquil surface of dead water ripples
Days pass,
But one scene from Shakespeare's play
Can't get it out of my inward eye
Now, I'm beginning to like the Apparition!"

The soft, gentle voice of Suu Myat Zaw echoed through the prison, as she recited the lyrics of the renowned revolutionary song with a sweet lisp:

> "We will die happy for our country, the blood of the Fighting Peacock, red as ruby.
> We will die happy for our country, the blood of the Fighting Peacock, read as ruby.
> Fight for our freedom, fight for our peace, and on and on we perform our Duty."

Her small voice may have been soft and delicate, but its echoes lingered throughout Insein Prison, reverberating even to this day.

Wall:

Inhumane Atrocities by the Tatmadaw

"Mom …! So painful ! Kill me right away, please! Can't stand it anymore …! Please !"

Little Maung Phone Teza, wounded in his hands and across the lower part of his body, lay murmuring in agonising pain. Beside him rested his G1 Maths textbook, its pages stained with his blood, and a dingy cotton sling bag. His bench, already broken, was splattered with blood as well. His aunt, a school teacher, humbly pleaded with the SAC soldiers, who eventually granted permission for his mother to see her dying son and hear his final wishes. "Kill me right away, please…!"

These were the last words uttered by this young child in his final breath, leaving those who heard them overwhelmed with a torrent of bewildering emotions. Like the Sibyl of Cumae in Greek mythology, the people of the modern age, grappling with stress, might often lament, "I want to die." Yet here was a seven-year-old child expressing such a desperate wish in his dying moments. He was too young to comprehend why those denizens of two rumbling, spinning rotor blades of hell hovering above—two Mi-35 helicopters—wanted to kill him.

Indeed, those damned souls in the sky cared nothing for the life of an innocent child below. He knew his mother had always indulged his requests, and now he pleaded with her to fulfil his one final wish. This child could bear the agonising pain no longer; he believed it would only cease with his death. Thus, he begged his mother to end his suffering. How shocking! The chilling truth of the connection between killing and death had dawned on this delicate mind.

On September 16, 2022, at a primary school in Let Yet Kon Village, situated 14 miles west of Dipèyin Town in Sagaing Division, a distressing event unfolded. The peaceful atmosphere was shattered by the sound of the school bell, signalling a chaotic turn of events for the school children.

Suddenly, the distant thrum of helicopters filled the air, prompting teachers and students alike to scramble for cover. Moments later, three heavy artillery bombs detonated within the school compound, sending shockwaves through the community.

Descending from the whirring helicopters, soldiers swiftly took control of the area. Amidst the chaos, the lives of innocent primary school children, such as Maung Phone Teza, were thrown into disarray. Machine guns and heavy weapons echoed through the air for an agonising hour, targeting not only the monastery compound where the primary school was situated but also the surrounding area, including the village dispensary. Seven innocent children were killed along with six adults.

Maung Phone Teza's mother pleaded with the troops multiple times, begging for the opportunity to retrieve her son's body for a proper burial, but her pleas fell on deaf ears. "We begged them to return the dead body," recounted Teacher Daw Aye Myint, as reported in a *Myanmar Now* article. "We kowtowed to them, his mother begged them to allow her to arrange a dignified burial for her son, but all her humble requests were rejected. 'No permission from above,' they replied."

Following the attacks, the SAC's five Mi-35 helicopters transported 17 students, including two severely injured volunteer teachers, to the hospital of indigenous medicine in Ye Oo Town, approximately 8 miles away, where the army was stationed. Additionally, six local individuals were taken captive, according to reports from local sources. The SAC justified the military raid on Let Yet Kon Village and its school by alleging that over 200 primary students from the local area and neighbouring regions were involved in arms trafficking orchestrated by the KIA and the PDF.

Among the victims were a father and his thirteen-year-old son, who were fishing in the Mu River, a young woman herding cattle on the pasture, and many other innocent lives. They were shot dead in the head. Witnessing the horrible scene full of gore, the school children were psychologically affected: they did not dare to go to school; the thrums of the helicopters still echoed in their eardrums, haunting them like a nightmare. On the following day, September 17, a comrade from the Ye Oo Township Comrades Group said: "In Ye Oo Cemetery, two sacks holding dead bodies were burnt. The dead bodies of two girls were already beheaded. They must be the bodies of young souls. These damned guys must have tried to wipe out the evidence of what they have committed in the massacre. We don't know how many victims there are."

In 2021, there were 9 instances of massacres where 5 or more lives were taken simultaneously at a single location, resulting in a total of 147 fatalities, as reported by the Ministry of Human Rights of the NUG. Among the deadliest incidents were a massacre on July 11, 2021, in Yin Village, Kani Township, Sagaing Division, where 34 civilians lost their lives, and another on December 24, in Mo So Village, Fruso Township, Karenni State, where 35 civilians were killed.

In total, there were 44 recorded massacres in 2022, leading to 515 deaths. Notable incidents included an attack on May 12, 2022, in Mon-Tai-Pin Village, Ye Oo Township, Sagaing Division, resulting in the deaths of 29 civilians, and another on August 8, in Hse Zin Village, Ye Oo Township, Sagaing Division, claiming the lives of 40 civilians.

The deadliest massacre occurred on October 23, at Anant Pa Village, Pha Kant Township, Kachin State, where more than 80 civilians were killed. This horrific act occurred during a music festival commemorating the 62nd anniversary of the KIO, without warning, when three jet fighters of the SAC dropped bombs on the site. The tragic victims included Kachin musicians, artists, and singers, among them the renowned Kachin Rock Star Aurali Laphai. Dr. Tun Aung Shwe, the Australian representative of the NUG, described the attack as a "barbaric act."

"The Shallow Graves of Myanmar"

The crows picked the corpse in the field
The villagers gathered at inspection revealed
A shallow grave that discerned
Five bodies dismembered and burned
Clothing, a watch and a medical bag
vouched for her, thus seen making a grab
for Open Country.

The infantry man, set to the village,
then made chase
of the defenceless young nurse.
Myanmar robbed of such spirit
and promise.

We are your countrymen and women too.
What sort of soldiers are you?

Dr. Jim Brockbank penned this poem, capturing the stark realities unfolding in Burma. Through his collaboration with Burmese medical professionals, he gained intimate insight into the country's struggles.

Columns of smoke reach to the sky
The villagers flee terrified
Another shallow grave another place
Another Community displaced.
Images on the mobile phone
Tell a widow she's now alone
Her man lies naked, decorated
in knife, wounds broken, desecrated
The infantryman strike once more
Looting, killing as villagers implore

We are your countrymen and women, too.
What sort of soldiers are you?

An excerpt from an RFA news article recounts the harrowing ordeal of a mother and her son from Pyan Kya Village, Dipèyin Township, Sagaing Division.

"Those damn soldiers call our village Pyan Kya the Den of the Rebels," said the mother, her tone mixed with anger and pride. "Well, let them label our village whatever they want. We resist injustice, and they call us rebels. We are proud of that. They set fire to our houses, but they can't set our iron spirit aflame! If we cry, it means we surrender. We will never surrender. Now, our house is gone. But I thought I'd find something so that I could pay for the carpenter's service." She and her son were scavenging, scratching through the piles of ashes in her compound with a stick fixed with a magnet to collect some scattered iron pieces.

It is an undeniable truth that the SAC has set fire to villages 282 times within one year, from February 2021 to January 2022, and 1,355 times within one year, from February 2022 to January 2023. During this period, air strikes and heavy artillery attacks increased twofold, while the number of arrests decreased by about four times, according to a statement from the Office of the High Commissioner for Human Rights (OHCHR). It is evident that the SAC has been resorting to the strategy of burning residential areas solely to maintain their grip on power. In other words, it appears that the SAC has struggled to leverage the on-the-ground situation to suppress the relentless armed resistance of the people.

Consequently, from May 1, 2021, to May 31, 2023, according to Data for Burma, the junta and its affiliated organisations torched 70,324 houses across the country, with Sagaing Division alone, the strongest resistance zone in mainland Burma, accounting for 53,816 of those houses. Perhaps the SAC believed that by burning residential areas, they could not only tarnish the image of local resistance groups in the eyes of the people but also create additional burdens for these armed groups in assisting affected communities.

Upon hearing that SAC troops were advancing towards their village in Sagaing Division, the local residents, already prepared with their essentials packed in small bundles, fled to seek refuge in a safe location. Upon arrival, the soldiers established a camp in the village, forcibly entered homes, looted belongings, and set fire to granaries and houses. Only after the soldiers had departed did the villagers cautiously return, confronted with scenes of devastation: rubble and debris, charred remnants, and smouldering wooden structures enveloped in smoke. Their livestock lay burnt to death, their possessions reduced to ashes. With no remaining rice from their recent harvest, they resorted to salvaging burnt peanuts scattered amidst the ashes to ease their hunger.

Children beaten and forced to endure
Mock executions by the score
Arrested is ransom in an attempt
to flush out a parental dissident
I saw my son's body on Facebook he said
Only 13, and he lies dead
For delivering food to local men.
I wanted to kill those infantry men,
Pick up a gun, but instead, one day
would take them to court. Seek Justice that way.
We are your countrymen and women, too.
What sort of soldiers are you?

The RFA news article recounted the firsthand experience of a resident from Pyan Kya Village: "Two houses in the village were reduced to ashes. Three motorbikes, a bullock cart, and a granary full of paddy, along with eleven oxen, all met the same fate. The soldiers fired their firearms and stormed into the village. Shells were falling all around, forcing me to flee, abandoning the oxen. I escaped with nothing but the shirt on my back. Now, look at this devastation. No cooking pots, no rice. Everything is gone."

Furthermore, the article detailed the meticulous preparations made by the army for their destructive mission: "Residents informed me that the soldiers brought along inflammable materials capable of reducing homes to ashes within hours. They used rubber pieces or incendiary rings to ignite the fires. Evidence of fire powders and iron rings was discovered."

The losses incurred were grave indeed. In the arid Dry Zone of the upcountry region, many locals struggled to eke out a living amidst profound poverty. Often, a family member would have to seek opportunities in a distant city, foreign country, jade mine, or remote area, working tirelessly for years, if not their entire lifetime, to send back earnings to their family. With these hard-earned savings, the family would endeavour to build a modest brick house or structure. Thus, for these individuals, a house reduced to ashes represented not just property loss, but a life consumed by flames.

An elderly woman, aged eighty, who had endured years of hardship, wept as she lamented the destruction of the towering tamarind trees in her yard. "Only charred stumps remain!" she cried. "I could rebuild a humble cottage with palm leaves, but the growth of such majestic trees takes a lifetime. What senseless destruction!"

Remarkably, amidst her sorrow, the elderly woman's concern for environmental conservation shines through. Her story highlights the poignant contrast between her sorrow for the loss of natural beauty and the devastation of her own dwelling. It begs the question: Does the SAC, consumed by power and violence, truly comprehend the significance of conserving the natural world within its borders?

The people dedicated to the cause of the Spring Revolution uphold the belief of Fight-Never-Flight, embodying an indomitable spirit akin to that of Invictus. They embrace a mindset of Win-and-Win-Again, fostering optimism for a brighter tomorrow.

A middle-aged woman from the upcountry region encapsulates this resilient attitude: "No matter what adversities they subject us to," she asserts, "victory resides within our hearts. Despite their attempts to destroy, we maintain a smile. It's not just me—our entire village shares this unwavering conviction. We refuse to shed tears; instead, we adorn ourselves with Thanaka paste and smile. We will never forsake our village, our birthplace. When we emerge triumphant, we will erect even grander structures. That is the belief that unites us all."

The woman's words resonated with unwavering determination and strength. She did not delve into complex discussions about the post-revolution era—questions of governance, rehabilitation programs, international aid, or justice. Instead, her focus was resolute and straightforward: "We will build better, bigger structures." Her resolve was steadfast and unshakeable.

Standing amidst the remnants of destruction, under the scorching sun, she declared firmly, "We will never abandon our village, our birthplace. Never!" What obstacles could possibly hinder the path of these people, armed with such high morale, as they march towards their well-deserved victory?

> "They might burn our village, but not our revolutionary spirit!"
> "They might burn our village, but not our morale and our land!"
> "Our houses may be burned to ashes, but never our revolutionary spirit!"
> "Stage the strike! Stage the strike!"
> "Down with the dictatorship!" "Our Cause! Our Cause!"
> "What must our Revolution be?" "A victory! A victory!"

The spirited slogans of the villagers rose above the scorched land of ashes, infused with newfound determination. The Spring Revolution had reignited the flames of spirit among those who had long been lost in the Maze of politics for decades.

Corner:

Predicament of the Spring

"My gosh!" muttered a young man as he settled into a chair at the tea shop. "Despotism everywhere! What on earth has happened to our country?" He was the youngest among his friends and had connections with members of the urban guerrilla forces. His physical appearance suggested he was a sickly-looking bookworm who often stayed indoors and made contacts online. In the early days of the Spring Revolution that erupted in 2021, he was thrown into jail for participating in the protests, but fortunately, he was released after a few years through an amnesty.

"You're speaking the truth, Bro," responded a middle-aged man who worked for a company. "Despotism, indeed! Just the other day, those damn guys showed up. They came to arrest a kid working at the lathing home industry, but he was nowhere to be found. So, what did they do? They grabbed his dad and sisters. Why? Because they claimed the kid had made an iron spring used in making a firearm. How could the kid have known that his work would be used to make a gun? They're arresting people for no good reason."

"I'd like to share some info with you," began the speaker. "Many members of the USDP are now appointed as new quarter administrators. They know who supports the Red (the NLD). In the evenings, at the junction of the main road, vehicles are stopped for licence inspection (only the vehicles belonging to the Reds) and they extort money. Yes, they'd extort money from the Reds, find fault with them, and threaten them with arrest. It's like a formula, you know."

"Well, if you happen to be sipping beer and having a good time with your pals by the roadside, you'll get arrested? By who? By the soldiers and the policemen whose mouths smell like hellish liquor! You'll be taken to the police station and fined. The maximum fine shouldn't exceed MMK 50,000, but they'd fine you MMK 200,000! What the heck, man! When you take a flight, there, at the international airport, an ordinary staff member will only be nice to you if you pay him at least MMK 30,000 or 50,000, sometimes even MMK 100,000! Otherwise, you'd be charged under the terrorist law. There's no rule of law at all!"

There was a collective click of tongues from their group, accompanied by a sigh in the blazing afternoon silence. New administrators were appointed in quarters to enforce the instructions of the SAC. Since they were not elected by the residents of the respective quarters, they did not garner any support or collaboration from the local people. Some administrators, locally called Oke-Gyi, were notorious for abusing their allotted power and suppressing the local people. As a consequence, they had become targets of the urban guerrilla forces and were often assassinated or badly wounded.

"Stronger and stronger resistance has been occurring these days! Resistance is not only happening in the countryside but also in urban areas. According to some political analysts, 'It could be considered as the largest operation in Burma after World War II.' There are approximately 250 armed forces of the PDF and urban underground resistance forces. About 50 groups have been engaged in fighting against the junta to the best of their abilities," wrote military analyst Anthony David in Jane Journal.

"What's wrong with our country? Well, we stand at the top of a sort of blacklist," said a young man, holding a cup of plain tea in his hand. "Here's one research finding, covering up until October last year. The research says Burma stands at the top with 60 percent in the world record of casualties of protesters during eight months' protests until October 2021. So, the SAC has broken the record as the most brutal army in executing civilians. My Gosh!" The cup in his hand thudded onto the wooden table, causing it to tremble slightly.

"Well," said a young man, with a smile playing at the corner of his mouth, "the number of casualties among SAC soldiers has reached more than a thousand. And the number of soldiers siding with the people is growing too. We must give credit for the largest number of deserters in history." He was the one who stayed busy at home, his phones and tablets arranged in a circle as he clicked through anti-SAC pages on Facebook.

"Well, I must admit," said the oldest man in the group, "I was a bit worried about whether our PDFs would be able to challenge the SAC forces. As you all know, the SAC is a well-established institution, fully equipped with guns and ammunition, but our poor PDFs only have unsophisticated weapons. But morale speaks volumes in the long term, you know. Our PDFs have been driven by the iron spirit of 'We must win!' Unbelievable! Even those on the periphery make contributions to the Revolution. They work overtime, keeping only a small amount of their earnings for survival, and pooling their cash to buy weapons for the sake of the Revolution." The man then shared his fears, based on past bitter experiences.

"My Gosh! Our young PDFs are quick learners, you see. They come up with their own innovations in firearms! Their drone strikes now pose a nightmare for SAC forces. Dropping hand-made mortar shells by drone! How clever! Now the country is being thrown into devastation, but maybe, after the Revolution is over, our Gen-Z's might build arms factories that manufacture 'money-saving firearms' for export! Well, just a joke!"

Their group burst into laughter. Mood swings have become characteristic of Burmese society these days.

"One sad thing is the art and entertainment industry has come to a halt. You know, even if we could restart this kind of entertainment industry, we're not sure we could free ourselves from the dictates of military dictatorship. Reviving this industry could also cause divisions among artists. It's going to be a big challenge."

"We all feel it's not the time for entertainment, so artists see it as a predicament. To be or not to be, you know. Even if the audience understands the artists, the SAC wouldn't grant permission if the entertainment programs don't fit their propaganda taste. So, where's genuine entertainment art gone?"

Their conversation shifted to another topic as a group of people came in and took seats near their table.

"There's one thing I can say. Publishing is thriving these days. Whether the books sell or not, I don't know. When I was behind bars, I had a chance to read a lot. My seniors offered books to me and organised the inmates to participate in movements inside. We all shared readings of books on the experiences of inmates, written by experienced political prisoners, as well as political articles."

"Glad to hear that, Bro. In fact, those experienced readers have their own world outlook. So, wherever you are, whatever decision you make, your action and decision could be the right decision, and the best action, too."

"I think writers have greater freedom than those in the entertainment industry who are bound to show up before the audience. Writers can change their pen names. Some use pseudonyms to write and raise funds for the Revolution, while others take things easy, promoting themselves in public shows. The latter type might even contribute writings to journals published by the SAC. Amazing! Can't believe it!"

"You know about the film directed by Ko Pauk, right (*The Road Not Taken*)? It was shot with an iPhone, but it's touring the world! It's been shown in many cities worldwide. Quite a hit! Movies with themes of the Revolution will soon follow. Some are documentaries. One positive aspect of the Revolution is that many artists have left for liberated areas, some struggling to make a living, but others still dedicated to the cause. Artists from various genres, you know. So, we have a party out there! Some artists remain on the mainland, labelling themselves as pure artists, but these celebrities have been aiding the SAC's propaganda network. Are they really pure artists? I don't think so."

"Maybe they thought the CDM was only for government employees. Actually, civil disobedience is the responsibility of every citizen. You are bound to do your bit. You can start right now. The important thing is to get involved in the network and exchange information."

"To be honest, I'm not quite satisfied with the NUG. I don't see many political moves on their side. Maybe they are now more focused on the armed revolution. They need to establish more diplomatic ties but are still weak in making political moves. The ongoing racial disputes are a clear signal that there's no good future ahead. One race, one dream. One individual, one dream. That's it! So what? Where's the union spirit gone?"

They all leaned in over the flask of plain tea on the table.

"How about the international community?" said the young man, drawing the attention of his friends. "They don't do much to get Daw Aung San Suu Kyi set free. Instead, they criticise the lack of unity among the revolutionary comrades, the weakness of administration and management, and the lack of collaboration among the EAOs." Their conversation topics seemed scattered, but they were discussing very seriously.

"Well, the international community is just a term. When has it ever acted as a community? Remember the Cold War days? Nations didn't wage war, but opposing forces were engaged in heated controversies and tensions. And the UN? Only the superpowers keep the ball in play, playing to their strengths. The international community expresses deep concern about what's happening here but takes no effective action. They got upset over the Rohingya crisis and put blame, but it's the military and authorities concerned who should take action. Instead, they leave the Myanmar people in a sea of troubles, just watching, like bystanders, how our people are tortured and killed. I'm afraid our people will sooner or later adopt a bitter attitude towards what you call the international community."

"The trouble is," said the middle-aged man, "we don't have many authorised persons in our society to get the world to hear our voice. Our language is like that of a minority in the international political scene. And our religion, too. Ukraine gets reactions from all parts of the world, but Myanmar doesn't. Why? It's not just the fault of tensions in our domestic affairs. Maybe, in their eyes, we appear like ordinary victims with dark hair, dark eyes, and dark skin, quite unlike those civilised Europeans with blue eyes, white skin, and blond hair. That's what I feel about it. Because we're not 'them,' not belonging to the same race. Maybe, I'm wrong. Maybe, if, in the news photos of top newspapers, magazines, and journals, we Myanmar people should appear with blue eyes, white skin, and blonde hair, and if they find just a few of us suffering living hell, then aid from our highly esteemed international community would flood in. I feel that way. Excuse me if I'm going too far, pals. Maybe, from their point of view, it sounds normal for people 'out there' to get into trouble, suffering in poverty just because they have yellow skin or dark skin. Hmm ..."

He had now run out of breath. He leaned against the back of the chair and turned his head upward, blinking his eyes. His friends knew he was trying to hide his tears welling up in his eyes. Silence fell.

"Sh...!" said the young man. "Those guys over there! The way they look at us is like they're pricking their ears and listening to us... checking suspiciously. They seem a bit fidgety, you see. Coming in and going out again. I feel they're heading over to the nearest table to us. I think we should break up, pals."

"Okay. Let's break up. See you soon. Stay safe, dudes. Let's carry on with what we're doing."

"Waiter! Bill, please."

There came the noises of a generator with no muffler box. The power supply broke down just before they finished their conversation. So, they had stopped their conversation just in time. They all knew that the Spring Revolution would be a victory with as few casualties as possible, only if it is executed with good timing. Meanwhile, the Spring has been struggling on and on, trying to find a way out of the Maze.

Passage:

Self-Funded Revolution

Mission One : succeeded
ID :
Player name :
Rank :
Exp :
Body count :
Bullets :
You can watch ad
To gain + 30 bullets   Reward ad   Next

On the phone screen were the silhouetted figures of six armed young men against the sombre background of ochre and rust colours. The data mentioned above were those of the Spring Supply Corps. These young men don't join the armed revolution underground, but this PDF Game offers a chance for gamers to even get promoted to the rank of general. However, it requires time. If you get bored with this app, or if you switch to a new platoon, other apps are waiting for you. In the End Game, you become a soldier of the KNU/KNLA shooting the "evil military forces," but you must watch the ads.

The Burmese youth, fueled by the revolutionary spirit, have developed such games, YouTube channels, and websites. These mobile games have generated dollars or MMK in gross revenue. Thus, young game developers have raised funds and sent "donations" online to the on-the-ground armed forces of the Spring Revolution for their needs. This monetization strategy doesn't burden the player but is a lucrative income-generating strategy for the Revolution, leveraging digital platforms and technology. Ads generate earnings from third-party sources. You buy time, pay a few charges for the internet connection, and make money. The total monetary value obtained from various ad channels exceeds the amount of individual donations. Plus, you can stay at home, play, and click, so, to some extent, there is little concern about security.

There are numerous channels on platforms like YouTube offering teachings of the Buddha, audio books on literature, and song and music channels. Additionally, there are over 20 apps such as Letsaung 4u, Thadin, Nwayoo Quiz, Nwayoo Candy, Nway Oo Videos, Squirrel Escape, Fruit of Victory, War of Heroes, Ahlushin, Ninja Jumper, Learn Word, Play 4Freedom, Dohkhit, Aung Pwae, VF Application, Mini Spring Revolution, Su Yadanar's Show, Su Yadanar's Adventure, Run Buddy Run, and PD Fitness. These apps are developed to generate income from ads based on the number of users, with some channels earning up to MMK 70 lakh (approximately $2,500) per day!

Both local users inside the country and the Burmese diaspora abroad engage in playing and clicking to raise funds for the Revolution. Local users often use devices like phones and Android tablets, choosing foreign locations for VPN app usage to increase income. However, not every internet user engages in clicking, and those who do must exercise caution. While clicking may seem harmless, if the security forces of the SAC discover apps like End Game or similar on your mobile device, they may arrest you immediately and charge you under the Terrorist Law for supporting what they term "terrorist groups," leading to potentially many years behind bars.

Despite the potential for online fundraising, there are significant challenges for those who wish to support the Revolution from home. Internet connections are often slow, power outages are common, and mobile internet charges have doubled since December 2021 due to pressure from the SAC. For instance, the 1GB charges of Telenor (now ATOM) have doubled from MMK 1,000 to MMK 1,999 for 965 MB. Additionally, the prices of commodities have been soaring, making the economic situation in Burma unpredictable. According to a report by the World Bank issued on July 21, 2022, 40 percent of Burma's population is now facing issues of poverty.

However, donations from the diaspora play a crucial role in supporting the Spring Revolution. Initially, it was challenging for the NUG to receive legitimate funds from abroad due to limitations in the monetary and international banking systems. To address this, the NUG launched a digital monetary system called NUGpay. Previously, supporters of the Revolution had to rely on the mobile cash transaction system of local banks, which were closely monitored by the SAC. Transactions made through these systems were traced by the SAC, resulting in the cancellation of accounts and action against their owners. With the introduction of NUGpay, supporters from abroad can now send funds directly to resistance groups and CDMs without using the international cash transaction system.

One noteworthy aspect of the NUG's fundraising program is its innovative use of technology, which is based on mutual trust between the people, both locally and abroad, and the NUG. This was analysed in a lengthy news article titled "Funding Myanmar's Spring Revolution" by Zachary Abuza in *The Diplomat*, dated August 1, 2022. A summary of the article is as follows:

The NUG initiated its first fundraising program, called the Nway Oo Lottery, in August 2021. Despite threats from the SAC, 50,000 online lottery tickets were sold within a few hours. The objective of the program was to raise MMK 20 million ($11 million) to provide aid to the CDMs. Although the income from selling the lottery tickets of the Nway Oo Lottery was only $8 million, 55 out of 78 prize winners generously donated their prize money to the NUG to contribute towards the victory of the Revolution.

The local accounts that sold the lottery tickets for the Nway Oo Lottery were cancelled by the SAC, causing disruptions in the online ticket sales. However, the NUG responded by introducing new fundraising programs.

In September 2021, the Representative Committee of the Pyihtaungsu Hluttaw enacted the Union Tax Law, which aimed to encourage corporate and individual taxpayers, both local and abroad, to pay taxes online through a self-assessment task program. The Ministry of Planning, Finance, and Investment (MPFI) reported in November 2021 that tax revenue had exceeded US $150,000. A columnist for *The Diplomat* noted that paying taxes to a governing body is a political statement, and as the

NUG progresses towards its political goals, it can expect increased tax payments from both corporations and individual businessmen.

On November 22, 2021, inspired by Kristo Käärmann's concept of a monetary system using the Ethereum programmable blockchain, the NUG began selling bonds priced at US $100, US $500, US $1,000, and US $5,000 with a two-year term. According to the NUG's report, within the first three hours of bond sales, the total income reached US $3 million. Within 12 hours, sales increased to US $6.3 million, and in just one day, the NUG earned US $9.5 million. The article in *The Diplomat* emphasised that the NUG's bond-selling efforts deserve recognition not only for fundraising but also for making a political statement.

According to the article, the NUG's ability to gain an advantage over the SAC depends heavily on its cooperation and collaboration with armed ethnic groups. The NUG has made a solemn pledge, stronger than any other government, to build a federal democratic nation as its ultimate goal. However, some minority groups and leaders of national races remain sceptical about the NUG's intentions. While the NUG now relies on armed ethnic groups, there are concerns that if the nation falls back under its control, it may not follow through on implementing a federal system that would distribute political and economic powers.

The article also highlights the importance of selling bonds in building mutual trust, but there may be issues with the bonds in individual states. For instance, there is a concern about the 100 percent rate provided by armed groups for the Kachin State and the Karen State. However, the majority Bamar group, represented by the Central Government, has kept its promise to allocate revenue shares to minority groups. In June 2022, the NUG transferred US $2 million in cash to Kayin groups in Kayah State. This helped alleviate the burden on armed ethnic groups, who had previously resorted to manufacturing narcotics, collecting loans from local people, or engaging in illegal drug trafficking, which hindered the flow of international aid.

The article also highlights that certain armed ethnic groups, which have historically rebelled against the central governments of Burma, have been involved in the manufacturing and trafficking of illegal drugs, as well as in collecting taxes. According to the UNODC, a record-breaking seizure of 1 billion stimulant tablets or 91 tons of Methamphetamine pills was made in Southeast Asia in 2021, with the majority of these substances coming from the Shan State. Presently, many armed ethnic groups in the Shan State are involved in what AP News terms as the "lucrative drug trade." These groups neither collaborate with the NUG nor openly criticise the junta. In fact, they maintain closer ties with the security forces of the SAC because they collaborate with them for the purpose of drug trafficking.

The article notes that the NUG has made significant efforts to minimise illicit income. It has successfully launched the first armed revolution, the revenue of which does not rely on the drug trade or drug trafficking within the country.

The article further highlights that the international community expresses concern about the activities of non-Bamar armed ethnic groups involved in the drug trade, while local and Facebook political pages demand financial transparency from the NUG and criticise its lack thereof. In response, on November 18, 2022, Acting President Duwa Lashi La delivered a speech, demonstrating foresight. He stated, "I, once again, solemnly pledge that the NUG and I will continue striving towards the goal of annihilating the dictatorship. I stress that starting from one Like, one Share of each and every individual citizen on social media, our people's desire can make a strong impact on the international community. That is why we all must do our bit in decrying injustice. I fully believe in the strength of our people. Our Spring Revolution, which has started from zero, has now reached closer to our goal of victory. Therefore, I urge you all to be more careful, more diligent, and more united and continue our mission."

The NUG has continued the "The End of Dictatorship (EOD)" programmes. In accordance with Articles 4 and 5 under the Fundamental Policies related to cantonment areas seized by the junta, issued on February 24, 2022, the NUG sold the shareholders: (1) the state-owned land, building, and property at 6½ Miles, Hlaing Township, and (2) the state-owned No. 14 building and property on Inya Road, Yangon, illegitimately seized by the coup leader Min Aung Hlaing. Moreover, the plots of land and the one-to-three-bedroom Condo Housing Projects were sold off under the urban development projects to be implemented in Yangon and Mandalay after the mission for the Revolution is successfully completed: the Nway Oo Yeikmon Project, the Nway Oo Mawkun Thit Project, Nway Oo Hninzi Project, the Nway Oo Taung Yeik Nyo Project, the Nway Oo Yaungzin Project, the Nway Oo Aung Hlan Project, the Tawwin Nway Oo Project, the Nway Oo San Yeik Mon Project, and the Yè Yint Nway Oo Project. All the allotted plots of land and apartments were sold out within a short period from the start of the sale.

In December 2022, during an interview with RFA, the NUG's Minister of Ministry of Planning, Finance, and Investment, U Tin Tun Naing, revealed that fundraising efforts had amassed approximately US $100 million. This achievement was credited to the unwavering determination of Myanmar's people, both domestically and abroad, who eagerly supported the resistance groups. Additionally, measures were underway to secure another US $250 million in the current fiscal year. Minister U Tin Tun Naing commended the resilience of the people, who endured pressures and sacrifices with fortitude. He encouraged continued contributions to expedite the success of the Revolution. Meanwhile, the NUG's upcoming project is the Early Partnership Programme, with its inaugural initiative focused on securing mining rights in the renowned Mogok treasure land. This project invites both local and foreign investors supportive of the Revolution to engage in joint-venture partnerships with the new State.

At the same time, various fundraising events, lottery ticket sales, and auctions of unique artworks and valuable items were organised. These included events like Hsan-Ye, where Daw Aung San Suu Kyi's son Kam Aris's wooden relief carving was auctioned, Ma-Ma Mya-nè Pwè Ka-me, "Nway Oo Aung Lan Lwint-tin-Pho Federal Drone-twe-pyan wè-so," and Metta-kan-let Aung Pwè set. Additionally, initiatives such as providing emotional and material support to prisoners of conscience during family visits, supplying basic necessities, and offering education and healthcare services to displaced families gained traction. Pages like Bon-sai Htaiyin Hlu, Cat Association, and Pan Hsai also saw some success. Notably, among international fundraising efforts, the Anar-gat Ah-hman Nyi-naung Group, composed of Burmese immigrants in Bangkok, Thailand, stood out. They collected recyclable plastic bottles, glass bottles, cans, and scrap metal, earning money by selling these materials to finance the PDFs and war refugees. Since its inception in October 2021, the group has generously donated over THB 2 million (approximately MMK 2000,000,000) to resistance groups and war refugees in just over two years!

Fundraising plays an incredibly crucial role in sustaining the momentum of the Revolution until its ultimate goal is achieved. In financing local resistance groups, both the NUG and individuals with a revolutionary spirit have made concerted efforts, blending creativity, ethics, and technological expertise harmoniously. Their endeavours undoubtedly deserve recognition in the annals of Burmese history.

Corner:

Geopolitical Maze

"I was used as yet another avenue to target Daw Suu and some of the other ministers," said Sean Turnell, an Australian economic advisor, in an interview with Frontier. "By arresting me, I think they were trying to demonstrate that Daw Suu (Daw Aung San Suu Kyi) and the government were excessively influenced by foreigners. A secondary reason was that the reforms, particularly the work I was doing on the banking sector, were starting to get close to some military-connected entities engaged in illicit financial activities, so they wanted to push back…"

"One thing that's really striking about this State Administration Council (as the junta names itself) is their lack of understanding of how modern economics work. I think they genuinely think that isolating Burma is the way to go, although what's very clear is that this is the quickest way to poverty. They have an idea of Myanmar exceptionalism, that what might have worked for the Asian tiger economies just doesn't apply to Myanmar (and) things like economic development are just fripperies. Economic liberalisation, the broad avenue through which the Asian tigers developed, is something that interferes with their project, which is binding Myanmar more tightly together under their control. So, they see Myanmar as an exceptional country that needs to be walled off from foreigners. But there's a degree of cynicism as well."

"The questions came from the people who didn't understand anything. I remember one moment when I was accused of being in communication with the International Monetary Fund, which of course was true; we worked alongside the IMF. But they didn't know what the IMF was, and when they asked me about the IMF, they said, that's George Soros! And I said, Well, no, it's not actually, and I went into an explanation of it. But I quickly saw I was making them all the more suspicious, because the explanation I was giving about complicated international finance was proof to them of too-clever-by-half foreigners being involved in

Myanmar."

"I think the first was raw political power," said this "mild-mannered little professor from Australia" about the attempted coup. "I don't think economic considerations matter much to them. However, the reforms were starting to bite. (The NLD was) in the process of creating a genuinely open and competitive Myanmar and that's the last thing that oligarchs, or various enterprises connected to the military and under the military, would want to see. The reform programme would have really accelerated if the NLD government has got a second term. If you're a crony who's cosy with the existing situation, enjoying market predominance, the idea that the industry you're in might be opened up to competition, or that laws might have come in requiring greater compliance, could be challenging."

The visit of Wang Yi, the Director of the Office of the Central Commission of Foreign Affairs, to Burma in the first weeks of January 2021, just before the attempted coup by the SAC, sparked speculation among political analysts. Some believed that China, operating behind the scenes, may have tacitly approved the military's coup. However, others questioned why China would involve itself in Burma's internal affairs, especially considering its positive relationship with Daw Aung San Suu Kyi and the NLD.

Several potential factors were brainstormed to explain China's possible involvement in the coup. First, the NLD government had amended the terms of the agreement for the Kyaukphyu Special Economic Zone (KP SEZ), a multi-billion-dollar Chinese investment project under the Belt and Road Initiative (BRI). Secondly, railway projects planned to accompany the natural gas and oil pipeline project were suspended. Thirdly, environmental impact surveys were conducted in regions where China sought permission to resume the Myitsone Dam Project. Fourthly, the proposal by the China Communication Construction Company (CCCC) for the Yangon New City Project was declined. Additionally, restrictions were imposed on jade and precious stone mining licences. Lastly, the promotion of investments by Japan and India in projects like Thilawa and Kalatan could have further strained China's relationship with the NLD government. These factors may have contributed to China's dissatisfaction with the NLD administration.

The cancellation of both the Shwe Kokko New City Project and the United Democratic Party, also known as Hnin-zi Party, by the NLD government further strained relations with China. The Shwe Kokko New City Project, submitted for approval to the Myanmar Investment Commission in April 2017, saw clearance work begin before official approval was granted, according to records cited by the MISP China Desk. This project, a joint venture between the Border Guard Forces led by Secretary General Colonel Saw Chit Thu and Yatai International Holdings Group, a Chinese company registered in Hong Kong, faced scrutiny when field surveys conducted by the Kayin State government in May and June 2019 uncovered eight infrastructure projects under construction that did not comply with MIC regulations and were thus temporarily suspended.

Special investigations were launched into allegations of corruption involving army officers who had allegedly accepted bribes for project implementation. Additionally, the NLD government took action against illegal Chinese citizens involved in drug trafficking, particularly of stimulant tablets, and online scams related to human trafficking. In response, on August 25, 2020, the Chinese Embassy in Burma issued a statement declaring that the Shwe Kokko New City Project was not part of the Belt and Road Initiative and emphasised China's support for Burma's handling of the project in accordance with existing laws.

Another case involved the United Democratic Party (UDP). In late September 2020, *Myanmar Now* revealed the background history of U Kyaw Myint, also known as Michael Kyaw Myint, Michael Hua, and Zakhung Zung Sau, the Chairman of the UDP. Consequently, the Union Election Commission, under the NLD government, revoked the UDP's registration as a political party. Additionally, U Kyaw Myint was arrested and sentenced to imprisonment on charges of money laundering, financial fraud against Myanmar's (Burmese) economic laws, and prison escape during the former pro-military government's tenure. This individual, with a questionable past, was born in China but raised in Burma. He served as a colonel in charge of a platoon in the Wa Corps and was previously affiliated with the Burma Communist Party BCP.

After fleeing imprisonment, he sought asylum and spent several years in the USA and Canada, where he engaged in numerous cases of financial fraud before fleeing again and entering China. Known for his ties to transnational criminal gangs involved in money laundering, he left China in 2013 and returned to Burma. During the 2010 Election, his party contested in 8 Hluttaw-level electoral districts, raising questions about why an ex-convict was allowed to register his political party during Thein Sein's government.

Despite its unsuccessful showing in the 2015 General Election, his party was registered to contest the 2020 Election nationwide, boasting millions of members and announcing plans to contest in 1,131 electoral districts with billions of Burmese currency. Interestingly, U Kyaw Myint, the ex-convict turned Party Chairman, had two personal meetings with Yang Houlan, a former Chinese ambassador to Burma. Xinhua, a news agency affiliated with the Chinese government and the ruling Communist Party of China, reported with accompanying news photos that on December 31, 2013, U Kyaw Myint and the former Chinese ambassador discussed political and economic matters.

Sean Turnell, the economic advisor to the NLD government, was optimistic about the prospect of the NLD securing a second term in office, believing that the real GDP growth rate, which had reached approximately 6 percent during the first term (2016-2020), could improve even further. However, it appeared that both China and the military harboured concerns about this possibility, sharing a common profit-driven perspective and experiencing unease. Thus, Burma's fate became entangled in the complex Maze of geopolitics.

Passage:

Facing the Terrorist Army

The Tatmadaw has, for years, established militias known as Pyithusit, or "Tatmadaw-supported local militia units," as described by John Buchanan in *Militias in Myanmar* (2016). The military has formulated strategies for these Pyithusits to implement in the local areas where they are deployed, aiming to establish a firm and solid organisational territory. These strategies include providing for the local people within their means, offering protection, and fostering a sense of unity and collaboration with the community. Additionally, they are encouraged to participate in rural development programs, learn the language and respect the customs of the local ethnic groups, and adhere to military principles and ethics.

In addition to the dos, there are clear guidelines on what the militias should avoid. These include refraining from taking what is not given, overburdening subordinates, engaging in insulting or rude behaviour towards civilians, and acting unlawfully or in a manner that may harm national unity. However, guidelines are only effective when implemented.

The stated strategic objective of the Tatmadaw's training regime is to instil the spirit of upholding the traditions, morale, and discipline of the military, as articulated by the Chief of Armed Forces Training Office (Sitpyinnyar Journal Vol. 37, No. 3, September 2003). However, the reality is that the SAC forces have failed to uphold these principles. This is evidenced by accounts from military personnel of various ranks, including soldiers, corporals, and officers, who have recently defected from the army and shared their experiences in interviews.

"Well, I'll switch to the topic of the interrogation process. There's this group of army men who handle arrests. We were assigned to keep watch over an arrested individual according to the duty roster, about two hours per assignment. Three sentry men are tasked with tying them with a rope behind their back and blindfolding them. Then the interrogation begins. The Special Branch (SB) and officers from the Office of the Chief of the

Military Security Affairs (OCMSA), known as Sa-Ya-Pha, are in charge."

"If a detainee is identified as a PDF member during the interrogation, that's the end for them. It's brutal. They unleash a volley of jabs to the body, face, chin, and deliver liver shots, knee strikes, and kicks to the ribs from all angles. As for me, I have no stomach for it. The Sa-Ya-Pha officers are the highest authority present, but if the victim is a suspected PDF member, they all join in the violence. They spew out laws from their foul mouths, but they don't care if someone dies during interrogation. A person's life in their hands is worthless, as insignificant as an ant. They wouldn't hesitate to crush the body and dispose of it without a trace. That's it."

"First, comes the interrogation. Then, they toss him into jail. The next day, the Sa-Ya-Pha officers take over the interrogation. The victim might not even be a PDF member, just someone with loose connections to them. Sometimes, they nab the wrong guys—elderly men, even women. The real trouble lies with the chief strategist (Army)—a real piece of work. He cracks open a bottle of the hard stuff, hits the karaoke joint, his favourite haunt, in the dead of night, and staggers back drunk, raising hell with the poor sentry on duty. The unfortunate fellow has to rouse all the detainees to line up for their inebriated master, who typically returns around one or two in the morning. By then, everyone's fast asleep, you know. Once they're all lined up, the drunken master unleashes a torrent of profanity. If he takes a dislike to anyone, he'll make them stand before him, balance a bottle of brandy on their head, and take potshots at it from a distance. I never participated in such brutality, but I was compelled to place the bottle on some poor soul's head. I've never encountered such a heartless officer. Never!"

"Our troops were then stationed at the hospital. That chief commander from No. 99 Regiment. As far as I know, the army men more or less abuse drugs. That's why they do all sorts of bloody things mercilessly! I found a middle-aged man with bruises all over his back. Too bad! The old man, his old wife, both about forty or fifty years old, and their young daughter. I was there inside the room of a ward. Another officer, too. Junior G3 officers. But the drunk and disorderly guy was the chief strategist. The most senior in rank. Who would stop him? He staggered into the room, where the old man, the old woman and their daughter were kept. He drove the old couple out of the room, came closer to the girl, and spoke vulgar language to her."

"There were cases of deaths due to the violent interrogation. I remember two guys who died during the interrogation. That night I was off duty. I was taking a break, but I could hear groans and moans. They were beating the poor guys to death. So, I discreetly positioned myself behind a large tree and began recording video. There were four, five, or maybe six of them. They were accusing two individuals of sabotaging a Mytel telecommunication tower and were subjecting them to brutal beatings. Tragically, the two young men lost their lives during the interrogation. My heartfelt condolences and utmost respect go out to them. They did not divulge any connections, and I felt utterly powerless in the face of such brutality."

"Those two individuals perished during the brutal interrogation. It began at 9:00 pm and persisted until 2:00 am, marked by relentless beatings and other forms of violence. Their hands bound behind their backs, they were dragged along the tar road by a vehicle. Yet, despite the torment, these two remained resolute in their silence. To exacerbate their suffering, military intelligence officers coerced other detainees to urinate into their mouths, claiming they were thirsty. Those who refused were subjected to severe beatings, perpetuating the cycle of violence within the army's routine. Regrettably, I too was compelled to partake in the beatings, despite my reluctance. When I escorted them for restroom use at daybreak, I seized the opportunity to apologise for my actions driven by duty. In response, they offered forgiveness, understanding the constraints of my role. Communication with detainees during duty hours was prohibited, but in moments of solitude, it was possible to engage in conversation. We were effectively authorised to execute detainees on sight, following the chief strategist's orders. Each strategist issued different directives, but the one I served under was undoubtedly the most ruthless."

"To be honest, I lost faith in the life of a soldier from the moment of the coup. I cast my vote for the NLD on November 11, 2020, despite the military's efforts to influence our choices. They distributed cards with instructions, one of which recommended voting for a party that maintained a favourable relationship with the Tatmadaw, clearly favouring the USDP. However, I disregarded this directive and voted for the NLD alone. There were others like me who made the same choice."

"Truth be told, after the attempted coup, I yearned to leave the military. During those days, we were cut off from information due to internet blackouts, especially in our regions. It was a complete communication blackout, leaving us isolated from the outside world. The military ordered us not to leave the cantonment area, threatening punitive action against anyone who disobeyed. I felt apprehensive and circumstances only exacerbated my anxiety. Consequently, I refrained from joining the Civil Disobedience Movement (CDM) for a period of time."

"On April 8, 2022, I made the decision to join the Civil Disobedience Movement (CDM). After completing my duty hours, I shed my uniform, donned civilian attire, and escaped. Thankfully, I had a supportive community that was aligned with the NLD. They assisted me for my safety, and I made my way to Mandalay. Boarding the 6:00 pm bus, I departed Mandalay for Myawaddy. However, I couldn't linger there for long as I had sensitive military data with me. Upon reaching Myawaddy, I established contact with armed ethnic forces, and that's how I ended up here."

These words were shared by a former air force personnel who had defected during the reign of the SAC. Many military personnel absconded during this period, each recounting similar harrowing experiences. Chiefs and officers, directly or indirectly, coerced subordinates to vote exclusively for the USDP. Additionally, various forms of electoral fraud occurred in the cantonment areas, including delayed notification of proxy votes and opportunities for double voting.

In 2015, while attending a training course, a member of the army personnel stationed at the arms factory under the South Command, Ministry of Defence Service, found himself in a compromising position. With his commanding officer overseeing inside the polling station, he was pressured to cast his vote for a representative of the USDP, earning such votes the local moniker "Pointing Finger Votes." Fast forward to 2020, all polling stations for military personnel were relocated outside the cantonment areas despite objections raised by army representatives in the Hluttaw citing security concerns. This relocation provided army personnel with the opportunity to vote without external influence or coercion. Propaganda proliferate within cantonment areas, urging soldiers to vote for a party that would protect their race, religion, and the Buddhist Sāsanā, while aligning with military interests. Soldiers reported receiving briefings and directives to vote exclusively for the USDP during weekly assemblies, indicating a pervasive influence. Additionally, derogatory remarks aimed at Daw Aung San Suu Kyi, labelling her as the wife of a foreigner, further fueled discontent. The interviewee, influenced by their recent experience of defecting from the army, was prompted to join the Civil Disobedience Movement (CDM).

"I found myself in a small town for about 17 days, where I bore witness to the despotic violence of the army. The arbitrary arrests and shootings that occurred at night, the callous disregard for human life – it was akin to squeezing the life out of a chicken or a bird. Witnessing such atrocities deeply troubled me. I was involved in the manufacturing of guns and ammunition, instruments used to end the lives of our own people. The realisation of my indirect role in these tragic events weighs heavily on my conscience. Despite not directly causing harm, the firearms produced in our arms factory contribute to the suffering of our people. This burden of responsibility weighs heavily on me." It may surprise you to hear the term "sense of responsibility" coming from someone with my background. Military leaders and soldiers are often perceived as lacking accountability, but I cannot escape the moral implications of my involvement."

One of the factors contributing to the deterioration of the military's reputation is likely linked to recruitment practices. The pay for soldiers, the lowest rank in the army, is lower than the daily wages of a labourer. While a common labourer experiences fatigue at work, they still have the privilege of enjoying "sweet recreation /And innocence, which most does please/ With meditation." In contrast, soldiers are often assigned various duties and deprived of a carefree social life.

Within the military, there exists a system described as a blend of "British structure with Japanese heart," where a strong sense of elder-younger relationships, known as Akogyi-Nyilay, is established. This institutional structure has perpetuated an age-old system of oppression, particularly affecting ordinary soldiers. Consequently, the core of the Tatmadaw has been predominantly formed by newly recruited individuals who may have been disqualified from other opportunities.

Despite the challenge of recruiting individuals for an institution with a long-standing and esteemed tradition, army officers resort to various methods to fill their units, often falling short of upholding the institution's values. This has resulted in a lack of senior-junior responsibility and a disregard for the duty to safeguard civilians.

Even worse, the so-called Akogyi-Nyilay relationship among army personnel of different ranks is not a blessing in disguise, but rather violence disguised as a norm. On May 30, 2022, *Myanmar Now* conducted an interview with a woman who was previously married to a captain but ended her five-year marriage through divorce. From her interview, it becomes apparent that the culture of relationships deeply ingrained among army personnel resembles more of a law of the jungle. According to the former wife of a captain:

"In my eyes, he seems like a criminal. Those indoctrinated army officers have lost their personal beliefs or convictions. After completing their education, their impressionable minds are filled with the philosophy of the totalitarian army. I've always believed that the Tatmadaw, originating from the people, was established solely to protect them. My ex-husband and I held different beliefs. Harming the people who should be protected is a crime, isn't it? But from his perspective, we were fighting because we didn't want military rule. When I got married, I found myself part of the 'Army Family' or the army community. The reality was, I was no longer free as a bird. My wings were clipped! I often felt despair. Violence was rampant everywhere. Punching, striking, kicking among them was commonplace. Even if you were a young officer, you could punch, hit, or slap an older man. As an outsider, I was shocked. They called it 'punishment'—excuse my expression—but it resembled incorrect punishment in dog training because, in my opinion, they should act according to the law, right? Punching is unacceptable, you know. It's quite disappointing. To these individuals, a human life isn't valued as much as that of a chicken or a bird. Their families know that. Mothers worry about their sons, but they also expect all the fringe benefits they believe they deserve."

"Everyone knows what the Tatmadaw soldiers have done and continue to do to the poor, helpless villages—burnt to ashes! But the mindset of the army personnel, whether senior or junior, remains unchanged. Poor villagers are now displaced, with no food or water. Just imagine working hard your whole life, saving money to build a wooden house, only to see it destroyed. The Army Community has always remained rather silent! I believe the Army Community is responsible for that. I feel I did what I could. I took the time to discuss things with my husband, warning him about the potential consequences in the future, but he rejected all my advice. However, I believe I was speaking the truth. Our young people—those younger than me—have been fighting for our country, sacrificing their rights to education, health, and everything else. These younger generations would even sacrifice their lives for the sake of future generations! They don't care if they get wounded or lose their limbs. I decided to get divorced because I thought that if he were to die in service, I'd feel a bit sorry for him, and that's all. I felt I needed to leave the community of war criminals. I will stand independently, free as a bird."

It can be assumed that anyone adopting humanist views would feel like a square peg in a round hole within the army community and seek a way out.

Interestingly, another aspect of military personnel's lives is their deep superstitions regarding the mystical powers of Vedic astrology and measures taken to appease negative planetary influences. Surprisingly, army officers have sought advice from astrologers and mystics for managing and administering manoeuvres. This is supported by interviews with CDM captains.

March 18, 2022, *Myanmar Now*.

Capt. Zay Thu Aung: "If you're going to fly, you must never wear anything black. If you do, there are issues awaiting. Before you fly, you have to get a drink of mystic water. If you're engaged in an operation, you must take a potato on board. Two Saturday-borns are not allowed to be on the same flight. There are some pieces of paper like Mantras, stuck on the surface of your plane, that you believe would dispel any evil consequences. Sometimes, you are bound to fold a piece of paper bearing a cabalistic square and swallow it with a gulp of water."

Corporal Myat Min Thu: "During a new ship launching ceremony, the monks who follow the mystic practices ask the officers to hold the Nat-propitiating ceremony and the ceremony of feeding the Naga (the mythical Dragon dwelling in water). In the navy, a crane is used to land on the surface of the ocean a gilded shrine of Shin Upagutta, supposed to be the Guardian of Floods and Storms. I participated in ceremonies like that, at No. 3 Navy Port, Thilawa Area, Yangon, and Navy Port, Mawlamyaing. Had to transport the Gilded Shrine in a truck from one place to another. It costs a lot of expenditure, you know. Whenever there's a political crisis, there goes the image of the legendary monk Shin Upagutta sitting cross-legged, with an alms bowl on his lap, checking the rising sun before noon, inside a shrine. Then you let go of the shrine on a raft afloat into water. Sometimes, something goes wrong, and the whole shrine sinks before you let it go afloat![4] The launching ceremony of the Mottama Ship belonging to the Navy was held in South Korea. For this purpose, a Buddhist monk was selected and brought along to South Korea. Poor monk! According to the safety precautions during the crane operation, the yellow-robed Sayadaw riding a crane had to go through a kind of transformations—a Buddhist monk in a PPE, wearing a hard hat, safety glasses, work gloves and hard-toe boots, and all that, before doing Pali incantations for the protection and safety of the new ship."

"When heading to the front lines, it's customary to carry a ballistic square piece and an amulet in your helmet and pocket. Every soldier

---

4. According to the revered Theravada Buddhist monks, who had a thorough knowledge of the Buddhist Scriptures, there existed no such monk as Shin Upagutta.

follows this practice. Additionally, the Chief Commander issued an order to refrain from consuming pork. During a clash in a remote area, our food supplies depleted, leading one soldier to discover a wild boar. We consumed its meat, but unfortunately, we failed in our mission and lost control of a well-fortified hill position. Consequently, we faced repercussions. Whenever we suffered defeat, red pieces of cloth appeared, and we were required to tie them around our arms. It's perplexing to witness General Khun Thant Zaw Htoo wearing a string of beads on his right arm while issuing commands to the artillery forces. It seems absurd to wear religious beads while commanding the taking of lives."

No wonder the SAC armed forces, equipped with years of warfare experience plus firepower and manpower, have found themselves defeated by the young PDFs. They are equipped with astoundingly high morale, have decided to wage an armed revolution, attended strenuous basic military training, and with unflinching iron spirit, have gone straight into war. Maybe their amulets and cult of mystic practices do not work. But what is certain is the low morale of these disqualified warlords that has led them into disaster. Capt. Nyi Thuta, who has joined the CDM, explained in the Pyithu Pantaing (The Goal of the People) Programme: "The downfall of the Myanmar Armed Forces is the lack of abiding by the military Code of Conduct." The CoC, he said, is of two parts: dealing with prisoners of war in accordance with the rules for POWs, and making "targeting decisions to take measures to limit harm to persons and property protected by the Law of War" and "preventing subordinates from executing an attack that would unlawfully harm those persons and property" (Nicholas Tsagourias (2016), Targeting and the Law of War, Oxford Bibliographies). Nyi Thuta stressed that the SAC armed forces have breached the CoC in so many ways, that the CoC is very important to put an end to hatred, bitterness, and oppression. All armed forces, including the PDFs, are required to follow the CoC, otherwise, revenge would come to a violator from the POW's families and supporters. If the violations continue for long, the groups of violators, who had based themselves not on justice, but on hate, would turn themselves into terrorists.

Captain Nyi Thuta's warning to the PDFs regarding the importance of adhering to the Code of Conduct (CoC) must be taken seriously by the comrades of the Spring Revolution. Meanwhile, within the army community, SAC forces of various ranks have fully committed to breaching the CoC, allowing their hatred and oppression to manifest unchecked.

On September 24, 2022, at 2:45 pm, an unexpected incident occurred: retired army officer Brigadier Gen. Ohn Thwin and his son-in-law Retired Capt. Yè Teza were assassinated. Brigadier Gen. Ohn Thwin, a graduate of the Defence Service Academy (Badge No. 15), held senior positions among present and retired generals. His assassination sent shockwaves not only through the military circle but also the public. The incident took place in his mansion, located in a secure environment for the elites, where he was shot to death. The assailants also confiscated his mobile phones.

The motive behind his assassination initially remained unclear, but Yangon Khit Thit News Article shed light on his background. It revealed that Brigadier Gen. Ohn Thwin was one of the masterminds behind the attempted coup. The article also highlighted his personality traits, suggesting a lack of adherence to the CoC, along with his tendencies towards hate and oppression.

Brigadier Gen. Ohn Thwin shared a close relationship with Vice-Senior General Soe Win. A source from military circles revealed that a year prior to the coup, he sent a note to Soe Win suggesting that the coup could be executed within the confines of the 2008 Constitution, framed as a transfer of power to the military. On his social media account, dated March 8, 2020, he wrote: "The Constitution is designed to prevent a coup, but if actions deviate from it and people refuse to accept the term 'coup,' a new term must be coined, such as 'transferring power.' This ensures that the original essence is not violated."

Brigadier Gen. Ohn Thwin welcomed the coup warmly. He stated: "There's a village named Daung Nang Kya ('Down the Fighting Peacock, the Emblem of the NLD, from its Palace'). I have a photo saved in my phone's gallery that I took, showing me standing before the welcome sign, 'Welcome to Daung Nang Kya.' That photo now holds significant meaning as of February 1, 2021, when Min Aung Hlaing initiated the coup."

Brigadier Gen. Ohn Thwin was known for urging the military to intensify violence against protesters during the Spring Revolution, with reports indicating that he encouraged the military to escalate their crackdown on the demonstrations. According to sources within the army community, he was quoted advising the military, "The more lives you take, the faster the suppression of the riots! Crush them swiftly, crush them thoroughly!"

On a separate note, Daw Aung San Suu Kyi made an appearance at the International Court of Justice (ICJ) where she defended her country's military against allegations of genocide. She stated, "[...] Regrettably, the Gambia has presented to the Court an incomplete and misleading portrayal of the situation in Rakhine State, Myanmar." (December 12, 2019, Transcript in Al Jazeera.) Brigadier Gen. Ohn Thwin shared a comment on his social media account dated June 2, 2018, stating, "So unkind as man's ingratitude."

"Now I'd die happy because I witness today what you call the 'International Prostitute.'"

This army officer also commented on the assassination of Lawyer U Ko Ni on his social media account, dated February 16, 2019, as follows:

"Nga Ni ('nga' is a derogatory addressing term in Burmese) got shot. Don't know for sure whether he'd go to Jannah and get 72 virgins (peace and blessings upon him). Are you now in Jannah, Nga Ni? Can you hear me? Don't know what would happen to the case of Ko Kyi Lin (the murderer of Lawyer U Ko Ni). Are you in Jannah, Nga Ni? Can you hear me? Sabbe sattā kammasakā (All beings have their individual kamma, good and bad actions as their own personal property)."

Such a male soldier, rotten at heart, did not receive any scathing criticisms from the army community. Instead, he was showered with praises, and when he got shot, of course, deep condolences, as well. Reputation of the honourable Tatmadaw, where is it gone? Honourable is the Tatmadaw "with a long, noble tradition!"

Corner:

The Views of the International Community

"Is Myanmar's Military on Its Last Legs?"

This is the topic of an article dated June 21, 2022, by Adjunct Fellow (Non-resident) Michael Martin, Southeast Asia Program, at the Center for Strategic and International Studies (CSIS) in the USA. The article highlights the deteriorating position of Burma military, noting significant defeats and casualties suffered in battles with Myanmar's ethnic armed organisations (EAOs) and People's Defence Forces (PDFs) nationwide. The Tatmadaw forces are now confined to their bases out of fear of being killed. Additionally, the military faces challenges in retaining existing soldiers and recruiting new ones to replace the deceased and wounded, as a large number of soldiers have deserted their units. The article underscores that military's authority has declined, with approximately 40–50 percent of Myanmar now under the control of EAOs or PDFs.

Ishaan Tharoor wrote an article titled "Burma's Junta can't win the civil war it started," published in *The Washington Post* on July 21, 2022. The article referenced findings from investigations by the International Institute of Strategic Studies (IISS) and Amnesty International, revealing the military's use of banned landmines in their harsh suppression of resistance forces. It highlighted the international community's limited response to the suffering endured by the people of Burma, noting a reluctance to escalate involvement in an already complex conflict.

The Economist, in an article dated August 18, 2022, titled "Myanmar's shadow government deserves more," urged the international community to support the National Unity Government (NUG), stating that international recognition and the financial support it would bring could serve as a positive initial step.

Former US Ambassador to Burma, Scot Marciel, penned an article on the online platform of the United States Institute of Peace (USIP) on August 22, advocating for support to the resistance movement. The article asserts that the brutal coup regime should not be considered a legitimate representative in discussions concerning Burma. It criticises the ASEAN's five-point consensus as "an incoherent initiative that was dead on arrival more than a year ago."

Marciel categorises the international community into three groups: the first, including Russia, China, and India, shamelessly supports the junta and supplies weapons; the second consists of ASEAN nations persisting with the five-point consensus; and the third comprises the West, which "has imposed sanctions, offered humanitarian aid, and taken a strong rhetorical position opposing the coup."

The article highlights the reluctance of the West to actively support the armed resistance of Ethnic Armed Organizations (EAOs) and People's Defense Forces (PDFs), favouring instead "the cautious, ineffectual path of supporting ASEAN's failed plan." It emphasises that the ongoing civil war is not merely a power struggle between political parties but rather a response to the "hated, corrupt, and bloodthirsty" Burmese armed forces. The military's long history of conflict with ethnic minority groups and the atrocities committed, including genocide against the Rohingyas, draw parallels to the brutality of the Khmer Rouge in Southeast Asia.

The article stresses that the impact made by the efforts of the international community has remained "neutral." The overwhelming factors contributing to this status quo are as follows: while China, Russia, and India have been supportive of the junta, including providing arms, the majority of the international community has shown "rhetoric, moral outrage toward the junta, and public support for the Myanmar people." The article suggests that the only way for Myanmar to emerge from this crisis with any hope of peace and stability is for the military to be forced out of power or at least forced into a position of such weakness that it seeks a face-saving departure from power to preserve itself. The military's planned bogus elections for 2023 aim only to transform Burma into a single-party state, or what the junta refers to as "disciplined democracy." It is also suggested that the ASEAN five-point consensus should be formally terminated according to Malaysia's proposal. Other suggestions include the United States reconsidering joining EU sanctions on Myanmar Oil and Gas Enterprise, which accounts for much of the junta's revenue. Such sanctions pose a supply problem for the US ally Thailand, but a dedicated team should be seeking creative ways to address the issue. Additionally, the UN Secretary-General should lead an international campaign to create a humanitarian assistance corridor via Thailand and India.

With the topic, "Is Myanmar's National Unity Government Ready to Govern?", Philipp Annawitt wrote an article in *The Diplomat*, dated September 6, 2022. The article commences with the observation: "Observers are slowly coming around to the realisation that the once mighty Myanmar military, or Sit-tat, can be beaten by the forces opposing Myanmar's military coup of 2021." As a leader of the International Institute for Democracy and Electoral Assistance (IDEA), the researcher conducted a study on the NUG's capacities and needs. It was discovered that the people of Burma support the performance legitimacy of the NUG, that the NUG "now controls significant territory, commands the loyalty of the overwhelming majority of its people, and provides security and justice in the areas under its control"; "The NUG provides services in areas it controls—and beyond"; and "The NUG is advancing a difficult transition to federal democracy that has a chance to succeed." In other words, the NUG has laid down plans for building a federal democratic nation through negotiations and agreements with ethnic groups, and through the National Unity Consultative Council (NUCC), composed of ethnic groups, Political Dialogues have been established. Therefore, the researcher has given his verdict that the NUG is ready to govern.

Regarding the inadequate global response to the crisis in Burma, The ReliefWeb, dated July 20, 2022, criticised the international community: "The Myanmar people are not receiving the humanitarian assistance they need." Heidi Hautala, International Peace Institute (IPI) Committee Chair and Vice-President of the European Parliament, called for an end to "inaction" and to prevent "the worst-case scenario for millions of people in Myanmar." Charles Santiago, IPI Committee Member, Malaysian MP, and Chair of ASEAN Parliamentarians for Human Rights (APHR), expressed his view: "[...] Reliance on ASEAN is not a strategy, but rather a disingenuous deflection of responsibility by international actors."

Additionally, in The Hill, Heidi Hautala, Iham Omar (representative of the 5th District Minnesota and committee member of the IPI), and Charles Santiago expressed their views in the article dated October 5, 2022, denouncing the actions of the US, European, and other democratic countries toward Burma as mere lip service, characterised by "regular statements of concern," while highlighting ASEAN's involvement. The article recommends a swift change in course by the international community. The IPI collaborated with lawmakers from seven countries in Africa, Asia, and Europe to conduct an International Parliamentary Inquiry into "the failed response to the crisis," which resulted in recommendations. The first step is to address the immediate humanitarian crisis by urging international donors to provide aid and resources through its civil society and Ethnic Armed Organizations (EAOs). The UN is recommended to encourage India and Thailand to accept refugees and facilitate aid flows without pushing them back. Secondly, the US is urged to adopt the EU's model of imposing sanctions on junta-owned companies such as Myanmar Oil and Gas Enterprise (MOGE). The IPI emphasised the importance of the international community unanimously recognizing the NUG and its partners as "the true representatives of the people of Myanmar." The article concludes that although the international community has failed to respond adequately to the crisis in Burma, it is not too late to take action for improvement because "the future of a whole country depends on it."

On December 21, 2022, the UN Security Council adopted Resolution 2669 (2022) (S/RES/2669(2022)) on the situation in Myanmar with a vote of 12 in favour, none against, and 3 abstentions (China, the Russian Federation, and India). The resolution demands an immediate end to all forms of violence throughout the country, urges the Myanmar military to release all arbitrarily detained prisoners, including President Win Myint and State Counselor Daw Aung San Suu Kyi, and reiterates its call to uphold democratic institutions and processes while pursuing constructive dialogue and reconciliation in accordance with the will and interests of the people of Burma. The council also calls for "concrete and immediate actions to effectively and fully implement ASEAN's Five-Point Consensus." The Secretary-General or his Special Envoy was requested to report to the Council by March 12, 2023.

During the statements from 15 countries, the necessity for "full, safe, and unhindered humanitarian access" was stressed, along with the importance of ensuring "the full protection, safety, and security of humanitarian and medical personnel." The Council emphasised the need to address the root causes of the crisis in Rakhine State and to create conditions necessary for the voluntary, safe, dignified, and sustainable return of Rohingya refugees and internally displaced persons. However, it was noted that the Council "should have directly addressed the severe violations of the freedom of religion and belief."

China, as well as the Russian Federation, explained their country's abstention, stating that "there is no quick fix for the Myanmar issue and the solution to the conflict depends on Myanmar itself." Ireland welcomed the adoption of the Resolution but pointed out that "the Council's actions in response to the violence in Myanmar have been inadequate." Ireland suggested that the Council "could have convened an open briefing," "could have recognized and condemned the continued sale and transfer of arms to Myanmar," and "could have directly called on the military to stop its assault on the people of Myanmar."

India made a statement in its explanation of its country's abstention, highlighting that "her country shares a long border with Myanmar, along with historic and cultural links with its people." India emphasised that "any instability in that country directly impacts India," and resolving the current crisis is a matter of national security. India stated that "the welfare of Myanmar's people remains India's priority," and "the complex situation in Myanmar calls for quiet, patient diplomacy."

On December 8, 2022, during the 117th Congress, the House of Representatives approved the National Defense Authorization Act 2023 (NDAA 2023), which authorises defence-related activities and addresses a wide variety of other issues, with 380 votes in favour to 50 against. On December 15, the Senate approved the Act with 83 votes in favour to 11 against. President Biden signed and enacted H.R. 7776 on December 23. The Burma Act of 2022 is included in the NDAA 2023.

In fact, the Draft was already submitted to both the House of Representatives and the Senate in October 2021. It was approved in April 2022 by the House of Representatives and has now been signed into law. This Act contains seven separate elements pertaining to the U.S. policy in Burma.

One section includes a general statement on U.S. policy, expressing support for "the people of Burma in their struggle for democracy, freedom, human rights, and justice." This section calls for support of the National Unity Government (NUG), but the ethnic armed organisations (EAOs) or the People's Defense Forces (PDFs) are considered only in the aspect of "non-lethal assistance."

The U.S. policy aims to "support a 'credible process' for the restoration of civilian rule, reform of the Burmese military, and the protection of the rights of minority groups." It also considers "the continued provision of humanitarian assistance for victims of violence still within Myanmar, as well as those in the surrounding region." The Act further calls for "the unconditional release of all political prisoners in Myanmar."

The term included in the Act related to taking action against the SAC covers 8 years, with no need for renewing the term for implementation.

Thus, in late 2022, the reactions of the international community to the political conditions in Burma tipped the balance in favour of the Spring Revolution. However, the outbreak of the Russia-Ukraine war has overshadowed the crisis in Burma, diverting attention away from it. Despite efforts by the Permanent Representative of Burma to the United Nations U Kyaw Moe Tun, the voice of Burma continues to reach decision-makers in the international community, but it must be acknowledged that sufficient information has not yet reached the public. Humans are prone to forgetting and forgiving, often moving on if news ceases to appear in the media. Consequently, the majority of the world population has overlooked the ongoing strength of the Spring Revolution of the Burmese people, which has persisted for over seven hundred days. The crisis in Burma remains largely unnoticed, stuck in the earlier phases of the Maze. Clearly, efforts to bring the struggles of the Burmese people to the attention of the world media have taken on a new form of strife.

Corner:

The People's Perspectives Towards the International Community

The evening lay there, like a patient etherized on a stretcher. A private room in a restaurant.

"In terms of geopolitics, you all know," began a middle-aged woman, initiating the conversation, "ours is a case of a country finding no way out in a Maze." She was a former university student who had joined the 1988 Democratic Uprising as an activist.

"Aha!" exclaimed a bespectacled young lady, a poetess, with playful expressions. "Look at the stance of our good old neighbours, I mean, our neighbouring countries. We are proud to have the superpowers as our good neighbours, sticking to opposing political policies. Aha! Armed to the teeth with opposing political policies, but sharing the same common interests of their own! The Crouching Tiger and the Hidden Dragon prowling for the same Prey! The Hidden Dragon–that's China–is exerting its power over the Golden Land of Myanmar, but the Crouching Tiger–that's India–and the Green Pheasant–that's Japan–are bound to deal with the SAC to stop the moves of the Dragon. Their common target is the Rakhine State with an amazing coastal line. That's the Dragon's 'String of Pearls' strategy, building a network in the IOR (Indian Ocean Region), surrounding India, you see! That's why the Dragon pushes the AA to make a ceasefire with the SAC. It isn't the idea of the AA, I suppose. I must say it's the move of China, as well as the move of Sasakawa, one of the wealthiest tycoons of Japan." She was a former activist who had joined the 1996 democratic movement.

Apparently, China, Japan, and India have heavily invested in the Rakhine State. However, during the rule of the SAC, these countries aim to justify their investment projects under the topic of Regional Peace and Stability. Despite Sasakawa, the Chairman of the Nippon Foundation, denying that he represents the government of Japan, Japan acknowledges and respects his efforts to restore peace and rehabilitation in war-stricken regions of Kachin and Rakhine States. This is seen as a strategy to counterbalance China's influence.

"Do you remember when Min Aung Hlaing met the Chief of Defence Forces of the Royal Thai Armed Forces in Rakhine?" said a dark-skinned, young woman, who was a former prisoner of conscience. "Their main topics of discussion might have been related to security in the border area. Perhaps, they discussed military air strikes, the situation of Burmese refugees, and, above all, the seizure of property belonging to Min Aung Hlaing's family following the arrest of Tun Min Latt." On January 19, 2023, the 8th Thai-Myanmar High-level Committee meeting took place on Ngapali beach, Thandwe Township, Rakhine State, where the junta leader Min Aung Hlaing met the Chief of Defence Forces of the Royal Thai Armed Forces.

"Yeah, I remember," said the bespectacled poet. "That was at the hotel in Thandwe, owned by Teza." Teza, a crony with close ties to former Senior-General Than Shwe, known as a military dictator, owns several international hotel chains.

"Anyway," said a political activist around sixty, who had previously been more pro-Chinese than pro-US, "if we mark on the map the areas free from clashes with the SAC, with no protests, you'll see all the EAOs that China has influenced. It's as clear as daylight!"

For the past two years, there have been few armed conflicts in border areas along China, where ethnic groups such as the Wa, Kokang, Ta'ang, armed Shan groups, and Rakhine regions where AA forces are stationed. Although some clashes occurred in Rakhine regions, the AA and the SAC recently declared a ceasefire. Propaganda news suggests that the SAC and EAOs, which signed ceasefire agreements, are engaged in peace processes. However, news of these negotiations has been overshadowed by reports of the SAC's brutalities against local people, including massacres, arrests, torture, and burning residential areas to ashes.

"In fact, you know," said the former pro-Chinese activist, "Russia and China could have exercised a veto on the Resolution, but wow! They abstained from voting, you know. From my point of view, Russia's political agenda perhaps doesn't prioritise Burma. When Russia invaded Ukraine, they needed partners to support their war crimes. Besides, Myanmar is a lucrative market for arms dealing. That's why Russia is interested in Myanmar." He gestured to the young waiter at another table to refill the pot of plain tea.

"Well," said the middle-aged woman, a former university student who still kept in touch with the academic staff of Yangon University, "we can't underestimate Russia's actions. I've heard that Russia is offering more scholarships for Myanmar students to attend universities in the Russian Federation. Those non-CDM students will surely welcome this opportunity. One amusing thing is, you know, for over the last 90 years, Myanmar military dictators have sent about a hundred officers to Russia on scholarships every year, but the Russian trainers and the Myanmar trainees have exchanged their bad habits—like bullying, cheating, and stealing from other trainees. You can compare the bad habits of the Russian army and Min Aung Hlaing's army side by side."

The Russian Federation, much like China, has distanced itself from democratic forces and has only engaged in joint military exercises with other nations. Therefore, it can be assumed that Russia remains somewhat unfamiliar to the Burmese people. During the term of the Burmese Socialist Program Party BSPP, the Burmese people became acquainted with Russia through translations of Russian works, which were the only form of literature permitted by the Press Scrutiny and Registration Office. While military relations between Russia and Burma were strengthened, the two governments failed to establish strong ties of friendship and goodwill. The Burmese people are now astonished to see Russia's lack of discretion in exercising military might in armed conflicts, which is now being compared to that of the SAC's armed forces.

"Yes, you're right," said the former prisoner of conscience, his dark-skinned figure barely visible in the dim corner of the shabby-looking restaurant. "I think India is an interesting case. Of course, the SAC's shells get into its territory, but they just ignore it as though nothing happens. Achchha! Achchha! In the UN Security Council, India stood among the abstentions. They also have cases of strong chauvinism and extreme religious beliefs in their own political and social situations, but from my point of view, they could do a lot more if they truly support democratic practices. Especially, instead of handing over humanitarian aid to the hands of the SAC, India, as well as Thailand, is the best channel for supplying direct aid to Myanmar refugees in troubled waters."

"But India is a federal democratic nation, isn't it?" said the bespectacled poet. "Thank God, the supplies are flowing in through the state governments. We are grateful to Mizoram, the state of India. We could learn from this, that if there's no democracy, it's hard to go federal."

Their conversation took place in a quiet atmosphere since it was a restaurant in the suburban area.

"In fact," said the pro-Chinese activist, "because the Chairmanship of ASEAN now goes to Indonesia, it's high time for the winds of change. Indonesia has tried out many ideas to sort out the problem. But the trouble is it's hard to make the first move since the SAC has not yet carried out even one single consensus out of five!"

"Oh, how I was impressed with what an Indonesian senior minister said, I think, on a panel at the World Economic Forum," said the bespectacled poet. "To use his exact words, mind, 'There are so many militaries in charge of the government, but if you are not qualified, why should you be president?' He also said, 'Let someone else who is qualified manage this country…' Remember he is a former military leader! Such a foresighted military leader! Quite different from our military personnel, ranging from the lowest rank of a soldier to the top. Not foresighted at all! Never think of doing good for the country! So disappointing!"

It was during the World Economic Forum, held in Davos, Switzerland, on January 18, 2023, that Indonesia's Coordinating Minister of Maritime Affairs and Investment Luhut Pandjaitan gave that pointed remark, as stated in *Bloomberg News*. It must be noted that during the term of the NLD government, with the economic growth of Burma, per capita GDP stood at 6-7 percent, but per capita GDP during the rule of the SAC has gone down to 18 percent. This is, undoubtedly, a clear indicator that, meanwhile, a disqualified military leader, seizing the power of the state, has been doing the management of the country.

"Poor, poor Myanmar people like us!" said the bespectacled poet, almost indignantly. "European countries have got themselves busy with the Russia-Ukraine crisis, the US is just giving lip service, having more interest in Taiwan. China, doggedly following its policy, doesn't bother about boosting up more democratic nations in the political scenario of the world. They could be making a straight bet, but they don't. What they do is backup one that will safeguard their interests, while letting their octopus's arms reach out for other sources just in case. What a cruel world! We have to rely on nothing but our own hands!"

Silence fell in this private room. They all nodded, looking a bit despondent.

"Well, if you recall and reflect," said the former prisoner of conscience, "our president U Win Myint did the right thing in 2018. He granted full pardon to those charged under Section 401(1). Otherwise, we all could have been arrested once again, without the need for new charges! Thank God, we can now meet again and talk." Some political prisoners were released, granted amnesty under Section 401, Article 1 (Power to suspend or remit sentences), but with conditions. The majority of the political prisoners, who were later elected as representatives of the Hluttaw, prime ministers, and the President, were released under this Section. On April 17, 2018, the President's Office issued a statement that, considering the social rights of the political prisoners released under conditions, President U Win Myint, exercising the power vested in the President, granted full pardon to all political prisoners. This amnesty must be well noted in Burma's legal history because it was granted to political prisoners only when a prisoner of conscience had been elected President. It was only after the attempted coup that the citizens of Burma realised the significance of such an unconditional amnesty granted to political prisoners.

"Yes, you're right," said the middle-aged woman, a former university student and activist. "I believe President U Win Myint did the right thing. He has dismissed the charges against him as false. The SAC has treated his detained family badly. I've heard that he's been moved to Taungoo Prison. His health conditions are not quite good. But not many have made strong claims for his case." Initially, the SAC had secretly confined the deposed President somewhere in Naypyitaw, but on January 14, 2023, he was moved to Taungoo Prison. The news of his detained family was no longer heard.

"Ugh..." said the bespectacled poet, "our people are getting sort of jet-lagged in this long flight of our mission. That's why Acting President Duwa Lashi La stressed in his speech that we should not forget that only the Myanmar citizens, both local and abroad, have been the main source of supporting the lifeblood of our Revolution. Yes, he's right. No other nations play a crucial role in the success of our mission. Do you remember what he said? 'If without the support of the people,' he says, 'no government can be sustainable in the long term.' We might take his words to heart, that the President was referring not only to the SAC but also to the NUG. The people's support can change over time, so the present is the most crucial moment. In the lifespan of history, two years is just a flickering moment, but our people have been going through miserable moments every second, every minute!"

"Well," said the pro-Chinese activist, "in some cases, there could be strategic dissensions caused by the SAC so that we could not build mutual understanding among ourselves. For example, getting the armed ethnic groups of Northern Shan State controlled via China, you know. What I do not understand about these armed ethnic groups is their mindset. They seem to believe that as long as they are getting along with the SAC, there would be peace in their regions, and they cling to the lame promise from the SAC that they would be granted autonomy and self-determination. On the other hand, what the SAC has calculated is more logical: Just a crack among the armed ethnic groups would topple down their armed uprising!"

They all fell silent once again. According to the data of the UN, there is already a displaced population of over one million. Still, there prevail 'shoot and run' protests in urban areas, as well as armed conflicts in border areas. The people of Burma firmly believe that they would be able to strive for their survival only after they have liberated themselves from the grip of the SAC. No wonder the Spring Revolution, already gaining momentum, will continue to advance forward in full swing.

Passage:

Spring 2023

"I must stress that 2023 will mark a crucial year for the turning point of Myanmar, and that we have consolidated our military and political coordinations with the revolutionary ethnic groups and other important organisations," said Acting President Duwa Lashi La of the National Unity Government, in his New Year Speech on January 1, 2023. He also warned the people to denounce the sham elections that the SAC has prepared, and to be vigilant about the possible dangers of the SAC's attempts to split up the allied revolutionary forces.

The National Unity Government (NUG) and the National Unity Consultative Council (NUCC) issued a joint statement on that day, urging all citizens from various ethnic backgrounds and regions to cooperate and coordinate to the best of their abilities, joining the ongoing Revolution that will ultimately determine the fate of the country. It was emphasised that all citizens are obligated to contribute to the current Spring Revolution, aimed at uprooting military dictatorship, establishing a genuine federal union, and resolving long standing political issues that have persisted for over seventy years. Eliminating the military dictatorship, the statement asserts, will also eliminate ethnic and racial privilege stemming from chauvinism, ensuring balance and self-determination for all ethnic groups and federal states. The joint statement includes a pledge to establish a federal democratic union that upholds the rights of citizenship, humanity, and minority rights in accordance with democratic principles.

On January 12, 2023, the NUG issued a statement denouncing the air strikes on the Chin National Front (CNF) headquarters, Camp Victoria, in Thantlang Township, located on the India-Myanmar border, from January 10 to 11. The NUG also urged the concerned countries, specifically India, to take effective action against the SAC for intruding into the airspace of neighbouring countries and launching air strikes.

These air strikes resulted in the deaths of 5 CNF soldiers and the injury of about 10 others. Additionally, the hospital ward where local people received healthcare services, as well as some residential buildings, were damaged. At least one bomb was dropped inside the territory of India. The NUG criticised the SAC for openly breaching the UN Security Council's statement calling for an immediate cessation of violence.

On January 13, 2023, Minister for Foreign Affairs of the Republic of Indonesia, H.E Retno L.P. Marsudi, made a declarative statement announcing the establishment of a new Office of ASEAN Special Envoy on Myanmar. The NUG welcomed this statement.

On December 23, 2022, at Areindama Hall, the Myanmar Police Force, Naypyitaw, at the No. 1/2022 Meeting of the Counter-Terrorist Central Committee, which was held secretly, Minister for Home Affairs Let. Gen. Soe Htut took measures to denounce the NUG, CRPH, and the PDFs as international terrorist groups and sought support from Interpol to collaborate with Myanmar in combating "terrorism." However, the global police body, declining its support at the request of the SAC, made a remark that it would not intervene in situations involving domestic politics. This left the home affairs minister in despair, as the leakage of this information was reported by Yangon Khit Thit News on January 15, 2023.

During these days, false news surfaced on Facebook and Telegram, spreading propaganda that the NUG was secretly negotiating with the SAC for an opportunity to participate in the SAC's elections.

On January 16, a demonstration led by Myanmar citizens was staged in front of the Embassy of Myanmar in Tel Aviv, Israel, protesting against the sham election planned by the SAC.

On January 18, the Special Advisory Council on Myanmar (SAC-M) reported that companies in Singapore are covertly aiding arms exports, which are either directed to the Directorate of Defence Industries (DDI) or to purported civilian companies. The report indicated that Australia, France, China, India, Israel, Ukraine, Germany, Taiwan, Japan, Russia, South Korea, and the USA are supporting "Myanmar's extensive weapons production network," providing the SAC with a supply of "raw materials, equipment parts, technology, and maintenance." It was noted that Singapore serves as a "strategic transit point" for such clandestine supply for the military production of weapons by the Myanmar military. However, the Ministry of Foreign Affairs of Singapore stated that Singapore "does not authorise the transfer of arms or items with potential military application" to Myanmar. A ministry spokesperson responded to the SAC-M report, stating that Singapore had only engaged in economic activities before the coup.

On January 21, with no armed clashes on the ground, a Mi35 jet fighter deliberately dropped bombs over Bahin Station Hospital in the controlled area of NUG. A 60-year-old woman died, and two PDF soldiers were wounded.

On January 21, coup leader Min Aung Hlaing attended the Chinese New Year celebration held at No. 1 Thuwanna National Indoor Stadium, Yangon. On this occasion, he remarked, "China has been an important neighbour to Myanmar, while Myanmar has been a reliable neighbour to China." Minister of Foreign Affairs Daw Zin Mar Aung conveyed a message of felicitations, dated January 22, to the Ministry of Foreign Affairs of China, expressing the NUG's gratitude to China for being a supportive neighbour to the Myanmar people on the international stage.

It is worth noting that following the military coup by the SAC on February 1, 2021, China has engaged in the most significant number of trading exchanges with the SAC. In the first six months of the 2022-23 fiscal year, the trading value with China reached over US $4.4 billion. China has constructed three new rail-road-sea cross-border trade routes connected with Myanmar: a rail-road-Indian Ocean route linking Sichuan province to Yangon port via northern Shan State to Singapore; a trade route connecting Chongqing to Laos, Thailand, and Myanmar; and a maritime route directly connecting the Beibu Gulf port in Guangxi province to the Yangon port.

On January 26, the SAC passed a new law regarding the registration of political parties, known as the Political Parties Registration Law. This new legislation is evidently more restrictive compared to the previous law. According to the new regulations, political parties intending to participate in elections must have a minimum of 100,000 party members and maintain a party fund totaling MMK 100 million 1,000. Parties entering the 2023 General Election are required to renew their registration within 60 days, beginning on January 26. Failure to comply with this law results in automatic invalidation of party status, leading to dissolution. Political analysts suggest that this law is aimed at limiting the number of political parties renewing their registration, except for the USDP, colloquially known as the "Stupid Rhinoceros."

On January 27, the CRPH and the Ministry of International Cooperation of the NUG conducted a video conference on the National Defense Authorization Act (NDAA) enacted by the USA. Meetings were held between the NUG, the Ministry of Home Affairs and Immigration, the People's Administrative Committees, and the People's Defense Forces, focusing on reducing the impact of revolutionary activities on civilian lives, addressing the threat of air strikes, and ensuring adequate emergency provisions.

On January 30, Farhan Haq, Deputy Spokesperson for the Secretary-General of the UN, issued a statement regarding Myanmar. In response to the Security Council's request, the Secretary-General's Special Envoy has been working closely with the new Chairperson of ASEAN and engaging all stakeholders to end the violence and restore democracy. Haq emphasised that the UN remains in solidarity with the people of Burma and their democratic aspirations for an inclusive society, including the protection of all communities, including the Rohingya. The UN will address issues stemming from the military's actions since February 2021, which have affected all people across the country. However, access is essential for the UN and its partners to deliver aid on the ground. Haq stressed the need for strengthened cooperation between the UN and ASEAN to pressure the armed forces to respect human rights and fundamental freedoms.

On January 30, in Monywa, campaigns were launched by the Letpadaung Hill Main Strike Committee to commemorate the 2nd Anniversary of the Spring Revolution. Pamphlets were distributed urging the public to participate in the countrywide Silent Strike on February 1.

In crowded places, the A-Nyar Pyit-taing-Htaung Groups affixed stickers to walls, promoting the message "Stay indoors on February 1. Join the Silent Strike." Additionally, the organisers utilised online platforms to promote the Silent Strike campaign.

On January 30, the World Bank issued a report highlighting the economic uncertainties and instabilities in Myanmar. The report noted that due to conflicts, frequent power supply disruptions, and policy changes, the country's GDP per capita has decreased by 13 percent compared to the period before the COVID-19 pandemic under the NLD government. According to the latest data from the UN as of January 30, the number of displaced persons in southeastern Myanmar has increased to 361,000. Across Myanmar, a total of 1.2 million people have been displaced due to conflicts and insecurity since February 1, 2021. Nonprofit organisations have provided humanitarian assistance to 4 million people across the country.

On January 31, the SAC convened the National Defence and Security Council in Naypyitaw. Present at the Council were Acting President U Myint Swe, members of the National Defence and Security Council led by the Commander-in-Chief, and Union Attorney-General Dr. Thida Oo as a Special Guest. Vice President U Henry Van Thio was absent on leave. During the Council meeting, the coup leader reported on the performances and achievements of the SAC, with a particular focus on the activities of the CRPH, NUG, and the PDFs. It was emphasised that the present political situation is considered extraordinary.

Section 425 of the Constitution states: "The National Defence and Security Council may, if the Commander-in-Chief of the Defence Services submits the extension of the prescribed duration by giving reasons why he has not been able to accomplish the assigned duties, on the expiry of the term of the Pyihtaungsu Hluttaw, normally permit two extensions of the prescribed duration for a term of six months for each extension."

According to Section 425, the SAC has extended its term twice, each time for six months. However, the coup leader's reference to an "extraordinary situation" during the recent Council meeting raises questions. This phrase was also noted in the declarative statement made on February 1, suggesting a deliberate motive to renew the SAC's term.

The inclusion of "normally" in Section 425 simply pertains to the renewal process without specifying the assessment criteria. Therefore, the adverb "normally" does not indicate whether the country is experiencing normal conditions. Additionally, the request for the resolution of the Constitutional Tribunal, necessary for interpreting constitutional provisions, was only made and approved during the Council meeting on that same day.

In light of these circumstances, it can be inferred that the SAC extended its term under extraordinary or abnormal circumstances, rather than following the usual process.

On January 31, 2023, the Asia Network for Free Elections (ANFREL), the International Institute for Democracy and Electoral Assistance (International IDEA), the National Democracy Institute (NDI), and the International Republican Institute (IRI) issued a joint statement. This statement, endorsed by International Election Experts and Organizations on Myanmar, provided detailed information and emphasised that any election conducted by the illegitimate Union Election Commission under the State Administration Council (SAC) would be deemed illegitimate.

It stated, "No recommendations that we could offer on this sham 'election' could cure the falsity of the process other than for the SAC to follow the call of the United Nations General Assembly to respect 'the will of the people as freely expressed by the results of the general election of 8 November 2020, to end the state of emergency, to respect all human rights of all the people of Myanmar, and to allow the sustained democratic transition of Myanmar.' The implementation of a sham 'election' will not bring stability. It will only contribute to increasing violence and polarisation, worsen the crisis caused by the military coup, and further threaten regional and international stability and security."

On February 1, 2023, the National Defence and Security Council issued the following statement:

"From February 1, 2021 to January 25, 2023, the losses and damage inflicted by riots to both state-owned and privately-owned property across Myanmar were significant. There were 4,917 instances of property damage, 8,527 explosions of grenades and man-made bombs, and 9,686 reported attacks. Additionally, there were 1,231 cases of residential houses and buildings being burned, resulting in a total of 19,444 acts of violence. Authorities also seized 17,697 firearms of various types, along with 1,382,627 bullets and 27,213 man-made explosives and bombs. These attacks resulted in casualties among government services, administrative officials, monks, children, and civilians, with a total of 5,443 deaths and 4,577 wounded.

Explosions occurred 1,021 times on roads, 66 times on railway lines, 137 times on bridges, 23 times on electricity towers, and 365 times on communication towers. Destruction by fire affected 58 roads, 12 bridges, 2 electricity towers, and 132 communication towers. Additionally, violence and murders led to 152 deaths, including 70 monks, 2 nuns, 66 education department staff, and 14 staff of the ministry of health."

This report was presented by the Commander-in-Chief, who is also the coup leader, to the National Defence and Security Council. However, given that the violence and brutalities inflicted by the SAC armed forces are not distinguished in the report, the accuracy and reliability of the data provided in the aforementioned account is highly questionable.

On the day marking the two-year anniversary of the military coup in Burma, foreign affairs ministers from over twenty countries, including the USA, the UK, Canada, South Korea, New Zealand, and the European Union, collectively urged the international community to take steps towards reducing arms transfers to the SAC.

Thus, the two-year struggle of the SAC has ultimately resulted in fruitless attempts to seize administrative power alone. In contrast, those involved in the Spring Revolution have been dedicated to missions such as overthrowing the SAC, dismantling the military apparatus, deliberating on the formation of a future federal democratic Union, and providing humanitarian aid to war refugees and victims of the SAC's coup. The tenure of the NLD government was criticised by pessimists as a period of miserable existence "under the high heels of the old widow" (referring to Daw Aung San Suu Kyi). Paradoxically, the Burmese people find themselves unable to articulate the profound misery of these two years lived under military oppression—ageing, surviving through a harrowing civil war, enduring displacement, and mourning the loss of countless lives among families, friends, and relatives.

Getting Out of the Maze or Getting Rid of the Walls of the Maze

"If you want to reach your goal, you must find a path. Whether it's straight or crooked, only a path can lead you there. Walking within the winding walls that block you on both sides, pausing when you reach a space, but then continuing on and on! Yet, after encountering numerous dead ends, you must step back, find another path, and venture farther and farther away from the starting point. But where does your goal lie?"

This sensation of being trapped in a dire situation has been all too common in the hearts of the Burmese people across two successive governments in the post-2010 election period. It must be stressed that the restrictions of the 2008 Constitution have contributed neither towards the development of democracy and basic human rights nor to good governance and the fair rule of law.

Even more troubling, the 2008 Constitution has ensnared the Burmese population in a labyrinthine Maze, where they embark on a journey but never make progress, let alone reach their destination. It appears that military leaders are determined to never surrender their role in Burma's political landscape. To achieve this, they have manipulated the law to suit their interests, blurring the distinction between the military as an "armed wing" of the government and the civil services.

The soldiers have been brainwashed. Their leaders have inculcated in them the motto, "The Tatmadaw is Your Mother, the Tatmadaw is Your Father." It's no wonder the soldiers have become entangled in the Military Maze, ensnared in the illusion of superiority, convinced they are better equipped to govern state affairs. With longstanding political tensions among the national ethnicities, civilians have been coerced into accepting the military's narrative. The military has strived to underscore its indispensable role, often invoking the term "the Union Spirit" for propaganda purposes. Over time, this phrase has become cliché and worn-out, losing its original significance, and, ultimately, undergoing a transformation in meaning.

The Tatmadaw has long been a state-level institution wielding military power and exerting authoritative control over the territory. For decades, this institution has systematically targeted the Bama-Buddhists, the majority group, as its main source of recruits. Consequently, minorities have been compelled to adopt the belief that they need to arm themselves and tightly control their territories to safeguard their race and autonomy. Over time, Burmese society has lost its way in the Maze, akin to Pandora's box, making it increasingly difficult to address the root problems.

Then came the illusions. A new government was formed, with some civilians assuming administrative power. These civilians were led to believe, "Finally, we've successfully navigated out of the Maze." Both the Burmese citizens and international political analysts fell into this illusion. They felt they could now relax, unaware that they were still within the confines of the Maze, blocked on both sides. They failed to recognize that they had become lost in the illusion, mistaking many dead ends for golden thrones and silver mansions.

In truth, the military has never wanted to see the emergence of a civilian government where civilians play a key role in politics. Ignoring the election results, a coup d'état occurred on February 1, 2021, as the military sought to manipulate state power. They justified their actions, using spoonerism, claiming they only wanted to control state power ("ah-nar-htein"), insisting it was not a coup ("not ah-nar-thein"). While confirming the validity of the 2008 Constitution, they also made a 'promise' to hold a new election and transfer power to the elected party. To their consternation, people now realise they are lost at the crossroads, neither advancing forward nor retracing their steps in the Maze with no exits!

"You must get back on the right track, the path leading to your goal. As long as you stay in the Maze, no matter how far you may have travelled, you will never reach your goal. A metaphor in the Myanmar language goes: this kind of complicated situation, or Gordian knot, is compared to a Thaput-U, a dried fruit of the sponge gourd with a stringy mass of fibres inside. However, the politics of Burma is much more complicated than a Thaput-U, since it is replete with so many misleading exits and blind alleys. Therefore, the slogan, 'Down with the military dictatorship' has been changed into the new slogan, 'Down with any form of dictatorship' because the Spring Revolution aims at reforming not only the political system but also all anti-democratic, outdated forms of culture that do not fit into modern times. In other words, you should not waste your time finding an exit out of the walls of the Maze, whether thick or thin. Instead, you and I and everyone are bound to ram and topple any part of the wall of the Maze that does not fit into democratic practices, that does not guarantee equality among our national races. The whole Maze must topple down! And we all must join hands to build the highway leading towards the federal democratic Union, shining under the sun. The road we want to take we will build on our own, and we will march towards our goal."

The Spring Revolution was first launched on February 1, 2021. It must be admitted that the Revolution has had unintended consequences: it has reinforced some parts of the Walls of the Maze. Meanwhile, the Spring Revolution remains an unresolved puzzle. Nevertheless, while some parts of the walls of the Maze have not yet been torn down, others will surely collapse within two years.

Even the NUG, the vanguard of the Revolution, represents the majority of national ethnicities but is still confronted with the Wall that impedes the inclusiveness of all ethnic groups. However, all have rallied under the same banner of the Spring Revolution: The Committee Representing the Pyidaungsu Hluttaw (CRPH), comprising elected representatives, the National Unity Consultative Council (NUG), comprising various organisations and groups, and the armed ethnic groups. The armed Revolution has been chosen as the last resort—the hardcore element of the Spring Revolution.

As a result, the role of armed ethnic groups has become more prominent than that of political parties. In particular, even the Bamas, who desire democracy and had previously staged peaceful strikes against the military dictatorship, have taken up arms on the largest scale in history. The armed revolutions of non-Bama ethnic groups, which have been waging war against the military for decades, have gained stronger ground than ever. Other armed groups proliferating rapidly in many parts of the country—resembling wild, vibrant growth in the deep jungle—are also integral to the Revolution's image. However, calls to the international community to grant legitimacy to the NUG instead of the military have yet to receive significant attention.

It can be assumed that it was the SAC that forced the Revolution to transform into an armed revolution. Clearly, there are both positive and negative consequences of this shift. While the majority believe that the armed revolution is the last resort, millions are unable to take up arms. Some actively support the revolution through supply efforts, while others are hesitant to embrace armed resistance. Therefore, convincing people that an unarmed political revolution still holds promise is a challenge. Political parties bear the responsibility of persuading the public that their unarmed efforts can contribute to political reforms, but their role remains unclear.

Factors such as the SAC's party registration law, the uncertain timing of the sham election, and changes to the electoral system contribute to public scepticism about the Revolution's potential success. Efforts are underway to find a political solution by introducing a new system where all organisations and groups accept the federal democracy charter, which will become the interim Constitution and ensure equal power distribution to all stakeholders. Additionally, armed revolutionaries are educating local communities about federal democratic concepts, promoting the right to engage in unarmed public politics.

Meanwhile, although the people of Burma hope to rely on the international community, anticipating that effective actions will eventually come, they now realise that the country is trapped in a Maze, a result of both its geographical conditions and the SAC's adeptness at "dealing with people," especially with "the Biggest Guns" of the world like China and Russia. While the Burmese diaspora abroad has provided strong support to the Revolution, efforts to establish more diplomatic relations with partner countries have encountered obstacles within the Maze of the international community.

In fact, the character traits of totalitarian dictators like "grandiosity" and "inflated self-importance" (to borrow from Seth Davin Norrholm's book *The Psychology of Dictators: Power, Fear, and Anxiety*), may not be readily apparent under normal circumstances in such a society. However, during challenging times, the personalities of dictators, with their "ultimate potential of human evil," are revealed across various layers of society. As trenchant racism has become a contentious issue during the Spring Revolution, efforts are underway to confront and dismantle this wall of racism as well.

It is essential to emphasise that the Spring Revolution embodies a grand vision. It extends beyond merely overthrowing the SAC; it encompasses a political, military, and cultural transformation aimed at eliminating all forms of dictatorship, including military rule. While the Revolution has made strides over the past two years, its ultimate outcome remains uncertain, with the timing of its conclusion even more elusive.

However, over the past two years, the Revolution has managed to dismantle a significant wall: the military's propaganda machine and dissemination of false information. Previously, the inner workings of the military were shrouded in secrecy, but now, injustices and confidential information within the military are being exposed to the public. This is largely due to defections from the army by individuals choosing to stand with the people, as well as informants still within the military, known as Pha-yè-thees. The role of these informants is pivotal, and their actions highlight the potential effectiveness of internal change driving external change. Thus, it becomes imperative to simultaneously dismantle the walls of the Maze from both within and without, ensuring their complete collapse.

The Spring Revolution continues unabated, pushing forward with unwavering determination and vigour. Its ultimate success hinges on the collective political outlook, speech, behaviour, and performance of every individual in Burmese society. The resounding motto echoed by the people of Burma is: "The Revolution must succeed! A genuine success!" To gauge the progress of the Spring Revolution, one must reflect on how the Burmese people have navigated through challenges and responded with courage over the past two years. These years have witnessed the trials and tribulations of the people at the onset, the midpoint, and the culmination of the Spring, as well as their unwavering resolve and efforts to dismantle the walls of the Maze.

Ma Thida (Sanchaung)
6 April 2023

Epilogue

Battering Down Some Walls of A-Maze: February–December 2023

Almost three years have passed since the SAC's atrocities began in Burma. As I was finalising the conclusion for this book, processing events up to February 2023, it became clear that I needed to provide updates on certain issues. The year 2023 was pivotal in the Spring Revolution, marked by significant changes in dynamics and the evolution of the SAC, especially in the latter half.

February

The SAC, which had announced an extension of the state of emergency on February 1, 2023, initially declared upon seizing power, once again extended its term on August 1. The declaration of martial law in 37 townships nationwide in February 2023 highlights the success of anti-coup resistance in hindering the military's attempts to strengthen its control. At the same time, the military persists in presenting legitimate elections as a political tactic to address the crises they instigated. This clearly indicates that it is unwilling to cede control but intends to tighten its grip through ongoing severe violence against civilian populations. One might wonder whether the SAC will initiate any country reform or engage in dialogue with resistance forces. What could be the exit strategy from this Maze?

March

The Union Election Commission disbanded the National League for Democracy (NLD) and the Shan National League for Democracy (SNLD) since the two parties did not re-register as political parties in accordance with the new political party registration law. It was observed that several other political parties have also not yet received recognition from the Union Election Commission. The new party registration law, which excludes other rival parties from the political scene, seems to ensure the status of the Union Solidarity and Development Party (USDP) as the sole well-established political party. To the Tatmadaw and Ming Aung Hlaing, it appears that the 2008 constitution contains some loopholes that have failed to protect them, so the Senior General needs to build another set of walls for a Maze.

April

On April 11th, a devastating airstrike by SAC troops claimed the lives of at least 100 people in the village of Pazigyi, located in Kanbalu township in Sagaing division. This marked the third significant civilian attack in Sagaing, and it turned out to be the deadliest assault in the country since the coup attempt in February 2021.

June

On June 21, the United States imposed sanctions on two banks controlled by military regime, namely Myanma Foreign Trade Bank (MFTB) and Myanma Investment and Commercial Bank (MICB). It was declared that transactions with these sanctioned Burmese banks must be concluded by August 5, 2023. Although the SAC appeared unaffected by this move, the central bank had to modify the foreign exchange policy in early December.

July

The SAC permitted Don Pramudwinai, the deputy prime minister and foreign minister of Thailand, to have an informal meeting with Daw Aung San Suu Kyi. Speculation arose that she might have been taken somewhere outside the prison for this exceptional meeting. However, the meeting yielded no discernible outcome, and Daw Aung San Suu Kyi showed no response to his offers or promises. Consequently, she was returned to her prison cell in Nay Pyi Taw. In September, reports indicated that prison authorities were notified about Daw Aung San Suu Kyi's declining health, prompting a visit from the prison's chief medical officer. Despite her worsening condition, the junta reportedly rejected her request to see a dental surgeon.

Initially citing the COVID-19 pandemic as a rationale, the SAC had prohibited prison visits by all visitors, including family members. However, due to significant pressure from both internal and external sources, family members have recently been granted that rare chance. *The Irrawaddy* reported that U Win Myint, the detained president, was permitted to meet his family in September. The legal team of Daw Aung San Suu Kyi applied for a visit on October 31, with the prison responding that she was "in good health." The team has not yet met with her personally. Their last meeting with her had taken place in December 2022.

August

A significant reshuffling of the junta-appointed cabinet unfolded. Lieutenant General Yar Pyae assumed the role of Minister of Interior, while General Mya Tun Oo took on the position of Minister of Transportation. The Ministry of International Cooperation was abolished, and Dr. Thet Thet Khaing, the former Union Minister for Social Welfare, Relief, and Resettlement, was appointed as the Minister of Hotel and Tourism. Though the Tatmadaw has a well-known history of bribery and corruption, few high-ranking officers have faced legal consequences until recently. In 2023, a notable shift occurred, resulting in the charging of several high-level military officers under corruption laws, including Lt. Gen. Moe Myint Tun, the seventh-highest leader in the SAC and chairman of various committees, and Gen. Yan Naung Soe, joint secretary of a central committee. These two high-ranking army officers were accused of committing bribery through dealings worth millions of dollars with traders. They were also charged with exploiting the disparity between Myanmar's official exchange rate (2,100 kyats to the US dollar) and the market rate, which deeply affected the value of the Burmese currency exchange. Another breaking news was that Lt. Gen. Soe Htut, the Home Affairs Minister, faced charges for involvement in the mismanagement of passport service and bribery, resulting in five years' imprisonment. Thus, the Tatmadaw has found itself lost in the middle of its own Maze of corruption.

October

On October 15th, the SAC commemorated the 8th anniversary of signing the Nationwide Ceasefire Agreement in Nay Pyi Taw. Present on the occasion were seven out of ten signatories, including the Karen National Liberation Army/Peace Council (KNLA), Pa-O National Liberation Army (PNLA), Arakan Liberation Party (ALP), the Restoration Council of Shan State, the Democratic Karen Benevolent Army (DKBA), New Mon State Party, and Lahu Democratic Union. However, three NCA signatories boycotted: the All-Burma Students' Democratic Front (ABSDF), Chin National Front (CNF), and Karen National Union (KNU).

Given the SAC's ongoing atrocities against civilians, it's imperative to reduce their capacity to produce weapons. Therefore, in late October, the United States imposed sanctions on Myanmar Oil and Gas Enterprise (MOGE). Additionally, the Office of Foreign Assets Control (OFAC) designated three entities and five individuals linked to the SAC. Furthermore, the United States, the United Kingdom, and Canada coordinated to impose additional sanctions on individuals and entities associated with the SAC.

Facing a dire need for US dollars, the SAC issued two orders in mid-October. Firstly, migrant workers who commenced migration from September 2023 with the aid of employment agencies must remit a minimum of 25 percent of their monthly salaries solely through the official channel recognized by the junta. Secondly, Myanmar nationals residing abroad are mandated to initiate tax payments in the foreign currency they have earned, per an amendment to the Union Tax Law

2023, effective from October 1, 2023. This move by the SAC resembles a carrot-and-stick strategy, with the "carrot" directed to the military and the "stick" aimed at its citizens working abroad. The SAC assumes that migrants abroad are major financial supporters of the Spring Revolution, thus framing tax as punishment. It's believed that the "carrot" may alleviate the SAC's financial constraints, particularly concerning foreign currency income, following sanctions against two banks.

1027 and beyond

The Three Brotherhood Alliance, consisting of the Myanmar National Democratic Alliance Army (MNDAA), Arakan Army (AA), and the Ta'ang National Liberation Army (TNLA), launched an offensive in northern Shan State on October 27th. This offensive caught the SAC by surprise, marking one of the most significant military challenges since the seizure of power in February 2021.

The Three Brotherhood Alliance's strategy aligned with China's objective to combat large-scale online scams based in Laukkai, northern Shan State. Even before Operation 1027 was launched, China had exerted significant pressure on the SAC to apprehend suspects involved in the scams. An escape attempt occurred on October 20th, followed by a massacre in Kokang Self-administered Zone (SAZ) where fleeing prisoners were killed by guards at a cyber-scamming facility. Among the 80 victims were four Chinese undercover police officers. These facilities were under the control of cybercrime leader Ming Xuechang, a former member of parliament of USDP, and three other Ming family members, who were issued arrest warrants by China on November 13th. On November 16th, the SAC eventually apprehended the individuals referred to as Chinese citizens.

However, Ming Xuechang was allegedly reported to have died in police custody, and Ming Guochang reportedly committed suicide. China also announced on November 21st that it had already received more than thirty thousand suspected Chinese criminals back from Myanmar. In his early December speech at the National Security and Defense

Council meeting, coup attempt leader Min Aung Hlaing said: "Among illegal foreigners exposed, 2,035 persons were transferred to China until November 28th. A total of 3,738 were arrested and handed over to China. A total of 37,936 persons left Myanmar under their arrangements. So, those illegal foreigners total 43,709, and some people remain." However, their announcement raised one significant question: How could a Chinese citizen (illegal foreigner) be a member of a political party and even become a member of parliament in Burma under the USDP regime during 2010-2015? In fact, he was even appointed to the second-highest position in the administration of Kokant SAZ. Although the SAC claimed he was a citizen of China, his Myanmar national identification card number was also disclosed. Myanmar's 1982 citizenship act never allows dual citizenship, and neither does China.

Ming Xuechang was a leader of Kokang armed groups under Bai Xuoqian's leadership, who pledged loyalty to the Tatmadaw in 2009, joining as border guard force number 1006. In 2010, he transitioned to politics, becoming a candidate for the Shan State regional parliament under the USDP. In 2011, he was elected as an executive member of the Kokang SAZ by the Shan State regional parliament. He won the election and served a full term until 2015. Enjoying the perks of a gazette officer, he received full salaries and benefits, later continuing as a pensioner. In fact, according to Article 407 of the 2008 constitution, the USDP infringed on at least one of four stipulations, as it stated that "directly or indirectly receiving and expending financial, material, and other assistance from [...] a person from a foreign country" and then, it "shall have no right of continued existence." Moreover, under Sections 10 (h) of the Political Parties Registration Law 2010, one of the qualifications of a member of a political party is "being a person who is not a foreigner or not a person who has assumed foreign citizenship;" and under Section 12 (A 6), it is stated that "a party shall not have the right to subsist as a political party if it is involved" in "concealing intentionally without dismissing from the party the person not in conformity with any fact contained in Section 10."

An intriguing fact is that U Thein Soe, who served as the Chairman of the Union Election Commission from 2010 to 2015, was reassigned to the same position in 2021 after the coup. As a retired military judge advocate general, he played a role in approving the re-registration of the USDP in 2023.

Maung Maung, a current member of the USDP, ran as a candidate in the 2020 election and was awarded an honourable title by the SAC in March 2023. He was recognized as the proprietor of a hotel and casino business in Laukai, Burma. He was part of a group of eleven business individuals apprehended by China's security forces on October 1. Invited by the Chinese authorities, they attended Trade Fairs in Lin Cang, together with Maung Maung. However, the citizenship status of Maung Maung, whether he is also a Chinese citizen, remains unclear.

On 10th December, Chinese authorities issued arrest warrants and lucrative rewards for the apprehension of 10 prominent figures (of four famous families, especially the "Bai" family members) heading telecom fraud rings in Myanmar's Shan State, particularly in the Kokang region. The list includes former Kokang region chairman Bai Xuoqian and various Kokang militia leaders aligned with the pro-junta faction. On 12th December, Chinese authorities also issued arrest warrants for "Wa" leaders Bao Yanban also known as Chen Yanban or Xiao Yankui and He Chuntian, for "violating Chinese Law." Then, instantly, the SAC also issued an arrest warrant. In response, Bao Yanban was withdrawn from the United Wa State Army (UWSA)'s politburo, and He Chuntian was dismissed from his former position as mayor of a district in Wa state. In the case of the four family members of Ming Xuechang, there were similar instances where the SAC issued an arrest warrant the day after the Chinese government issued an arrest warrant. However, in the case of Bai Xuoquian and the ten, there was still not a follow-up arrest warrant by the SAC, and no side has yet announced any update about these Kokang SAZ leaders.

Another remarkable fact about the relationship between Min Aung Hlaing and Bai Xuoqian, also known as Bai Suocheng, could be detected in his speech at the meeting March 2023 of the National Security and Defense Council. Bai Xuoqian indeed assisted Pheung Kya-shin, former leader of the Myanmar National Democratic Alliance Army (MNDAA). However, in 2009, Bai Xuoqian allied with the Tatmadaw to oust Pheung Kya-shin when Min Aung Hlaing was the Regional Military Command of Triangle Regional command in Eastern Shan State. The remnants of the MNDAA were then organised into Border Guard Force 1006, with Bai's younger son Bai Yingxiang becoming the leader. He was also elected as an MP of Amyotha Hluttaw, representing Laukai constituency during the 2010 general election. He became the first head of the Kokang SAZ in August 2010 after its formation. Bai's elder son, Bai Yingneng, also known as Khin Maung Lwin, became a member of the Shan State regional parliament from USDP in both the 2015 and 2020 general elections. After the coup attempt in 2021, he became a member of the SAC of the Kokang region. It would be a challenging task to unravel the intricate connections among Min Aung Hlaing, other senior military leaders, USDP party leaders, certain ethnic armed forces, and the Chinese authorities. However, following Operation 1027, the barriers within this Complex of the Maze appear to have been dismantled.

Cross-border trade with China was suspended due to the military operation, leading to disruptions in traffic on vital trade routes to the Chinese border and the closure of border posts in Muse and Laukkai. Cargo was redirected to Loi Je in Kachin State, but trade volume remained significantly lower compared to northern Shan State's border trade with China. The disruption of trade is estimated to cost the junta approximately US$423,000 in tax revenue daily, according to estimates by *The Irrawaddy*. In a press conference held in Beijing on December 14, Chinese Foreign Ministry spokesperson Mao Ning announced the commencement of negotiations between the military and the Alliance, expressing satisfaction with the positive outcomes from the peace talks. Despite the negotiations, clashes continued in the regions, with the TNLA and AA engaged in intense battles, capturing additional cities and ammunition. By December 22, the TNLA had seized control of nearly 90 percent of the Taáng region. Additionally, there were indications that a delegation from the SAC had returned to China to seek further negotiations for a ceasefire.

On the other hand, there were simultaneous attacks in Sagaing, Mandalay, Magway, and later Pegu divisions, as well as Chin, Karenni, Karen, and later Mon States. The People's Defense Forces (PDFs), the Kachin Independence Army (KIA), the Chin Defense Force (CDF), the Bamar People's Liberation Army (BPLA), the People's Liberation Army (PLA) (of the former Communist Party of Burma CPB), the Karen National Liberation Army (KNLA), and the All-Burma Students' Democratic Front (ABSDF) are also effectively cooperating in this operation. Therefore, the US Institute of Peace (USIP), a Washington-based think-tank focused on conflict prevention and resolution, stated in its report in November that it was a display of "unprecedented cooperation among outfits that come from different parts of Burma, speak different languages, and traditionally have had different priorities."

Since November 29th, the situation has tipped the balance to the Alliance: at least two Light Infantry Battalions (125 and 129), comprising at least 300 Tatmadaw soldiers and over 200 family members, surrendered in the region of Kokang SAZ. The total number of surrendered soldiers was at least 600. So far, the division commander of Division 99 was killed, while the one in charge of Division 101 was arrested by resistance forces during these days. Additionally, at least two tactical operation commanders and seven battalion commanders were also killed. Moreover, at least 12 military tanks, 9 Howitzers, and several other ammunition have been seized. More than 20 cities are already under the control of revolutionary forces. Furthermore, more than 300 military and police outposts and bases were conquered.

On December 8th, the 12th Military Operations Command Chief, Brigadier General Aung Zaw Lin, was reported to have been killed in Konkyan Township in northern Shan State. On November 11, 2023, Operation 11.11 was launched by the KNDF. After winning battles in over half of Karenni state, their aim was to capture Loikaw, the state capital, located just 138 miles west of Nay Pyi Taw. On November 19th, a K-8 fighter jet was allegedly shot down by KNDF and crashed in the state. One of the two pilots of the military aircraft was Major Khine Thant Moe. He found himself arrested by the KNDF. The SAC's spokesperson, Zaw

Min Tun, and other pro-military media denied the news of the arrest. However, Khine Thant Moe's video went viral: he gave a detailed account of the incident, disclosing information on how the SAC airstrikes targeted him and his co-pilot to eliminate all evidence.

Consequences

It must be stressed that the Tatmadaw, an institution that the SAC has always been proud of for its military might, is now disorganised. In November, according to the report by the Security Force Monitor SFM, "Under Whose Command," since 2011, more than 60% of the senior commanders of the Myanmar Army have faced allegations of disappearances, killings, rape, or torture allegedly committed by units under their command. Since Min Aung Hlaing became Commander-in-Chief in March 2011, 79 senior commanders, who had been in control of the entire army operations, are responsible for giving commands to their subordinates and committing crimes against humanity. The research findings disclosed that out of 64% (51) of senior commanders who have served under Min Aung Hlaing, 54% (28) of these commanders, who were in charge of at least one alleged human rights violation, were promoted in rank. The others could not be promoted further in rank (9), promotions could not be determined (11), or may be promoted in the future (3). This report highlights how the Tatmadaw itself is a Maze or an institute of human rights violations.

Under Operation 1027, the resistance forces, fighting hand in hand with the Alliance, have been achieving significant victories. According to the Burma Affairs and Conflict Study, 14 towns and more are now under control. By the end of the year, 21 towns had been seized: 7 towns in Shan State, 7 towns in Chin State, 3 towns in Sagaing Division, 3 towns in Karenni State, and 1 town in Bago Division. Additionally, most of the border trade gates at both the China and India borders have fallen under the control of the resistance groups. On the other hand, almost 600 SAC troops have surrendered, while over 250 army and police bases were seized, along with tons of ammunition, a dozen military tanks, and more than a dozen rockets.

Under SAC, Burma has fallen into disgrace. According to the UN report, it now stands as the world's biggest producer of opium in 2023, surpassing even Afghanistan after the Taliban government's crackdown on the trade. Forbes reported that the Myanmar military killed more than 100 people in a single airstrike. According to the Armed Conflict Location & Event Data Project (ACLED) 2022 report, Myanmar recorded the highest number of events of violence targeting civilians by state forces operating domestically, second only to Ukraine. Additionally, Burma recorded the highest number of battles globally in 2022. With the military's ongoing targeting of those who resist its rule and Operation 1027 by Brotherhood Alliance forces in the northeastern Shan state, 2023 was a year of violence and chaos in Burma.

From 2021 to 2023, there were numerous deadly airstrikes (around 2000 in total) and severe arson attacks (resulting in more than 85,000 houses burnt down) by the SAC troops, with the number of victims doubling up into the thousands. Since the escalation of armed conflict since October 27, 2023, it is estimated that over half a million people have become newly displaced. Some attempted to return and stay for a period, only to be compelled to flee again due to SAC airstrikes and arson attacks. This has exacerbated the situation for over 2 million people who were already displaced. In many parts of the armed conflict areas, particularly along the China-Myanmar border, little to no basic humanitarian assistance has reached the war refugees. The UN and its partners have found it challenging to fulfil their missions, partly due to the decline in international funding and partly due to the SAC's restricted rules and regulations. Additionally, there are many more challenges such as road closures, movement restrictions, safety and security concerns for aid workers, fuel shortages, serious banking issues, and soaring commodity prices.

What has exacerbated the economy of Burma is the decline of natural gas reserves, which have been a crucial revenue source for the SAC. Projects involving prominent investors like the French company Total and Australia's Woodside were aborted, raising alarms among the generals. Diesel imports were urgently hoarded to maintain military operations, leading to more power shortages and a deepening fuel crisis. On December 5, gasoline and diesel importers were deprived of US dollar reserves. The central bank of the SAC declared that it would no longer control exchange rates. Consequently, the situation has worsened: the shortage of essential commodities, particularly fuel, cooking oil, and medicine imported from abroad, has intensified. Burma now finds itself grappling with an intensified shortage of electricity and fuel.

Paradoxically, the SAC, which constructed the walls of the Maze, now finds itself trapped within its own confines. The military strength has been declining, with the total population of the Tatmadaw estimated to be around 150,000, including approximately 70,000 combat troops and an additional 20,000 reservists. Though obtaining accurate figures is challenging due to manipulations by subordinate officers, the military has been rapidly losing its strength. On December 3rd, the SAC announced that it would accept individual serving sentences of desertion or absence without leave if they returned to the Tatmadaw. As part of an amnesty on December 7th, marking Myanmar National Day, 239 prisoners were released, with pressure to rejoin military service. However, since over 200 pardoned deserters declined to do so, they were returned to their "mother units," i.e., prisons. These data highlight the desperation of the SAC for manpower.

In fact, the recorded number of police and army personnel who have joined the Civil Disobedience Movement (CDM) is over 13,000, although the total number of CDM civil servants has decreased from more than 800,000 in 2021 to 300,000 in 2023. On the other hand, the Ministry of Education of the NUG has almost 4,000 schools (with more than 550,000 students attending) and 77 online basic education programs (with around 90,000 students attending) running with the support of almost 60,000 CDM teachers and volunteers. Additionally, 113 online programs are provided for university students (with more than 40,000 students attending) with the support of over 14,000 CDM university teachers. Furthermore, more than 4,000 undergraduate students are attending Education Degree College supported by 250 experts and academics. The

Ministry of Education of the NUG has also recently declared to open more than a dozen universities online with a new curriculum adjusted to the needs of educational reform in line with federal democracy policies. However, many other education programs and schools, both online and offline, are being run by other independent resistance groups. Thus, despite the Tatmadaw's destruction of around 200 schools and their establishment of a brainwashed education system, the resistance forces are striving and tearing down the walls of the Maze of Education.

For almost three years, the Tatmadaw has attacked almost 400 medical facilities. Conversely, the Ministry of Health of the NUG and the resistance groups are operating 66 hospitals, over 150 health posts, and approximately 250 mobile health teams with more than 4,000 healthcare providers. Additionally, they have trained around 7,000 community volunteers under basic emergency care training. Their telemedicine services have already served at least 150,000 patients.

At the same time, under the Ministry of Justice of the NUG, more than 100 judges are serving at almost 30 courts. Additionally, 20 detention centres have been built, where approximately 60 prisoners and around 400 detainees are kept in line with community confinement standards. The National Unity Consultative Council (NUCC) has also recently published its principles on Transitional Justice (TJ).

The National Unity Government (NUG) has also made efforts to formulate a new governance structure for the country. It established the People Administrative Team (Pa Ah Pha) in regions controlled by the resistance to carry out governmental functions in these areas. In regions where non-Bamar ethnic groups are the majority, newly formed resistance groups and long-standing ethnic resistance groups have established public administrations. Recent fundraising activities, such as the Spring Development Bank share of the NUG, raised more than 10 million US dollars. With this funding, the NUG's Ministries of Humanitarian Assistance and Disaster Management, Health, Education, and Women, Youth, and Child Affairs are coordinating efforts to assist the general public affected by the SAC's violent attacks. According to the report by the Ministry of Foreign Affairs of the NUG, 52% of humanitarian assistance went to IDPs, 15% were used for food security for the victims, and at least 3.6 million USD has already been distributed.

The **media** continues to wield substantial influence for both the SAC and the Resistance. "Manipulation via translation" has emerged as a new form of disinformation by the SAC. Its leader, Min Aung Hlaing, delivered a speech at the State Administration Council meeting June 2023 at the SAC Chairman's Office in Nay Pyi Taw. His speech was published in both Burmese and English in state-run newspapers, but some discrepancies were obviously found between these two versions.

In the Burmese version, it was stated, "Last month, TNLA, KIA, AA, and other Kokang groups and 6,500 foreign drone experts attacked security posts of the Tatmadaw in the Kokang region of northern Shan State." However, in the English version, the translator deliberately left out the number of foreign experts, stating, "Last month, TNLA, KIA, AA, and other Kokang groups *and foreign drone experts* attacked security posts of the Tatmadaw in the Kokang region of northern Shan State." This example simply shows that the SAC knows how to manipulate both internally and externally. Recently, *The Irrawaddy* published "Fact Check: Exposing the Myanmar Junta's Lies on Operation 1027" and disclosed the SAC's disinformation.

Despite the SAC's restrictions on Facebook usage, it leverages platforms like Telegram, YouTube, TikTok, and other social media channels. The Resistance groups also operate numerous social media channels in both news and entertainment forms. In addition to mainstream news agencies, other informal news-like outlets from both sides play a crucial role in presenting news with unique angles but without in-depth analysis. While diverse news sources provide a comprehensive view of events, the lack of critical thinking and cross-referencing information to ensure accuracy and reliability can confuse news consumers and lead to increased bias in their views on the current situation and political decisions. However, the emergence of citizen journalists and informers from the SAC (called "Watermelons") contributes to offering more reliable data for analysis and clearer predictions.

UN and international community

In 2023, Timor-Leste (East Timor) added its name to the list of supporters of the Spring Revolution, giving recognition to the NUG. In July, President Jose Ramos-Horta, who delivered a compelling speech at the UN General Assembly in September 2022 highlighting the crises in Burma, officially invited the Foreign Minister of the NUG, Zin Mar Aung, and her team to attend his government's inauguration. In response, in August, the SAC issued an order for the expulsion of its Charge d'Affaires in the country by no later than September 1. Since then, Timor-Leste, the eleventh member of ASEAN, has emerged as a conscientious voice in Southeast Asia. People of Burma have commended Timor-Leste for its steadfast commitment as it willingly takes risks for its long-anticipated opportunity to join ASEAN.

In September 2023, Indonesia hosted the Association of Southeast Asian Nations (ASEAN) summit and its related meetings with dialogue partners, including the East Asia Summit, in Jakarta. The absence of major ASEAN partners like China's Xi Jinping and U.S. President Joe Biden dampened the proceedings. During the meeting, the five-point consensus was reviewed. ASEAN's legitimacy and reputation have been compromised due to its inability to stop the junta from continuing violence against civilians. One of the decisions made was that the ASEAN Chairmanship in 2026 shall be assumed by the Philippines instead of Burma. However, no concrete outcomes were reached. Indonesia, which had conducted over 180 engagements with Myanmar multi-stakeholders, including the SAC, during its chairmanship, introduced a "troika mechanism"—an arrangement between outgoing chair Indonesia, future chair Malaysia, and incoming chair Laos to work collectively to identify a solution.

Regarding the international community, despite the UN's rules of engagement for UN agencies operating inside the country instructing them not to participate in junta-staged events, it seems that many UN representatives in Burma are practising leniency in dealing with the SAC. This has disappointed the people of Burma and led them to believe that ASEAN and the international community, whose efforts to persuade the military regime for cooperation and collaboration have consistently failed, are experiencing "fatigue." Additionally, according to the report by the Ministry of Foreign Affairs of the NUG, the scale of the airstrikes and destruction of civilian properties carried out by the SAC far exceeds the demands of ASEAN and the UN Security Council to stop these atrocities. Surprisingly, however, the people of Burma do not express any "fatigue." On the contrary, they exhibit an iron spirit in their ongoing struggle against the military regime and its dictatorship. Having strong faith in the people's power that could bring about real change, the people of Burma maintain unwavering confidence in their ability to address the core issues. Therefore, an intriguing puzzle remains as to why the international community, including ASEAN and the EU, have displayed "fatigue" and have been so slow and sluggish in their support for Myanmar's Spring Revolution, as though acting out the role of "To be or not to be."

It is noteworthy that the research findings of the United States Institute of Peace (USIP), a think tank from the USA (November 2023 report), have concluded that the Spring Revolution has "characteristics that would contribute to stability in a post-junta period." The key findings highlighted that "the assumption of fragmentation and warlordism among resistance groups is unlikely because the intercommunal conflict is mainly driven by exclusionary governance structures and divisive political dialogue of the past, and the resistance motivated by a desire for a new political paradigm is well connected to communities in which social cohesion is strong." However, it will take years of national dialogue for the process to reach its desired goal. A chance for the new generation of leaders within the resistance structures is also awaiting, as they have plans for a post-coup interim administration: a more secular governing structure and other positive socio-political visions. This will lead one to reflect on how the resistance forces are trying to tear down some walls of the Maze.

On the other hand, growing evidence suggests that Myanmar is becoming one of the most urgent and swiftly intensifying threats to global security. Alarmingly, transnational criminal organisations have already been established, largely under the protection of the Tatmadaw's border guard forces in <u>Kokong on the China border</u> and in <u>Karen on the Thai border</u>. These criminal entities have been involved in human trafficking, affecting tens of thousands of victims from ASEAN countries, China, and beyond. Additionally, intricate online fraud schemes aimed at a worldwide population have been occurring at an alarming speed. If this issue is not solved in a timely manner, the entire population might become lost in another Maze of transnational crime structures originally hosted in Burma.

All in all, the most significant breakthrough in dismantling some walls of the Winkapar (maze) has been the revelation of the intricate dynamics among the Tatmadaw, its political party USDP, Chinese-speaking ethnic armed forces, and Chinese authorities. Some analysts posit that the Chinese Communist Party (CCP) is assuming a dual role, acting both as an instigator and a peace negotiator in this relationship (as a Burmese proverb says, "A torch in one hand and a cup of water in the other"). The military ties between Russia and Burma have grown stronger over the past two years, and the Tatmadaw has also maintained connections with the Iranian military.

Nevertheless, numerous internal and external catalysts and stakeholders contribute to the complexity of Burma's situation, adding more walls to the Maze. Burma should no longer be overlooked, even if there is no apparent international interest in its political, economic, and social affairs. While the path to democracy remains uncertain and the fate of this intricate Maze is yet unknown, the Spring Revolution persists in dismantling its walls and barriers as it approaches the conclusion of its third year.

Ma Thida
26 December 2023